UNDERSTANDING STREET PHOTOGRAPHY

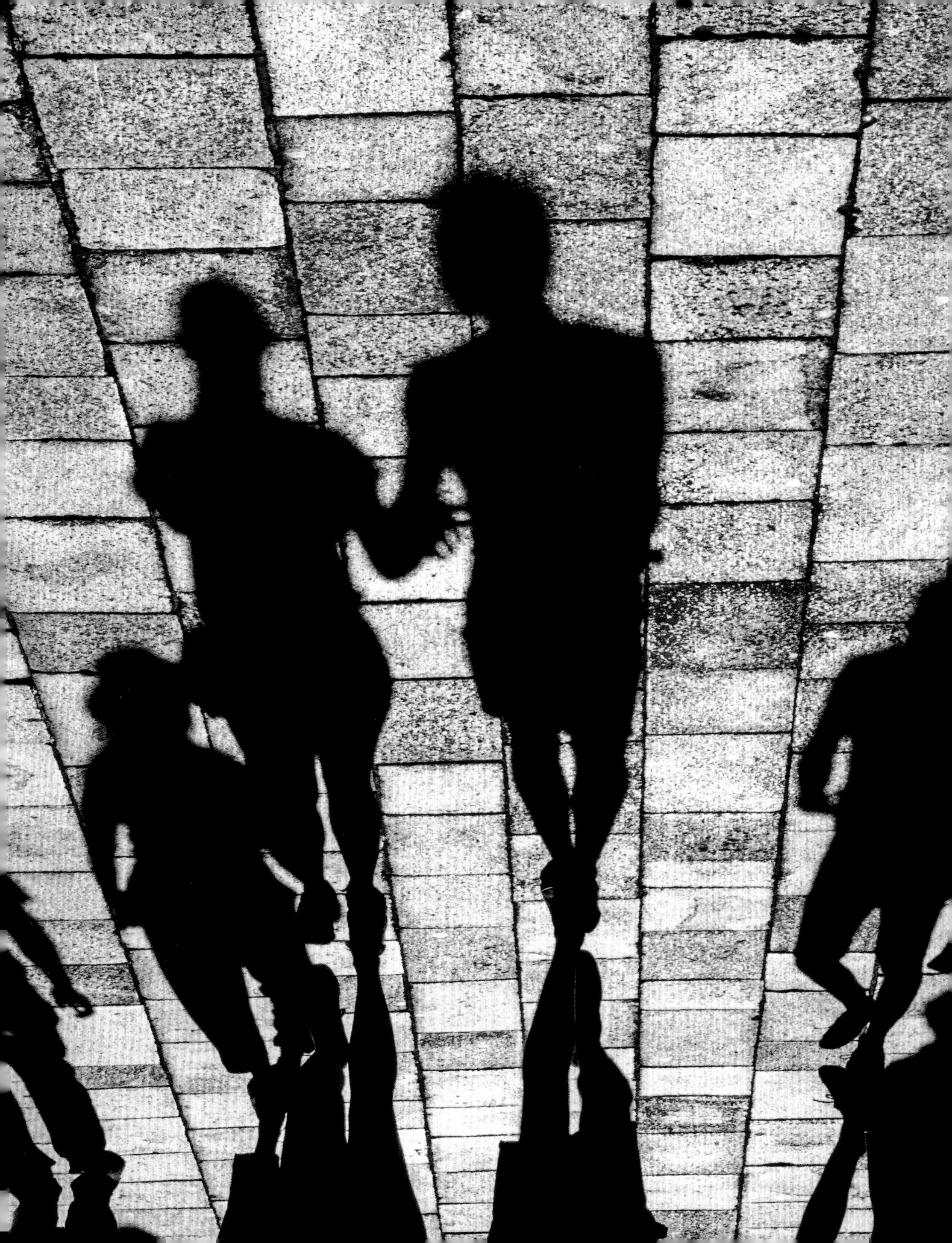

UNDERSTANDING STREET PHOTOGRAPHY

An Introduction to Shooting Compelling Images on the Street

Contents

Introduction–1

LIGHT AND SHADOW—5

Seeing Like a Camera: Shadow Pockets–6

Backlight and Transparent Color–22

Dappled Light–28

Light and Shadow Are *Not* the Holy Grail–32

COMPOSITION—37

Mergers–38

Connections–46

Framing with a Frame–54

Point of View–62

Scale–72

Pattern and Color–78

PEOPLE—89

Posed–90

Candid–106

MOTION—125

Freezing Motion–126

Blurring Motion–130

Panning–142

SEEKING THE ABSTRACT—149

Abstracts–150

Texture and Macro–164

Graffiti–170

USING FLASH—177

Flashes of Inspiration—178

About the Author—184

Index—185

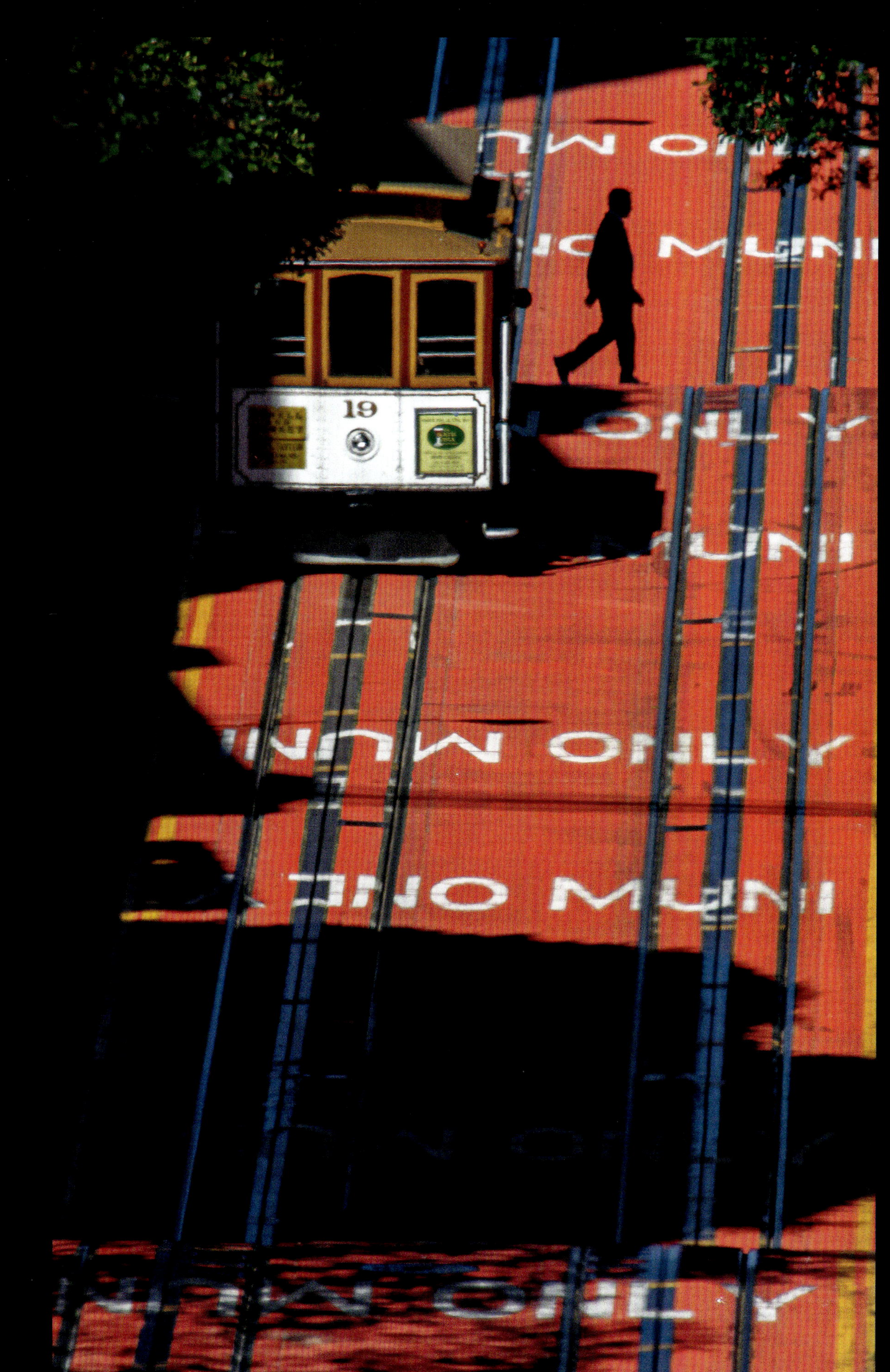
MUNI ONLY

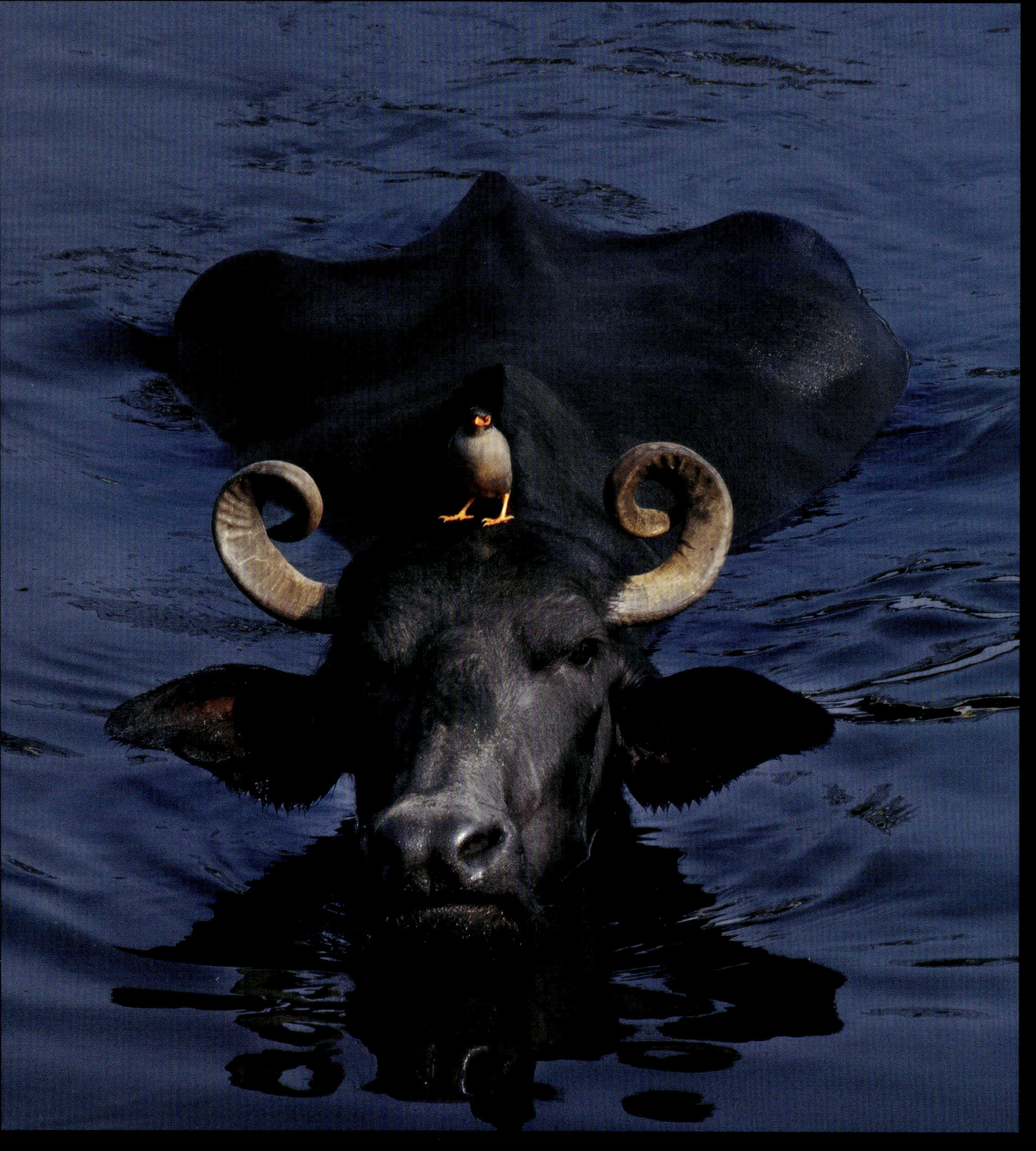

Creating photographic art has always been about clicking the shutter, while creating digital art will always be about clicking the mouse. Street photography, thankfully, remains a great place to create photographic art. To all of the photographers out there, I hope you continue to enjoy the sound and the click of that shutter!

Introduction

Street photography has become a very popular subject in today's photographic community, whether shot with a DSLR or a smartphone. On Instagram, street photography is the second most searched photography category after travel photography. And it could easily be argued that much of the travel photography being done in recent years is in fact just street photography shot by tourists. Today, everyone is a photographer, and whether you are shooting in your own hometown or halfway around the world, you are, at least in my mind, a street photographer!

What is street photography? I define it as photography done in the streets, avenues, lanes, and urban environments of cities of all sizes and shapes. It is observations of life on the street: people, abstracts, still lifes, motion-filled subjects, color. Most street photography compositions include people, whether posed or candid, someone the photographer met or saw passing by, or figures that appear small and distant in the overall composition. Architecture is another common thread in street photography, featuring lines, patterns, and the dramatic play of light and shadow. Street photography can also be abstract: a crushed bottle cap lying in a crosswalk, or the car scrapes left behind on the concrete walls that line the narrow entrances of public parking garages. While people are certainly not a requirement in street photography, most compositions do convey the evidence of human interaction, such as a half-eaten sandwich sitting on a restaurant counter in low-angled sidelight against a backdrop of blurred yellow cabs seen through the restaurant's window.

I am often asked what kind of photographer I am: nature, industrial, abstract? Fashion, nude, or fine art? Corporate or advertising? Truthfully, I have been all of those at one time or another, but at a recent photo conference where I presented, I was told (not asked) at least a dozen times that I am a street photographer. And it's true that I have been a street photographer off and on for twenty-five years, traveling to cities worldwide and accumulating more than three million frequent flyer miles along the way.

One thing I have learned about street photography, especially in these past five years of shooting in cities all over the world, is that much of its photographic gold remains hidden from a lot of photographers. I have met many amateur photographers over the years, most of whom live near or in cities large and small. They usually tell me how much they love shooting nature, and that they dash off to the countryside, beach, or mountains whenever they have free time to shoot. When I ask why they don't just shoot in the city where they live, or in other cities that are not familiar to them, I'm almost always met with something like, "Other than a possible city skyline during the 'blue hour,' what else is there to shoot?"

Throughout the pages of this book, you will find ample proof that cities of all sizes are treasure troves of photographic gold. A walk or slow drive down any street, lane, alley, or dirt road will reveal a visual feast, from people and architecture to abstract subjects that, once discovered, will broaden your creative vision. It is in the cities that skyscrapers sit next to buildings of much smaller height, and the hustle and bustle of organized chaos offers up a constantly changing buffet of photographic potential. No other genre offers as many opportunities to capture what Henri Cartier-Bresson called the decisive moment.

In this book you'll find more than one hundred mini tutorials for street photography, each sharing the story behind an image, covering a vast array of subject matter that is certain to appeal to every reader (even nature photographers!). In each mini diary (as I like to call them) I describe my thought process and *why* this scene caught my attention, along with considerations such as the arrangement of the composition, the psychology of the colors, and the visual weight of the image. Each tutorial concludes with the camera, lens, aperture, shutter speed, ISO, and white balance (WB) used.

Whether you have just picked up an interest in street photography or you have been on the street for several years, this book will help you gain a better understanding of both exposure and composition. You might also find it beneficial to refer to my previous books, such as *Understanding Exposure*, *Understanding Shutter Speed*, *Learning to See Creatively*, and *Understanding Composition*, for more in-depth explanations. *Understanding Exposure*, now in its fourth edition, would be a useful companion to these mini tutorials, as it helps readers understand the difference between a correct exposure and a *creatively* correct exposure, offering in-depth explanations of, for example, a "Who cares?" aperture versus a "storytelling" aperture. If you are a smartphone user, you are probably familiar with the creative exposure limitations of your smartphone; this book will serve to expand your vision and point of view and help you create far more compelling compositions.

Street photography requires a keen awareness of your surroundings and how people, vehicles, and bicycles interact with light, shadow, architecture, and signage—providing endless opportunities to play with photographic potential and the creative use of shutter speeds, whether through implying motion, freezing action, or the simple act of panning. It allows you to capture the human condition in all of its good, bad, joy-filled, sad, tragic, celebratory beauty. Once you've absorbed the mini tutorials in this book, I believe your senses will be awakened to all of the amazing possibilities for image-making on streets the world over.

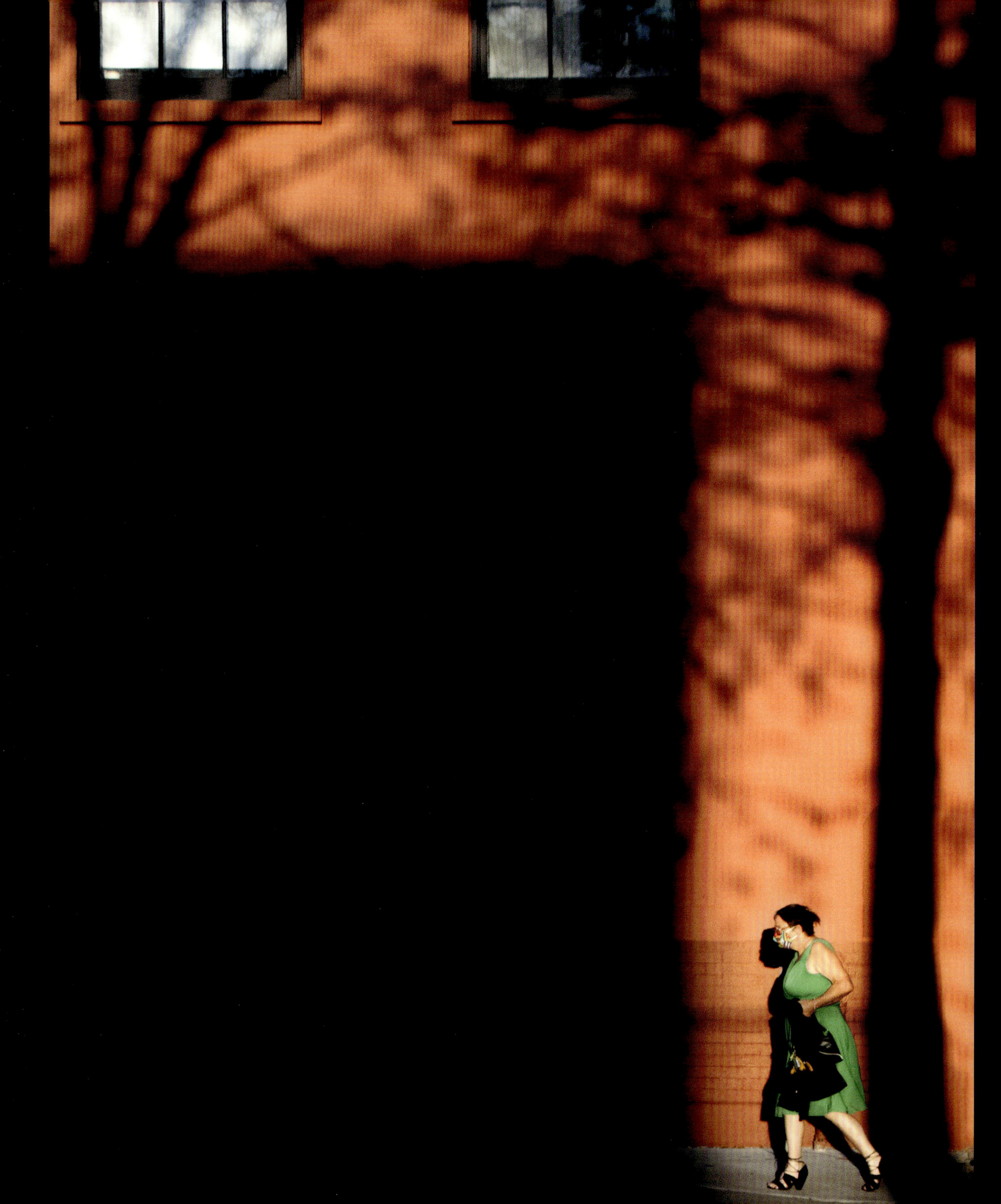

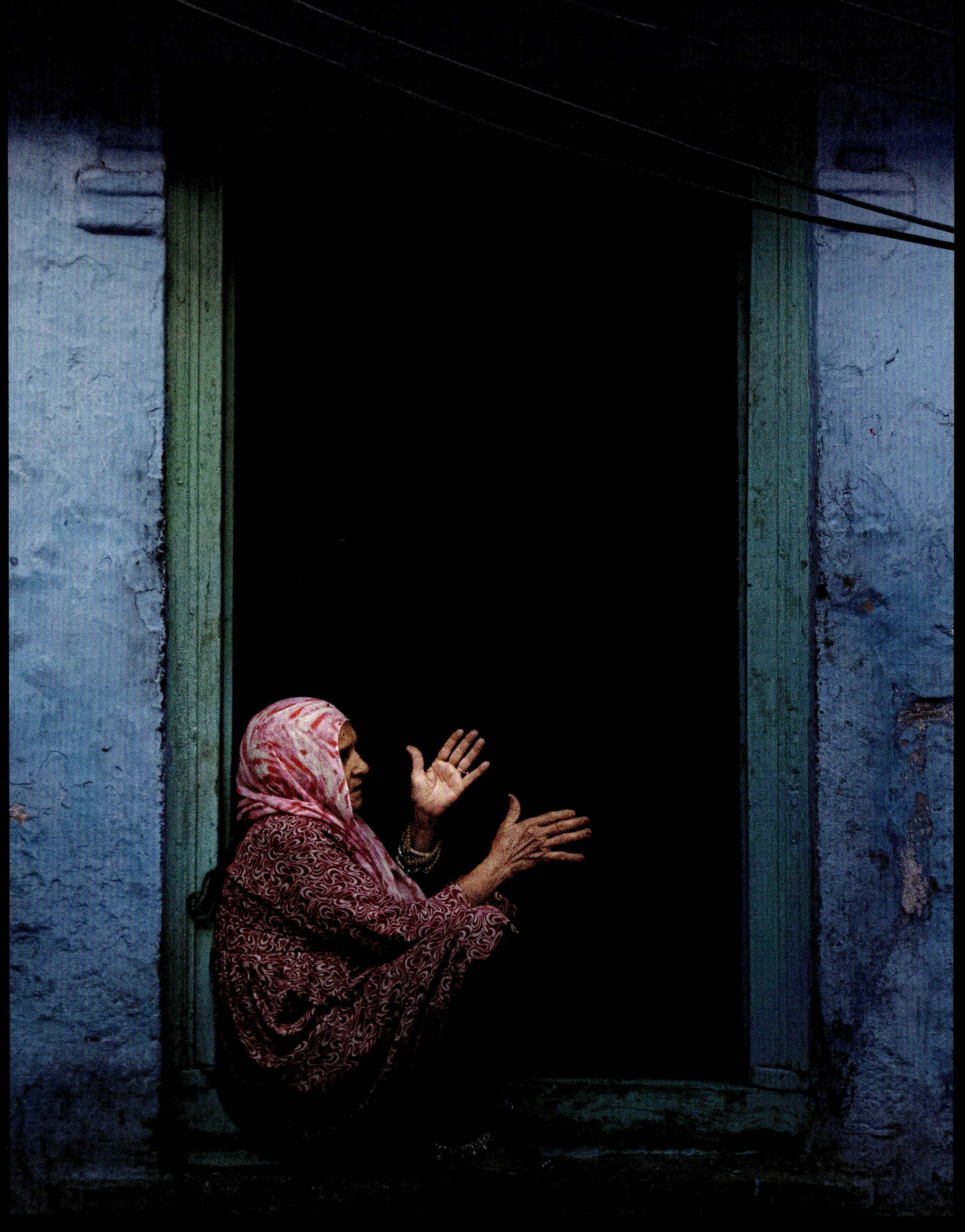

LIGHT AND SHADOW

Seeing Like a Camera: Shadow Pockets

Thanks to the architecture of cities worldwide and the many tall buildings that define them, "shadow pockets" are especially prevalent, more so than in landscapes. In these very pockets of "black gold"—and the brightly lit features around them—you can find a wealth of impactful images. Yet to reveal these treasures, you must learn to see as a camera does.

The human eye can see a range of light and dark that is equivalent, in photographic terms, to 16 to 18 stops. This means you will often walk past the black gold, because your eyes and brain can clearly see, for example, both a frontlit tricycle and the long, dark shadow of the alleyway behind the tricycle. But what if, on the other hand, you could "see" like your camera's light meter does, with only about a 9-stop range of light to shadow? Then you might see the shadowed alleyway behind the tricycle as an opportunity. By setting a manual exposure for the sunlit tricycle and composing it against the alleyway, you would reveal the great volume of black gold behind the tricycle.

And the reverse is also true: shaded figures in front of a brightly lit background can become velvety dark silhouettes if you expose for the lit background. Do you remember the first time you shot a sunrise or sunset at the beach with a friend or family member walking in the foreground against the rising or setting sun? Or how about that country scene at sunset where you shot a large oak tree or barn against the bright red-orange sky? It was exciting, I know, to see such stark contrast between the vivid colors of the sky and the often pitch-black silhouetted shapes of people, trees, or the proverbial barn. If you have yet to realize that you can create that same type of image without an actual sunrise or sunset, perhaps that defining moment can happen now.

These are just two examples of why it's imperative that you learn to speak and see like a camera, in much the same way that you will go much further in any foreign country when you speak that country's language. Your camera and lenses speak a unique photographic language, one that many photographers, especially with today's proliferation of smartphones, are failing to learn.

Are you familiar with the new language translation recorders that allow you to say something in your native language and then play it back in a different language? Perhaps you own such a device. For many photographers, Photoshop serves the same purpose, replacing any need to speak the language of photography. And similarly to the language translation apps, Photoshop—as smart as it may be—is actually undermining the personal self-esteem and uplifting feeling of empowerment you can gain from creating an image and photographic style that you can honestly claim as your very own. Prior to the digital age, most photographic creations were the result of investing the necessary time to learn about metering light and shadow, the potential

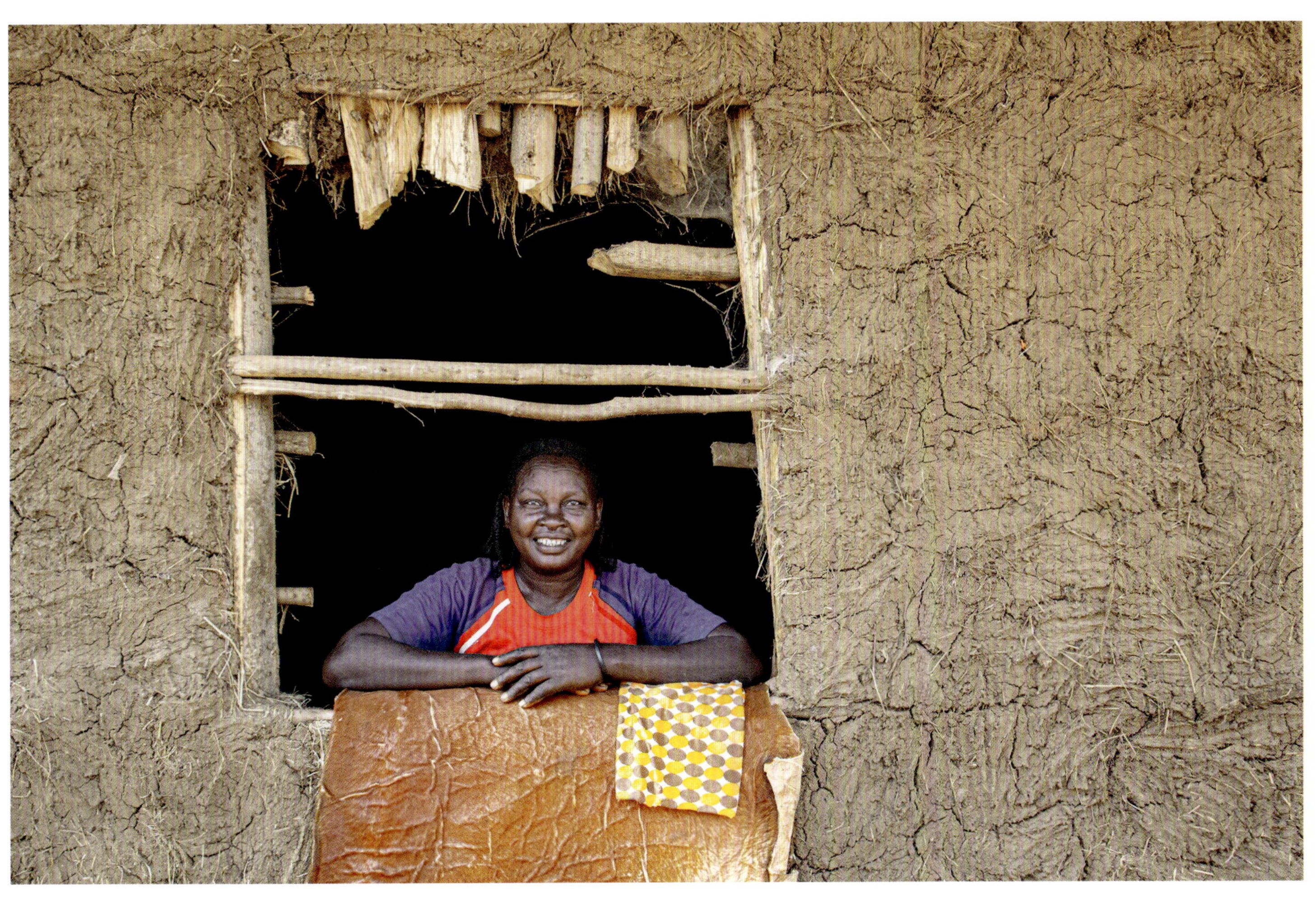

In both this composition and the one on the preceding spread, I made use of the camera's limited range of light and dark, mining the "black gold" behind the subject. This young woman, from the Konso tribe in Ethiopia's Omo Valley, was lit by the overcast light of midday, with the much darker interior of her small home behind her. I exposed for the brighter, softer light on her face, recording the background as a severe underexposure and adding a welcome dollop of contrast!

◘ Nikon D850, NIKKOR 24–120mm lens, *f*/8 for 1/100 sec., ISO 200, Daylight/Sunny WB

visions of apertures and shutter speeds, the unique visions of all of your lenses, the various focal lengths, and finally how to combine your personal style and love of line, pattern, texture, color, and people and/or landscapes with fresh and unique points of view, all leading to what was hopefully an impactful image, a compelling composition.

I should note here that because smartphone cameras can encompass both light and shadow simultaneously with a more extreme dynamic range, they do not offer the same opportunity to capture pockets of black gold. (DSLRs and mirrorless cameras are headed for that extreme dynamic range, and I'm hoping that manufacturers will install a kind of dimmer switch to tone down the dynamic range when necessary.) If you're using a standard DSLR, it should be really important to you to develop your vision, abandoning what your eye and brain have led you to believe and embracing with fervor the vision of your camera's more limited sensitivity to light and dark. Once you do this, you will discover the black gold that is often right in front of you, if not behind you!

The Photographic Triangle

Before we go further, let's review some fundamentals. Just as it was one hundred years ago, every camera, whether a DSLR or the one in your smartphone, is nothing more than a lightproof box with a lens at one end and a light-sensitive receptor (formerly film; today, a digital sensor) at the other. When light is allowed to enter the opening in the lens (the aperture) for a certain amount of time (the shutter speed), an image called an exposure is recorded. A correct exposure is a simple combination of aperture, shutter speed, and ISO (the sensor's sensitivity to light). I refer to these three factors as the photographic triangle.

The size of the aperture, or lens opening, determines the volume of light that reaches the digital sensor during an exposure. The *smaller* the *f*-stop number (for example, *f*/2.8, *f*/4, *f*/5.6), the *larger* the lens opening and the more light is allowed in. The *larger* the *f*-stop number (for example, *f*/16 or *f*/22), the *smaller* the lens opening and the less light. For more on aperture, see page 44.

Shutter speed controls the amount of time light is allowed through the camera's lens to stay on the digital media. The slower the shutter speed, the more light is allowed in. Today's cameras offer shutter speeds from a blazingly fast 1/15,000 sec. to as long as 30 seconds. Smartphone cameras have a more limited range, from approximately 1/1000 sec. to 1/60 sec. For more on shutter speed, see page 126.

The third part of the photographic triangle is the ISO, or the sensitivity of the film or digital sensor to light. The higher the ISO, the higher its sensitivity to light. For example, ISO 400 is more sensitive to light than ISO 100. For more on ISO, see page 12.

If you're new to these concepts or just need a refresher, you can also check out one of my previous books, such as *Understanding Exposure* or *Bryan Peterson's Photography School,* for more in-depth explanations.

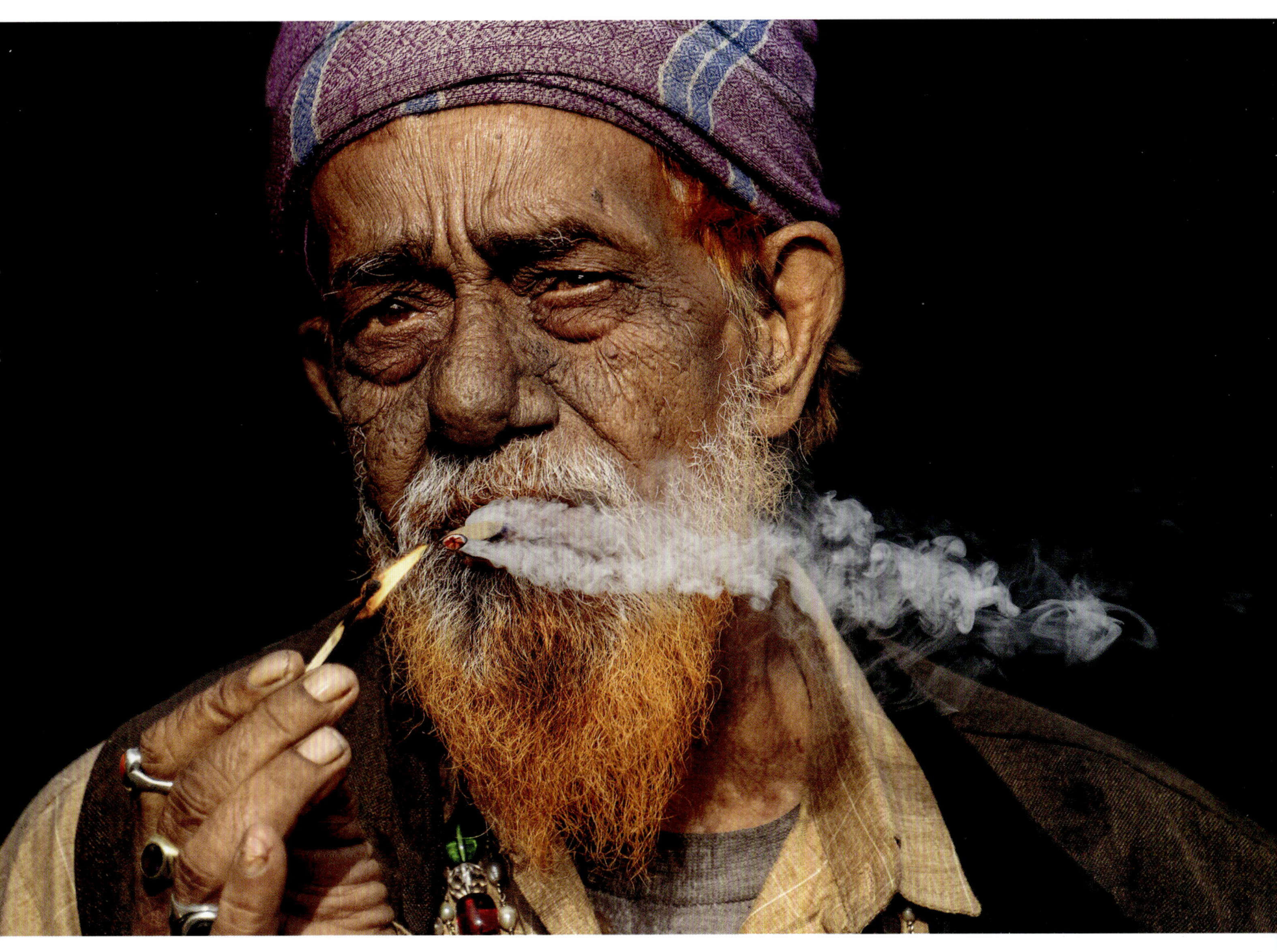

I had just completed a ride with this taxi driver in Jodhpur, India, and we were still engaged in a discussion about life in Jodhpur when he began to smoke, standing beside his tuktuk. He was sidelit by the strong early morning light, with a large alleyway about ten feet behind him. Since my exposure was set for the much brighter sunlight on him, the darker area of open shade behind him recorded as a welcome and contrasting black background.

◘ Nikon D850, NIKKOR 24–120mm lens, *f*/11 for 1/400 sec., ISO 200, Daylight/Sunny WB

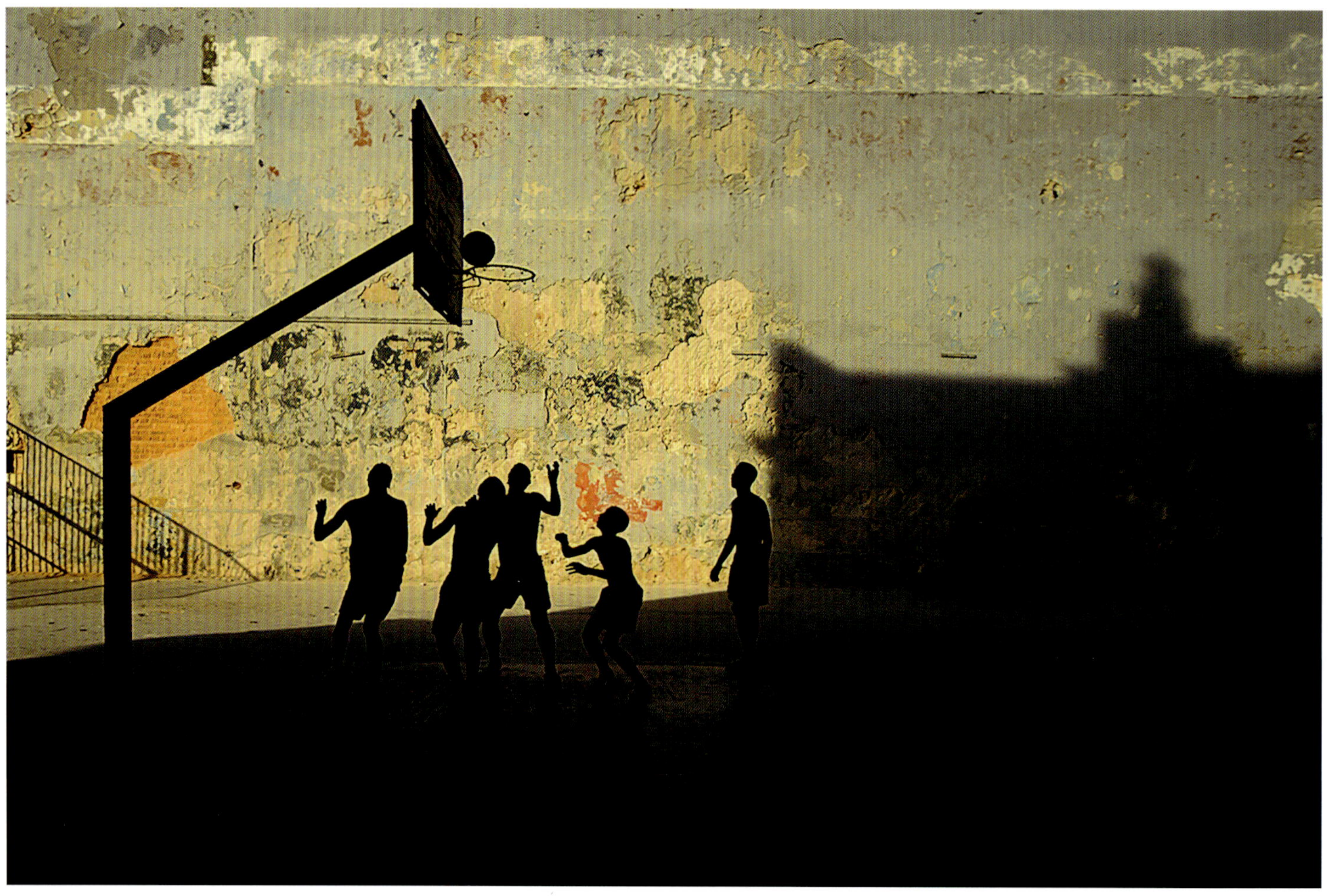

Throughout my photographic career, I have had perhaps a half-dozen defining moments that changed my approach to image-making. One of those moments took place while on assignment for CNN in Havana, Cuba, in August 1993. I was there as a silent observer, to photograph still images while the CNN journalist interviewed Fidel Castro—an interview that unfortunately never took place, as Castro's office staff said simply, "President Castro is no longer interested in being interviewed."

I say "unfortunately," but in retrospect it was good fortune. That canceled interview soon found me out on the streets of Havana with an unexpectedly free afternoon. Shortly afterward, my ears caught the loud, competitive voices of teenagers and the familiar sound of a basketball hitting the pavement. Turning a corner, I saw a large open courtyard bathed in golden light and a group of boys playing a pickup game. I wasted little time, moving down into a low position near the concrete pavement to push the young men higher up in my frame. I began to fumble with the manual exposure settings on my Nikon F3, not quite certain how to meter the scene. Within seconds, feeling like an idiot, I chastised myself for failing to realize the obvious: the scene before me was a Sunny 16 opportunity!

I had learned of the Sunny 16 formula all the way back in 1973. The formula was simple: when using any film—color slide, color print, or even black-and-white—to photograph a frontlit or sidelit scene (when the light source is illuminating the front or side of your subject), you can always obtain a correct exposure by setting your aperture to *f*/16 and your shutter speed to the same number as the ISO—meaning if the ISO is 100, the shutter speed should be 1/100 sec.; if the ISO is 400, the shutter speed should be 1/400 sec.; and so on.

Since then, I had applied the Sunny 16 rule to many frontlit and sidelit *nature* scenes, but like a bumbling idiot, my initial reaction to these young boys playing basketball was like walking into a foreign land, a land unlike anything in nature. I just stood there, cursing the fact that the wall behind them was in bright, golden late-afternoon sunlight while the boys were in open shade: a metering nightmare. Then, as if struck by a bolt of lightning, I realized this was the same "golden" opportunity I had shot in nature countless times. A Sunny 16 exposure would correctly expose the wall, thus rendering the teenage boys as a striking and stark silhouette against the urban inner-city wall.

But there was a bit more to understanding the Sunny 16 rule: the use of *f*/16 was merely a starting point, meaning that *f*/16 at 1/100 sec. was merely one of *six* possible correct exposures with ISO 100. The quantitative value of *f*/16 for 1/100 sec. is the same as *f*/11 for 1/200 sec., the same as *f*/8 for 1/400 sec., and the same as *f*/5.6 for 1/800 sec. and *f*/4 for 1/1600 sec. As I stood there watching the basketball game unfold, I grabbed my Nikon F3 film camera loaded with Fujichrome 100 slide film and, using my NIKKOR 35–70mm lens, set my exposure to *f*/8 (for a "Who cares?" aperture) and 1/400 sec. (which was fast enough to freeze the action). Over the course of fifteen minutes, I managed to get a number of images of extreme contrast, one of which is shown here.

The biggest takeaway from this afternoon in downtown Havana was the realization that Sunny 16 was *not* only for nature landscapes. In fact, ever since that day, I have often called upon Sunny 16 while shooting street photography all over the world. Set your exposure for the sunlight (aka Sunny 16) and anything in the shadows between your point of view and that sunlight will record as a severe underexposure, often resulting in a silhouette. For more on Sunny 16, see page 12.

◘ Nikon F3 with Kodak Slide Film E100S, NIKKOR 35–70mm lens, *f*/16 for 1/100 sec., ISO 100, Daylight/Sunny WB

The Sunny 16 Rule

The Sunny 16 rule is a formula almost as old as photography itself, a formula used countless times *before* the advent of the in-camera light meter. I still use this formula today, despite having a highly sophisticated digital camera at my disposal with no fewer than three built-in light metering choices.

Sunny 16 simply means this: If your subject is basking in the front light or sidelight of full sun (meaning that the sun is not obscured by any portion of a cloud or object), then to correctly expose any part of that subject and/or scene awash in sunlight, set your aperture to *f*/16 and choose the same number for your shutter as your ISO setting. For example, at *f*/16, with an ISO of 100, I would shoot at 1/100 sec. With an ISO of 200, I would shoot at 1/200 sec.; with an ISO of 400, I would shoot at 1/400 sec.; and so on.

"Ah," you say, "but what if I don't want to shoot at *f*/16? What if I don't want that much depth of field?" No problem! You can shoot at any aperture and shutter speed as long as the quantitative value of the aperture and shutter speed are the same as in the original (*f*/16 for 1/100 sec. at ISO 100). For example, let's say you are using ISO 100 and want a limited depth of field, so you choose *f*/5.6. You have opened up the aperture of your lens (made a much wider opening) by a total of three stops: from *f*/16 to *f*/11 (1 stop), from *f*/11 to *f*/8 (2 stops), and from *f*/8 to *f*/5.6 (3 stops). So now you must also decrease your shutter speed (the duration of time) by three stops: from 1/100 sec. to 1/200 sec., from 1/200 sec. to 1/400 sec., and finally from 1/400 sec. to 1/800 sec., making your final settings *f*/5.6, 1/800 sec., ISO 100. To make learning your progressions easier, I have created a simple Sunny 16 chart based on an ISO of 100.

f/32	1/25 sec.	ISO 100
f/29	1/30 sec.	ISO 100
f/25	1/40 sec.	ISO 100
f/22	1/50 sec.	ISO 100
f/20	1/60 sec.	ISO 100
f/18	1/80 sec.	ISO 100
f/16	1/100 sec.	ISO 100
f/14	1/125 sec.	ISO 100
f/13	1/160 sec.	ISO 100
f/11	1/200 sec.	ISO 100
f/10	1/250 sec.	ISO 100
f/9	1/320 sec.	ISO 100
f/8	1/400 sec.	ISO 100
f/7.1	1/500 sec.	ISO 100
f/6.3	1/640 sec.	ISO 100
f/5.6	1/800 sec.	ISO 100
f/5	1/1000 sec.	ISO 100
f/4.5	1/1250 sec.	ISO 100
f/4	1/1600 sec.	ISO 100
f/3.5	1/2000 sec.	ISO 100
f/3.2	1/2500 sec.	ISO 100
f/2.8	1/3200 sec.	ISO 100

The Sunny 16 rule is in full force from about ninety minutes after sunrise to ninety minutes before sunset. It can be an effective exposure setting for any frontlit or sidelit subject that requires little, if any, tweaking in post-processing—regardless of the person's skin color, from the fairest white to the darkest brown, or whether a person is dressed in white or black.

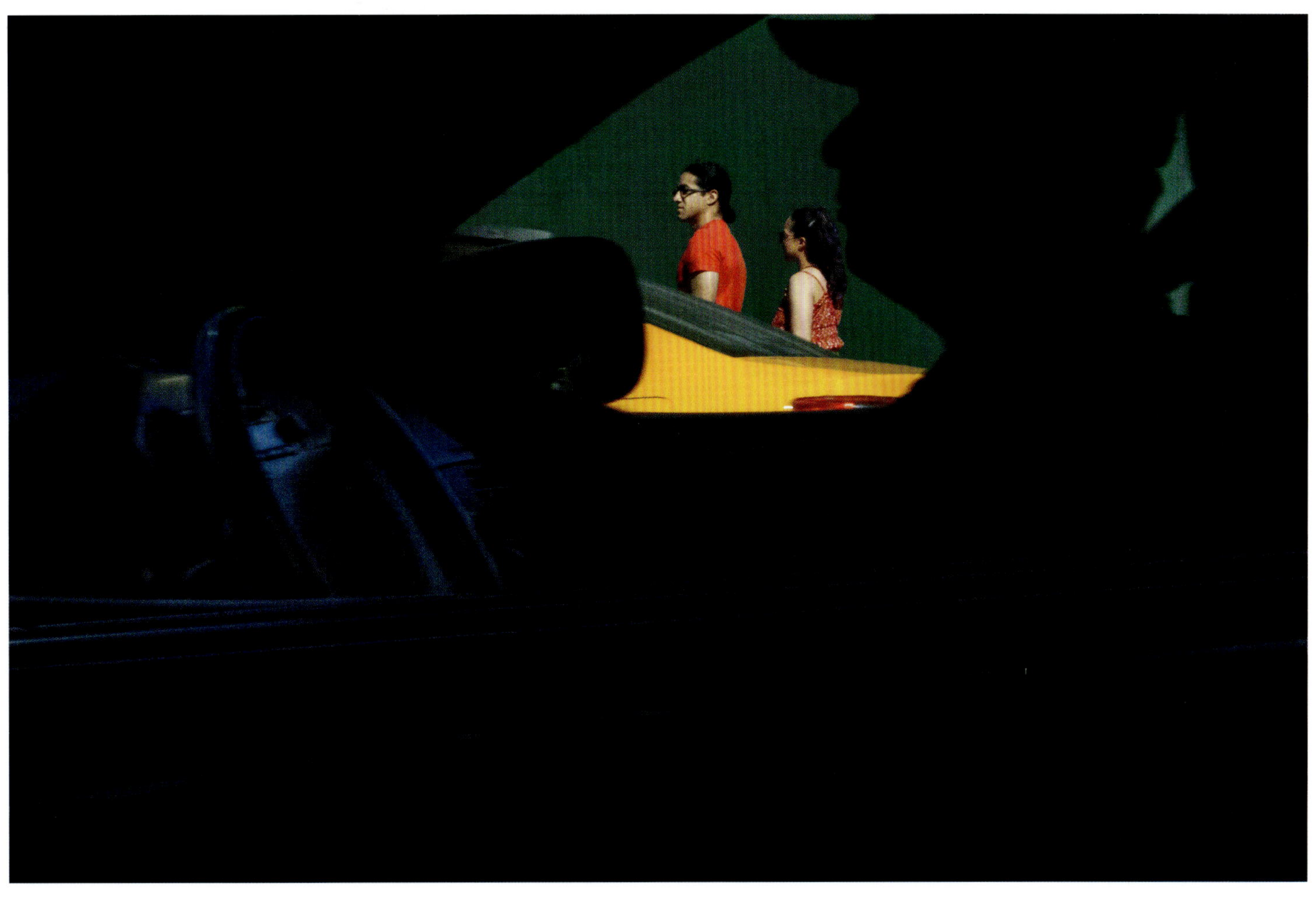

It was a hot June afternoon and I was on West 33rd Street and Tenth Avenue in New York City, a favorite city of many street photographers. The lane of traffic farthest from me was basking in full sunlight, while the two lanes nearer to me were blanketed by large shadows being cast by the Hudson Yard high-rises directly behind me.

I could see the possibility before me: a layered exposure of dark shadows near me becoming silhouetted shapes in front of the brighter sunlit background—assuming I trusted the Sunny 16 rule and didn't overthink it. In less than fifteen minutes, color, form, and shape all worked in concert together as a lone man in his car pulled up to the red light, stopping in the lane nearest to me with his front window down, a taxi behind him in the far lane basking in full sun. Then, talk about timing—wow!—a young couple in that same full sunlight walked into the scene from the right. Wait, wait—now, fire!

◘ Nikon D850, NIKKOR 24–120 lens, *f*/22 for 1/200 sec., ISO 400, Daylight/Sunny WB

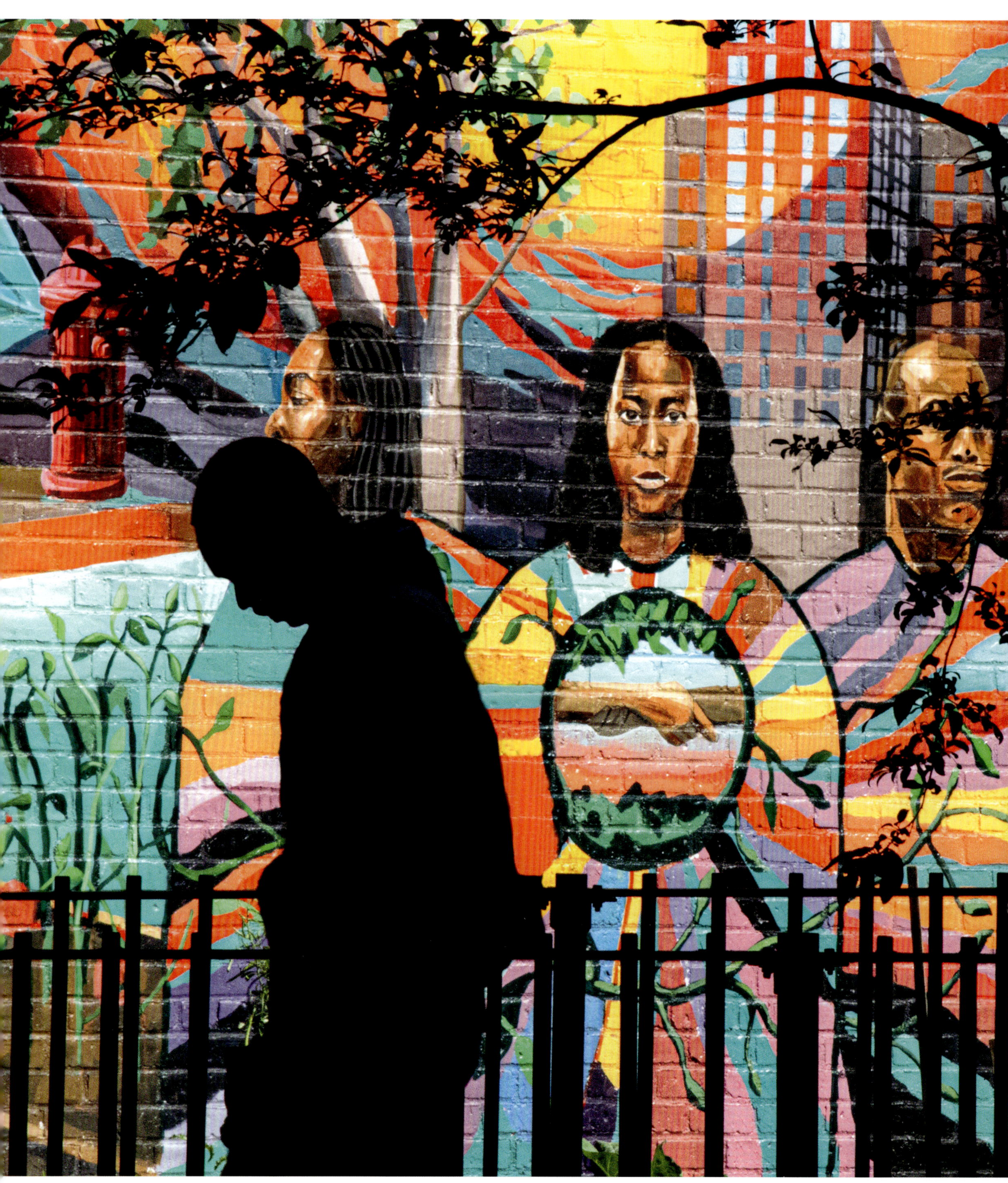

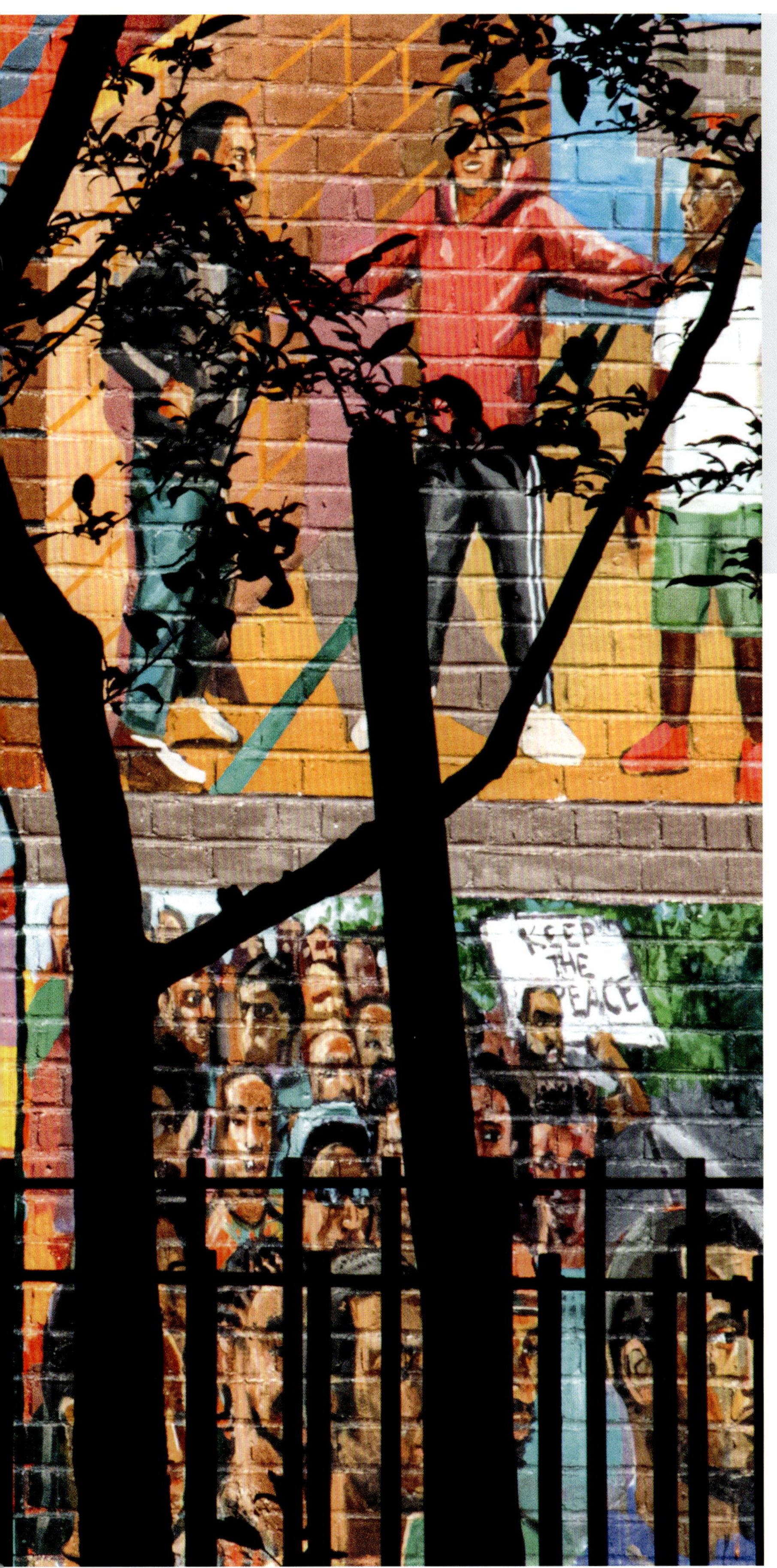

The Art of Staying Put

When it comes to street photography, there are two schools of thought on finding subject matter. One approach is to place one foot in front of the other, and with a bit of luck you will eventually come upon something compelling—often fleeting, but compelling nonetheless. The other approach is to find a compelling scene and then just stay put; give it at least thirty minutes and wait for the hoped-for subject to come to you. More often than not your thirty-minute wait will be amply rewarded. Do I have a preference? Despite my impatient photographic nature, I embrace the stay-put approach, with fingers crossed.

A student and I were enjoying an early summer morning in Harlem, New York, when I saw a bright mural basking in the full sunlight about a block away. As I got closer, I began to look for points of view that would allow me to use the mural in much the same way as one might use a sunset sky: metering for the bright mural with objects or people in front of it in open shade. It didn't take long to find just such a location. A local park directly faced the mural and, thanks to a six-floor building, there was a large shadow cast onto the park's fence, its few trees, and the lone pathway at the edge of the park, about twenty feet in front of the beautiful mural.

Minutes passed, and soon I began expressing my impatience. "Why can't somebody please walk down that path?" I grumbled. "It would lend so much to the overall interest in the composition." Just as my student volunteered to be a model and walk down the path, a young man appeared and just as quickly disappeared—but not before both of us got the much-wanted composition of a real human shape contrasting with the painted human shapes in the mural!

◘ Nikon D850, NIKKOR 24–120mm lens, *f*/16 for 1/400 sec., ISO 400, Daylight/Sunny WB

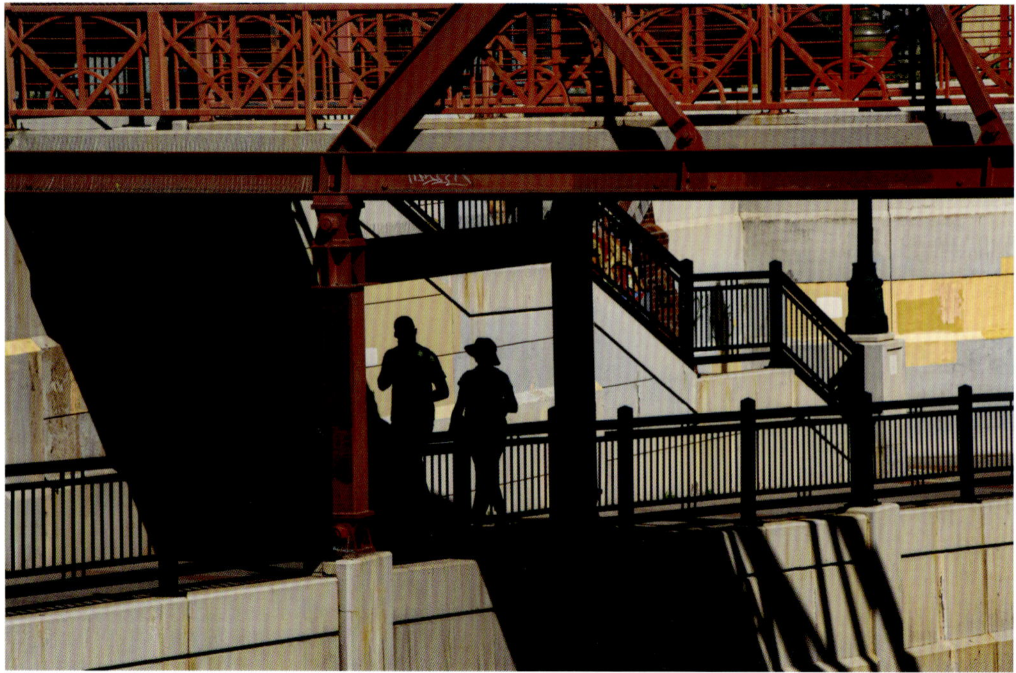

Get to know the Sunny 16 rule and you'll be amazed by how often it comes into play. This time I was in Denver, Colorado, shooting a potentially tricky mix of sunlight and shadow as pedestrians and bicyclists passed beneath the Denver Bridge. With my camera in Manual mode, I exposed exclusively for the sunlight, resulting in a perfect exposure of the sunny parts of the scene and a severe underexposure of the shadow areas, including the people. I fired away while they were briefly in the shadow, and voilà: a graphic composition of light and dark.

◘ Nikon D500, NIKKOR 18–300mm lens, *f*/16 for 1/400 sec., ISO 400, Daylight/Sunny WB

I discovered early in my photographic career that I was not cut out to be a wildlife photographer. I didn't have the patience that is so often necessary to get the perfect wildlife shot. Yet, while shooting in San Francisco recently, it occurred to me that maybe I was ready to try my hand at wildlife photography again, as I found myself shooting for the better part of an hour on the famed Powell Street, showing tremendous patience as I waited for the various elements of this composition to come together. I was hoping to capture silhouetted shapes of people disembarking from the famous cable cars, which required them to disembark in a shadowed area. While a number of people did disembark, it was always into the sunny part of the street. Finally, sixty-five minutes later, I got my wish. In hindsight, I think my patience had more to do with the color red, as it often is a real attention-getter in the world of color photography. As Kodak was fond of saying in their ads and how-to guides back in the days of Kodachrome slide film, "Include a subject with a lil' red in your composition and people will take notice." Well, here is a lot of red—and chances are good that you noticed! Here again was a Sunny 16 opportunity; I exposed for the brightly lit street and let the shadows and pedestrian become silhouettes.

◘ Nikon D500, NIKKOR 200–500mm lens on a monopod, *f*/22 for 1/320 sec., ISO 640, Daylight/Sunny WB

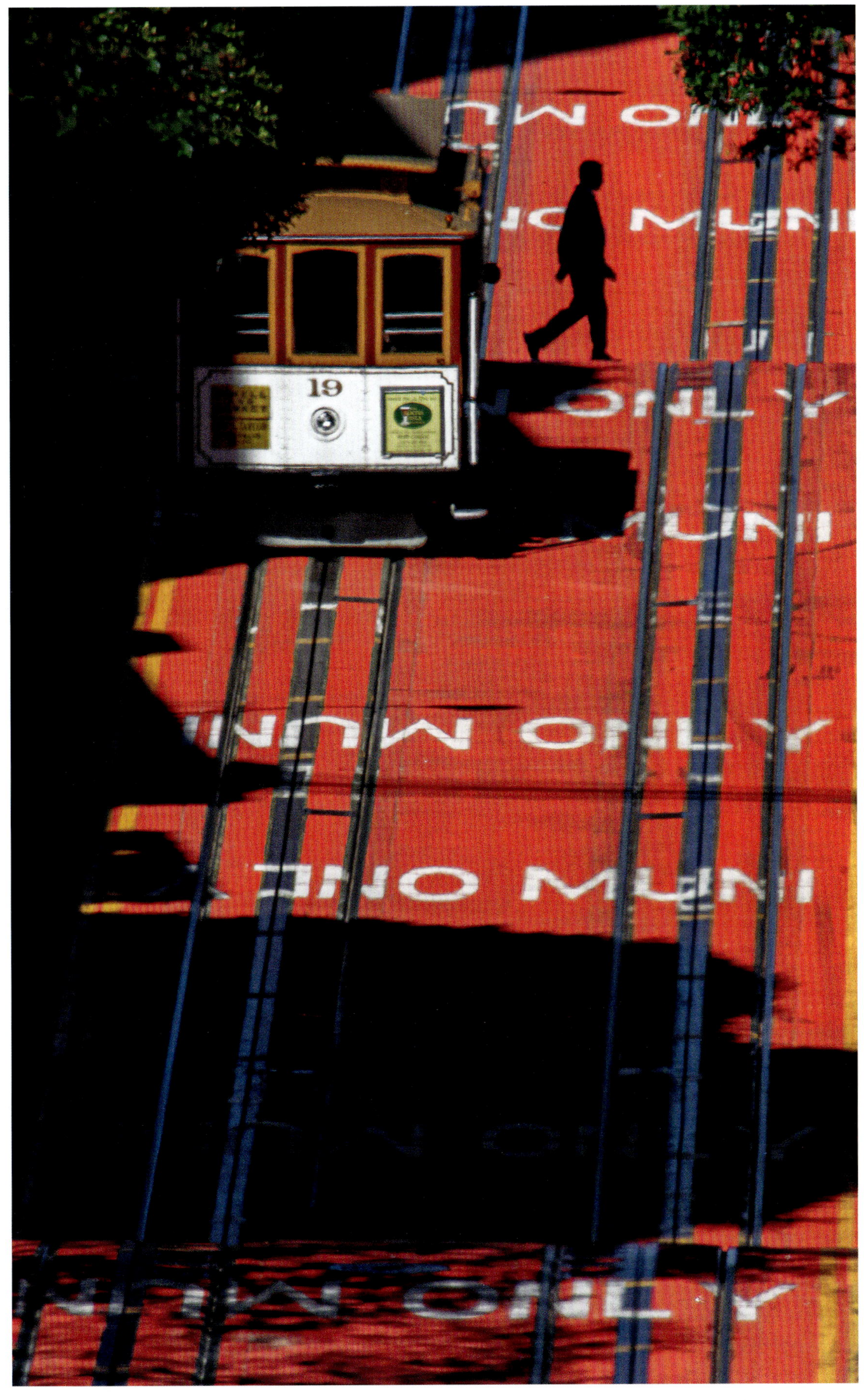
19
MUNI ONLY

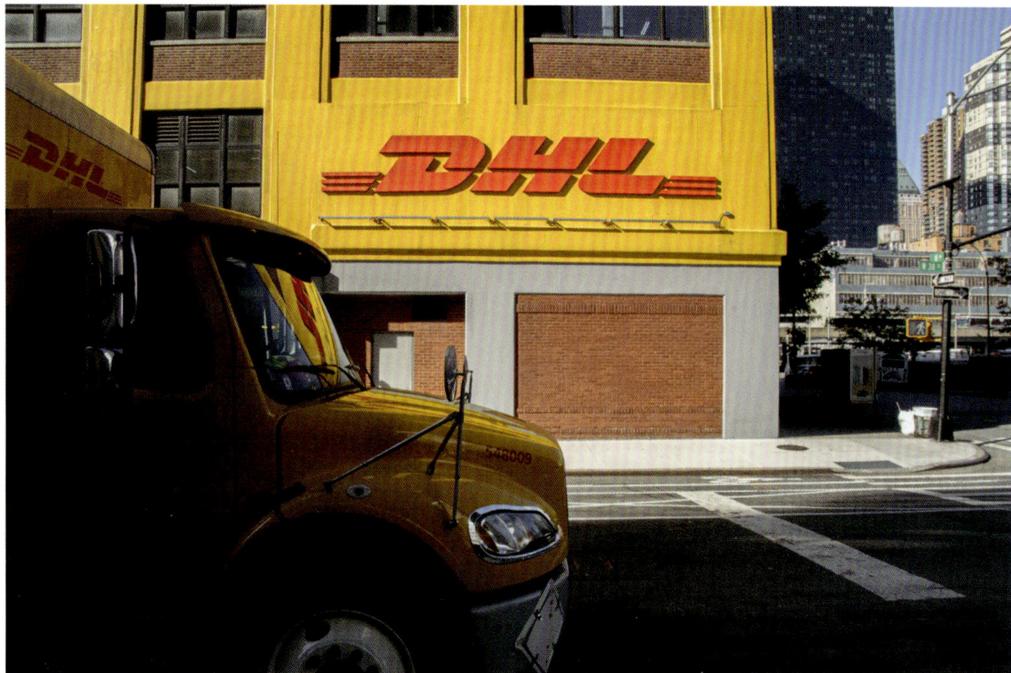

Street photography can be like wildlife photography, and sometimes the waiting can really test my patience. On this particular Monday afternoon, I was about to give up after a mere ten minutes, as I watched the low-angled late-afternoon sun getting lower and imagined all the other shots I was missing by hanging out alongside a DHL truck. But then a lone man entered to my right, and just before he emerged from the shadows, headed toward the much brighter street and sidewalk, I caught him in stride, taking his last step before walking into the light. Patience rewarded!

Once again, this is a Sunny 16 exposure. With my camera in Manual mode, I exposed for the sunlit building. I took full advantage of the wide-angle focal length of my 18–300mm lens by shooting at 18mm, very close to the hood of the parked DHL truck to gather the reflection of the DHL office across the street, much like shooting at the edge of a lake to capture a mountain reflection. A lucky afternoon on an unusually quiet day in Manhattan!

◘ Nikon D500, NIKKOR 18–300mm lens at 18mm, *f*/16 for 1/400 sec., ISO 400, Daylight/Sunny WB

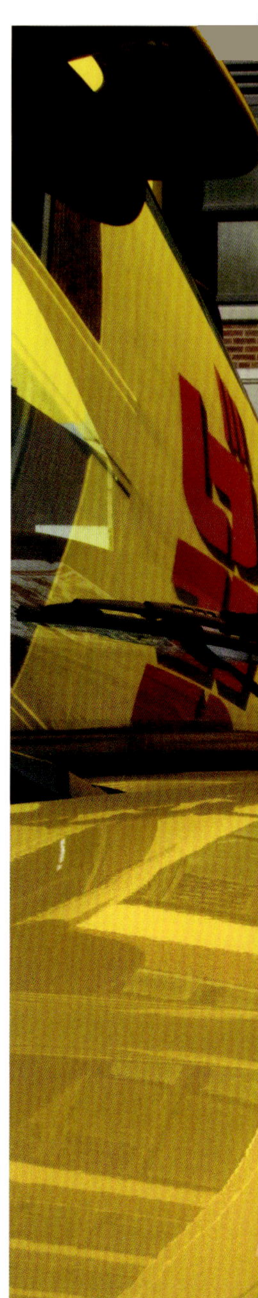

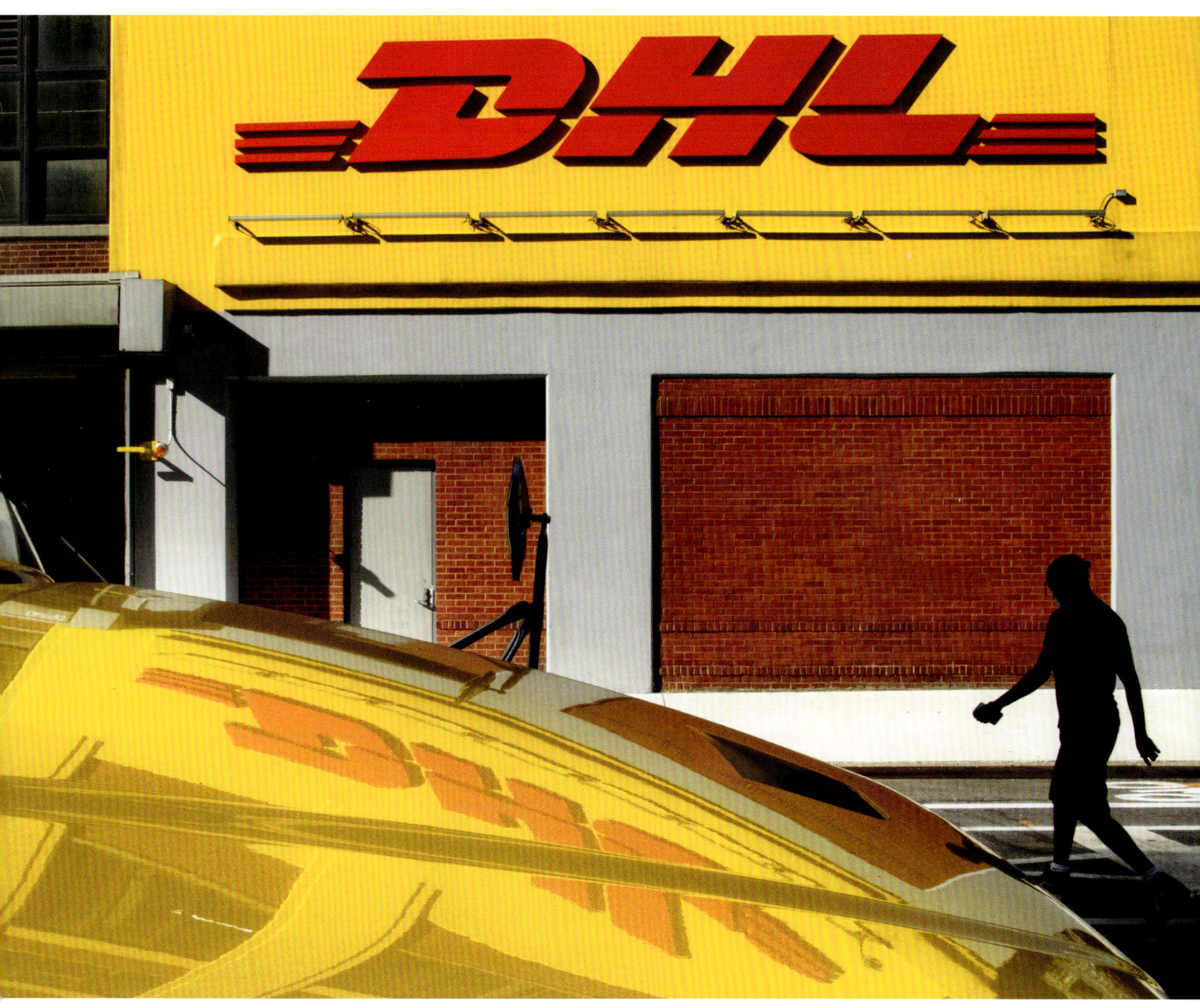
DHL

According to legend, the eleven rock-hewn churches of Lalibela, Ethiopia, were carved out of the rocky hillsides by forty thousand laborers by day and forty thousand angels by night. Regardless of who carved them, they are a UNESCO World Heritage site and truly a wonder of the world. The churches are connected by narrow passageways, uneven stairs, and archways, some of which might be too narrow for some, too steep for others, too short for the tallest among us, and a bit precarious for anyone with balance issues.

How ironic that in one of the holiest of places in all the world, I found myself thinking about the parallels between street photography and gambling in Las Vegas. Both involve chance and luck, hoped-for payoffs, observing the ever-changing scene before you, patience as the cards are shuffled or the chips tossed on the table, and then—maybe on the first hand, maybe several hands in—the gamble pays off. At least it did on this day, as three gentlemen came walking in from the right in the foreground shadows while a lone woman prayed in full sun against the background wall. Perhaps the main difference is that, unlike in Vegas, if you keep shooting you will eventually win far more then you could ever lose. And yes, this is yet another example of the Sunny 16 rule.

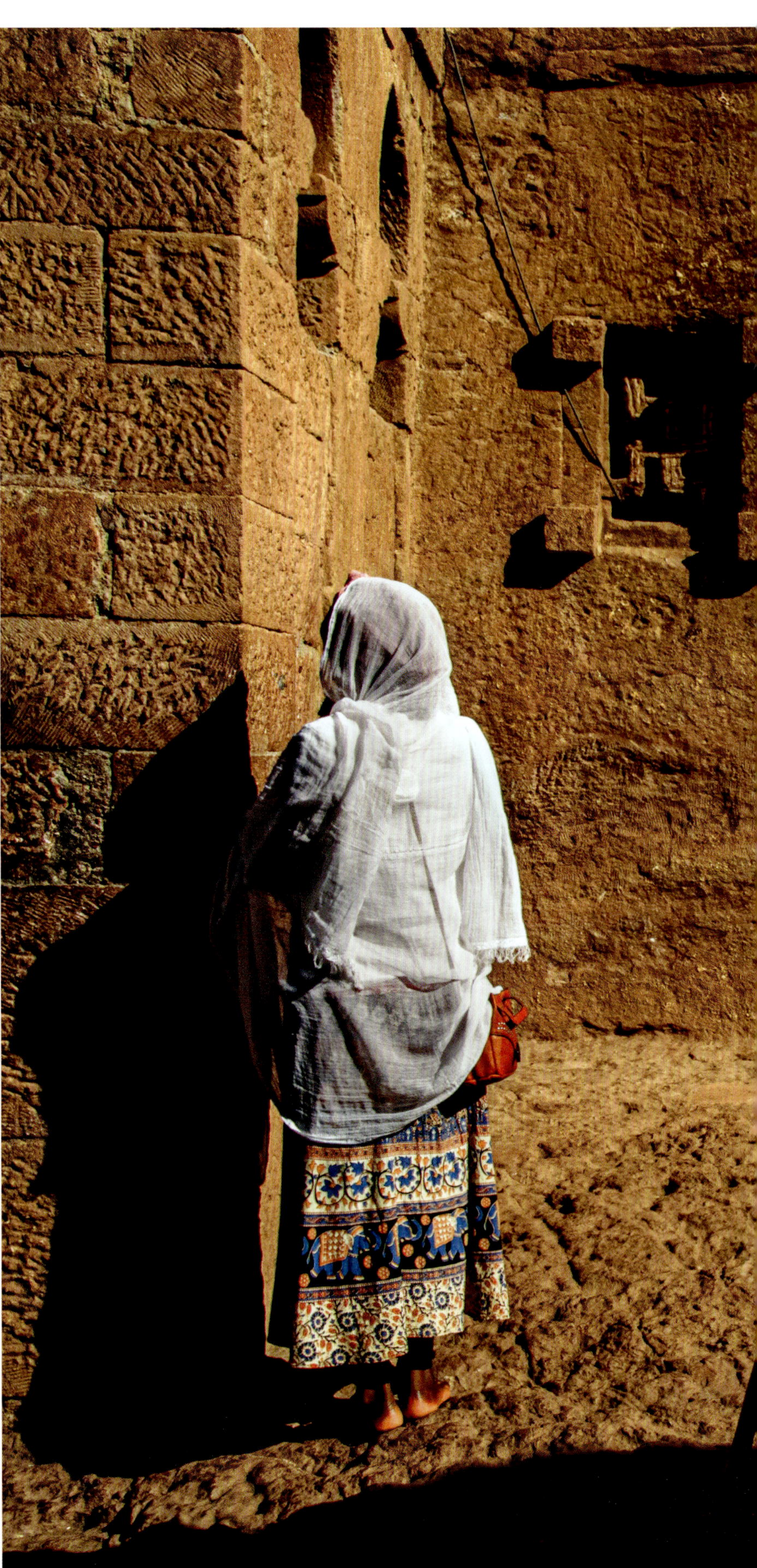

Nikon D500, NIKKOR 18–300mm lens, *f*/22 for 1/400 sec., ISO 800, Daylight/Sunny WB

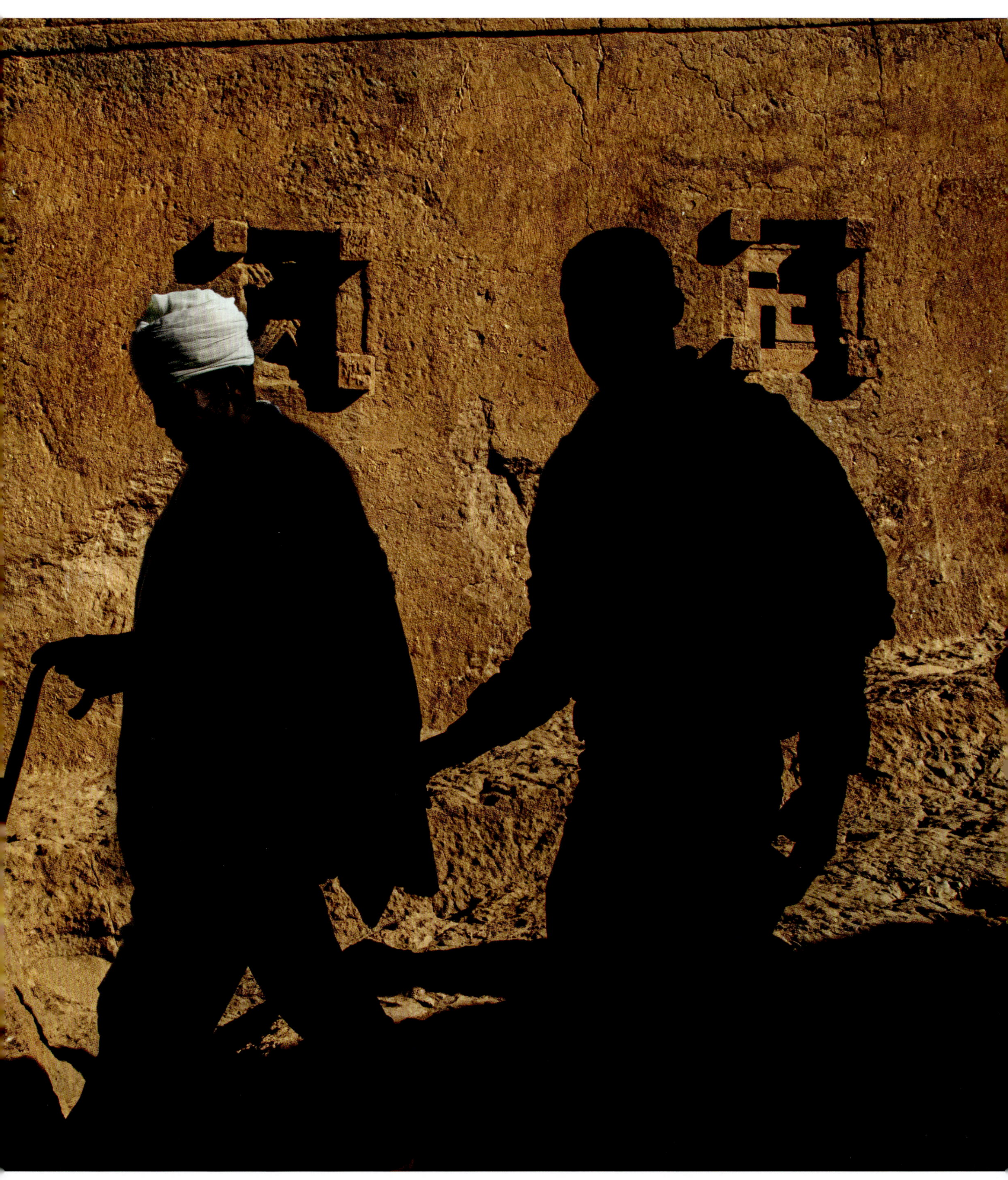

Backlight and Transparent Color

One of my favorite compositions is a backlit scene that includes a person or persons rendered as silhouettes in stark contrast to transparent, often colorful subjects. Low-angled backlight is best for shooting these compositions, along with a wide to moderate telephoto lens (especially the wide-angle lens) used in conjunction with an aperture of *f*/22 to create a "starburst" effect. To substantially reduce or eliminate lens flare when shooting into the sun like this, be sure to remove any filters! If you shoot these scenes in Aperture Priority, using *f*/22 with a setting of -2/3rds exposure (-0.7) along with an ISO of 200 or 400, the bold, dark shape of the human form will be in marked contrast to the transparent objects, which add vital color and contrast to the overall composition.

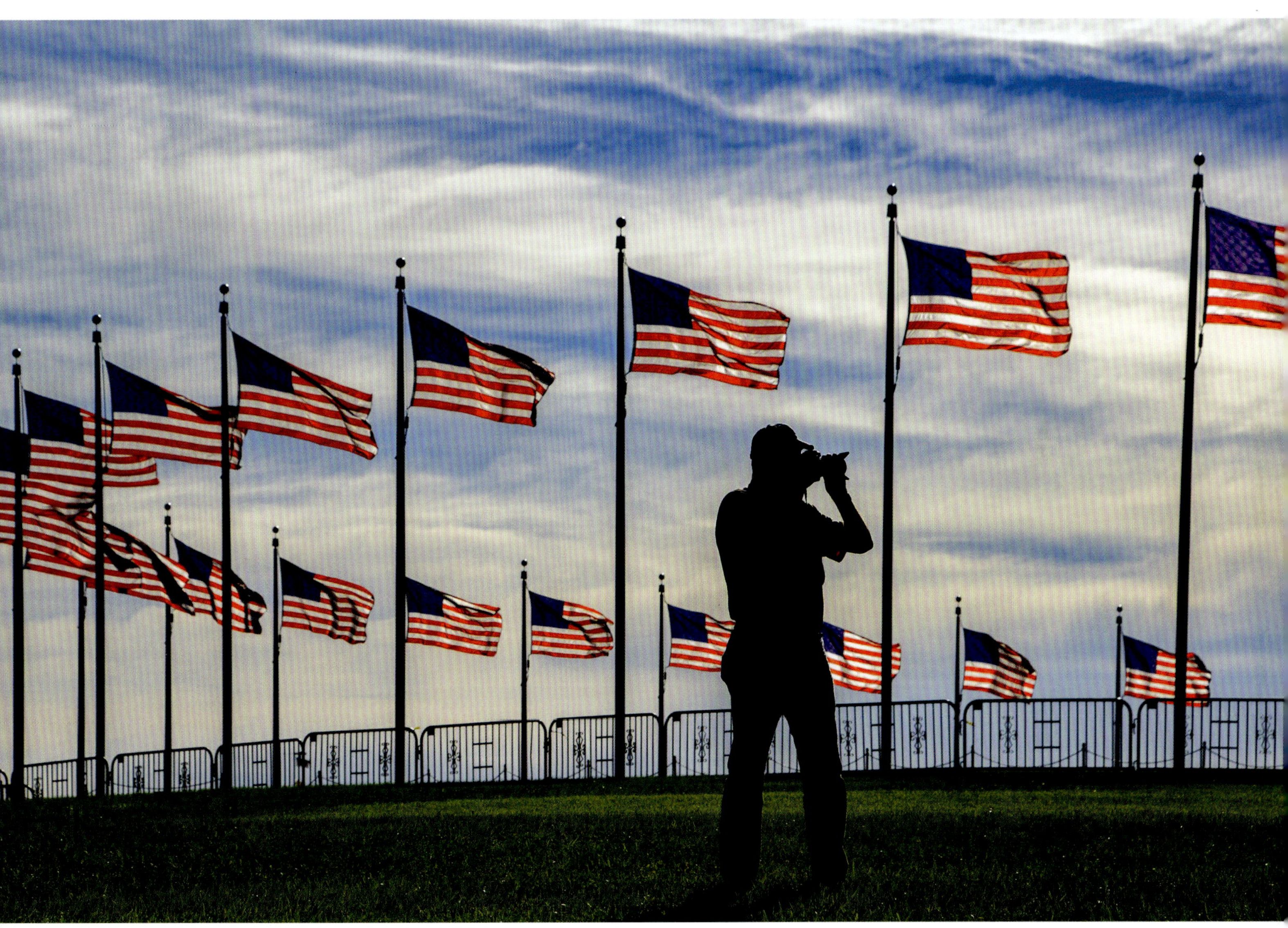

It was early morning on the first day of a Washington, DC, workshop, and I had not as yet learned much about the ten students in attendance beyond their obvious interest in photography. As we were shooting these backlit flags, I asked one of my students, a man named Bob, if he wouldn't mind standing in the foreground of my composition, just to add some human interest. I wasn't aiming for a starburst effect, so I chose an aperture of *f*/16 rather than *f*/22, providing more than enough depth of field and sharpness throughout.

It was only later, over lunch, that I learned that Bob was a retired airline pilot for United Airlines and had served with the US Air Force as a young man, so here's a salute to Bob in front of the flags he proudly served. Thank you for your service!

◘ Nikon D850, NIKKOR 24–120mm lens, *f*/16 for 1/320 sec., ISO 200, Daylight/Sunny WB

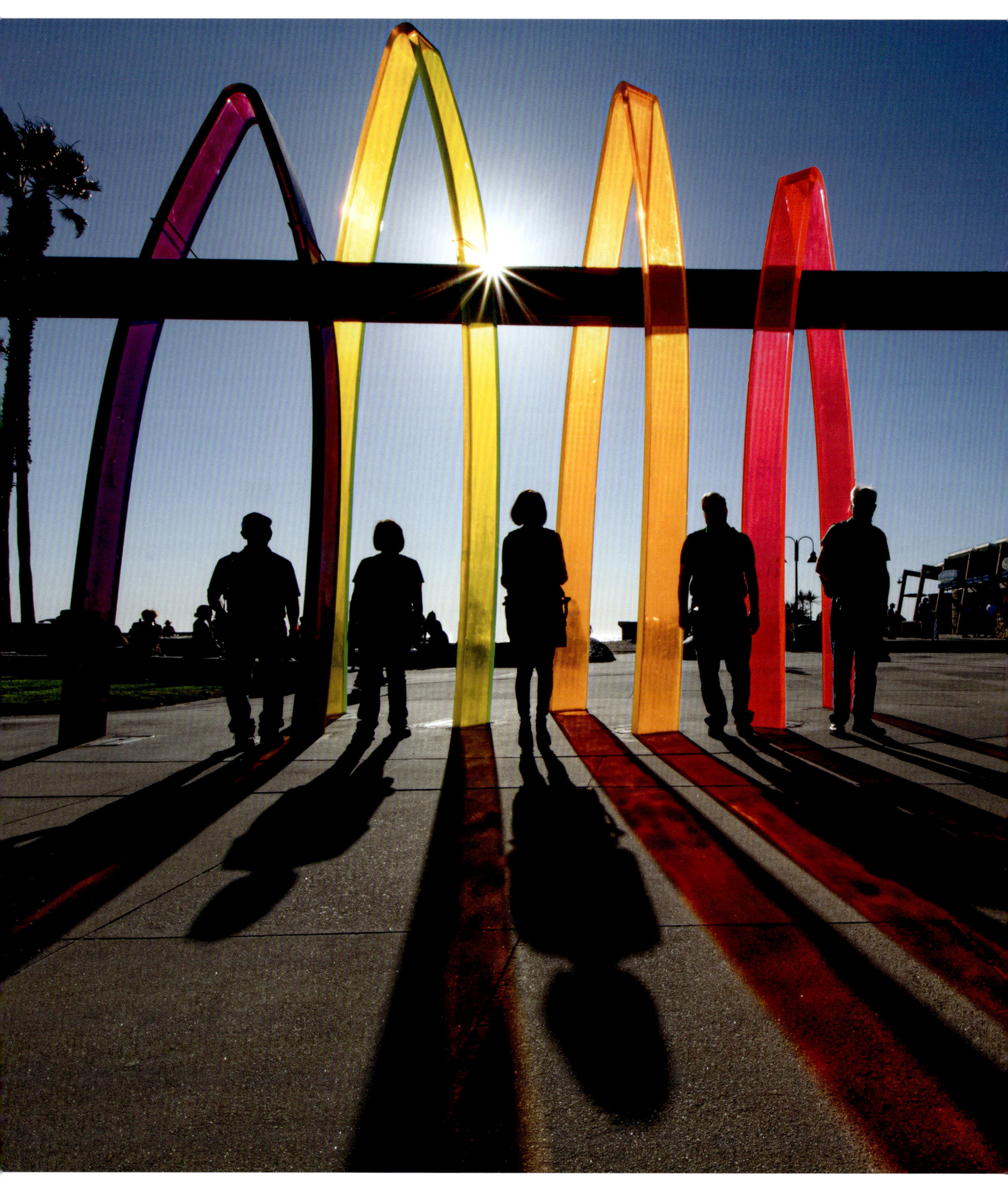

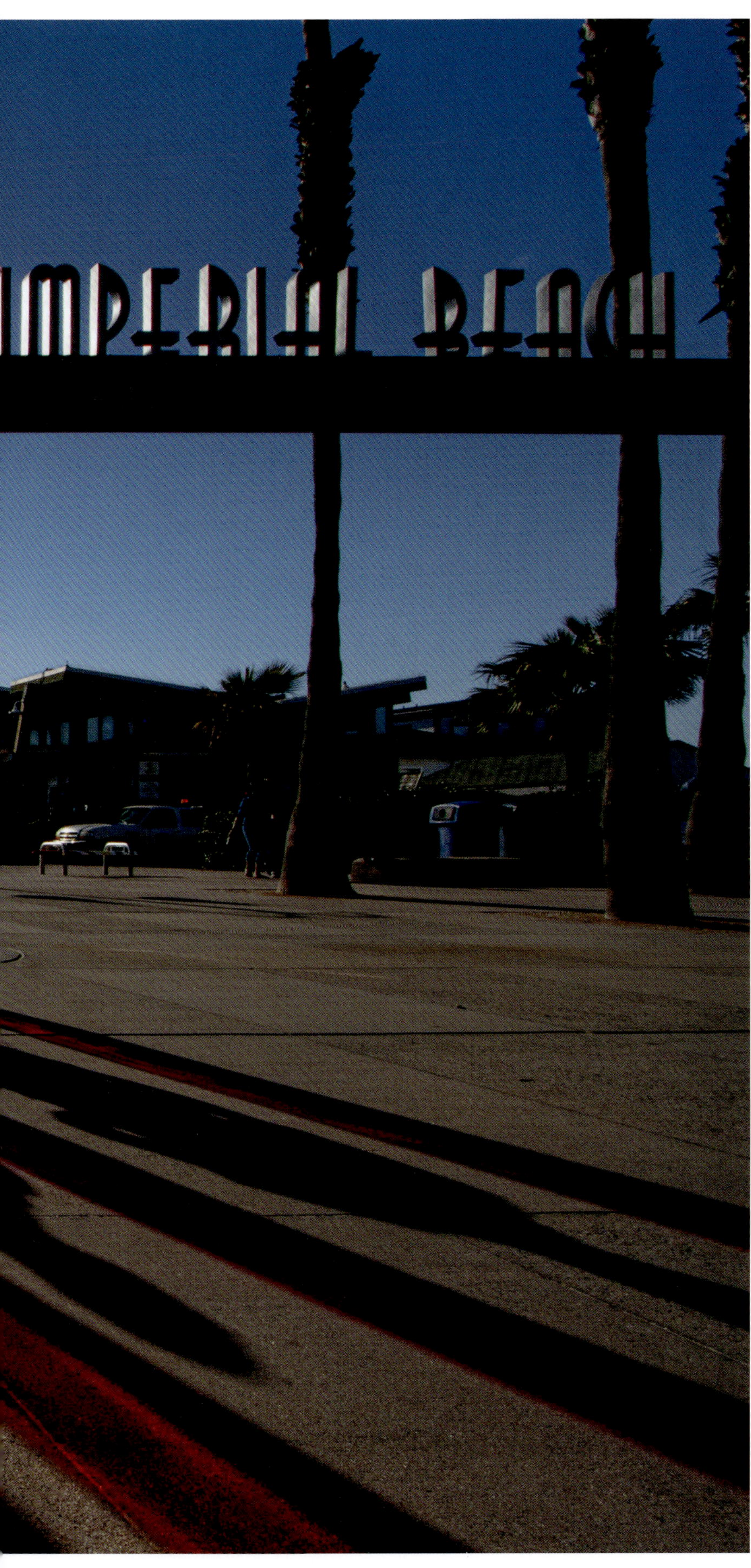

Although there was a seven-year gap between my first and second trips to Imperial Beach, California, it felt like I had been there just a week earlier, since the concessions, the entrance, even the palm trees were exactly as I remembered them. If you should catch a wave on your surfboard at Imperial Beach and it blows you farther south than you wish, make sure you have your passport around your neck in its waterproof enclosure, as you will need it to get back into the United States; Imperial Beach is but a mile north of the US/Mexico border.

On this late afternoon, I knew upon reaching the entrance to the popular beach that I would be shooting these colorful arches with my students as models, and they in turn would shoot their own group shots as we rotated from one shooter to the next. But to get *the* shot, we had to wait at least another hour, as I wanted a starburst of the sun to be breaking at the horizontal bar that ran through the arches. By that time the colorful shadows on the ground below would also be even longer, thus creating the illusion of greater depth, since we would be using those long foreground lines as immediate foreground interest. Line, color, and shape are an unbeatable and surefire combination when generating a compelling street photography composition. And as is shown here, returning an hour later proved to be the correct decision. The massive depth of field was obtained by setting the distance mark on the lens to one meter and focusing manually, as explained in "Storytelling Apertures," page 26.

◘ Nikon D500, NIKKOR 12–24mm lens, *f*/22 for 1/320 sec., ISO 100, Daylight/Sunny WB

Storytelling Apertures

There are three picture-taking situations in which attention to aperture choice is paramount. The first is what I call a storytelling composition—an image that, as the name implies, tells a story. And as with any good story, there's a beginning (the foreground subject), a middle (the middle-ground subject), and an end (the background subject). Such an image might contain stalks of wheat (the foreground/beginning), which serve to introduce a farmhouse fifty to one hundred feet away (the main subject in the middle ground/middle), which stands against a backdrop of white puffy clouds and blue sky (the background/end).

Once you start focusing your attention on storytelling compositions, you may find yourself asking a perplexing question: "Where the heck do I focus?" When you focus on the foreground stalks of wheat, for example, the red barn and the sky go out of focus, and when you focus on the red barn and the sky, the foreground wheat stalks go out of focus. The solution to this common dilemma is simple: you don't focus the lens at all, but instead preset the focus via the distance settings.

There was a time when most photographers used single-focal-length lenses instead of zooms simply because those lenses were sharper. Additionally, all single-focal-length lenses had—and still have—what is called a depth-of-field scale. This scale makes it very easy to preset your focus for the scene before you, and it offers tremendous assurance that you'll get the area of sharpness that you desire in your image. But with the proliferation of high-quality zoom lenses, most photographers have abandoned single-focal-length lenses in favor of zoom lenses. The trade-off, of course, is that we are running around with lenses that don't have depth-of-field scales.

But what we do have are distance settings. These settings are similar to the depth-of-field scale in that they allow you to preset the depth of field before you take a shot. And since every storytelling composition relies on the maximum depth of field, you would first choose to set your aperture to *f*/22 and then align the distance of one meter directly above the distance-setting mark on the lens. This one-meter setting applies only to the following: when using the focal lengths of 16–24mm on a full-frame camera (FX sensor) and when using the focal lengths of 10–16mm on a crop sensor camera (DX sensor). Again, it is vitally important that you set the distance mark to one meter (or three feet) and that you turn off autofocus whenever you wish to record storytelling sharpness. When you do this, the resulting depth of field will be between fourteen and twenty inches and infinity, depending on which focal length between 14mm and 24mm you are using with your full-frame camera (FX) or which focal length between 10mm and 16mm you are using with your crop sensor camera (DX).

For more about storytelling apertures and the other two picture-taking situations where aperture choice is important, see page 44.

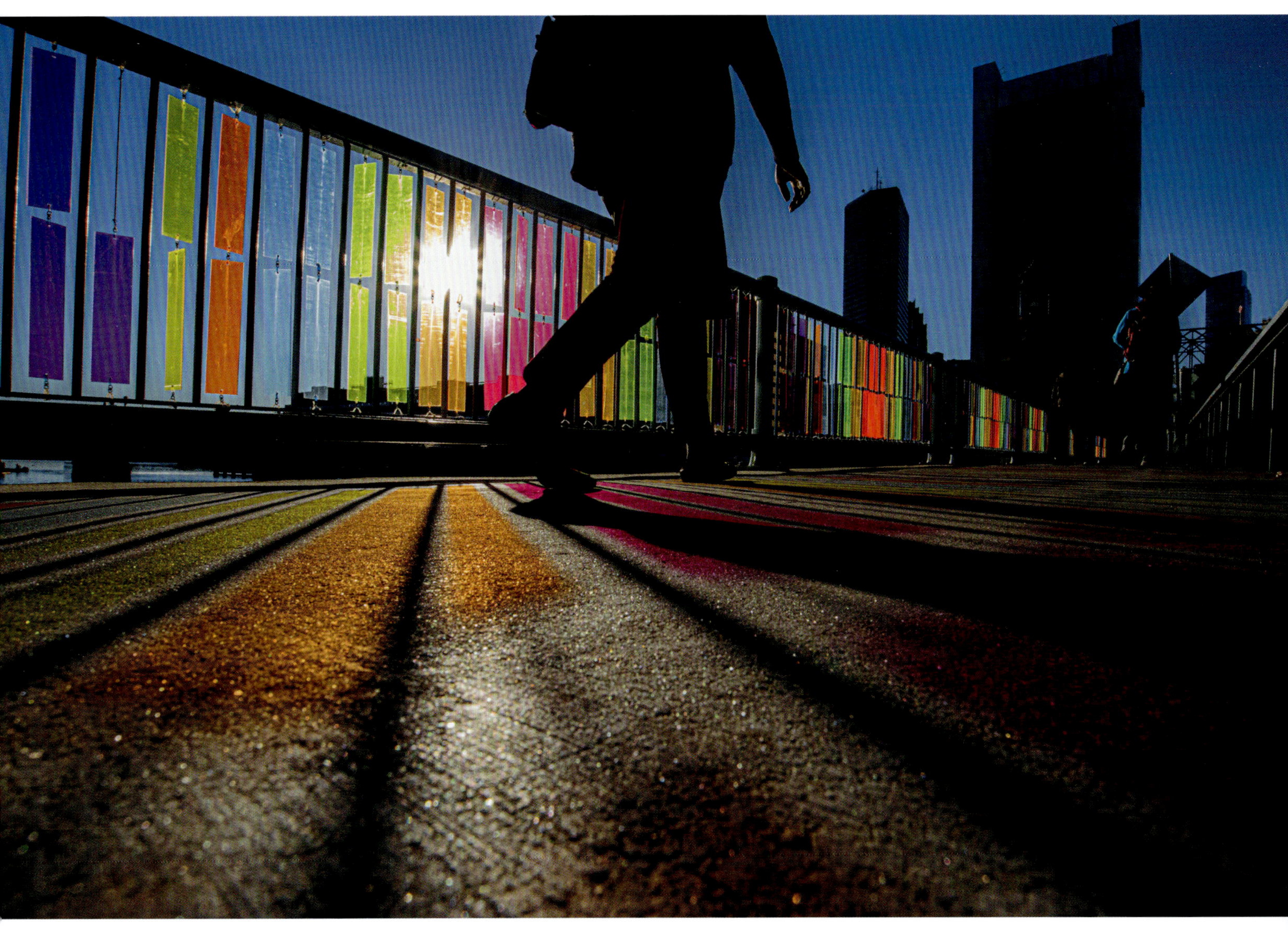

It was my first trip to Boston, so how was I to know that the extremely colorful bridge I found myself shooting was going to be this colorful for only a few weeks? Unbeknownst to me, I was party to an art installation that would be on display for just a few weeks, which in retrospect means that I now have rare images from that Saturday afternoon. It was much like the *Gates*, a 2005 art installation in New York's Central Park for which Bulgarian artist Christo Yavacheff and French artist Jeanne-Claude installed more than 7,500 gates covered in saffron-colored fabric and that, similarly, was taken down only sixteen days later—vroom, vanished, gone forever, never to be repeated! Get it while you can, right?

I am a huge fan of working the subject, which means shooting from varying points of view: up, down, from the side, lying on your back, shooting down from above, and so on. But on this day, there really was only one compelling point of view: from down low. As in the Imperial Beach image on page 24, this allowed me to use the leading lines to propel the viewer into the scene. It was now only a matter of waiting for pedestrians—correction, waiting for the *right* pedestrian. I wanted a pedestrian whose stride matched up with a snippet of the sun's light to get an elegant starburst along the starkly colorful bridge, creating contrast with the equally stark silhouetted shape of that lone pedestrian.

◘ Nikon D850, NIKKOR 14–24mm lens, *f*/22 for 1/320 sec., ISO 100, Daylight/Sunny WB

Dappled Light

Many of us are familiar with the "big three" lighting conditions—front light, sidelight, and backlight—but aren't yet exploring the beauty of dappled light, primarily because it may seem harder to find or shoot. Dappled light is well worth looking out for as it often imparts a striking combination of soft light and soft shadows, bringing a quiet impact to any subject within it.

One common place to find dappled light is under trees during midday, from 10 a.m. to 3 p.m. As the sunlight cascades down through the leaves, the light is scattered and softened. In the absence of trees, you can also find dappled light in the early morning or late afternoon, especially near buildings made of dark reflective glass. As the sunlight hits that dark glass, it bounces off and scatters down onto the streets and fronts of nearby high-rise buildings.

With its often even distribution of light and shadow, dappled light can easily be metered using Canon's Evaluative Metering mode or Nikon's Matrix Metering mode, as either will average the two and render an exposure that is—much like Goldilocks' choice of porridge—just right. (Sony, Fuji, and Pentax also have Matrix or Evaluative Metering modes; consult your manual.) Do not set an exposure that is under or over. As a side note, I recommend keeping your metering mode set to Evaluative or Matrix for 99.9 percent of your photography; the other 0.01 percent of the time is when you want to sound like a pro and point out to people that you are using the Spot Metering mode, but don't forget to return to Evaluative or Matrix when you are done.

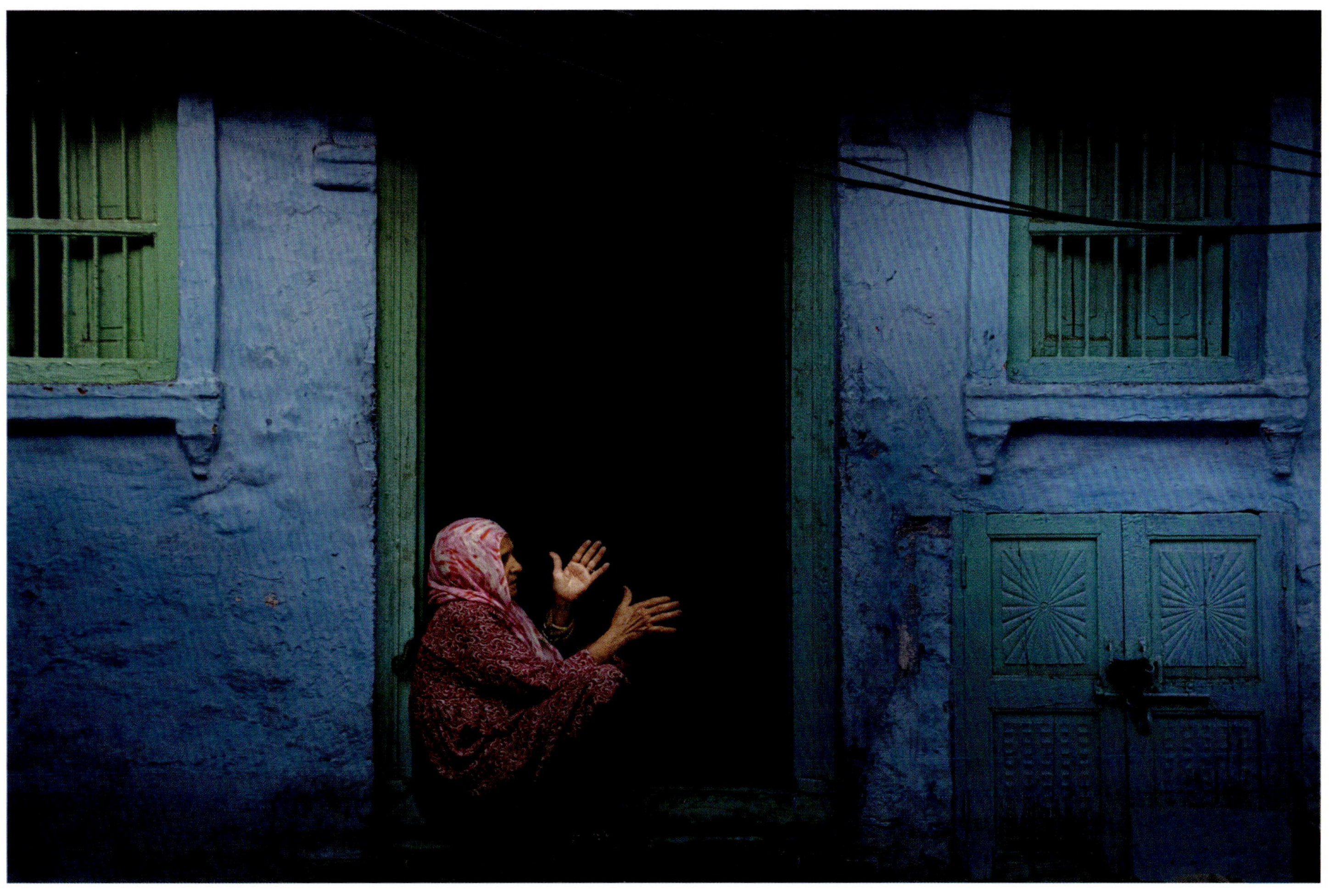

Perhaps she was conversing with someone inside the house, which would explain her very animated hand gestures, yet I did not see her lips move. Or perhaps she was wiping her hands clean after finishing a meal, or shooing away a fly. From across the street, and during a brief gap between the many motorbikes, tuktuks, and bicycles flying past, I was able to fire off several clean frames. Directly across the street from this house was a three-story bank with golden-colored reflective glass windows, and the low-angled sunlight hitting those windows engaged in a game of ping-pong as it bounced off the glass back toward the sun, dropping glistening particles of light onto the woman and her house.

◘ Nikon D500, NIKKOR 18–300mm lens at 210mm, *f*/13 for 1/320 sec., ISO 1000, Daylight/Sunny WB

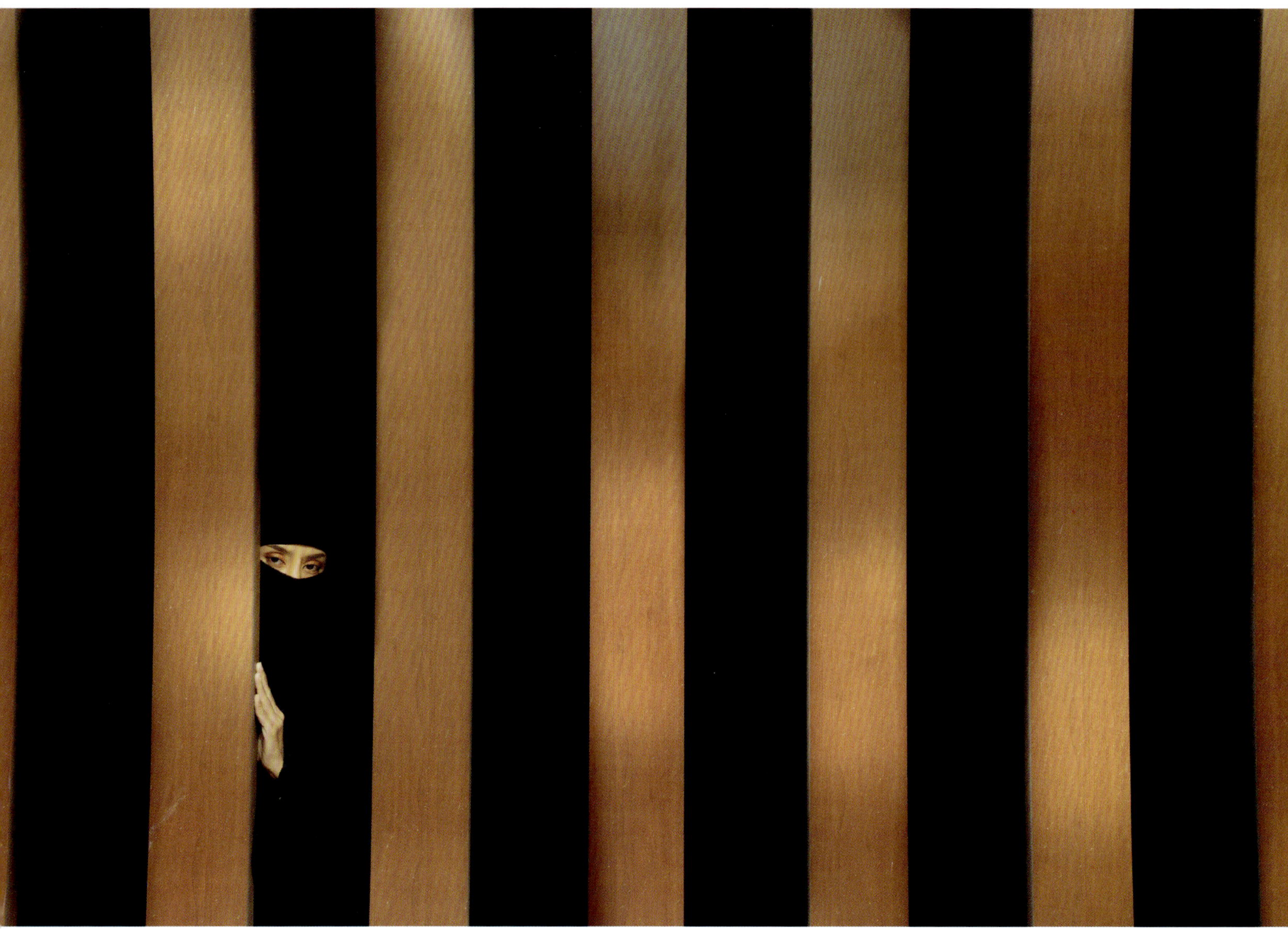

A parking garage in Dubai became the unlikely location for a quick portrait shoot of one of my students. What caught my attention was not so much the bold, clean lines of the wooden wall surrounding the parking garage, but rather the dappled light cascading down the vertical columns of wood from a glass building directly behind me. I asked my student to stand in the dappled light and vertical columns, and because she disrupts the pattern of lines and light, she of course becomes the focus of the overall composition.

To expose this image, I did switch to Spot Metering mode. I pointed at the exact dead center of my student's face since that was the light I was most concerned about, and that one-degree spot was all the light meter took into account. I then adjusted my shutter speed until a correct exposure was indicated and fired away.

◘ Nikon D850, NIKKOR 24–120mm lens, *f*/11 for 1/160 sec., ISO 400, Daylight/Sunny WB

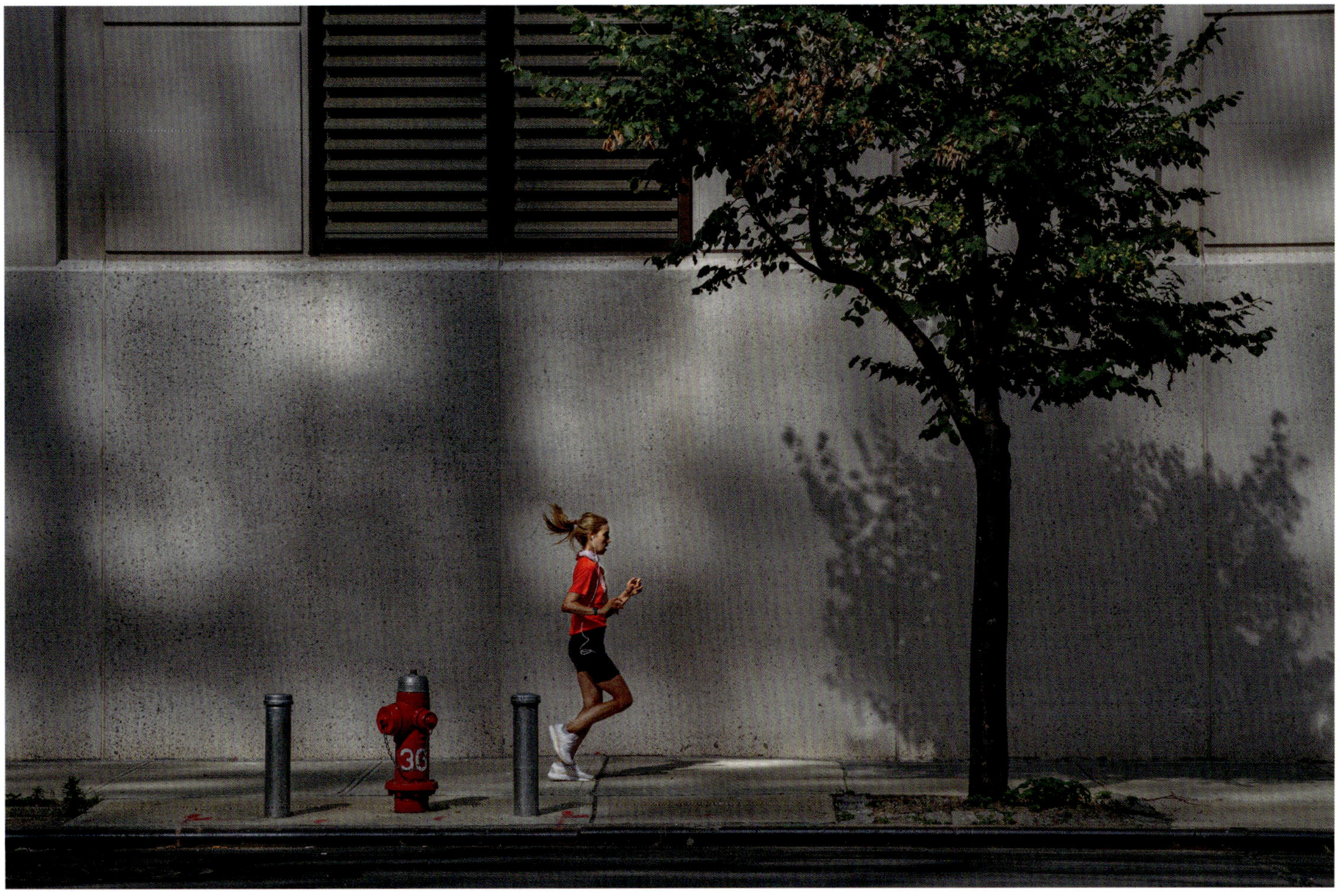

It was an early Sunday morning as I walked around the West Side of Manhattan, and the sunrise was soon reflecting off the high-rise buildings of Hudson Yards behind me. After taking notice of the strong dappled light, I felt the frustration of looking at incredible light yet having nothing to work with. Time was not on my side, as the sun rose higher in the sky, the intensity of the dappled light diminishing with each passing minute, much like a steamed-up bathroom mirror clearing as soon as the bathroom door is opened. A quick look at my watch told me the sun had already been up for thirty minutes, and to add to my level of frustration, it was a Sunday! Where were the dog walkers, the early-morning joggers, the bicyclists?

Five minutes later, my wish for someone, anyone, was granted: a lone jogger. To freeze the action, I called upon an ISO of 800 and the "Who cares?" aperture of *f*/8 (for more about the "Who cares?" aperture, see page 44). Aperture Priority gave me a 1/400 sec. shutter speed, plenty fast enough to freeze the jogger's stride. I was grateful for this woman who appeared in my canvas of dappled light, with the bonus of that gesture of her bouncing blonde ponytail.

◘ Nikon D500, NIKKOR 18–300mm lens, *f*/8 for 1/400 sec., ISO 800, Daylight/Sunny WB

Light and Shadow Are *Not* the Holy Grail

I have sat through a number of talks by well-known and not so well-known photographers who espouse a common mantra: when it comes to the art of the image, light is everything, and without attention to light, you will not succeed. You may be surprised to learn that I do not agree. I don't believe that light is everything. My feeling—and you can quote me on this—is that great light *rarely* salvages a poor composition, but a great composition will, almost without fail, salvage poor light!

Am I anti-light? Hardly! Without light—whether the source is the early-morning sun, studio lights, or the flame of a Zippo lighter—we cannot take a photograph. Light is absolutely essential to the making of a photograph, just as milk and cream are essential to making vanilla ice cream. Yet even if you use the highest quality milk, cream, and vanilla to create the most desirable vanilla ice cream, it's doubtful you will sell a single scoop if it's the color gray and has the texture of broken glass! Yes, all of the ingredients are there, but the final arrangement of the ice cream, its composition, does not look appealing. Each and every time you create an image, your goal should be for the viewer to feel overwhelmingly compelled to visually consume your work—to eat it up, as they say. And if you place all of your emphasis on the light and not on the composition, you might as well try to sell just the frosting without the cake (good luck with that, by the way).

If you struggle with composition, make that your number-one priority. And if the light is still a struggle, don't worry; over time, even without any formal education, you will get ever closer to the light. With each experience that falls a bit short, you will learn, until finally light will become second nature, even as you continue to keep the image's arrangement—the composition—in the forefront of your mind.

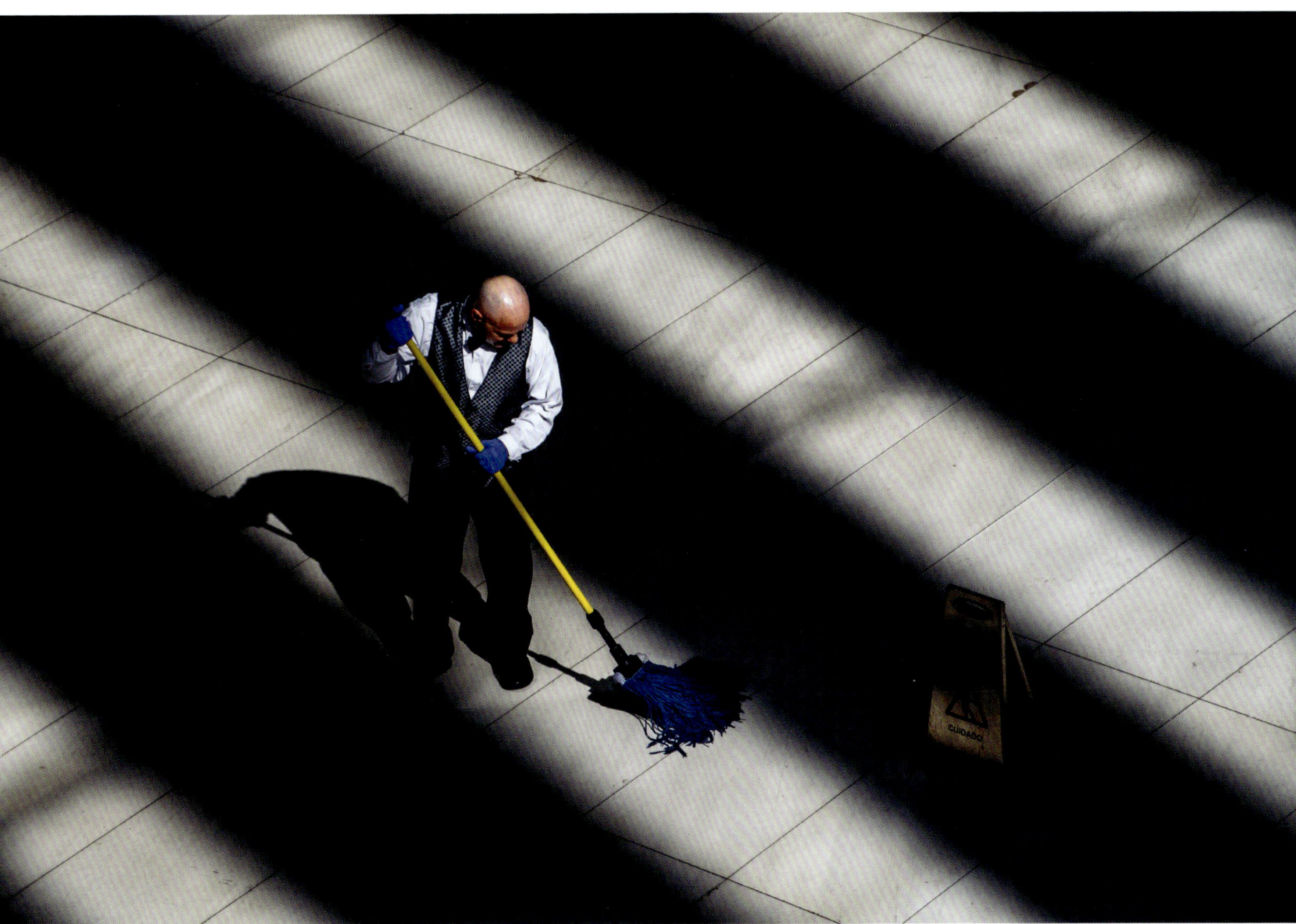

Like most photographers, I love light and shadow, and their combination is no doubt compelling. But even when great light does happen, a poor composition will dilute its effectiveness.

In both this image and the next, it is the composition—the familiar Rule of Thirds, also known as the Golden Section—that is truly responsible for making the photograph compelling.

It was late in the day on a fall Saturday when I entered the Oculus in Lower Manhattan and was quick to go to work from the overhead staircase landing, which affords views to the floor below. The relatively equal combination of light and shadow made the exposure quite easy; the meter deduced that the subject was equal parts light and dark and correctly balanced the exposure—another argument for using Evaluative or Matrix Metering and not underexposing or overexposing. I will add that strictly from a wardrobe perspective, the custodian's tuxedo-like vest and bow tie elevate this scene into a kind of janitorial elegance.

◘ Nikon D500, NIKKOR 18–300mm lens, *f*/16 for 1/100 sec., ISO 400, Daylight/Sunny WB

In Washington, DC, another custodian was preparing the Lincoln Memorial for the onslaught of Saturday visitors, running his wide dust mop across the marble floor under the watchful eye of Lincoln himself. Perhaps he was unaware of how the low-angled early morning sunlight was streaming in like a spotlight, elevating his importance to that of a play's main character on stage. It's an example of how light can control and direct the visual weight of a photograph's importance.

◘ Nikon D500, NIKKOR 18–300mm lens, *f*/11 for 1/100 sec., ISO 400, Daylight/Sunny WB

Exposing for Mixed Light and Shadow

The light meter in all cameras and smartphones is what we call a reflected light meter—it reads reflected light. And regardless of whether your camera left the factory thirty years ago or your smartphone left it last week, that light meter was primarily programmed to generate a reading based on the simple principle that the world is a neutral gray color, from the North Pole to the South Pole. When light hits a neutral gray color, approximately 82 percent of the light is absorbed and 18 percent is reflected. And whether the light is direct sunlight or light on an overcast day, most of the time the light we see is in fact reflected light, equaling the 18 percent reflectance of a gray card.

However, you will come upon many compositions that are a combination of sunlight and shadow. These can be tricky, not only for you but also for your camera's light meter. Since this is not a book about science, I will cut to the chase. When you're confronted with a mix of light and shadow, such as in a sidelit scene, look at your subject. Is it in sunlight or in shade? Or is it under the umbrella of an equal distribution of light from an overcast day? Whatever the dominant light source is for your subject—full sun or open shade—set your exposure exclusively for that light, assuming, of course, that you want to record the most dramatic exposure. Determine your subject, determine the light on your subject, and expose exclusively for that light.

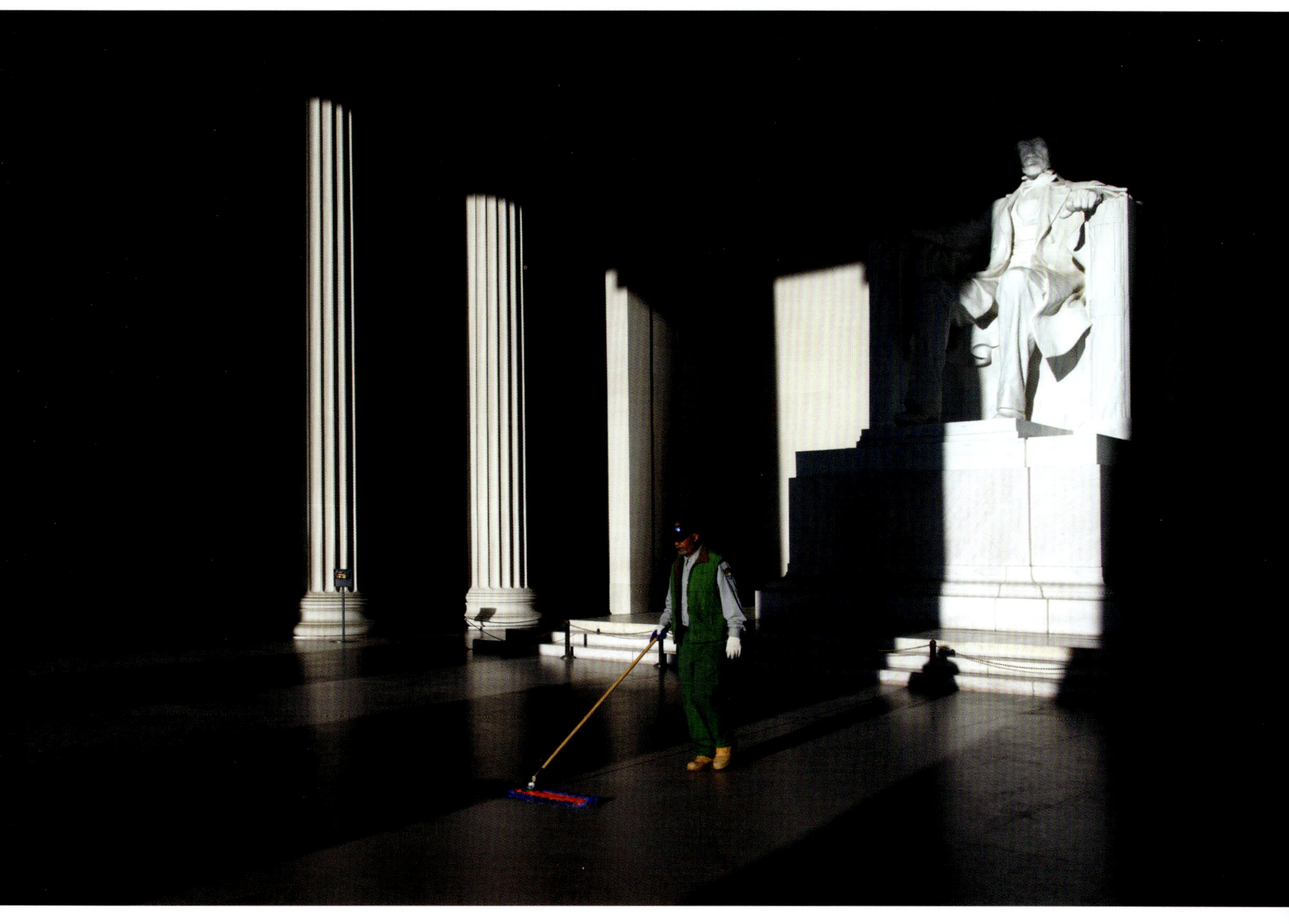

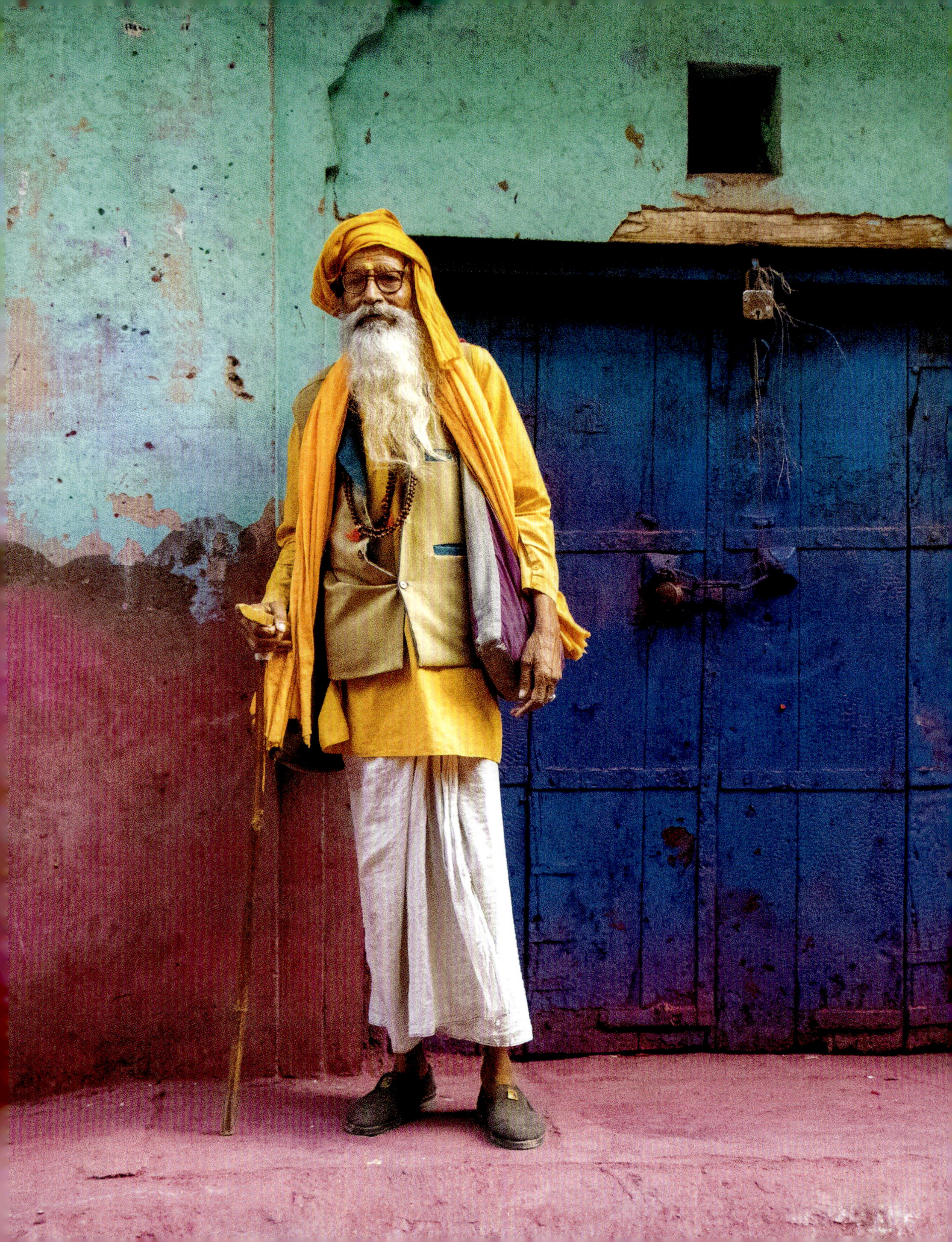

COMPOSITION

Mergers

When discussing composition, many photography books describe the common mistake of "mergers," such as a tree in the background appearing to grow out of a person's head in the foreground. Yet experienced street photographers embrace and even deliberately seek out mergers to create humorous compositions and make visual statements about social issues.

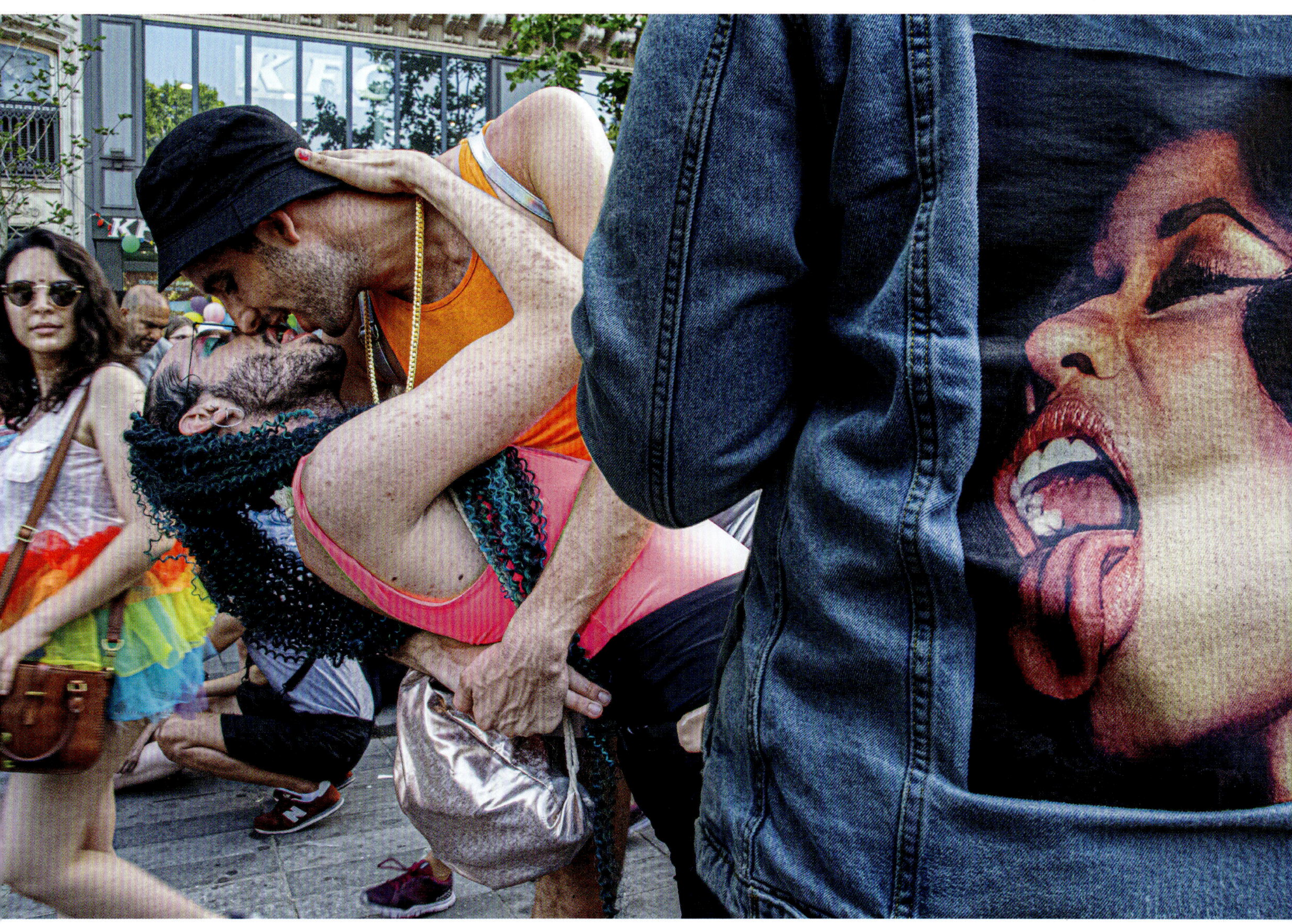

One of my many deliberate mergers, which I consider one of my best, was shot during the LGBTQ+ Parade in Paris during the summer of 2019. I had caught sight of a young woman wearing a jacket bearing a photo of a woman with her tongue extended, as if licking a phantom ice cream cone. I was quick to ask the woman if she could stay put while I framed up the back of her jacket as the foreground to my composition, and it wasn't long before two parade participants came into view, obviously celebrating the day and "sharing the love." I quickly fired, and only later made the discovery that I'd also captured another woman passing by, expressing surprise at what she was witnessing.

◘ Nikon D850, NIKKOR 24–120mm lens for 28mm, *f*/22 for 1/200 sec., ISO 640, Daylight/Sunny WB

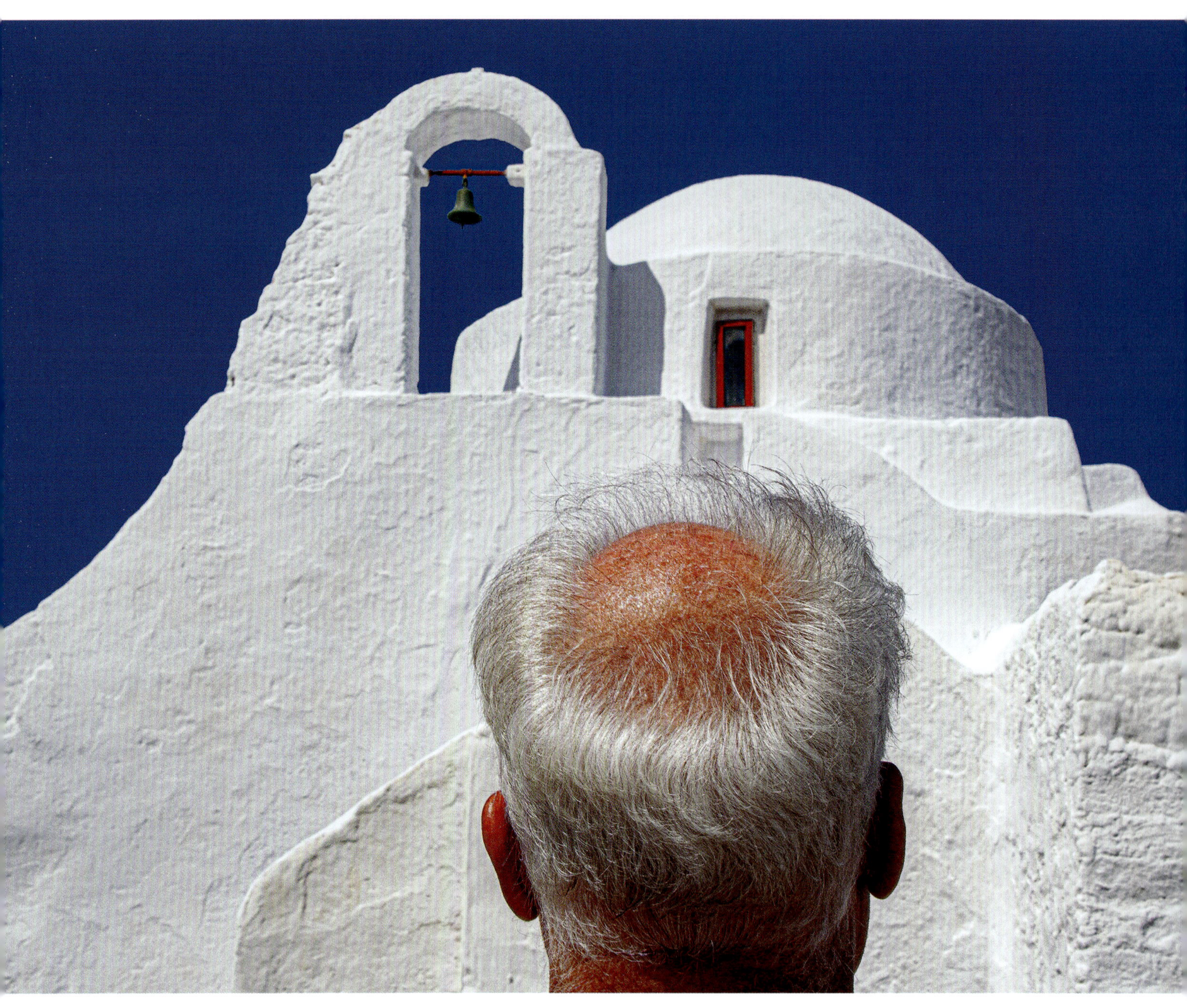

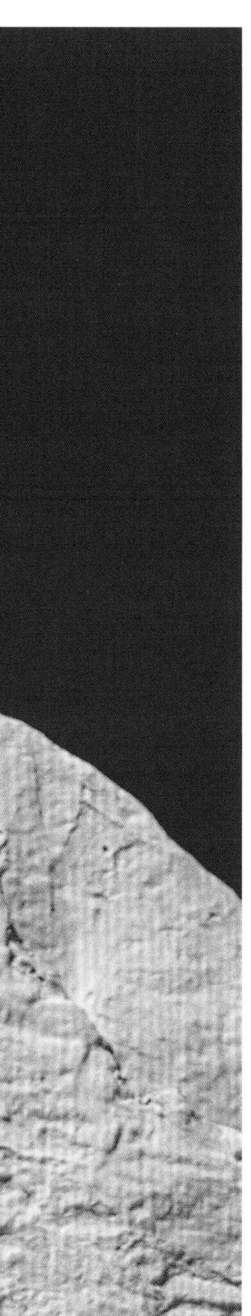

On the Island of Mykonos in Greece, you will find, at the water's edge, in the Castro neighborhood, the Paraportiani Greek Orthodox Church. It is actually five little churches, one built atop the other, or side by side, depending on which century the construction was done—kind of like adding on a room or a second floor to an existing house over several centuries. It claims to be one of the most photographed white churches in the world, a claim made by the Greek tourism body. I am not sure how that claim can be substantiated, but it makes for good press. The argument of it being one of the most photographed could be justified, based on the number of tourists. On my most recent visit, I was accompanied by several students, including one balding student, Jerry, who had just turned away from me to photograph the church. With his back now toward me, I was immediately struck by the relationship between the "two white domes," and I was quick to ask Jerry to just hold still for a second or two. As he faced the church, I quickly composed the shot you see here, in the name of humor, of course. As you might imagine, all of that really bright reflecting white could have played havoc with my camera's light meter, but nope, nothing to worry about here. It was all frontlit, thus a Sunny 16, with ISO 200, 1/200 sec. Since I also wanted front-to-back sharpness, I called upon that "dreaded *f*/22" again and was able to record exacting sharpness front to back. The Sunny 16 correct exposure is now at *f*/22 for 1/100 sec. If you want to see pictures of the entire church(es), just Google "Paraportiani Church" and you'll see hundreds.

◘ Nikon D500, NIKKOR 18-300mm, *f*/22 for 1/100 sec, ISO 200, Daylight/Sunny WB

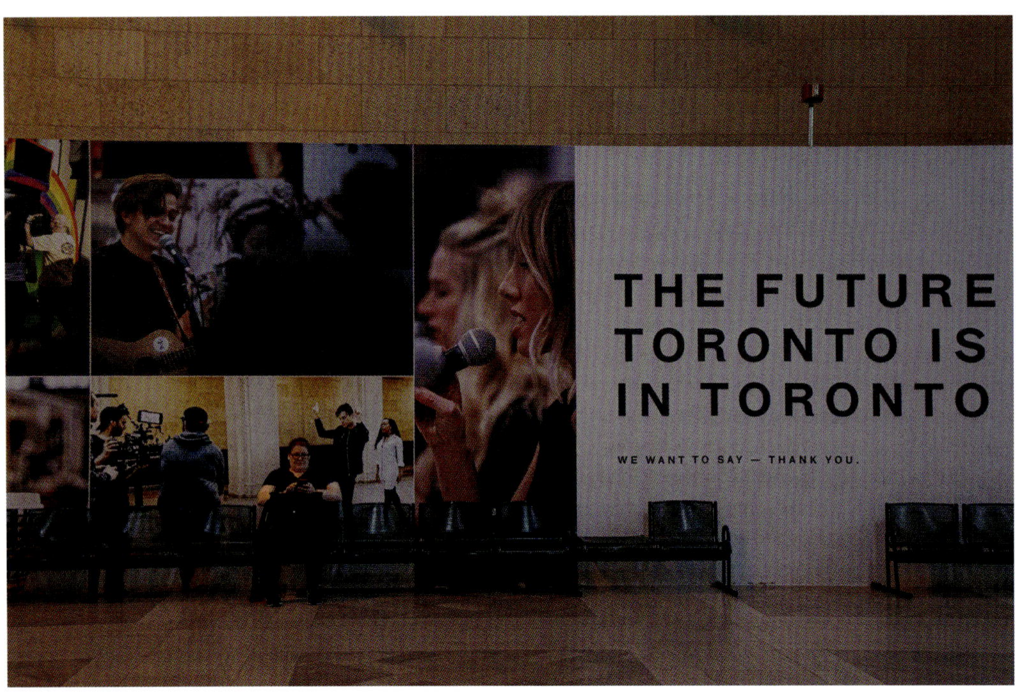

Seeking out deliberate mergers is one way to add humor to your images. I spotted one such merger in the train station in Toronto, Canada, where a woman sat in the waiting area in front of a big billboard promoting Toronto. I quickly moved so I was shooting straight at her. At first glance, it appears that she is feeling the brunt of the "kick" from the guy behind her, but of course it's merely the illusion created in part by a carefully planned point of view. As luck would have it, she is reacting with surprise, perhaps, and this is a guess, to something she saw on her phone, which coincided with perfect timing of my pressing the shutter.

◘ Nikon D500, NIKKOR 18–300mm lens, *f*/11 for 1/100 sec., ISO 3200, Daylight/Sunny WB

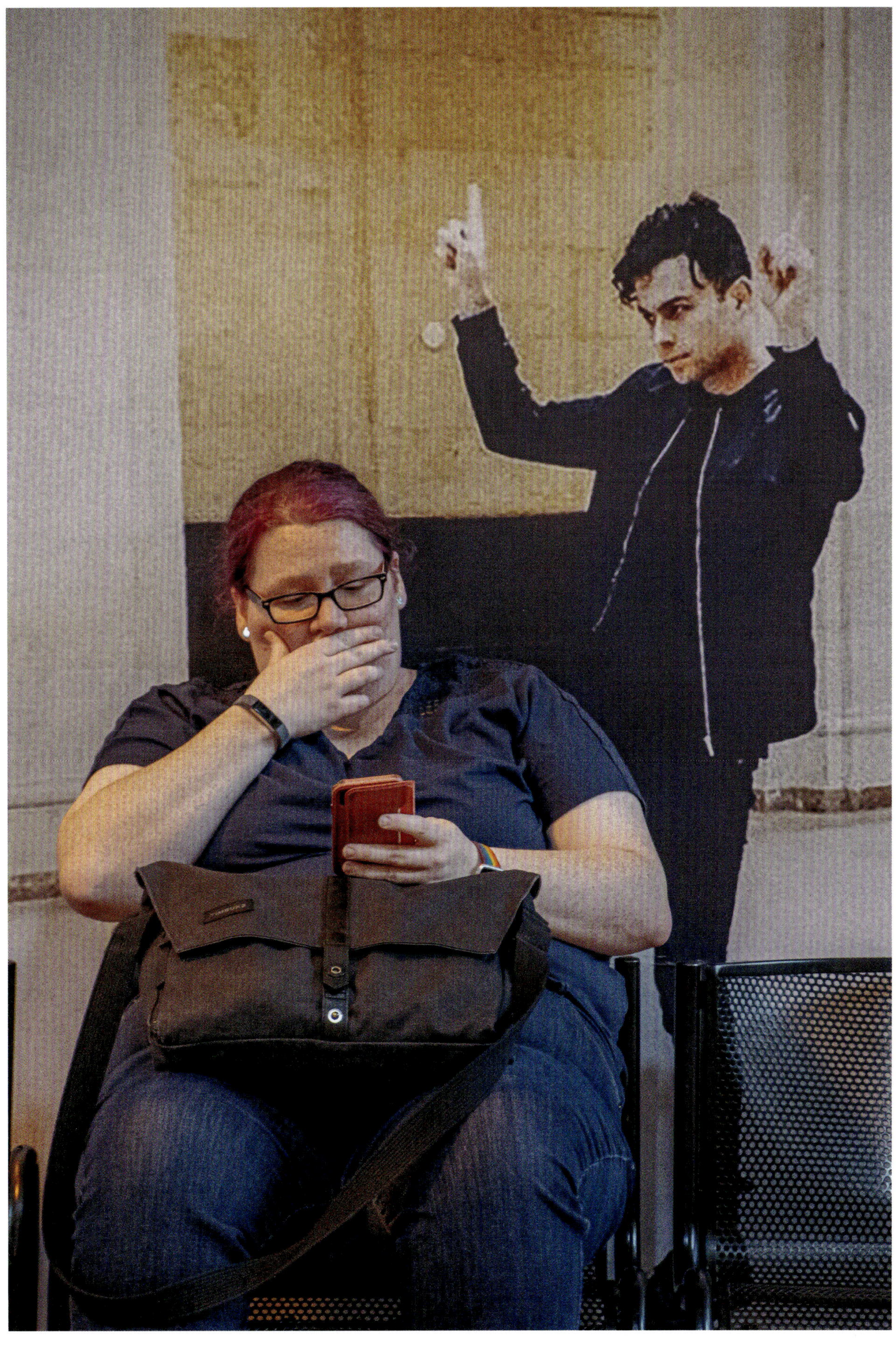

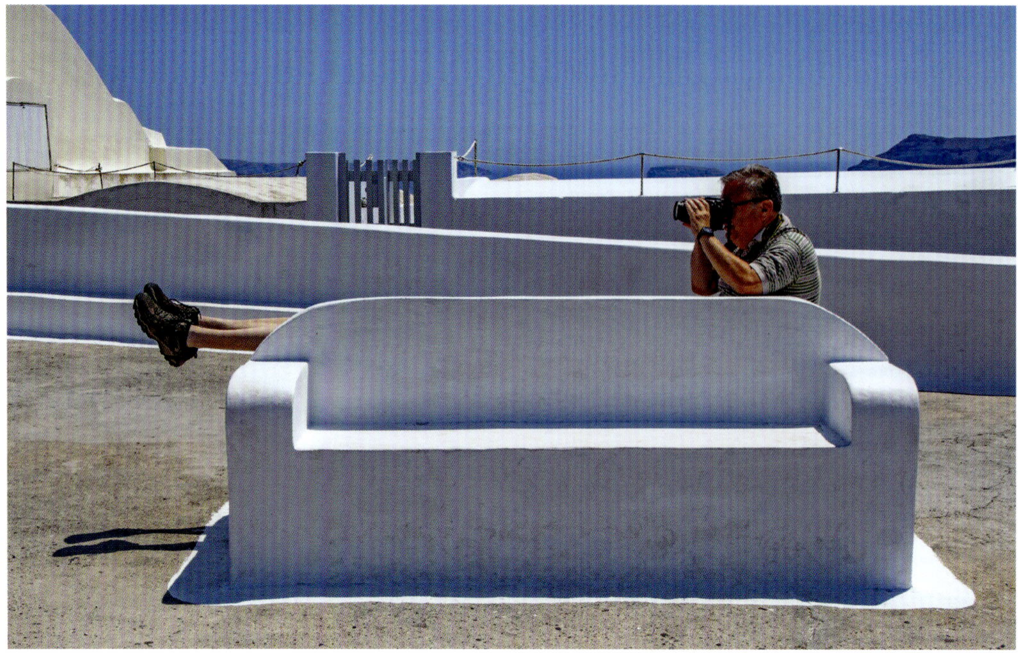

The Greek island of Santorini has never disappointed me. It seems a compelling photograph can be made at every turn, especially during the peak tourist season of May through September and particularly in the village of Oai on the island's west end. Long white benches invite fatigued tourists, including two of my students, to take a break and soak up some sun. How funny it was to see the head and torso of one of my students on the far right while another student stretched out with her legs and feet hanging off the left, merging into one very long-legged person.

◘ Nikon D850, NIKKOR 24–120mm lens, *f*/16 for 1/200 sec., ISO 200, Daylight/Sunny WB

Understanding Aperture

The aperture, or opening, in the lens has many functions, the most obvious being to control the volume of light that passes through the lens and onto the film or digital sensor. Whether you push buttons, turn a wheel, or rotate a ring on the lens to select the size of the aperture, you'll see a series of numbers in the viewfinder or on the lens itself, as explained earlier in "The Photographic Triangle" (see page 8). (On smartphones, these numbers are usually seen only when choosing the Portrait mode setting.)

But the aperture plays a far more important role than just determining how much or how little light travels through the lens. It is your choice of aperture that determines how much more of the scene behind and in front of your point of focus appears sharp, an optical phenomena called depth of field. Put simply, the bigger the aperture number (such as *f*/22), the larger the area of sharpness in front of and behind your subject; the depth of field increases. I call these storytelling apertures, as they allow you to keep all of the visual information, from foreground to background, in sharp focus. (For more on focusing storytelling compositions, see page 26.)

A smaller aperture number (*f*/4) gives you less sharpness in front of and behind your subject, creating a shallower depth of field. I call these singular-theme apertures, as they allow you to isolate one piece of visual information (generally your subject) and focus the viewer's attention.

And what about when everything in your frame is the same distance away? In these situations, depth of field isn't a concern. The best apertures for critical sharpness and great contrast in these situations are what I call the "Who cares?" apertures of *f*/8 and *f*/11.

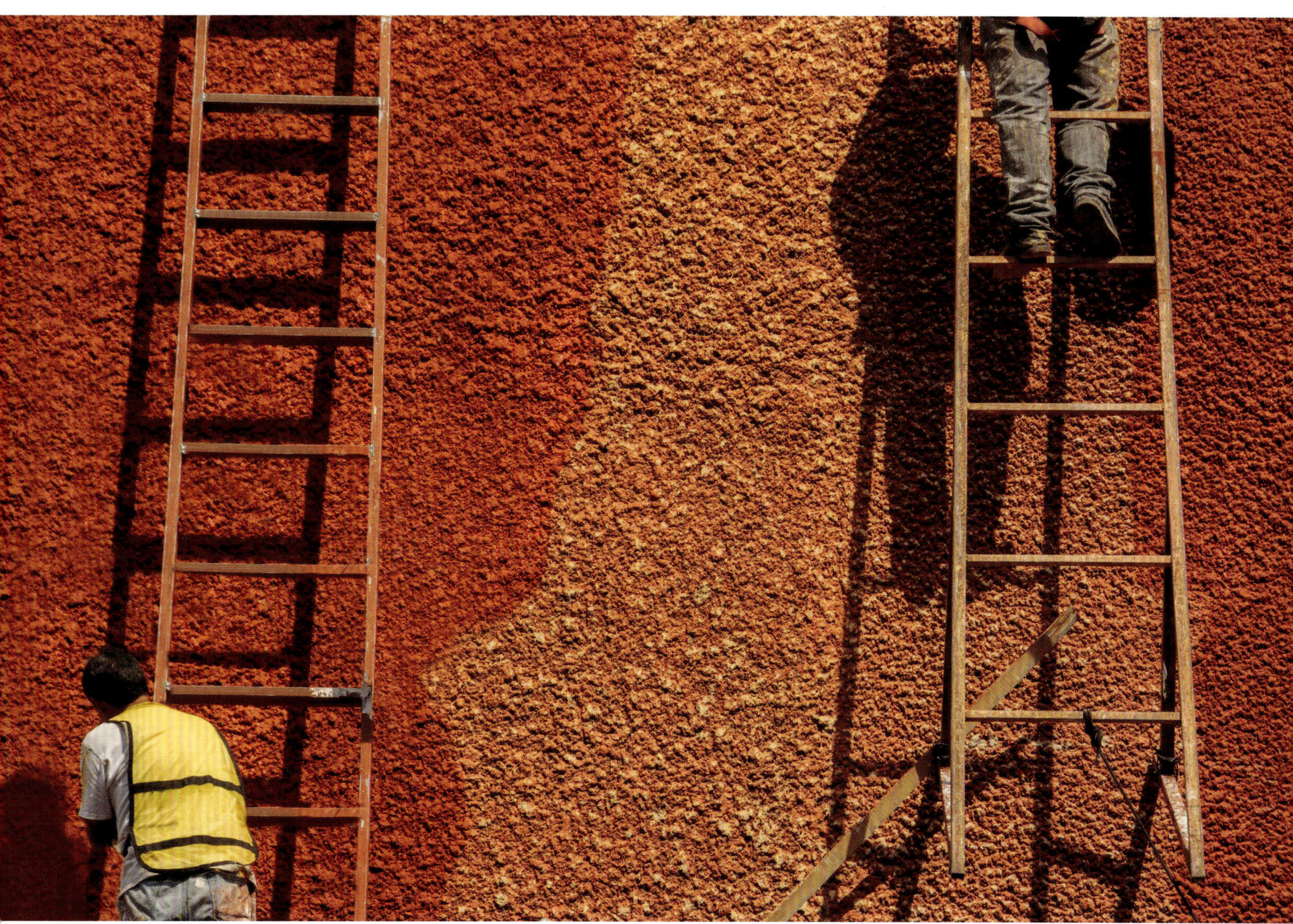

I came upon a few construction workers painting a church, and I noticed that one worker was much lower on his ladder while the other was working at a higher point on the wall. I waited for the man on the right to come down one rung on his ladder so his lower body juxtaposed almost exactly with the other man's upper body, creating a humorous merger of two half bodies.

Nikon D500, NIKKOR 18–300mm lens for 220mm, *f*/14 for 1/250 sec., ISO 200, Daylight/Sunny WB

Connections

We're all familiar with the expressions "six degrees of separation" and "it's a small world"—both are often invoked when we discover an unlikely connection, sometimes between friends but more often between strangers having a seemingly random conversation. Maybe you discover you are both are from the same town, went to the same high school, or once dated the same person. In one documented case, two strangers met and, during the course of a conversation, discovered not only that they both had a long-lost sibling but that they *were* each other's long-lost sibling.

When it comes to street photography, many shooters spend hours, days, and even weeks searching to capture that same feeling, combining the right point of view with the most pleasing compositional arrangement to render an obvious connection that conveys how we are all in some way connected, not only to each other but also to our surroundings.

Being sensitive to these connections is almost second nature for some photographers, while for others it takes a great deal of visual study. Seeing the potential connection is one thing, but the key is timing, knowing when the decisive moment presents itself and then having the instinct to press that shutter release. I have had more than my share of missed connections, but much like the occasional par and even rarer birdie in my golf game, the ones I do catch are what drive me to keep returning to the streets and raising my camera to my eye.

Capturing these connections often relies on factors completely out of the photographer's control, namely the behavior of the complete strangers who are unknowing participants. Much like wildlife, people's behaviors, especially on city sidewalks, are often unpredictable and a challenge that will test the will of any hopeful street photographer.

It is no secret that I love color, which is probably why many of my connections involve color, especially those between my subjects' clothing and their surroundings. It doesn't matter whether I am in India—arguably the most colorful country in the world—or the concrete jungle of New York City, opportunities to shoot connections in color abound. As you begin to seek out connections, rest assured that some opportunities will be immediately obvious, while others, especially if you are not a skilled photographer and quick to react, will challenge your level of patience.

Compositions of connections are the norm for my great friend and internationally known street photographer Vineet Vohra. I recommend checking out his feed on Instagram, which will have you asking yourself how he discovers these amazing, humorous connections over and over and over!

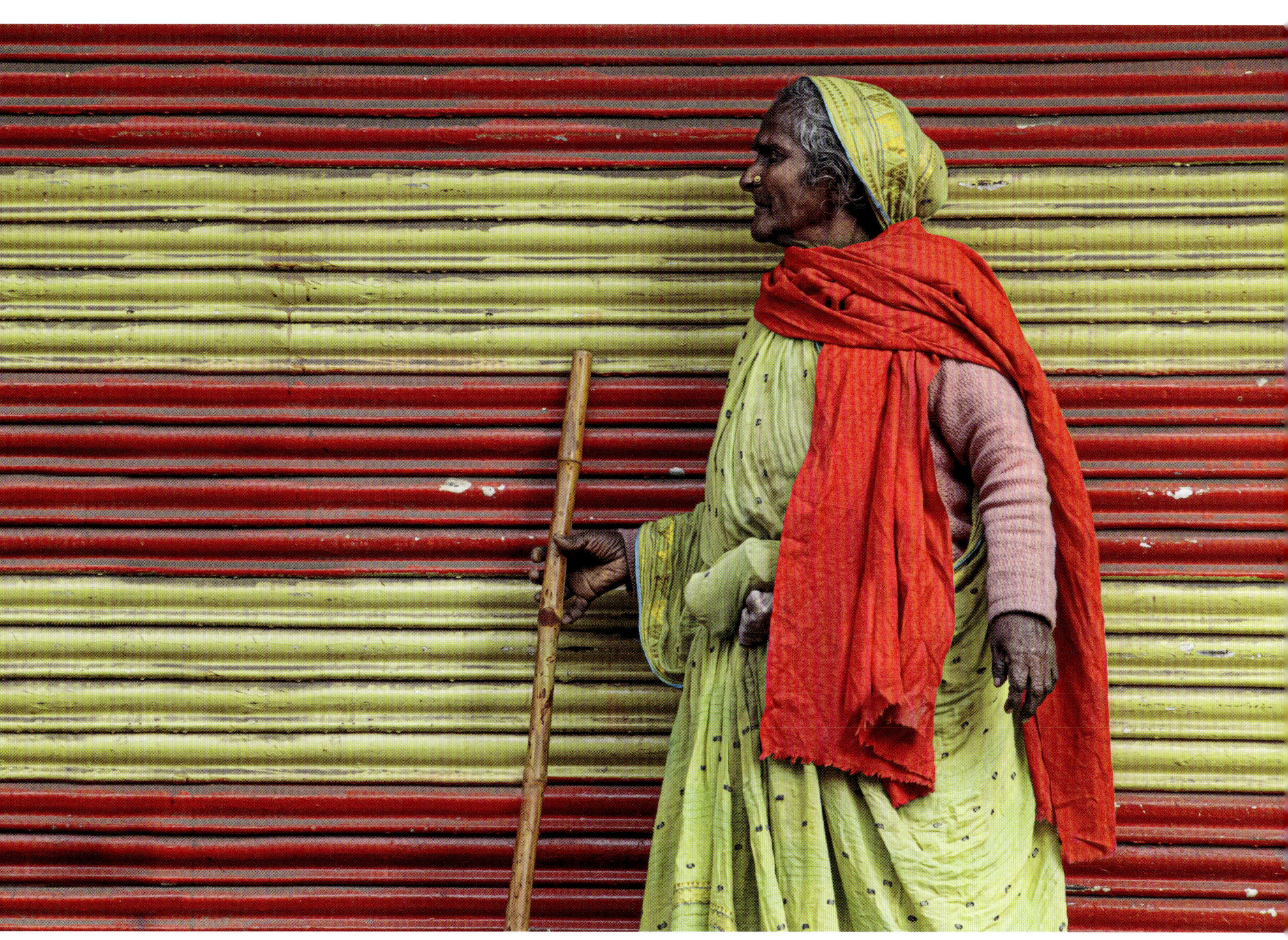

While shooting in the Chandni Chowk market in Old Delhi, I saw a woman standing and talking to another woman about ten feet to the right of a similarly colored corrugated door. Lucky me, because when she finished talking, she headed toward the matching colored doorway, and it was a simple matter of firing my camera on its usual setting of Continuous High (CH), which meant I was firing at a frame rate of almost eleven frames per second, assured that one would capture the perfect gesture or expression as she passed in front of the door.

◘ **Nikon D500, NIKKOR 18–300mm lens, *f*/14 for 1/320 sec., ISO 1250, Daylight/Sunny WB**

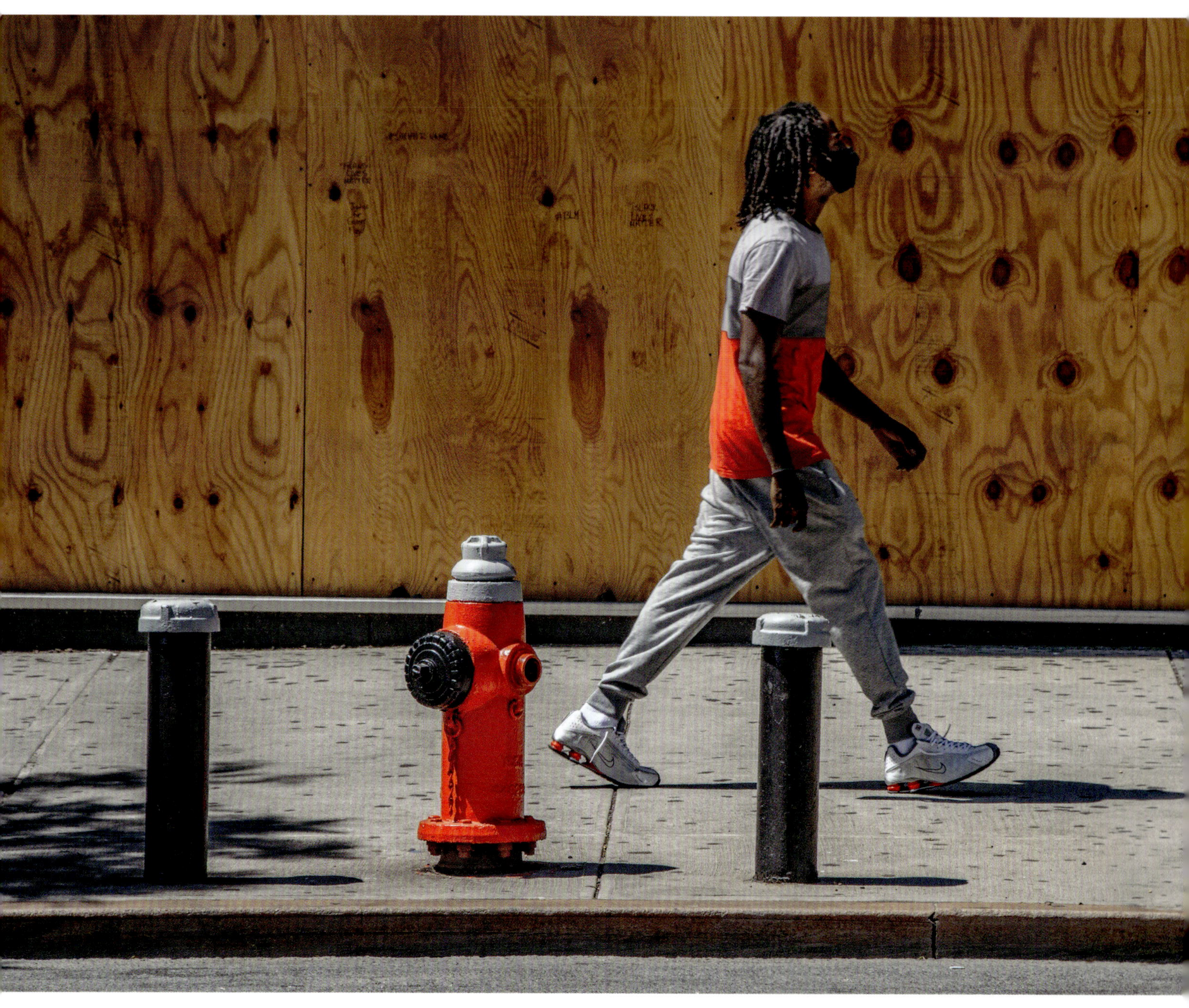

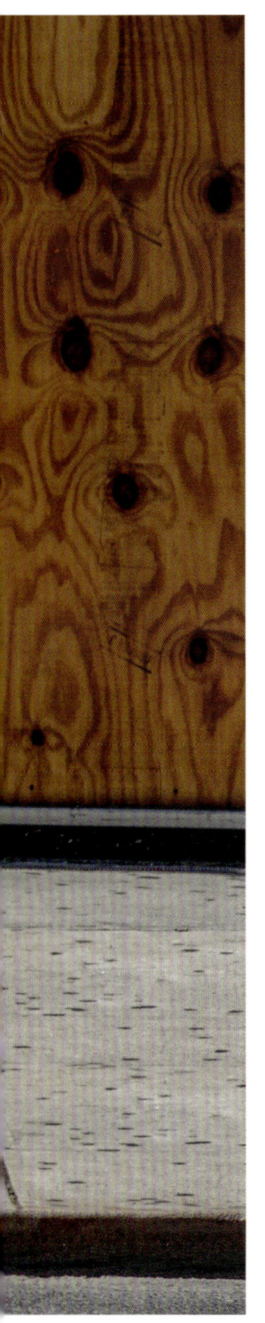

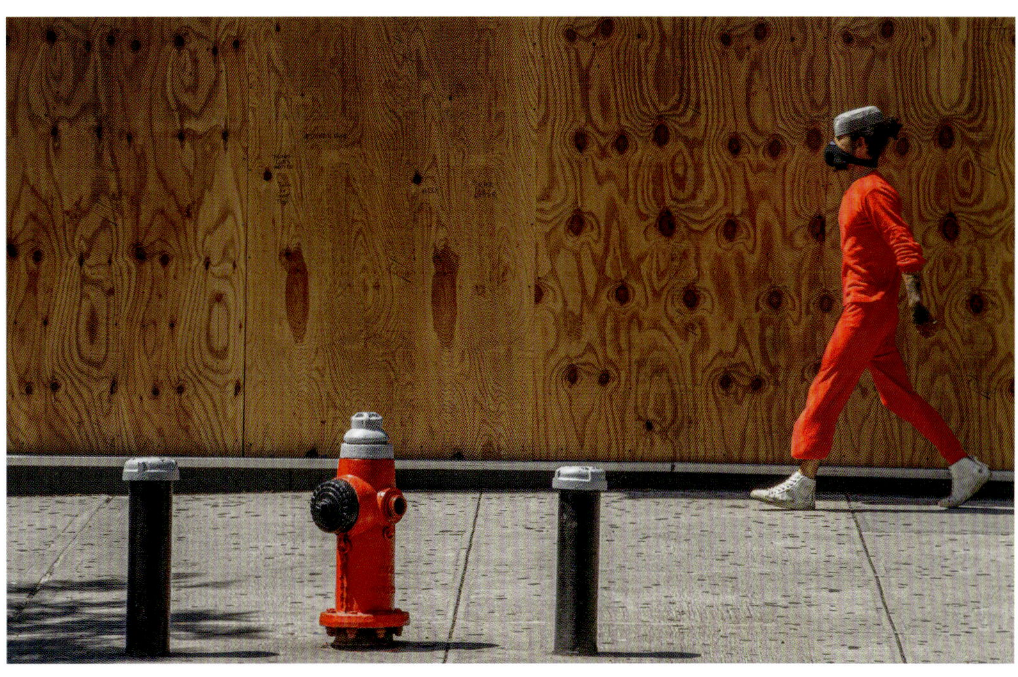

One hour had already gone by, and I still had nothing to show for my hoped-for composition of this red, gray, and black painted fire hydrant in Harlem. The thought of giving up kept pestering me, yet I could not let go of my initial reason for stopping at this location: a man dressed in gray sweatpants, a red shirt, and a black mask who had drawn me to this otherwise empty section of sidewalk. Right as I was about to move on, a black-masked, bearded young man entered the frame from the right, who—talk about dumb luck!—was also dressed in red, gray, and black. No more than a minute later, the young man I had seen earlier, who had started this hour-long quest, returned, walking in the opposite direction. After photographing him in another fleeting moment, I felt the joy of a five-year-old sneaking an extra cookie from the cookie jar. It's this kind of success that keeps me returning to the streets in hopes of capturing more insanely lucky connections.

◘ Both images: Nikon D500, NIKKOR 18–300mm lens, *f*/11 for 1/500 sec., ISO 200, Daylight/Sunny WB

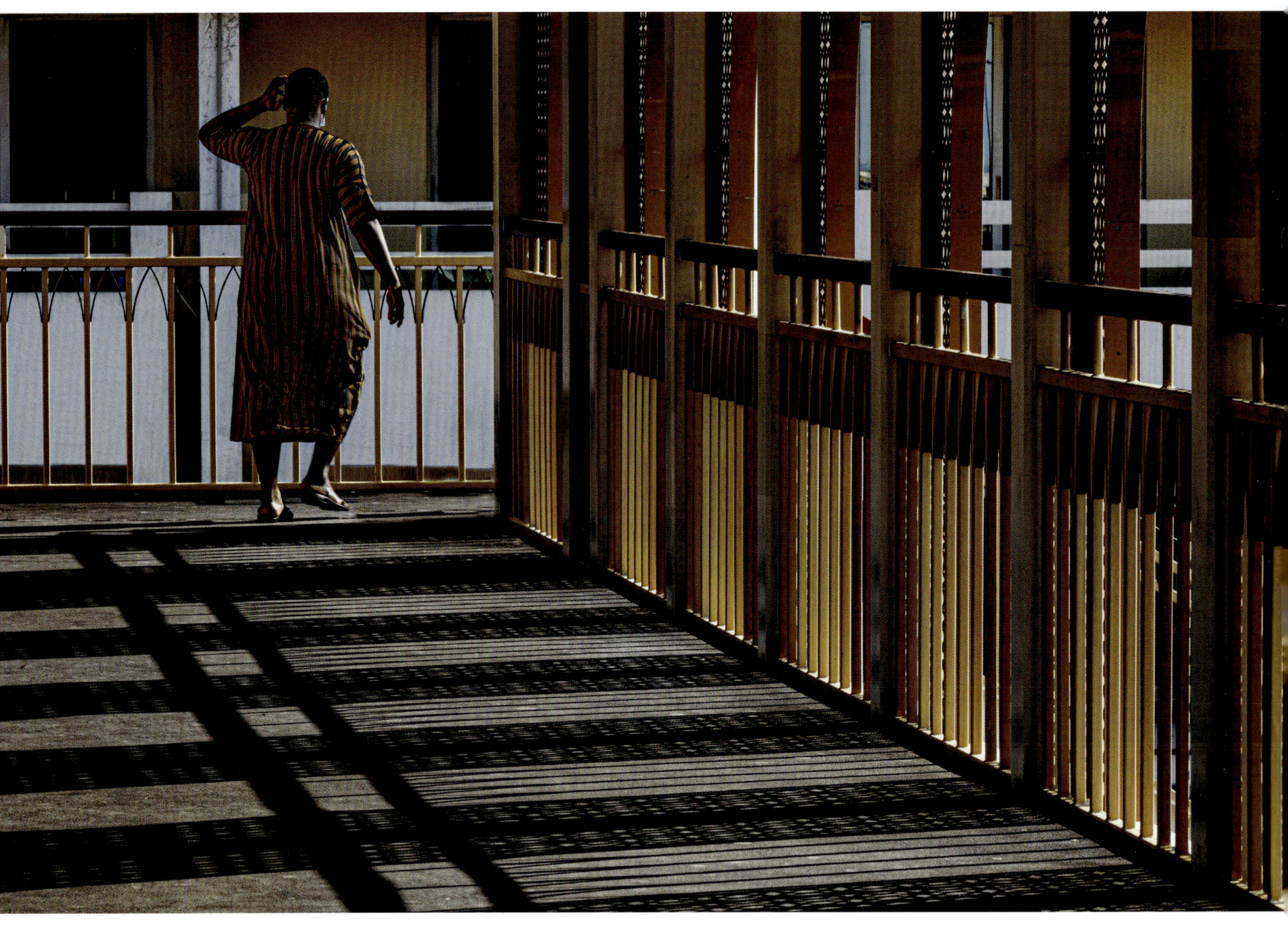

On another trip to Dubai, several months later, I was on a pedestrian overpass, attracted by the shadows falling across the carpeted floor and the countless compositions of feet on the move through the pattern of light and shadow. It wasn't until thirty minutes later that I noticed one such pair of feet belonging to a man wearing a striped robe. I looked up and realized that his robe was very much connected to the light, shadows, and colors on the overpass, and just before he disappeared from view, I fired off two quick frames.

◘ Nikon D500, NIKKOR 18–300mm lens, *f*/22 for 1/250 sec., ISO 500, Daylight/Sunny WB

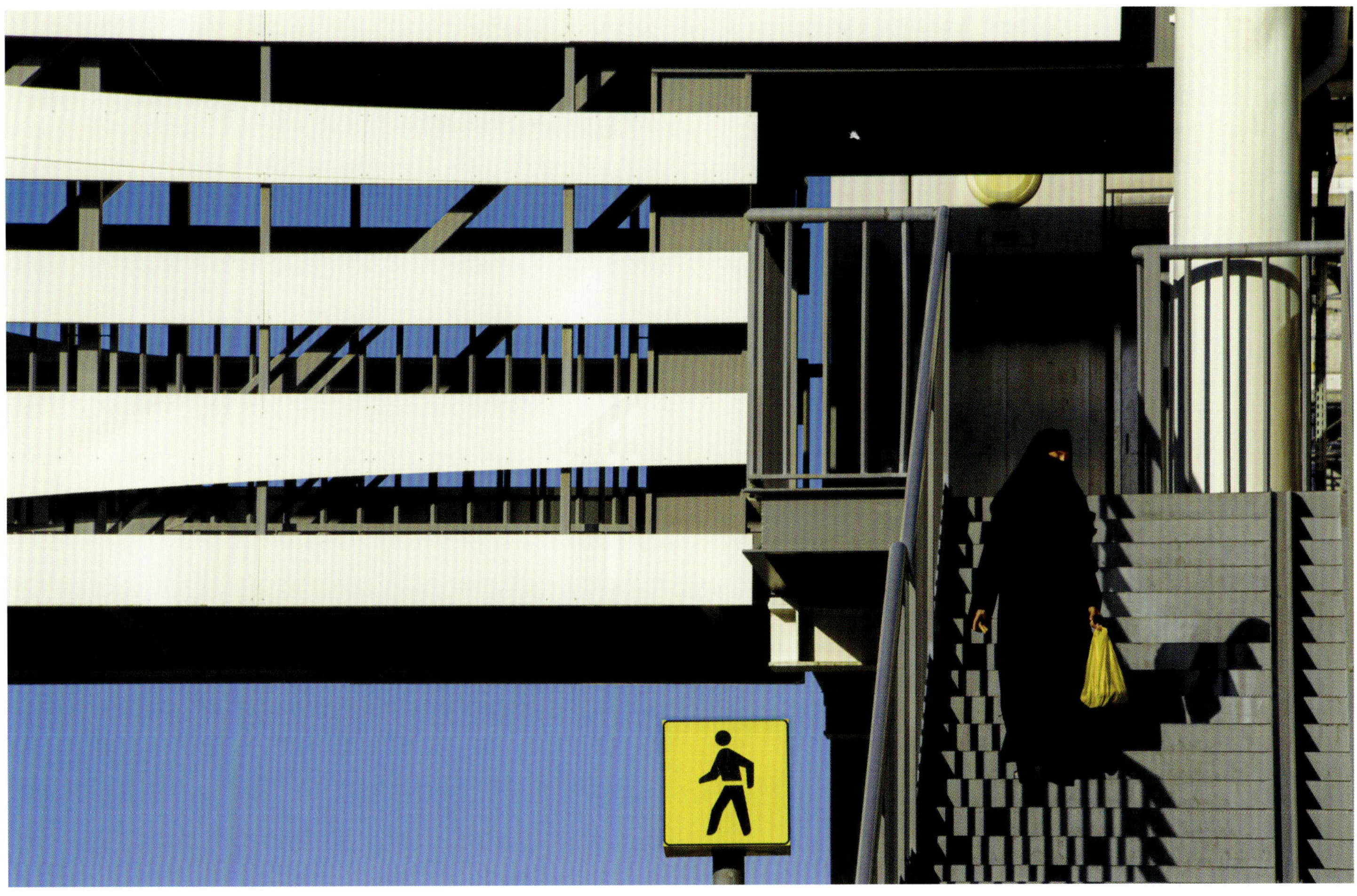

It was late afternoon when I caught sight of this stairway connected to a pedestrian overpass, which would soon be full of people commuting home from work. What caught my eye was the pedestrian sign, a silhouetted shape of a person against a bright yellow background. Oh, how I wanted to capture someone wearing yellow in front of that sign—and within twenty minutes, I got something completely unexpected: a woman wearing a black burka and carrying a bright yellow shopping bag. Another connection of color and contrast!

◘ Nikon D500, NIKKOR 18–300mm lens, *f*/16 for 1/320 sec., ISO 400, Daylight/Sunny WB

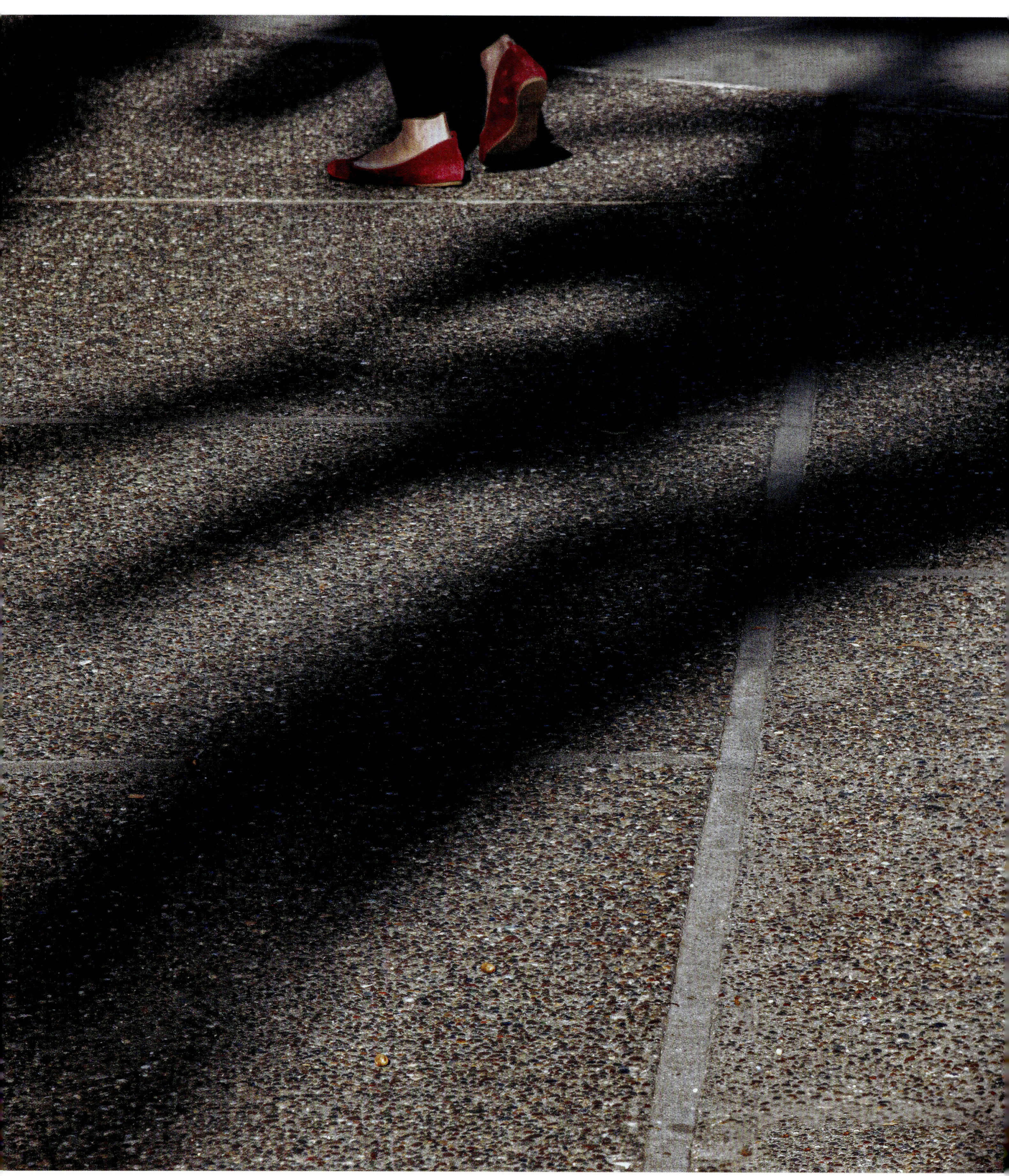

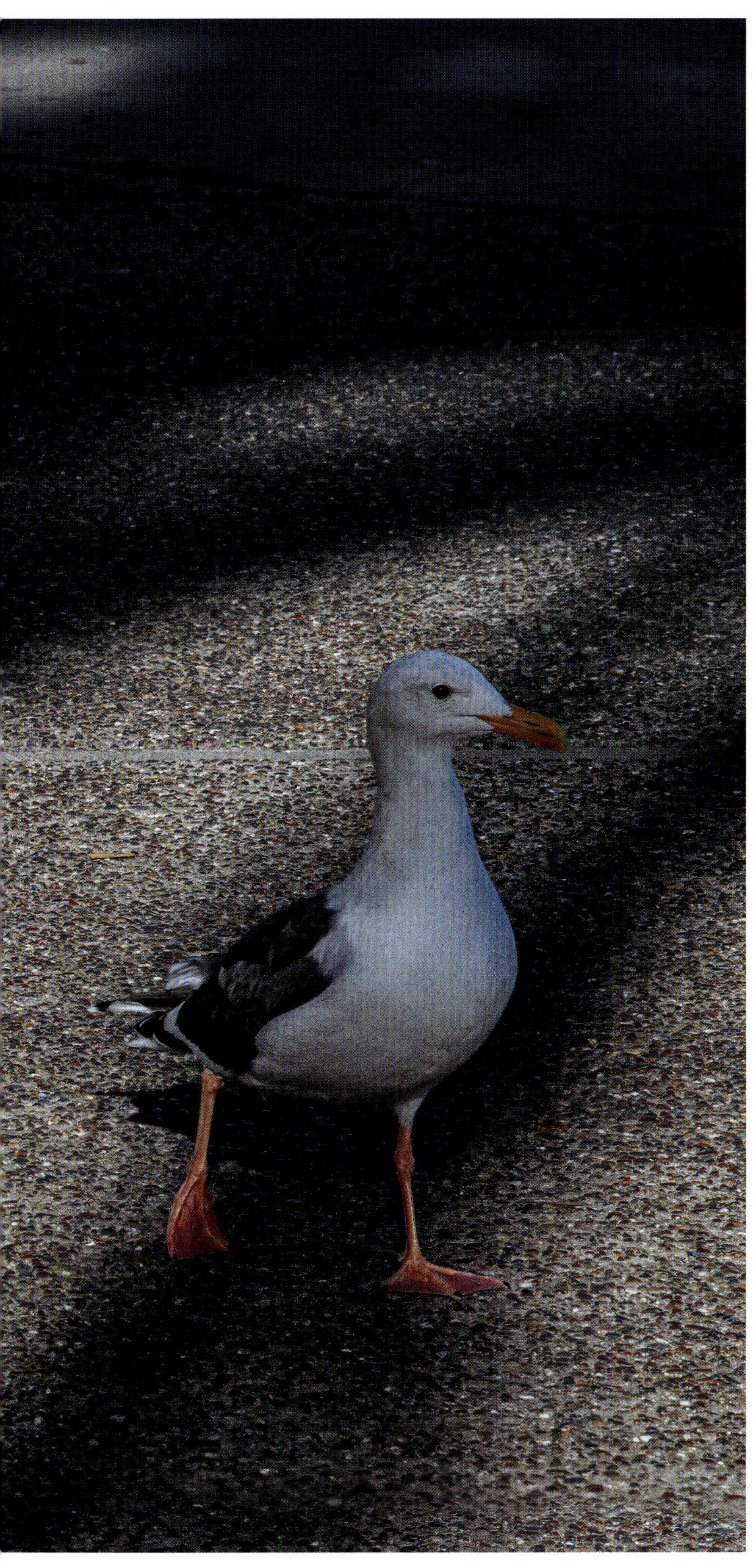

It was the second day of a three-day shoot on the streets of San Francisco, down near the Embarcadero, where in the morning light large palm trees cast their shadows onto the large aggregate sidewalks. A lone seagull had all of my attention; it was very accustomed to humans, and as it walked through the shadows and low-angled sidelight, I caught sight of a lone pair of pinkish-red shoes entering the frame in the upper left. Despite making a quick compositional adjustment, I could get off only three frames. In my favorite, seen here, one of the woman's shoes and the seagull's foot are in the same elevated position.

◘ **Nikon D850, NIKKOR 24–120mm lens, *f*/16 for 1/250 sec., ISO 400, Daylight/Sunny WB**

Framing with a Frame

In cities big and small, the streets are filled with numerous opportunities to frame within a frame. Whether you are framing a person, a car, or a dog or cat, a well-executed frame always elevates the subject's importance, in much the same way many artists and photographers call upon a cardboard mat to frame their work.

Framing with a frame is an often-overlooked opportunity to create depth in a photograph. More often than not, the frame is created by a foreground object, which can be either in focus—like a window frame or a doorway—or out of focus, calling attention to the focused subject behind the out-of-focus foreground. A foreground frame can also add color or texture.

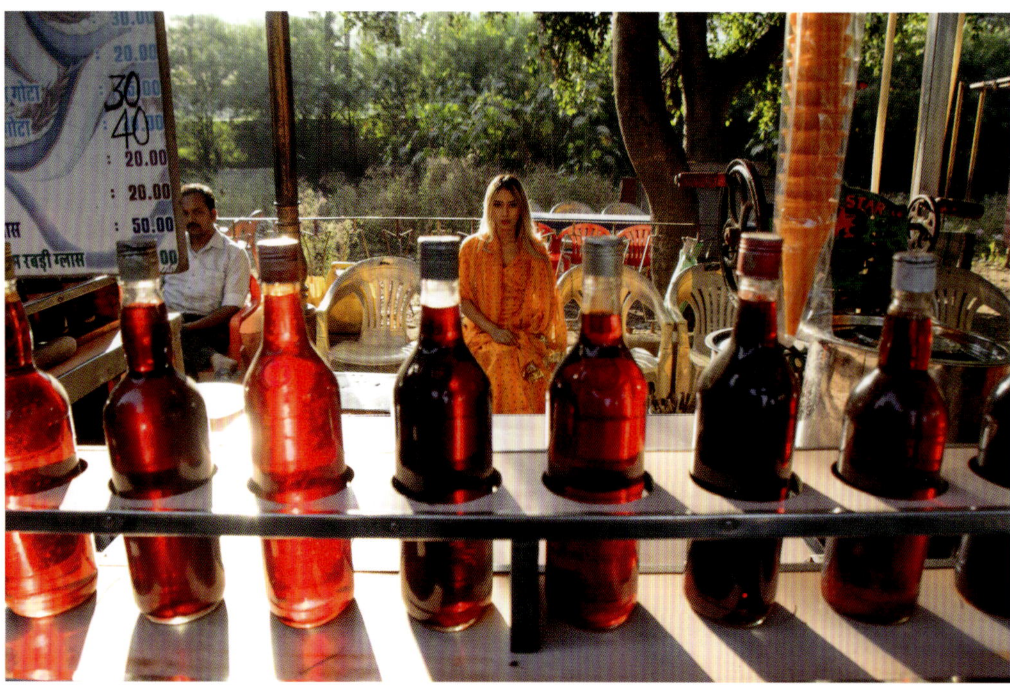

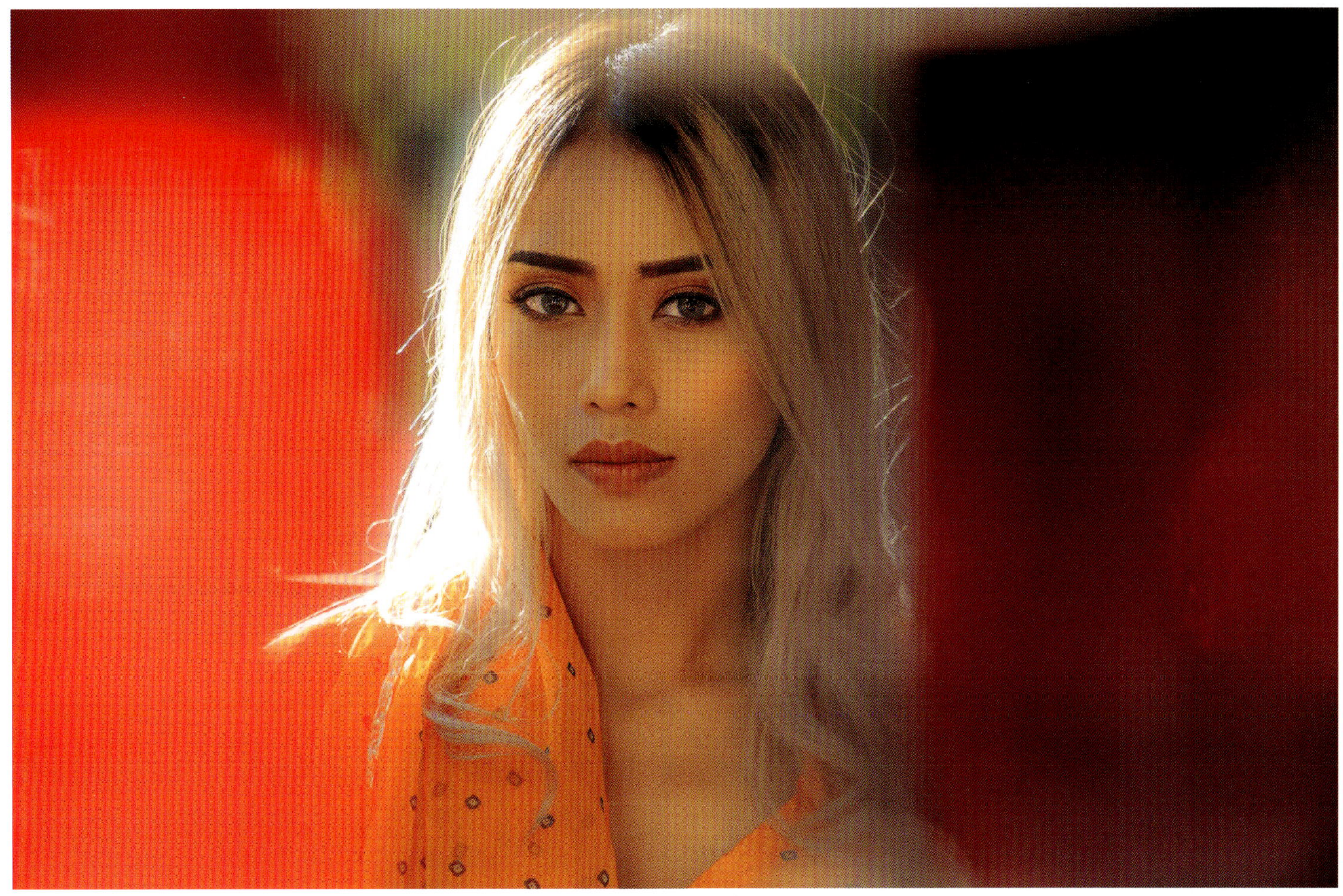

What you choose to use as a foreground frame will dictate how defined or undefined it should be. In this instance, I chose to frame the subject between two colorful bottles, rendering the bottles as out-of-focus blocks of color by using a large lens opening for a shallow depth of field. Framing with a frame brings order and structure to the overall composition and, in this case, further elevates the model's face and strongly sidelit hair.

◘ Nikon D500, NIKKOR 18–300mm lens at 300mm, *f*/6.3 for 1/640 sec., ISO 200, Daylight/Sunny WB

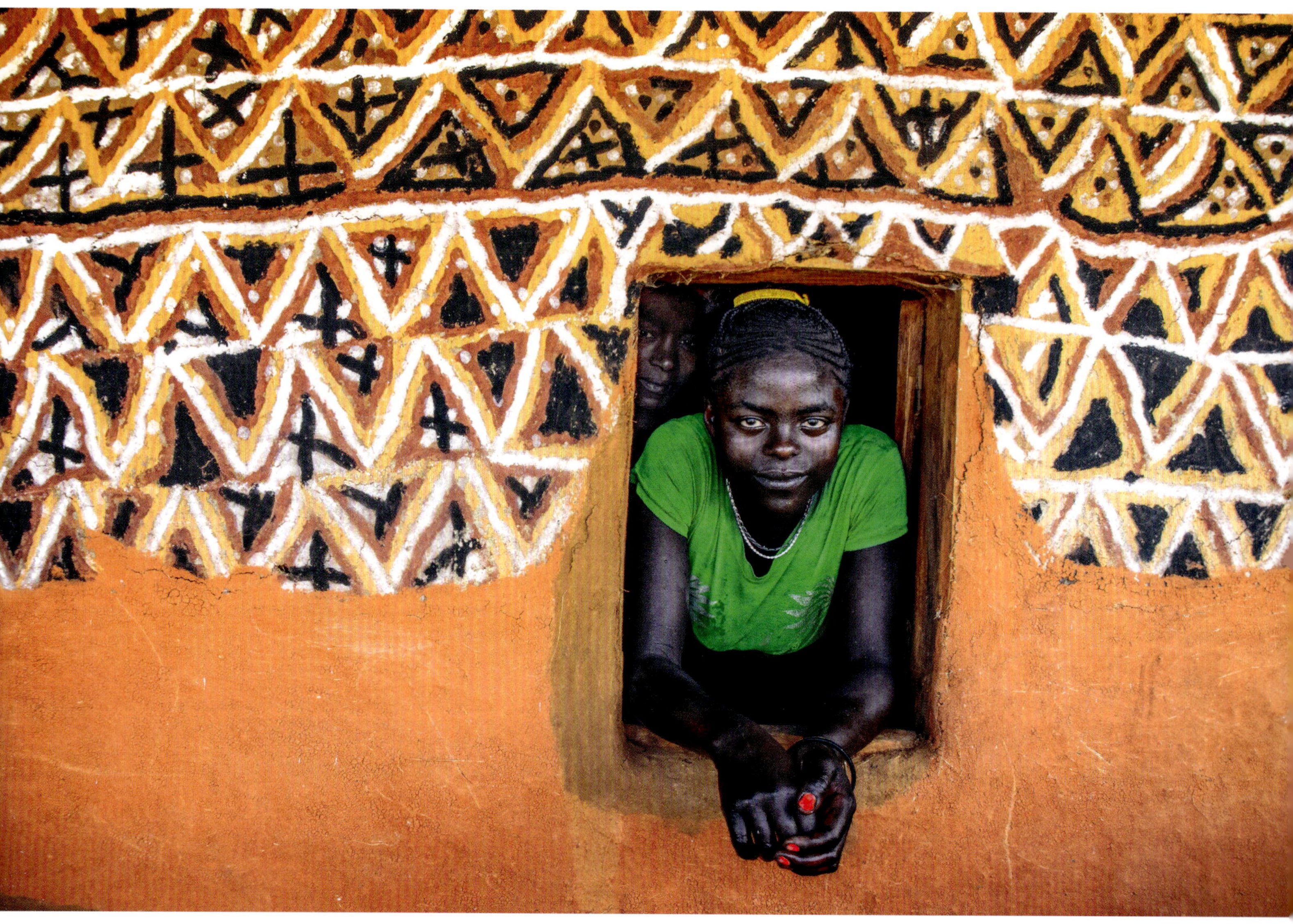

"Before you take my photo, I want to put on my red fingernail polish," she said. Ten minutes later, with freshly painted nails, this young Ethiopian woman in the Omo Valley posed in one of three windows of the house she shared with a sister, three brothers, and her parents. Framing with a frame—in this case an actual window frame—is used to visually direct the viewer to focus on the main subject.

◘ Nikon D810, NIKKOR 24–120mm lens, *f*/11 for 1/200 sec., ISO 1600, Daylight/Sunny WB

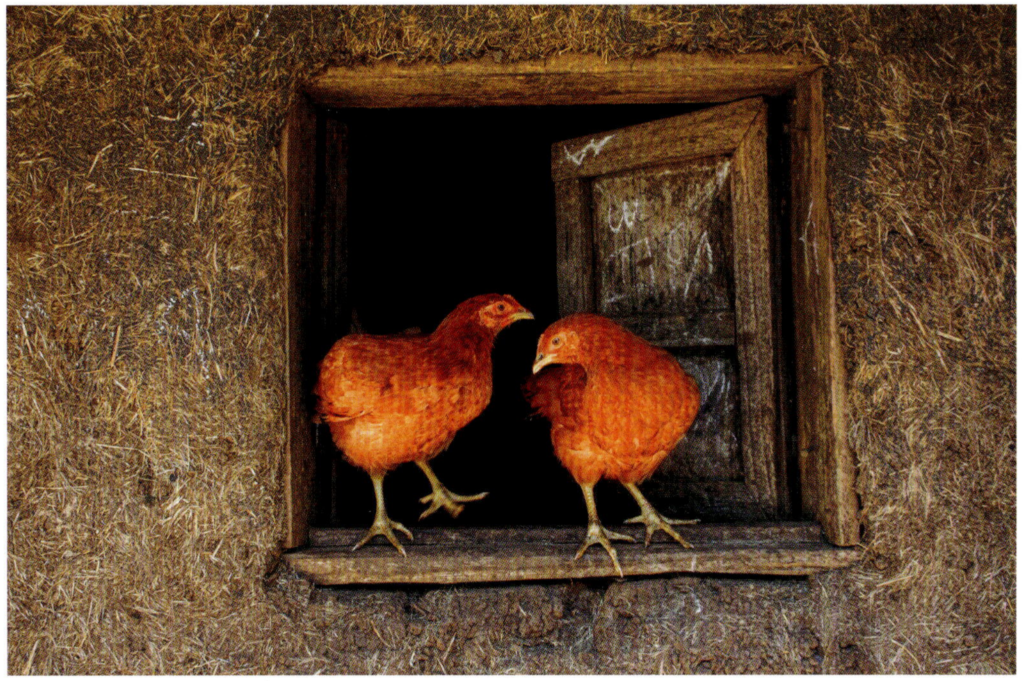

Other than the fading roar, a thick cloud of dust was all that remained of the double-trailered diesel truck that passed through the otherwise sleepy town of Turmi, Ethiopia. As I walked her few streets alone on this early November morning, the roosters in town were making it known sunrise was upon us. Turning toward one small house, I could see several roosters engaged in what I surmised was a fight for who would rule the roost. As I approached, a number of hens flew up from out of the darkness of the coop and onto this small window ledge. I hurried closer, facing the window head-on as I managed to get off about a dozen frames of "poultry in motion" before the coop was emptied.

◘ Nikon D500, NIKKOR 18–300mm lens, *f*/14 for 1/250 sec., ISO 1600, Daylight/Sunny WB

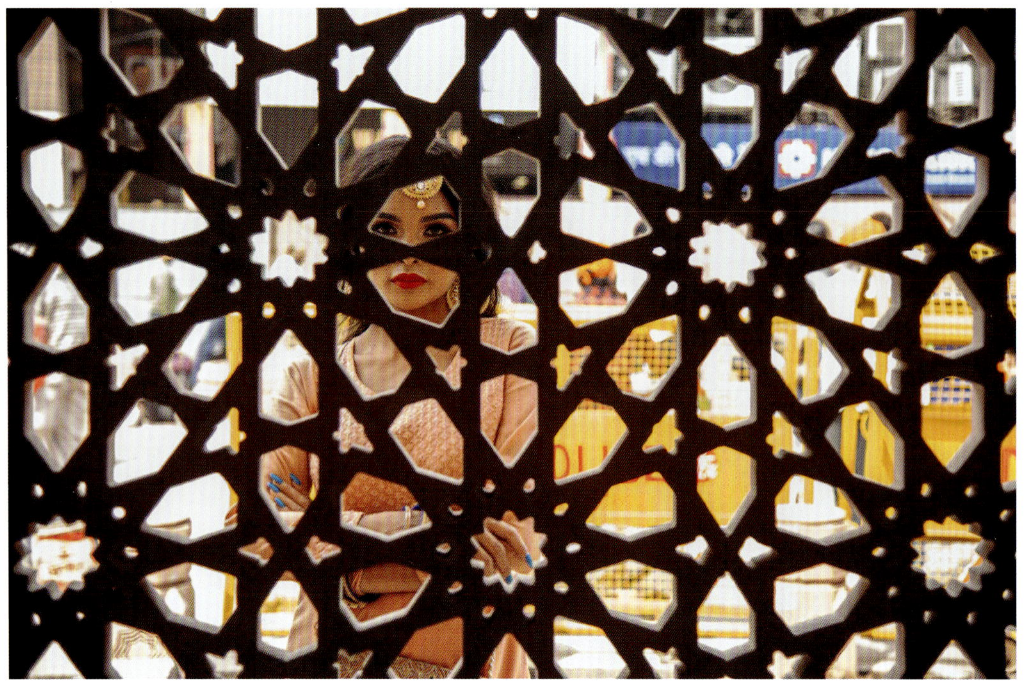

It was on the streets of Delhi that I saw these star-like openings in the latticework surrounding the Gurudwara Bangla Sahib, a Sikh temple. As I was here to shoot street portraits of my model and makeup artist Nattakun Plaengdee, I asked Natt to move into position facing one of these stars from about one foot away. I wanted to keep the focus literally and figuratively on Natt, so I shot with a wide-open aperture of *f*/4, rendering the edges of the star as a soft shape. Because the star is out of focus, the implication, as far as the eye/brain is concerned, is that its role in the overall composition is secondary to the in-focus Natt. Our visual processing is quick to deem any out-of-focus element in a composition irrelevant and whatever is in focus as the subject.

◘ Nikon D850, NIKKOR 24–120mm lens, *f*/4 for 1/640 sec., ISO 100, Daylight/Sunny WB

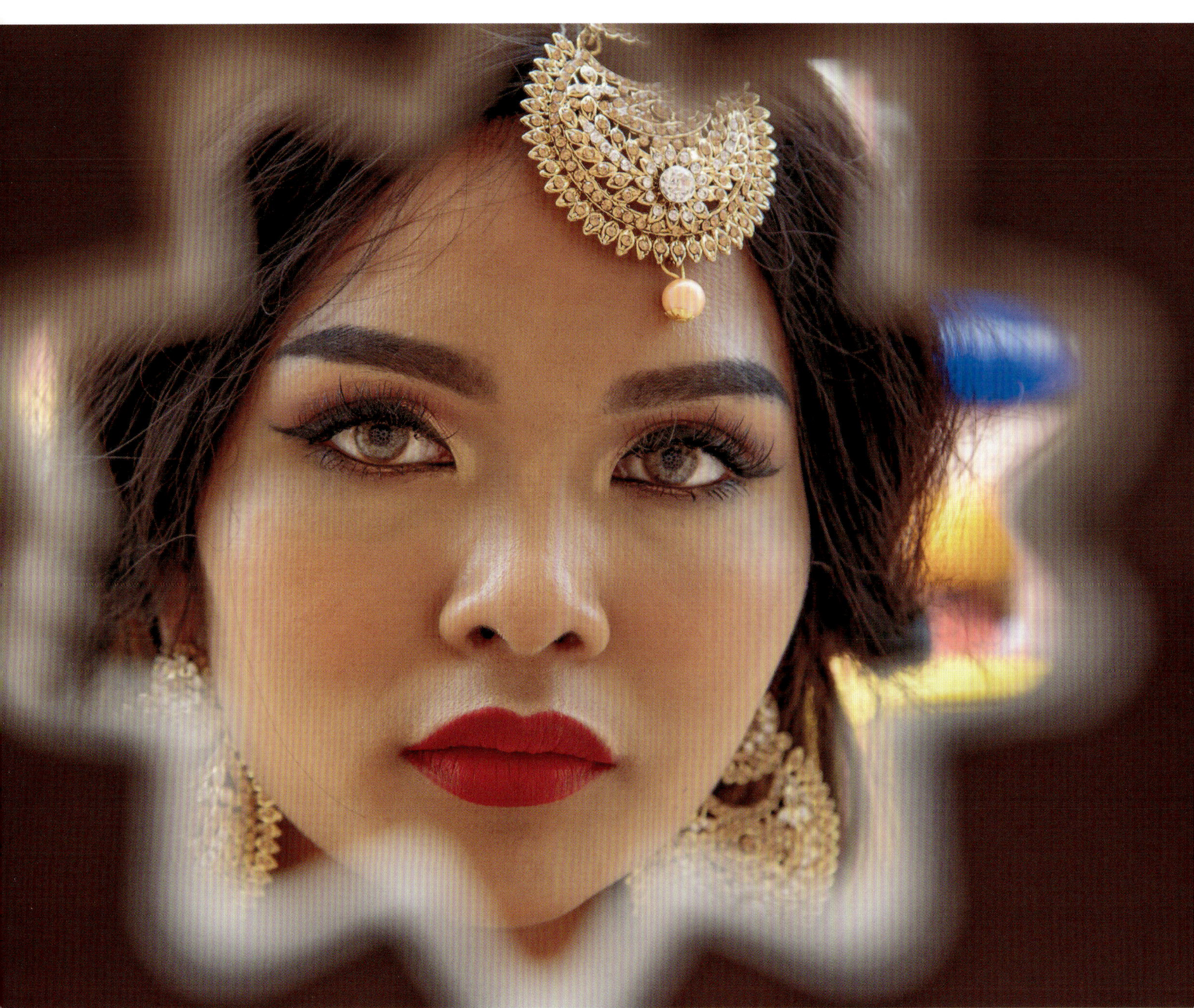

Guyzahn is a security guard at a small construction project near Jima, Ethiopia; he lives on the job site 24/7. At my suggestion, he posed for me inside his bedroom window. This was a quick no-brainer, using the bedroom window and the white, textured wall around it to call attention to Guyzahn. If your portraits lack impact, consider seeking out frame within a frame opportunities, which are far more common than many street shooters realize.

◘ Nikon D850, NIKKOR 24–120mm lens at 120mm, *f*/8 for 1/200 sec., ISO 100, Daylight/Sunny WB

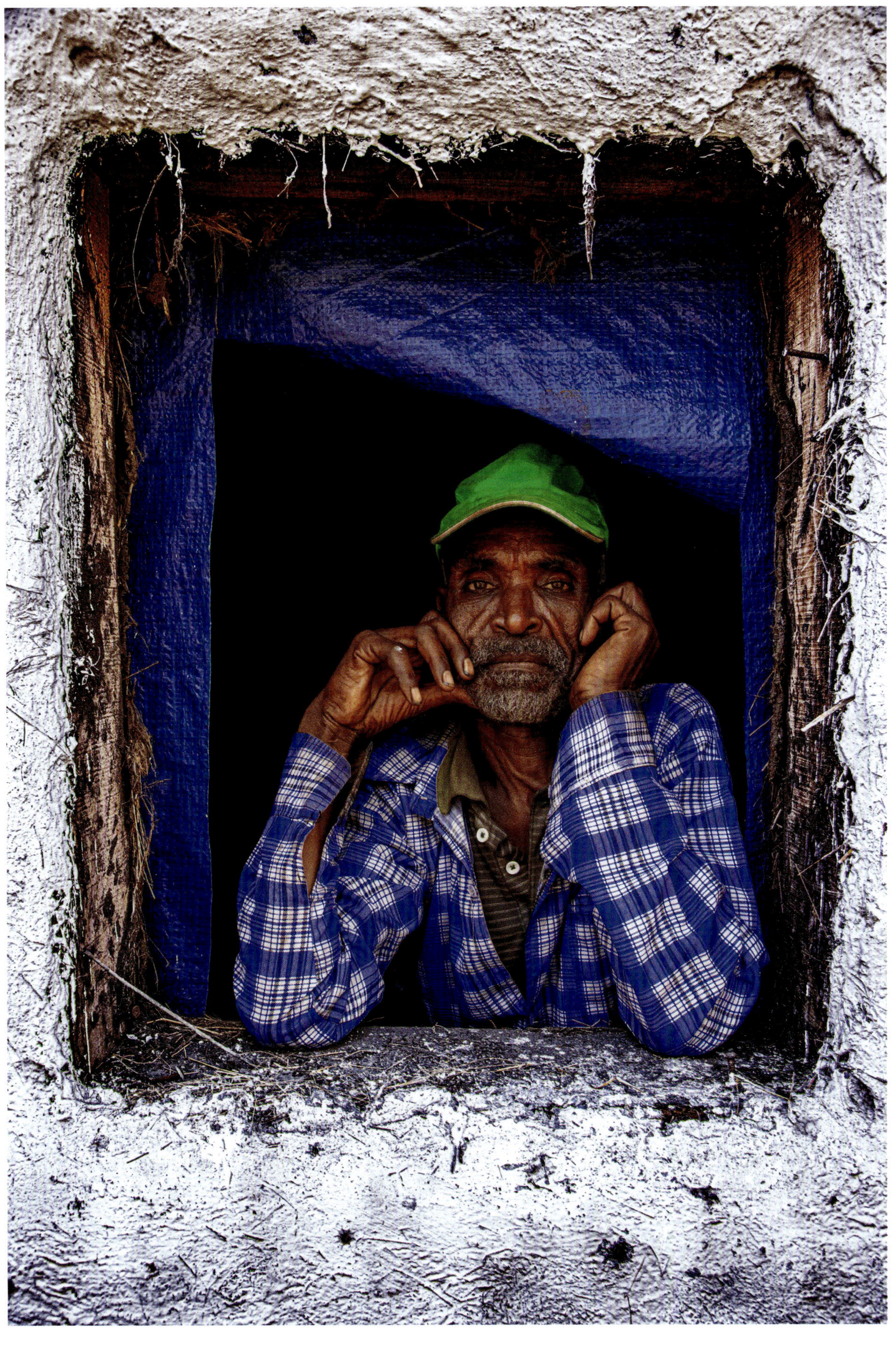

Point of View

If I were to choose my top three tips for improving one's overall composition, one of them would surely be to look at the world from points of view that are *anything* but eye level. When was the last time you climbed the steps of a parking garage and shot down onto the street below? Or lay on your back on a bus stop bench and shot straight up? Or lay flat on the ground and shot at the level of the feet of passing pedestrians? Granted, when getting into position for these points of view you might get the odd stare, but I will take an odd stare any day in exchange for a possible thousand stares and reactions of "*Wow!*" to the photograph I took from that odd point of view.

By seeking out points of view that are anything but eye level, you'll not only turn predictable and possibly mundane subjects into something fresh, but you'll also discover subjects in which lines and textures are made more apparent. For example, perhaps shooting down from above reveals a striped crosswalk you hadn't noticed when you were walking on the same street moments before. And while point of view also conveys distance—if you are far away and using a wide-angle lens, the subject will appear distant, whereas being right up on your subject will convey a feeling of intimacy—it is about much more than that, as you are about to discover.

On a visit to San Francisco, I found an elevated plaza near the Embarcadero, putting me in a great position to shoot from above. The street below was in strong midday sun, with a number of trees casting random shadows on the sidewalk's radial designs. It was a very busy, if not chaotic, canvas that needed just the right person to enter. Within the hour in which I shot down into this chaos, a number of pedestrians walked on the canvas, unknowingly adding great interest. The two images you see here, both with subjects wearing a smidgen of red, are my favorites. The chaotic symphony of shape, line, and texture is interrupted by the loud "voice" of the unique human shape, the added touch of red disrupting the canvas much as a small rock tossed into a pond disrupts the surface of the water.

It's all about patience, nothing more than patience. Yes, I know, it's hard to wait in one place, but bring your headphones and listen to your favorite podcast or music while enjoying the view. Choose your spot, and the image will come to you.

◘ **Both images: Nikon D500, NIKKOR 18–300mm lens, *f*/11 for 1/400 sec., ISO 200, Daylight/Sunny WB**

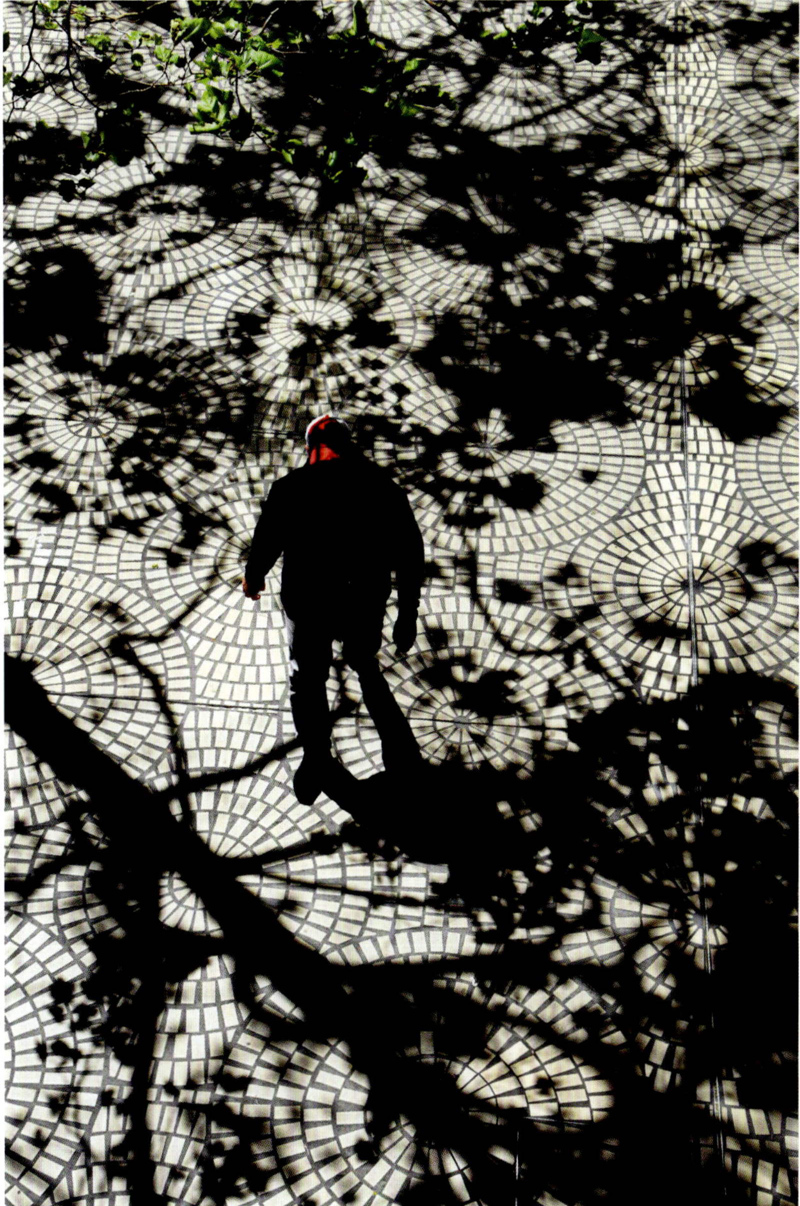

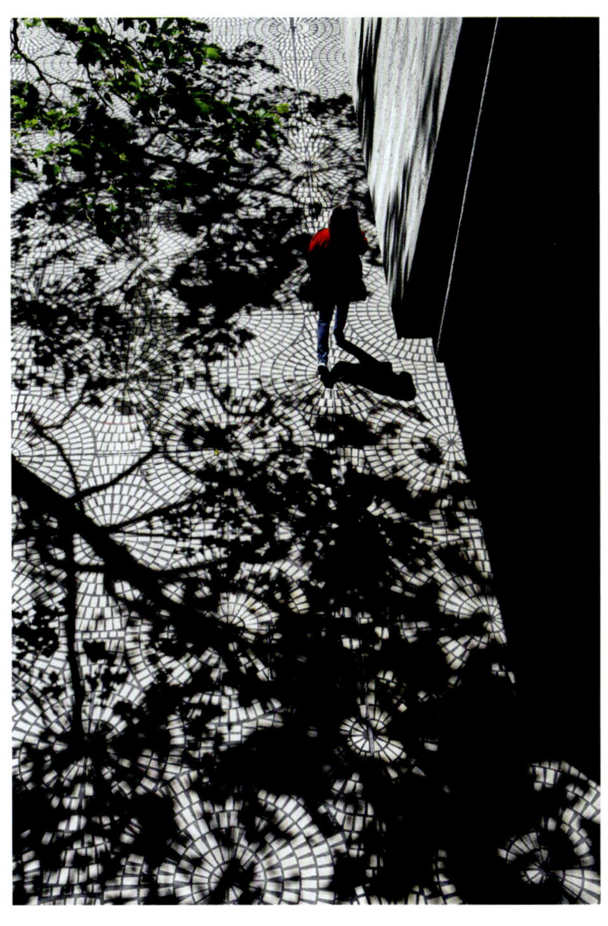

It was an extremely windy Saturday afternoon in Dallas, Texas, several years ago when the idea for this photo was born, though the actual photo wasn't taken until the next day. My youngest daughter, Sophie, had accompanied me and my students for the weekend, and she stood very still, arms outstretched while holding an umbrella that had been deliberately inverted. Although unlike the day before, this day of overcast skies was windless, but a fast-moving tram entered the frame and blew a bit of Sophie's hair. A 3-stop neutral-density (ND) filter allowed me to use a slow 1/2 sec. shutter speed to capture the sense of motion without overexposing the image.

Note also the deliberate diagonal point of view, which serves to accelerate the train even more. Funny thing about a diagonal line: it's always on the move.

◘ Nikon D810, NIKKOR 24–120mm lens, *f*/22 for 1/2 sec. and a 3-stop ND filter, ISO 100, Daylight/Sunny WB

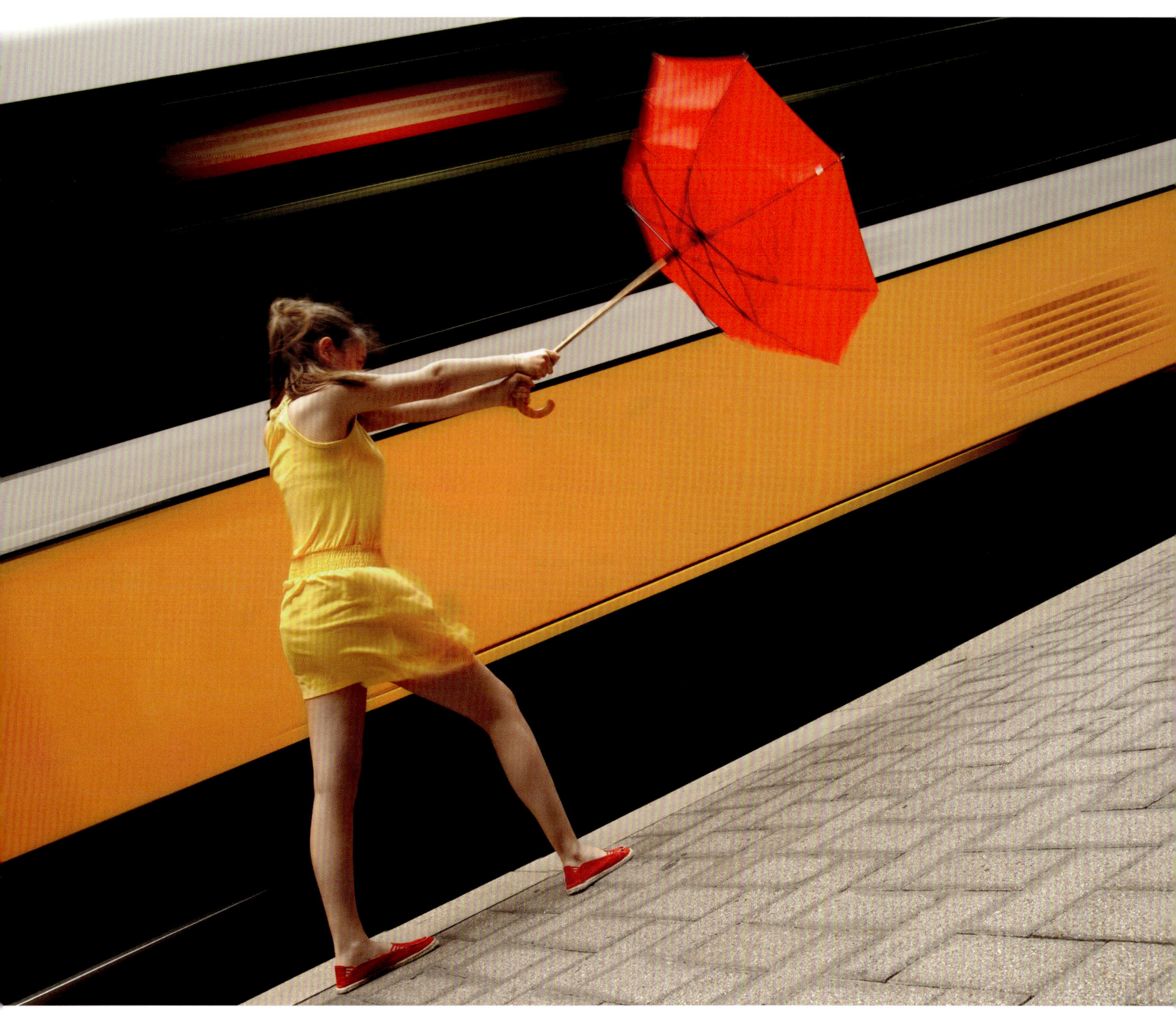

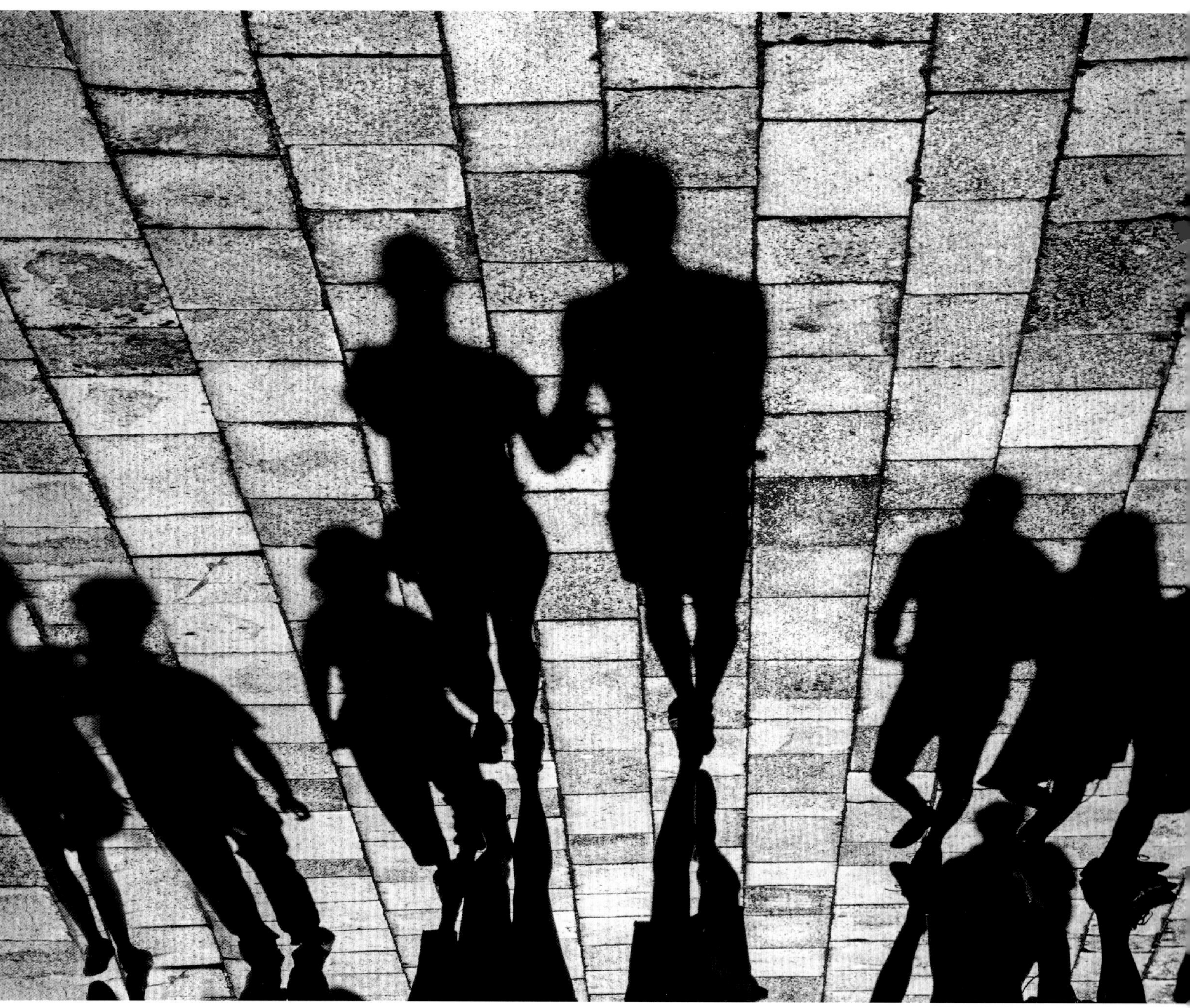

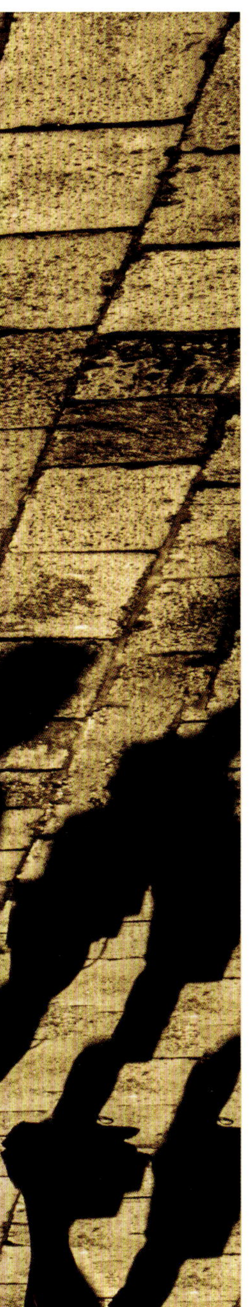

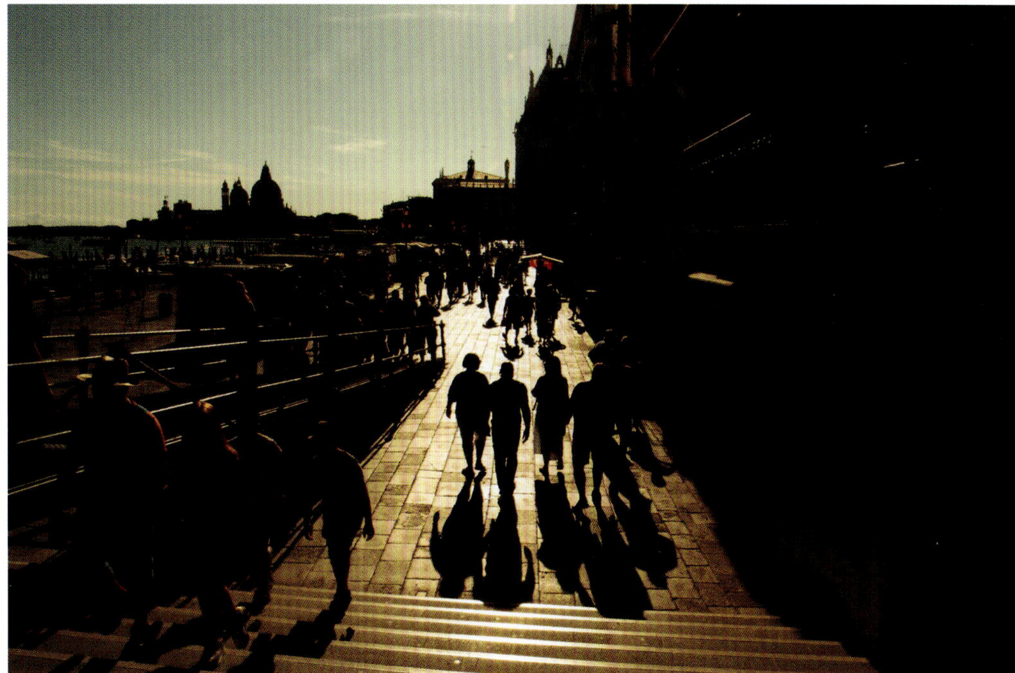

Most photographic compositions, when turned upside down, will cause the viewer to remark, "Hey, your photograph is upside down." But that is hardly a reason to abandon this idea! Some photographs actually do look better when turned upside down (or even sideways), and the idea of flipping an image is certainly not limited to abstracts, though abstracts may be better suited to it than other subjects.

It was late afternoon in Venice, Italy, and crowds were swarming the boardwalk. From atop one of the many pedestrian canal overpasses, I turned around to be greeted by the strong backlight of the late afternoon light. After several tries to capture the scene, a light bulb went off in my brain, and I changed my white balance (WB; see page 68) to the absurd setting of 10,000 Kelvin. If my hunch was correct, this would render the bright areas of the backlit boardwalk a deep golden color, in contrast to the stark, silhouetted shapes of the people coming my way. After fifteen or twenty shots, I had all the proof I needed that the exposure and WB setting had achieved the desired effect. And as I turned the camera upside down and viewed the results again, I felt that at least three of the images would benefit from being displayed upside down, one of which is shown here. The idea is to playfully disorient the viewer, to cause you to take a second look, as if the group of people in this composition are members of the Gumby family out for a stroll. And as far as the overall warmth of the image, give all the credit to that setting of 10,000K, which is readily available to any DSLR user.

◘ **Nikon D500, NIKKOR 18–300mm lens at 220mm, *f*/32 for 1/500 sec., ISO 1000, Custom WB (10,000K)**

Understanding White Balance

The option to choose your white balance (WB) at any given moment is probably my second favorite feature of shooting digitally. (My favorite? Changing ISO from one shot to the next; this coming, of course, from a guy who shot film for thirty-plus years.) Let me go on record, hopefully for the last time (at least for the foreseeable future), to say emphatically that you should *not* use the Auto WB setting. It almost always generates an image that suffers from an overall cold, blue cast—and a portrait cast in cold blue light is usually far from flattering.

Ninety-five percent of the time I shoot in Daylight/Sunny WB, though when shooting those red-orange sunrises or sunsets, I sometimes make one or two exposures with my WB in shade, just to see how much warmer and deeper the orange and red can go. Some will argue that it is best to leave it on Auto and then adjust it later in post-processing, yet I have found that, more often than not, my students end up adjusting the WB to end up around the Kelvin color temperature of 5200, which happens to be Daylight/Sunny. So why not eliminate at least one step from your post-processing? If on a rare occasion you do want an image to be more blue or yellow, you can make the changes accordingly.

Having said that, changing the WB *can* be a fun way to alter the overall mood of an image, and I am all for opening up an image to experimentation. For example, the Custom WB setting (K) allows you to set your WB at a number beyond shade (7600K) or below Tungsten/Incandescent (2800K), resulting in a much warmer, golden color cast or a much bluer (ice blue, in fact) color cast.

I also use a Custom Fluorescent WB for the dawn sky and the blue hour, especially when I have forgotten to bring along my FL-W filter. This is a Custom WB setting that comes close to rendering the blue/magenta colorcast that the FL-W filter is known for. If you'd like to learn how to set this Custom WB setting, check out my instructional video "FLW FILTER WB SETTING", on my Bryan Peterson Youtube channel.

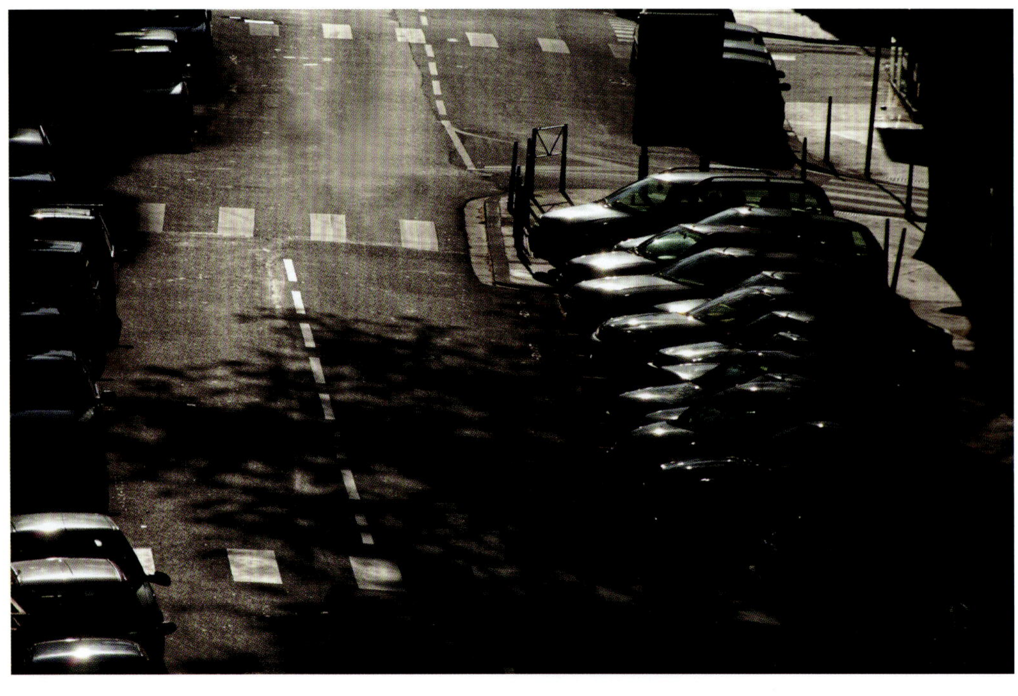

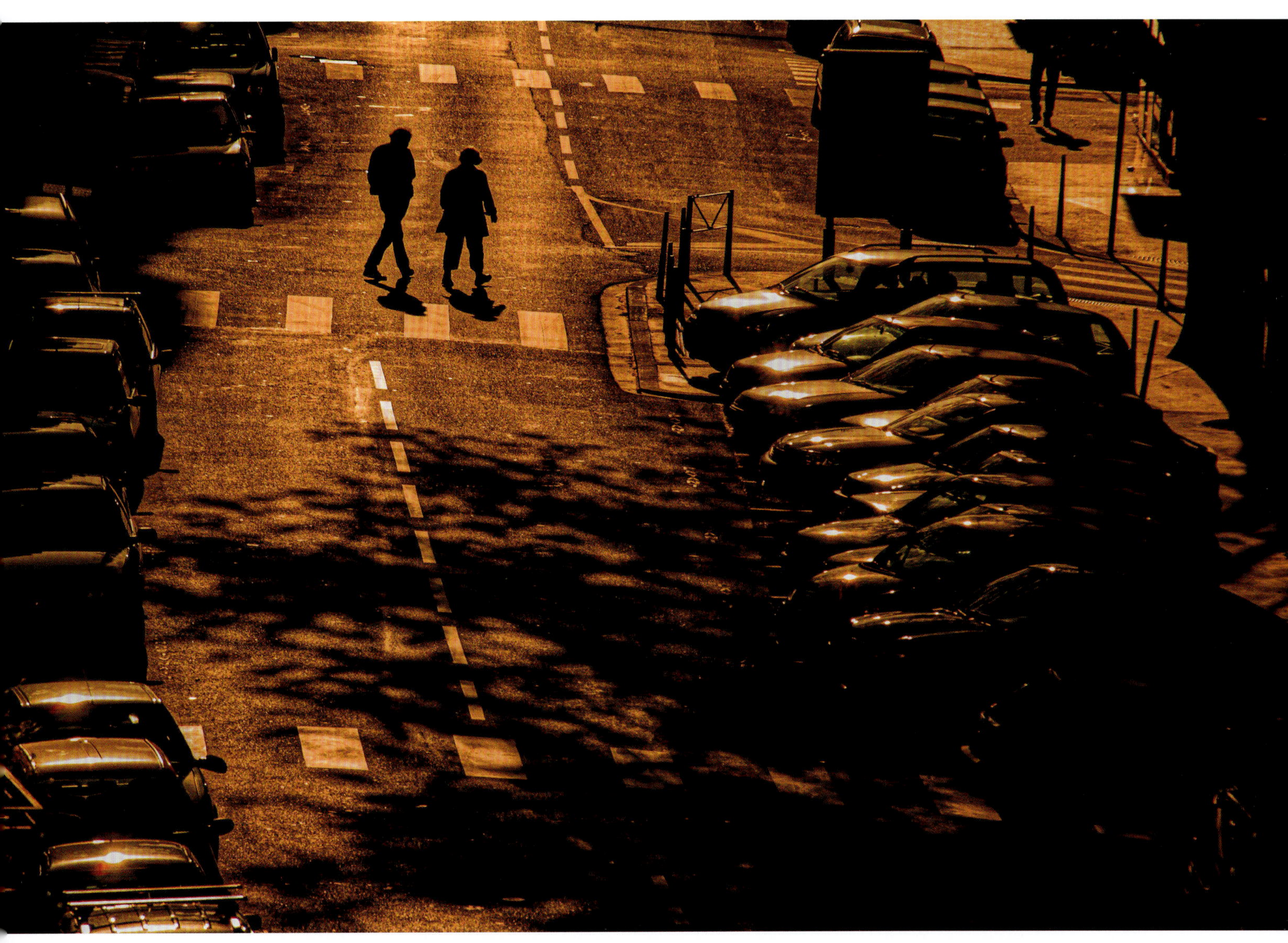

One way to increase the dynamic appeal of a backlit image is to use the Custom WB setting (K) and run your WB up to 10,000 Kelvin. This imparts an incredible golden hue to the image, suggesting that one is shooting just minutes before the sun sets or after it has risen. The intensity of the golden hue is influenced by the time of day, intensified as the light of late afternoon naturally becomes more and more golden as the sun nears the horizon.

This was certainly the case in this image of two gentlemen crossing the Quai St. Vincent in Lyon, France, on a late winter afternoon. The comparison shot taken before the two men showed up was done with Daylight/Sunny WB, dramatically illustrating the jump from cool to warm as I went from 5200K to the much warmer 10,000K.

◘ Nikon D300S, NIKKOR 70–300mm lens, *f*/22 for 1/250 sec., ISO 400, Custom WB (10,000K)

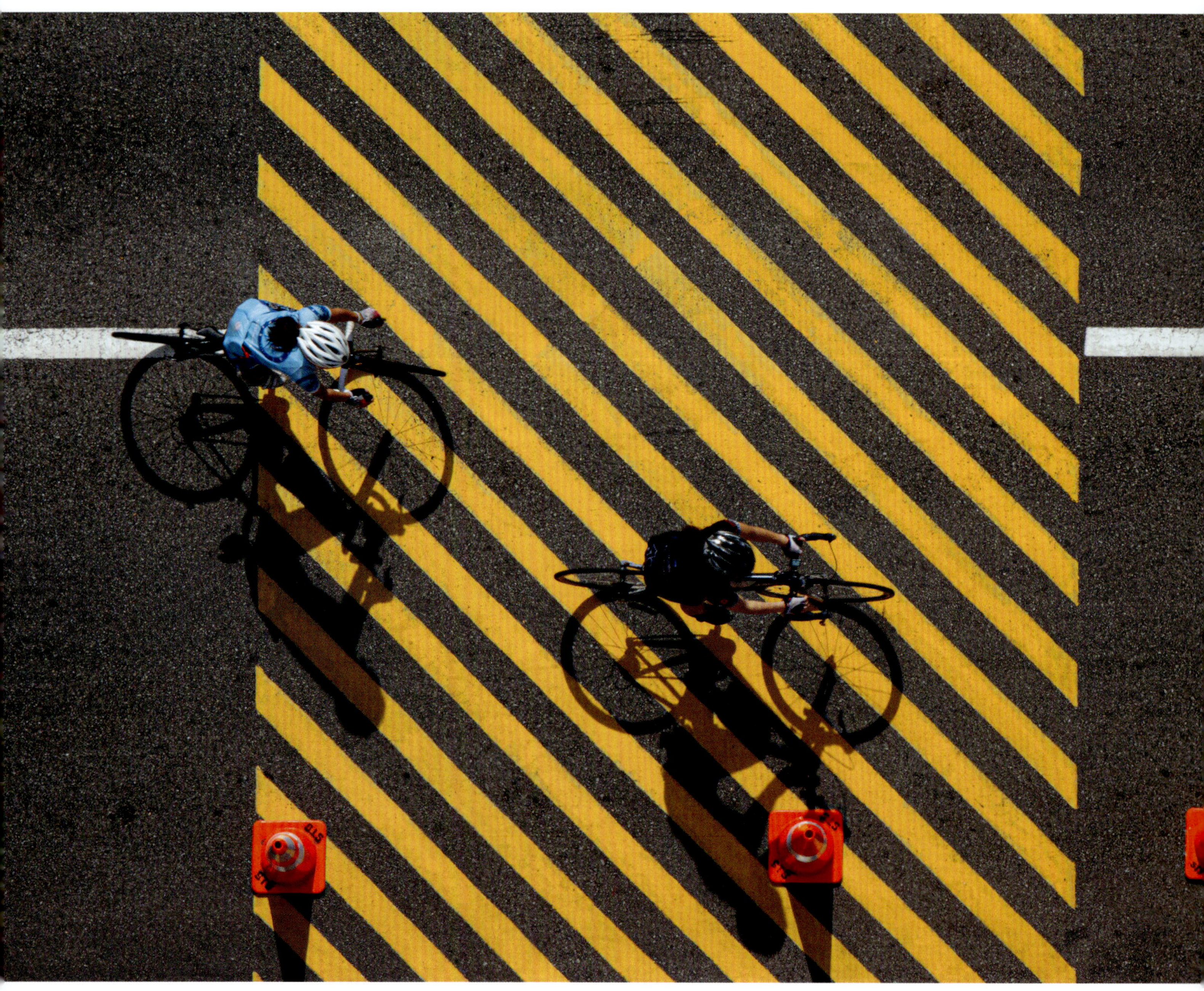

Sounds on the street travel far, including straight up to the forty-fifth floor of my Singapore hotel room, where the sounds of a street protest came through the sliding glass door of my outside terrace. A protest on the streets of Singapore is rarer than steak tartare, so, like a moth to a flame, I quickly went out onto the terrace. Looking down to the street, I could see several hundred bicyclists riding past the hotel. The scene was mesmerizing from forty-five floors up, so much so that I forgot to rush back inside and grab my camera until it was too late. By the time I did grab my camera and the attached 200–500mm lens, I managed to capture only two stragglers riding at a pace normally reserved for a relaxing afternoon stroll. Perhaps they were Sunday afternoon riders, perhaps not.

In retrospect, I was fortunate to record *only* the two of them, as the orange safety cones, numerous diagonal yellow lines, and asphalt create a strikingly graphic background that does a nice job of showcasing the two bicyclists and their shadows.

◘ Nikon D850, NIKKOR 200–500mm lens, *f*/14 for 1/400 sec., ISO 320, Daylight/Sunny WB

Scale

Think of scale as a thermometer that tells us how cold or hot it is. The thermometer is a tool, and the information it gives us has a huge impact on our emotions as well as the course of action we choose to take: "I'd better wear long underwear and take a scarf, now that I know it's only eight degrees outside!" Much like the information from a thermometer, the eye and brain get information from scale. When primitive people stood outside the entrance to their cave looking up at a lone tree on a distant hillside and a saber-toothed cat appeared, they could quickly tell the size of the cat by its relationship to the tree, which lent *scale* to the cat standing next to it.

The shape of the human form is so recognizable that we often, without giving it any thought, can determine how far away someone might be or how big or small they are based solely in comparison to other nearby objects. In a photographic composition, it is not uncommon to call attention to a large piece of machinery or an airplane by including a person in the image. "Wow, is that a big piece of machinery!" you remark as you see the tiny figure standing next to it, or "That's a huge cliff!" as you notice the two rock climbers scaling the cliff face. Think about using scale when shooting on the streets to call attention to the big structures and buildings around you.

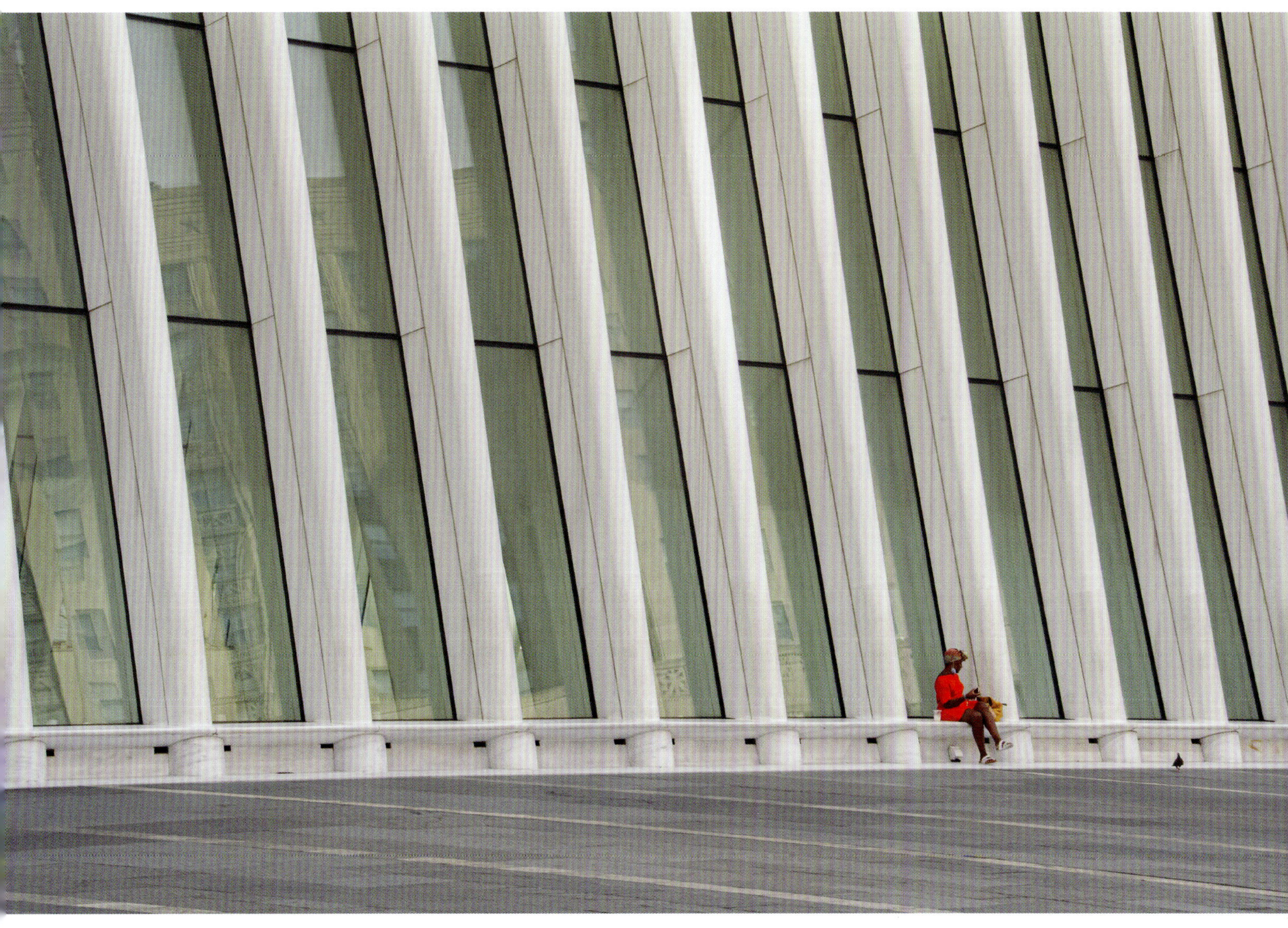

The Oculus in Lower Manhattan continues to provide great fodder for both street and architectural photographers, whether they are shooting inside or outside. On this overcast June day, the COVID-19 pandemic had created opportunities rarely seen in New York: empty streets, empty sidewalks, and a long stretch of "empty" at the Oculus. There was a lone woman—in red, no less—calling attention to the great size and scale of the building's outer walls.

◘ Nikon D500, NIKKOR 18–300mm lens, *f*/16 for 1/100 sec., ISO 400, Daylight/Sunny WB

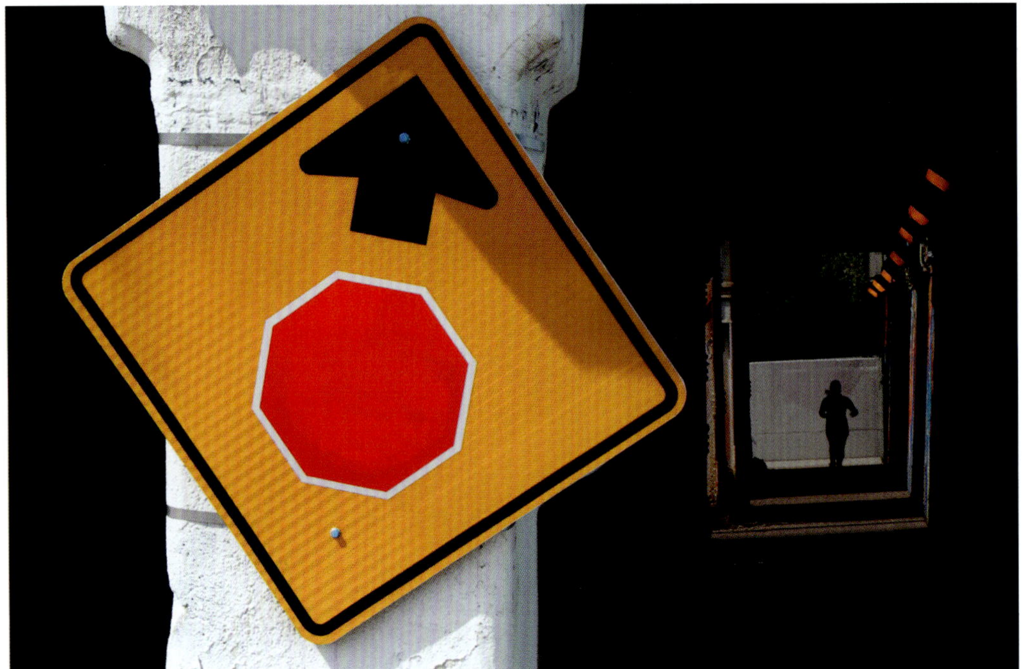

An overpass built for the many trains that pass through Chicago's Pilsen neighborhood creates a dark tunnel of light on the street below. Lucky me to have a bright yellow road sign to call upon as a foreground subject. As I framed the tunnel beyond, I knew that the element I needed to emphasize the depth of the composition was a distant pedestrian. My patience was rewarded ten minutes later when a lone jogger passed me. Just before he popped out into the light at the opposite end, I fired off several quick shots, the best of which is seen here. Because my exposure was set manually for the bright sign outside, the runner in the darker light is recorded as a silhouette.

◘ Nikon D500, NIKKOR 18–300mm lens at 20mm, *f*/22 for 1/320 sec., ISO 640, Daylight/Sunny WB

As my students and I walked the streets of downtown Denver, I spotted this black-and-white billboard. I then asked Taylor, a young woman who was merely accompanying her friend attending the workshop, if she would mind walking across the vast empty parking lot to pose against the wall with her arms folded and legs crossed. If my hunch was correct, we would end up with an interesting composition of scale and contrast. When Taylor saw the image, she shared her excitement. What do you think?

◘ Nikon D500, NIKKOR 18–300mm lens at 38mm, *f*/8 for 1/500 sec., ISO 100, Daylight/Sunny WB

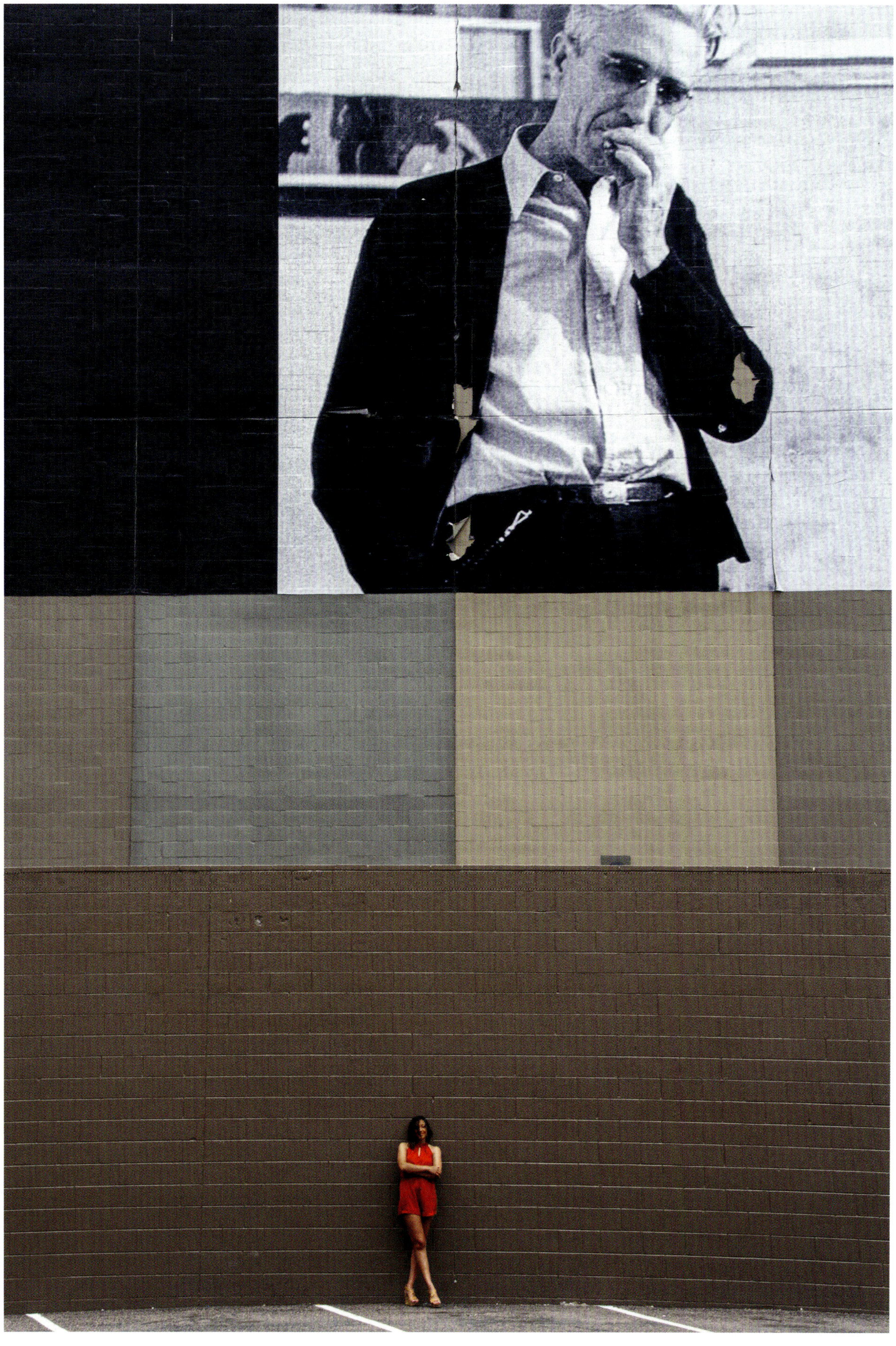

La Défense is the modern-day business district of Paris, France, arguably a dream location for any architecture photographer as well as, surely, for any street photographer—and in particular, those of us who like color. Installed along the very wide pedestrian walkway is *Le Moretti*, a very colorful sculpture by Raymond Moretti that comprises 672 colorful fiberglass tubes. Thanks to its size, *Le Moretti* is hard to miss and draws people like moths to a flame, yet most people have no idea that the sculpture is actually covering a ventilation shaft. Imagine if art could be used to hide other eyesores around the world in similar fashion!

On this particular day, one of my students got caught up photographing the sculpture, and as I watched her express a gesture of surprise at the sculpture's size, I fired off several quick shots. Whether friends or strangers, planned or candid, humans bring a sense of size and scale to a composition. Often there is nothing better than the unmistakably identifiable human body.

◘ Nikon D850, NIKKOR 24–120mm lens, *f*/11 for 1/320 sec., ISO 200, Daylight/Sunny WB

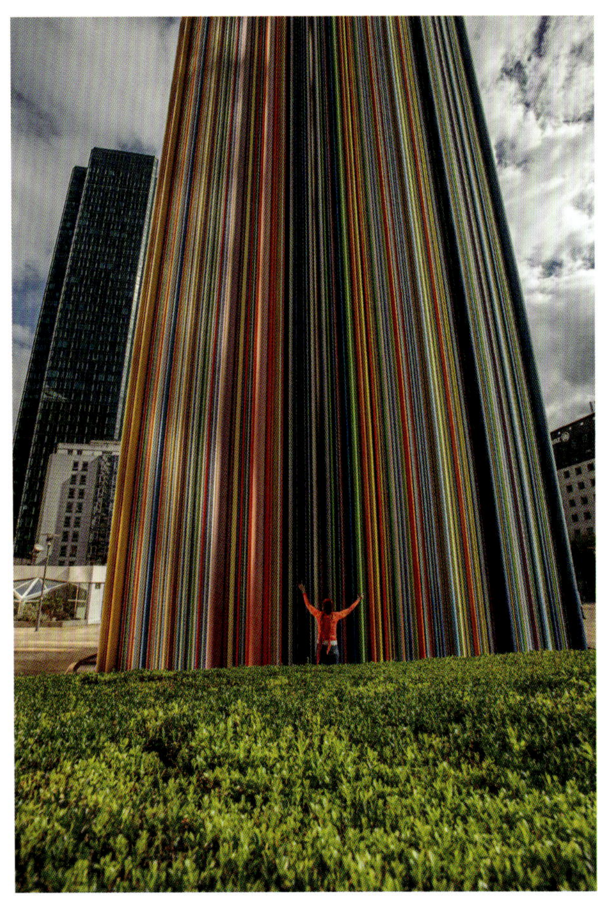

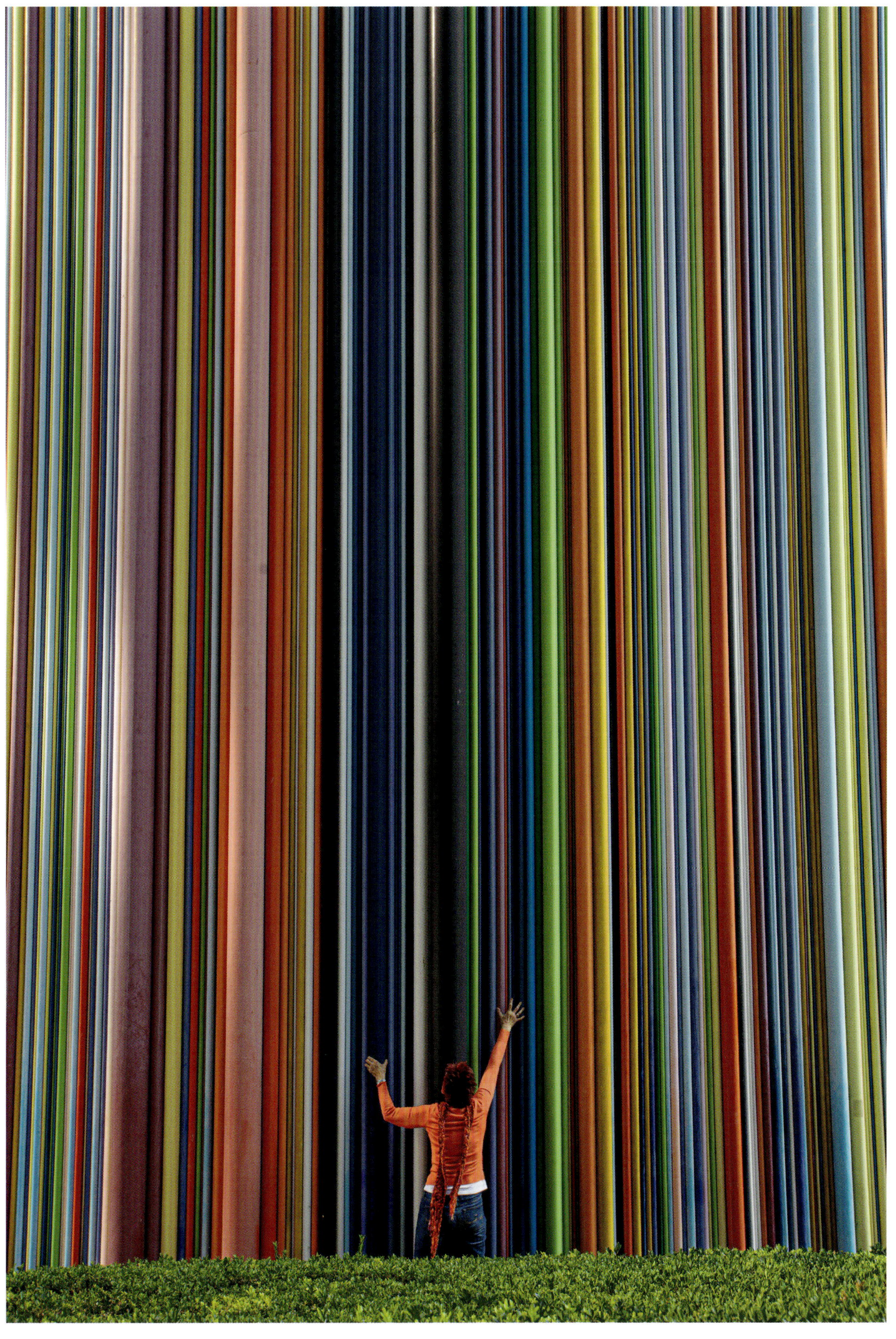

Pattern and Color

Most of us are wired with a desire for the world to operate in an orderly manner. When chaos erupts, our blood pressure rises, our heart rate increases, and nerves fray. Obviously, one person's chaos might be another one's joy, but chaos is essentially a breakdown of structure, and at its extreme a complete disregard for law and order.

Not surprisingly, a photograph of chaos is a photograph without order, in which it's not clear exactly what the subject is. We might see lines, textures, and colors that indicate the photographer's intent, but we can't get past the disarray of the composition: lines that lead us away from what we sense to be the subject, textures that clash or merge with the intended subject, hot spots of bright light that call attention away from a subject in open shade, colors that are more dominant than the colors of the intended subject, and so on. Photographic chaos is akin to trying to hear the players on stage at a Broadway play while seated next to a baby in the throes of colic!

Of all the elements of design, pattern places an exclamation point on an orderly composition, amplifying what is already a well-composed single line, texture, shape, or color and turning up its volume substantially. Pattern calls attention to itself by being *extremely* loud.

Color, another element of design, is evident on city streets big and small, whether in cars and motorbikes, newspaper boxes and trash cans, or people in colorful dress.

Let's take a look at how you can capture pattern and color for compelling street photographs.

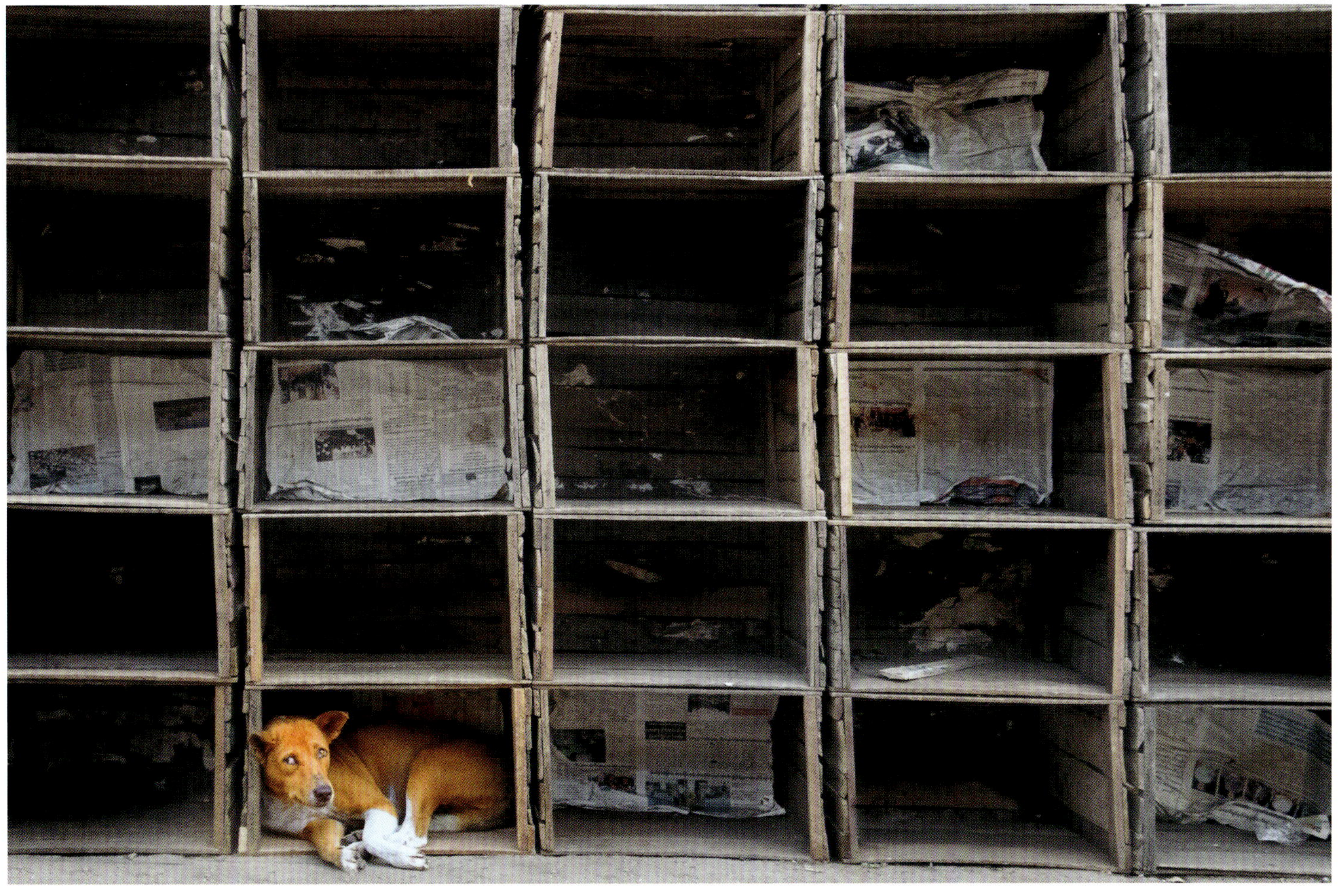

As I rounded a corner of one of the many narrow streets surrounding the flower market of Mandalay, Myanmar, I noticed a wall of nondescript wooden boxes, approximately fifteen feet long and ten feet high. I have always been drawn to pattern, and this group of boxes were certainly a pattern, but "nondescript" is an appropriate descriptor: I couldn't find anything of value in photographing them, unlike the numerous patterns of color and texture in the bouquets of flowers I had photographed moments before. As I continued my trek, I came upon the vegetable and fish markets, both also known for offering opportunities to photograph pattern. Several hours later, my route back to meet my driver took me past that same wall of boxes, only this time a lone dog was holed up in one of them. Contrast that breaks up a pattern's predictability like this can be used to amplify the volume of any subject. Obviously, this is just one dog, but it could be the loudest nonbarking dog you have ever seen. Think of the wooden boxes as the background choir, with the dog the lead singer.

◘ Nikon D500, NIKKOR 18–300mm lens, *f*/14 for 1/200 sec., ISO 400, Daylight/Sunny WB

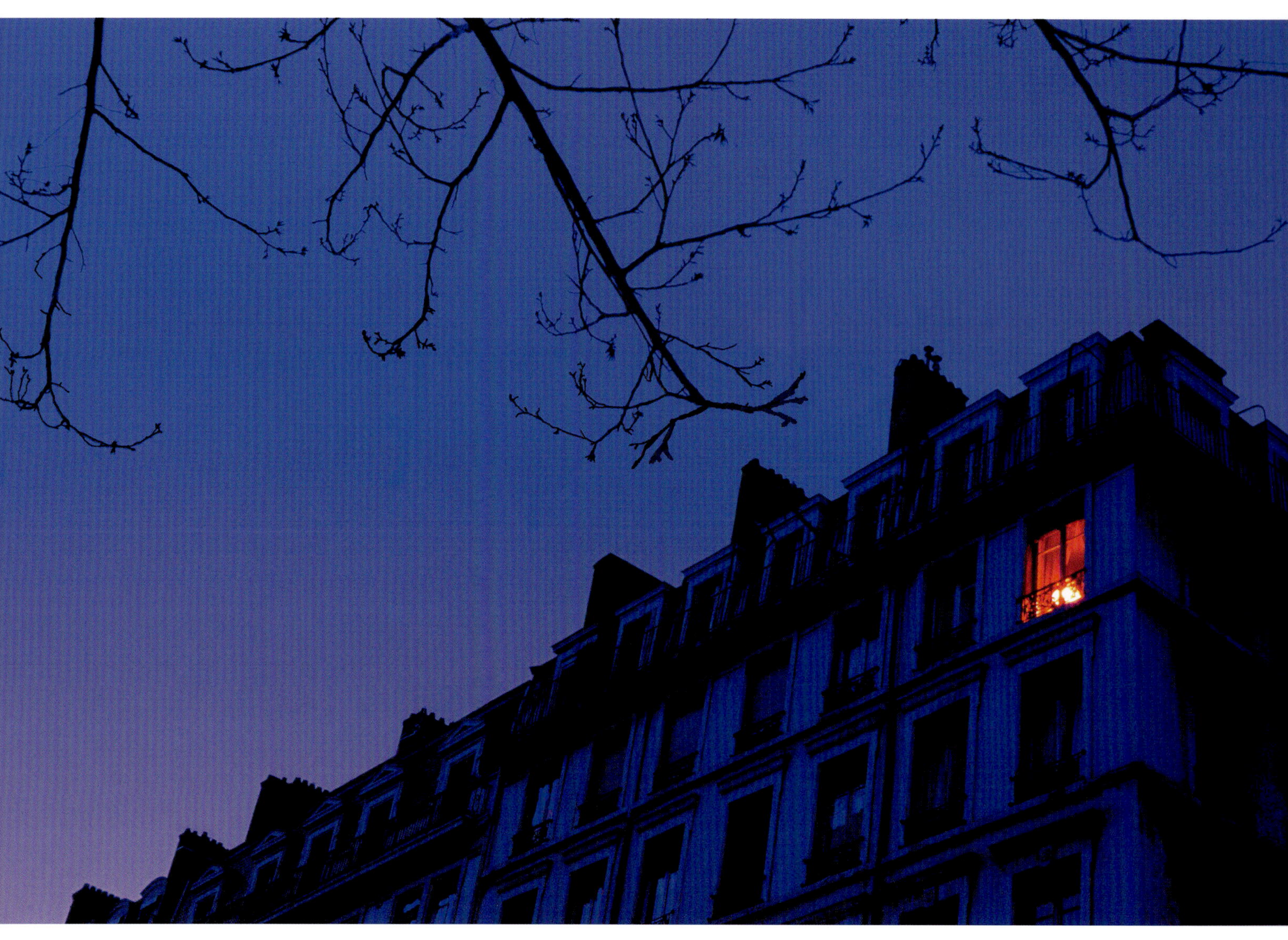

Pattern has an uncanny ability to draw attention to itself when something in the pattern steps out of line. As I was walking the streets of Lyon, France, before sunrise on an early winter morning, an unmistakable chill in the air, my eyes darted up to a lone light illuminating a sixth-floor corner apartment. Insomnia? Early morning flight? Hungry baby? Confronting the truth about a relationship? Unexpected phone call? Stomach pain? A poet burning the midnight oil? I have no idea. What do you imagine is going on in that sixth-floor apartment?

I opted for the Fluorescent WB to impart an even greater sense of chill on an already cold morning. I deliberately used a low ISO (and thus long exposure) for the sole purpose of trying out a new tripod I had just bought.

◘ Nikon D810, NIKKOR 24–120mm lens on a tripod, *f*/11 for 1/2 sec., ISO 100, Fluorescent WB

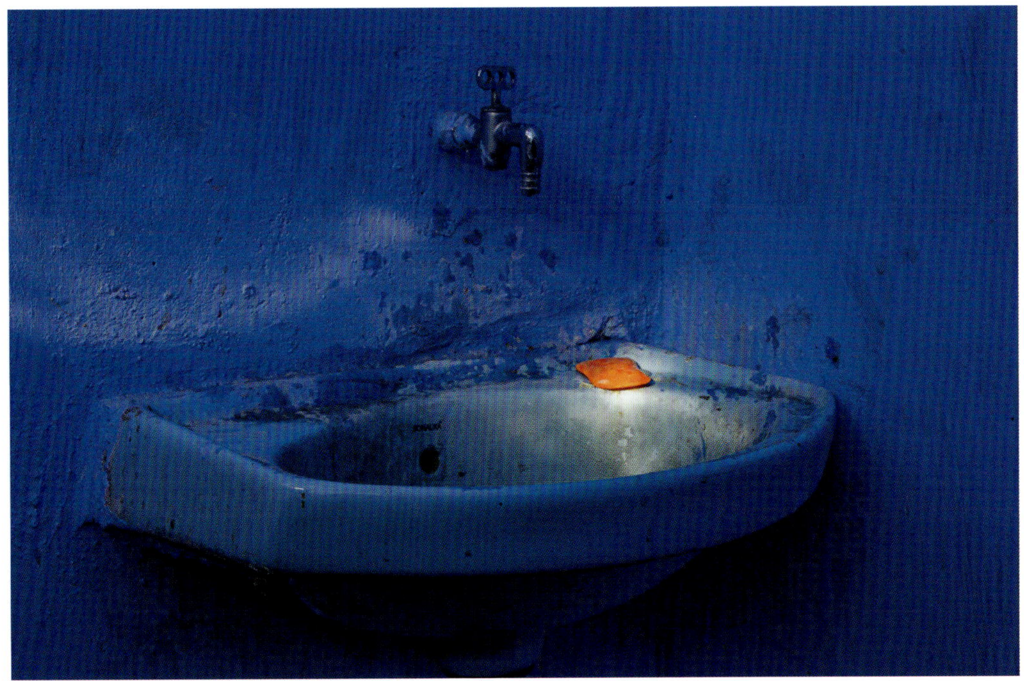

A homeowner shouted down from her second-floor window, "Would you like to see my home?" I smiled at her invitation to a total stranger, reaffirming the friendliness of residents of Jodhpur, India. "How can I say no?" I replied. Several seconds later, I was walking through the outer courtyard headed for the actual entrance to her home, and as I followed the stone path to the left, *there* it was: an outdoor washbasin and wall in Jodhpur blue with a bright orange bar of soap illuminated by sunlight that first struck a bedroom window and then ricocheted onto that small corner of the washbasin. What were the odds? I could not help but succumb to the feeling that I was witnessing something extraordinary. I quickly raised the camera to my eye and used Aperture Priority and *f*/16. Seconds later, the "spotlight" had moved on. If you are familiar with the color wheel, you'll know that orange and blue are color complements. Life on the street once again demonstrated its ability to perform magic.

◘ Nikon D500, NIKKOR 18–300mm lens, *f*/14 for 1/200 sec., ISO 200, Daylight/Sunny WB

After a relatively short climb, this wide path in Santorini, Greece, opens up into a small terrace. Once you've counted nine cats, your first thought might be that you have stumbled on a shelter for cats. But these nine cats are waiting, with certainty, for the arrival of an elderly woman who has been faithfully feeding *all* the cats in this village for years. She reaches this terrace shortly after sunrise every day, removes a weathered padlock from an even more weathered wooden door nearby, enters the small, darkened room, and fills stainless steel bowls with dry cat food, setting them down on the terrace outside the doorway as fast as she can. As the bowls hit the stone surface they make a clanging sound, a sort of breakfast bell that alerts cats near and far, and soon the stone terrace is a wall-to-wall carpet of cats. The food is gone in fifteen minutes, tops, and the cats have dispersed, returning to their familiar resting places, including the many stone steps found on the island.

Chances are, blue is your favorite color—because it's the color favored by 75 percent of the world's population. The beauty of blue lies in its soothing, calming ability. It also creates a great deal of depth, as in this scene, with a lone black-and-white cat appearing to jump out from the expanse of blue.

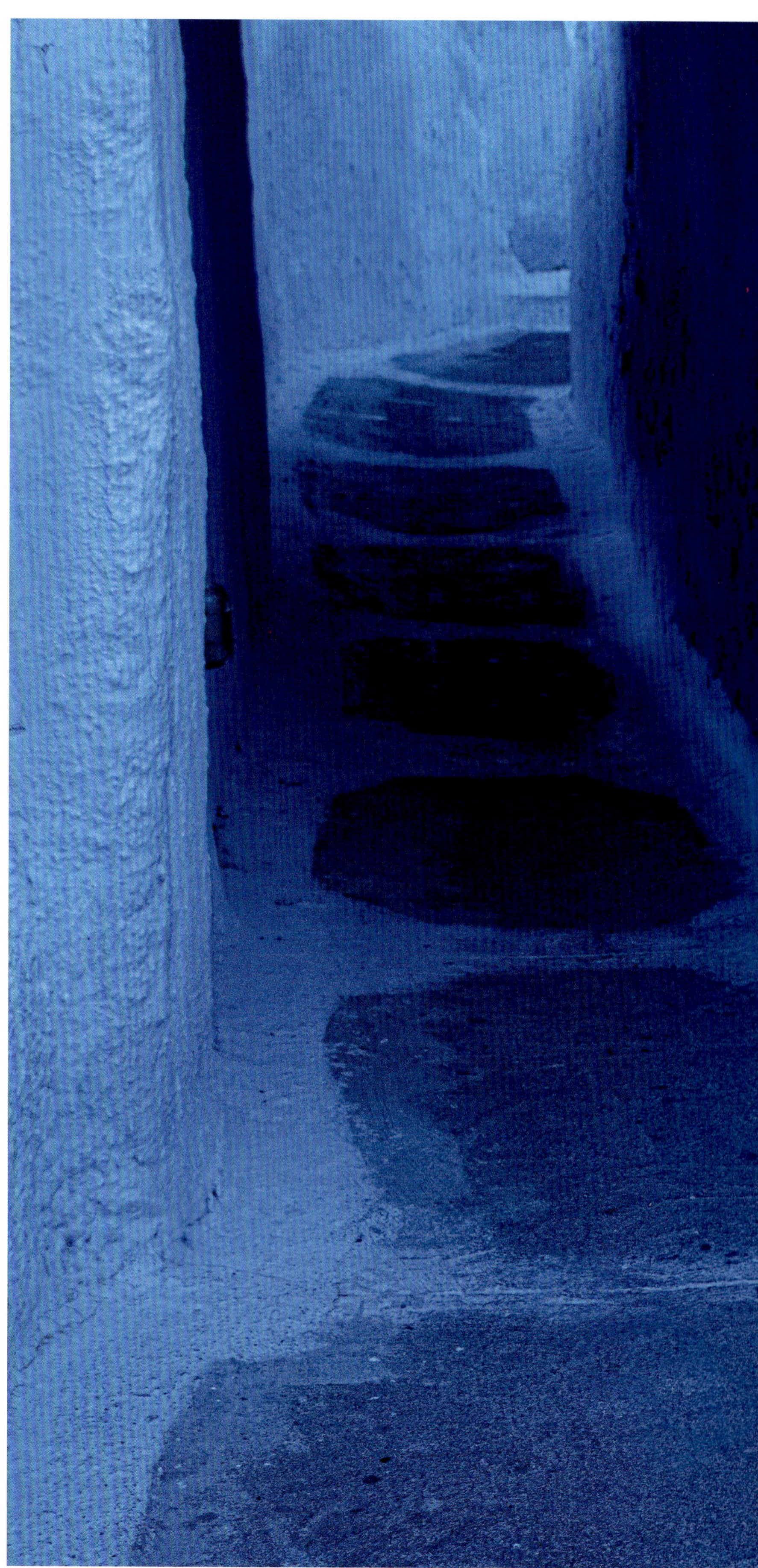

◘ Nikon D500, NIKKOR 18–300mm lens at 18mm, *f*/16 for 1/80 sec., ISO 1250, Daylight/Sunny WB

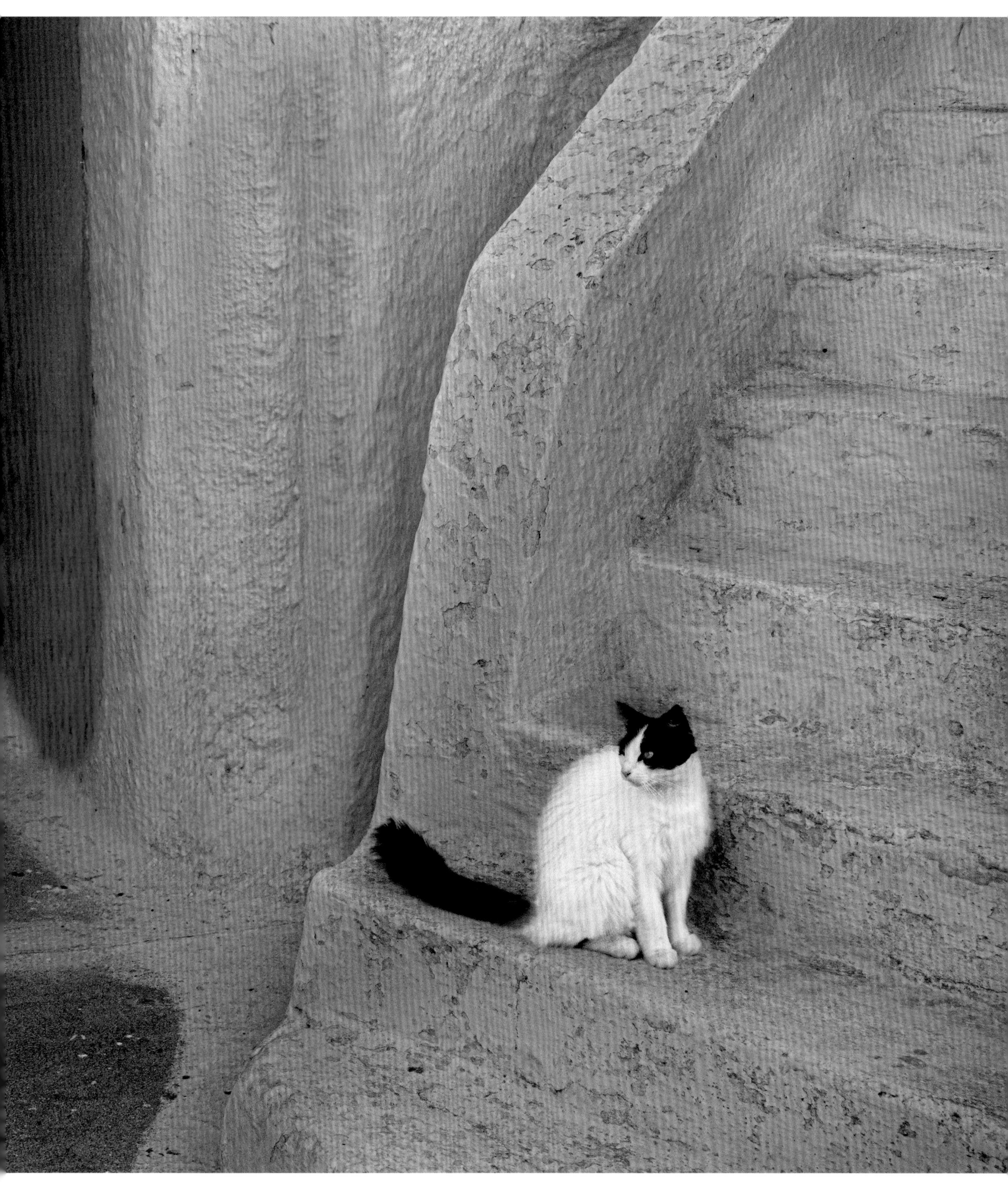

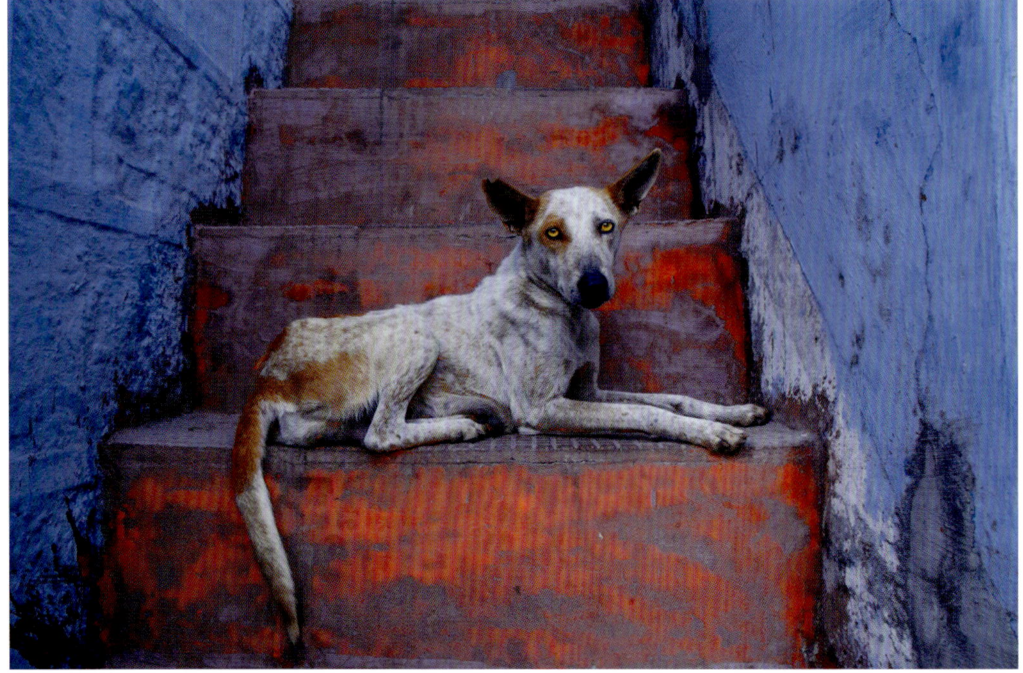

One morning in Jodhpur, India, several students and I froze when we came upon the dog you see here. None of us had ever seen a dog with such intense yellow eyes. With the blue walls and red stairs it was lying upon, it was a fantastic display of triadic color, and the dog's intense yellow eyes contrast vividly with the much calmer, receding light blue walls. Right place, right time, no doubt.

◘ Nikon D500, NIKKOR 18–300mm lens at 18mm, *f*/16 for 1/80 sec., ISO 400, Daylight/Sunny WB

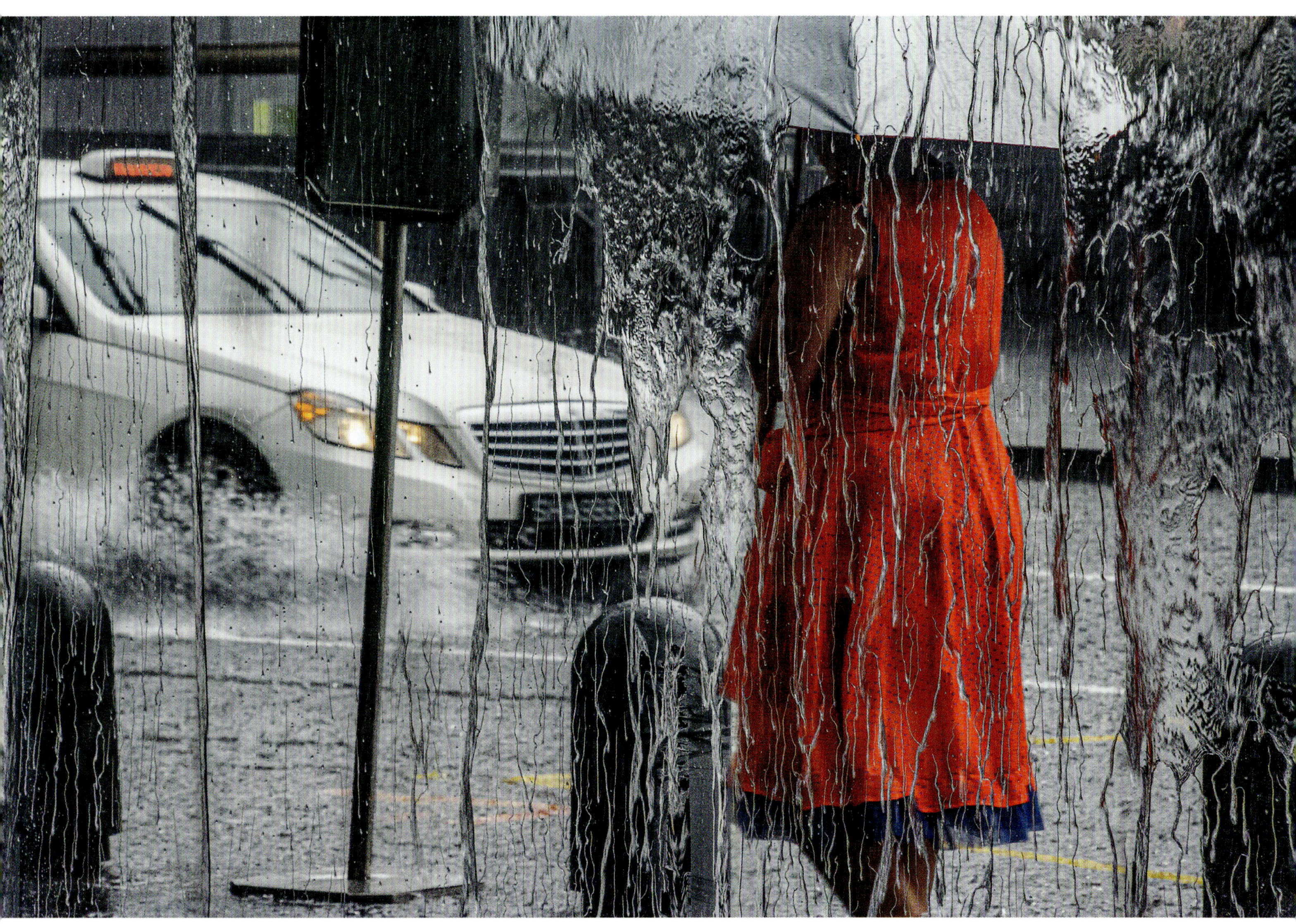

If you like downpours of tropical rain, then book an airline ticket for Singapore between November and February, as the rainy season will offer not only heavy rain but also some good lightning displays in the evenings. One November, I stood inside the Raffles Shopping Center waiting for one particular cloudburst to let up before venturing out to a nearby restaurant. As I stood near the large windows on the ground floor, a sheet of rainwater was coming down the windows like a waterfall. A few minutes later, a woman showed up in an orange dress, with taxis and hired cars behind her making their way toward the nearby Swiss Hotel. I chose a high ISO of 1600 because I needed both depth of field and a fast, action-stopping shutter speed on this day of dark skies. Although it was over quickly, I was really happy to have captured this image during that brief fifteen-minute downpour.

◘ Nikon D850, NIKKOR 24–120mm lens, *f*/16 for 1/320 sec., ISO 1600, Daylight/Sunny WB

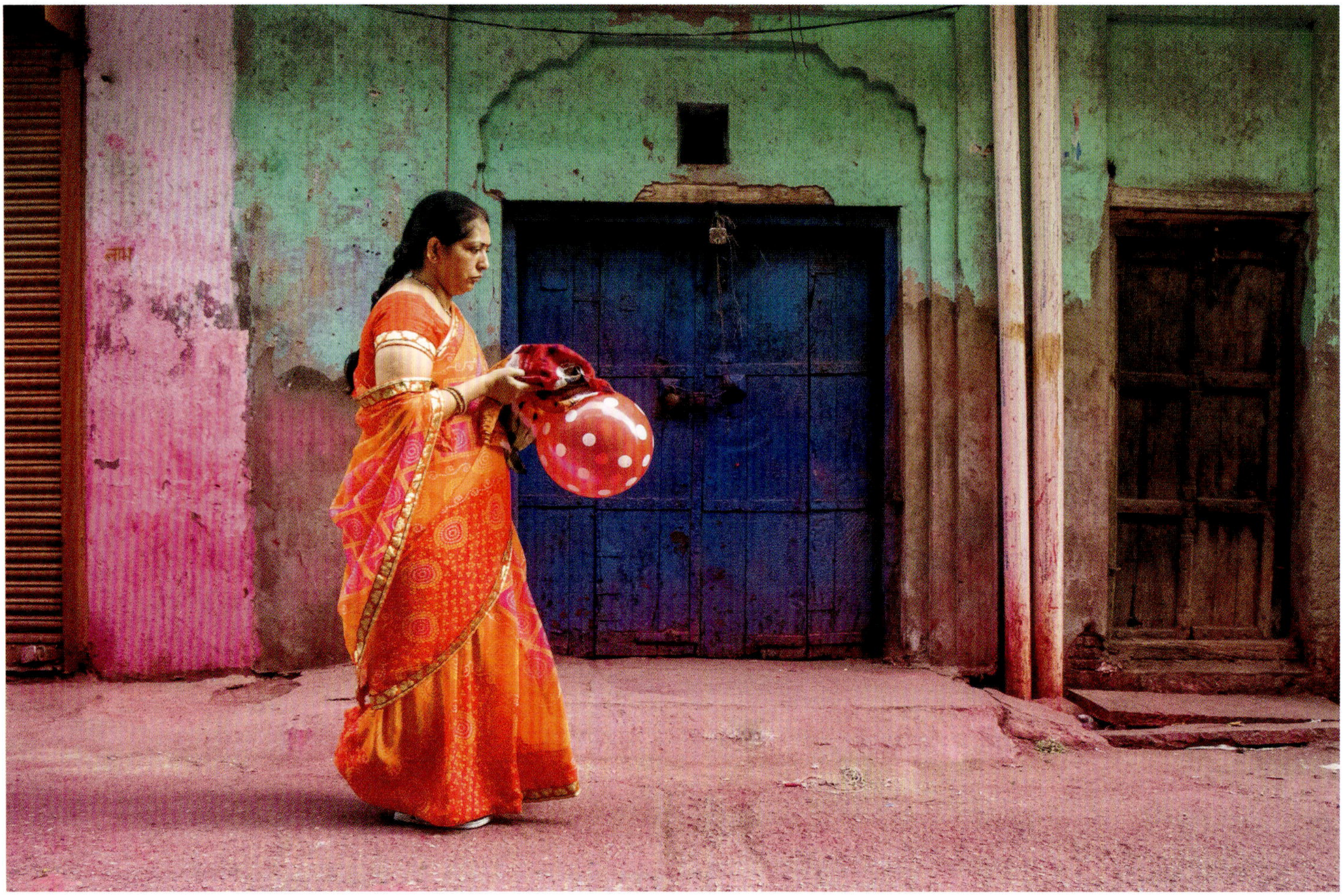

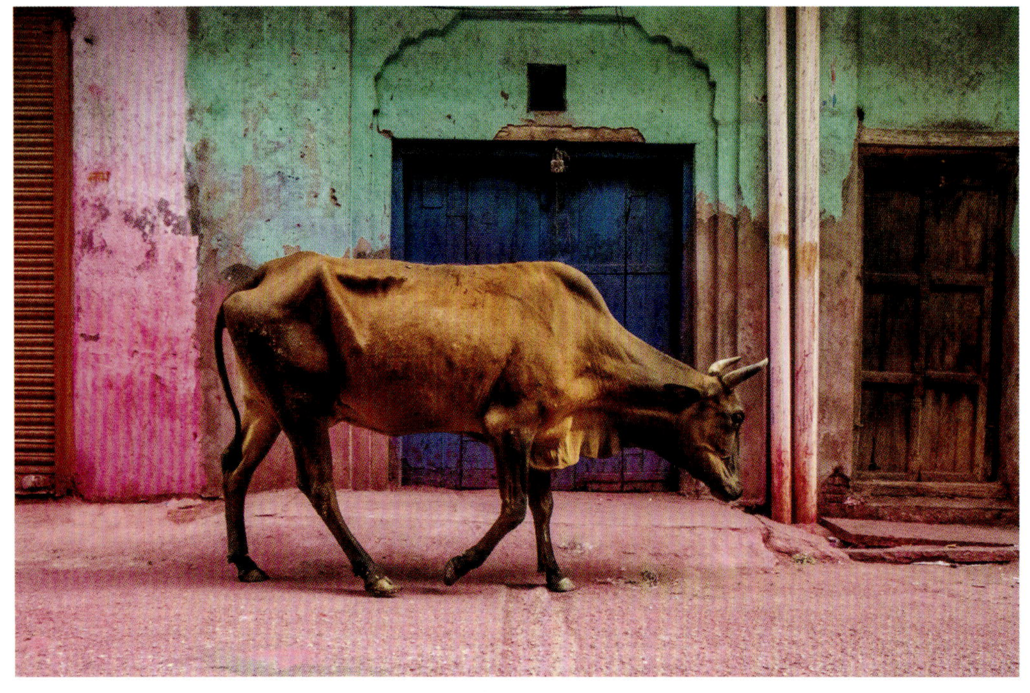

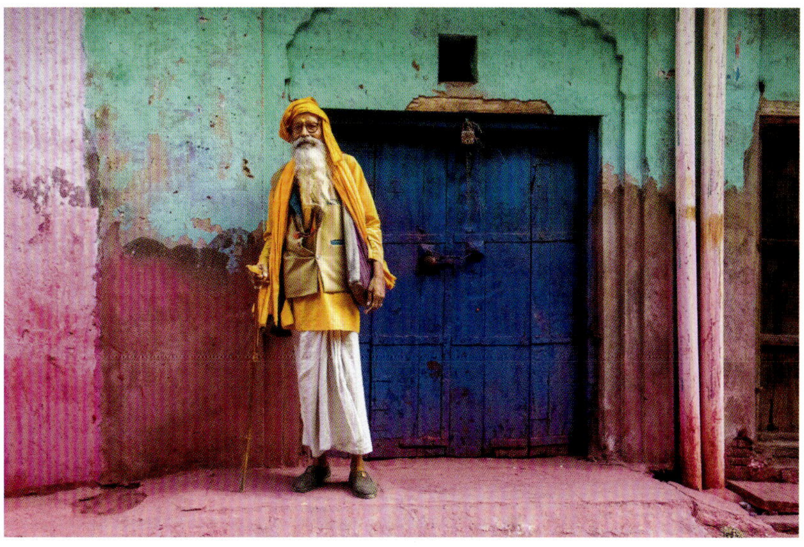

India's Holi festival had taken place just two days earlier, leaving a wash of magenta on the walls of this quiet street in Agra. As often happens when I come upon a setting with great color, light, or texture (or a combination of all three), I took up a position and chose my composition (or "canvas"), then patiently waited for subjects to enter the canvas. Over the course of thirty or maybe forty-five minutes, a number of people and animals—dogs, cats, cows, and one monkey—passed through the frame in front of me, four of them shown here. (The monkey entered from the left, but once he saw me he quickly went vertical, grabbing a nearby downspout and disappearing onto a nearby rooftop.) This was an easy setup in terms of exposure. Because the overcast morning cast an even light throughout that hour, I shot everything in Aperture Priority mode at the "Who cares?" aperture of *f*/11.

Rather than expending the personal energy of walking the streets looking for a shot, stake your claim and take up a comfortable position in front of what you deem to be a perfect "canvas," then let your subjects come into your composition. Shoot these nuggets of gold and experience the richness of a morning well spent.

◘ Nikon D500, NIKKOR 18–300mm lens, *f*/11 for 1/320 sec., ISO 800, Daylight/Sunny WB

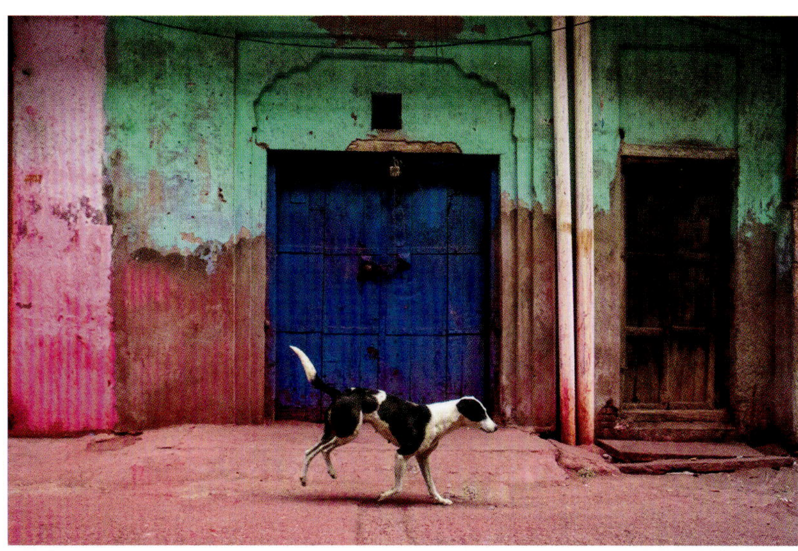

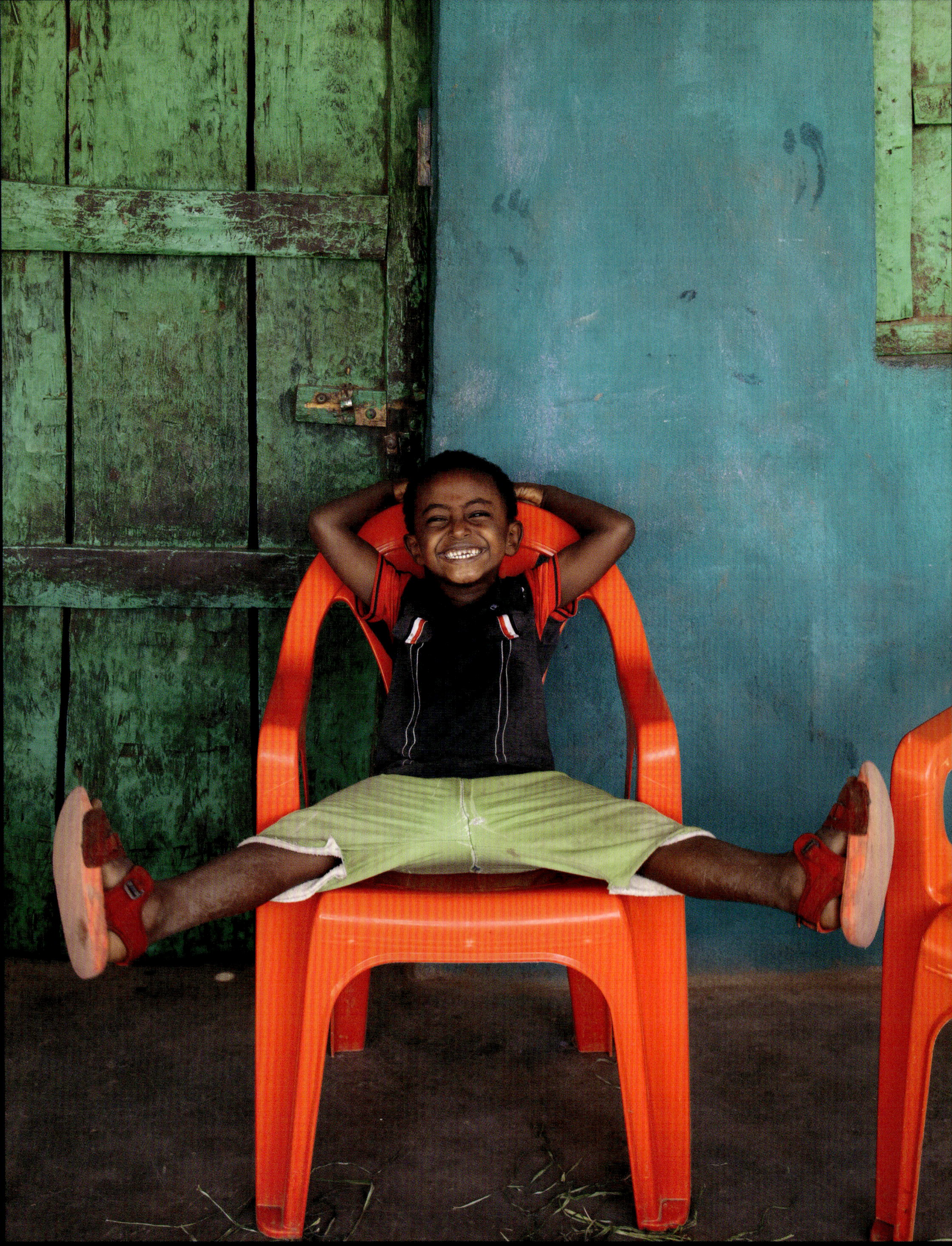

PEOPLE

Posed

Photographers frequently debate whether posed or candid portraits are more pleasing. I think that either can be appealing when the photographer's primary goal is to depict the subject as accurately as possible. Posed portraits are those for which the photographer directs the subject(s) to move, stand, or sit a certain way; to tilt their head this way or that way; and then, hardest of all, to look right into the lens and smile.

One of the greatest challenges street photographers face is learning to break through the shyness barrier; for some photographers, that means not only subject shyness but their own shyness as well. Assuming you've gotten past the internal obstacle that keeps you from asking others to pose for you, how do you convey your intentions with sincerity, certainty, and confidence to the subject you wish to pose?

After talking with subjects for several minutes and getting a sense about them, I often ask this provocative question: "How do you define or see yourself?" Obviously, this question can't be answered with only a simple yes or no. It invites more conversation, and it's here where the experienced photographer has the edge—and now you will, too. At some point, you follow that question with this one: "If you could look any way you want, wearing what you want, and do anything you want while being photographed, what would I see in the final image?" The purpose of this question is, of course, to draw the person into the photographic decision-making process, thereby opening them up to the idea of being photographed. For me, taking an interest in my subject—a *sincere* interest—has taken me further than any offer of payment or promise of a copy of the photo.

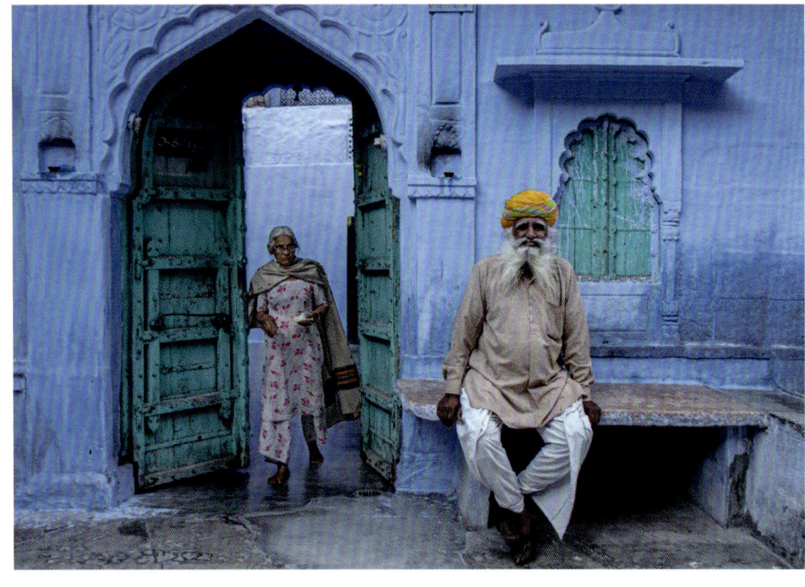

Nikon D850, NIKKOR 24–120mm lens, *f*/8 for 1/500 sec., ISO 400, Daylight/Sunny WB

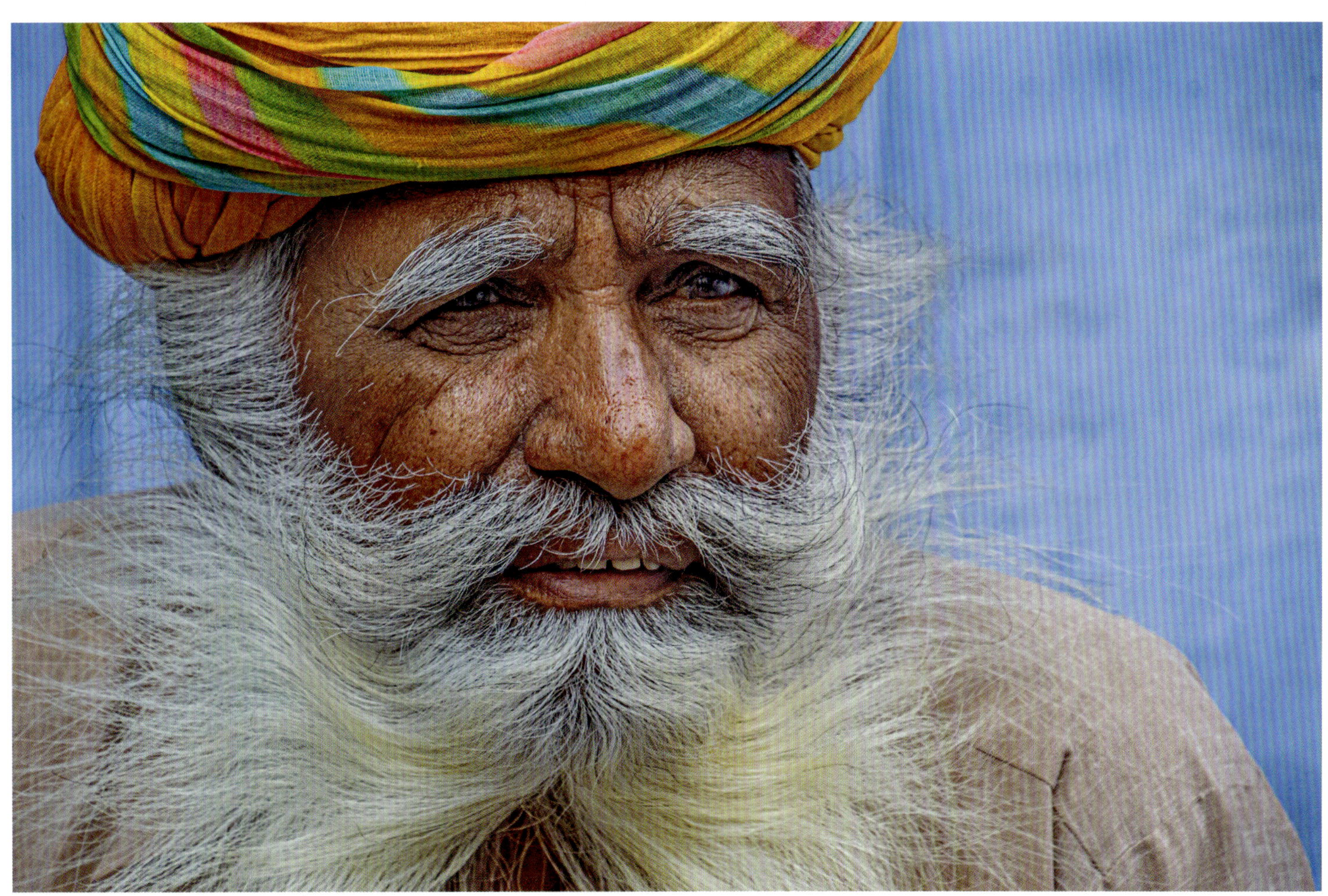

Once you have a subject's trust, relax, take your time, and explore all of the possible compositions, mindful of never crossing the finish line until you have that one portrait that spills out of the frame.

From a safe distance away on a narrow street in Jodhpur, India, I saw this man sitting on a stone slab bench against a sea of blue. I pointed to my camera and then to him, and he nodded his approval. With camera now raised, I fired off a shot or two, nervous as hell, overwhelmed by the feeling that I was intruding on his morning. Then the door to his right opened, and despite my nervousness, I recognized *that* moment and fired away as the unsuspecting woman unknowingly added a welcome jolt to the composition. Poof, it was over, my nervousness now replaced with joy, satisfaction, and the reassurance that I had what it took—well, assisted by luck, but luck rewards the prepared, right? Smiling, I approached the man and showed him the picture on the camera's monitor. He nodded approvingly and I thanked him. Since I felt a bit of trust had now been established, I asked if I could take a few tighter portraits, and again, he willingly agreed.

On more than one occasion in my early years as a photographer, I would move on quickly after taking my first shot, nervous that I was taking up the subject's time, but I have since realized that whenever possible I should share the results and, if nothing else, thank the person for sharing the moment, since it would never have happened without their willing participation. It's frustrating to realize hours, if not days later, *Oh damn! I never shot a frame-filling portrait of just his face, even though I had obviously earned his trust!* It's a hard lesson, but one you will never repeat.

◘ Nikon D850, NIKKOR 24–120mm lens, *f*/16 for 1/125 sec., ISO 400, Daylight/Sunny WB

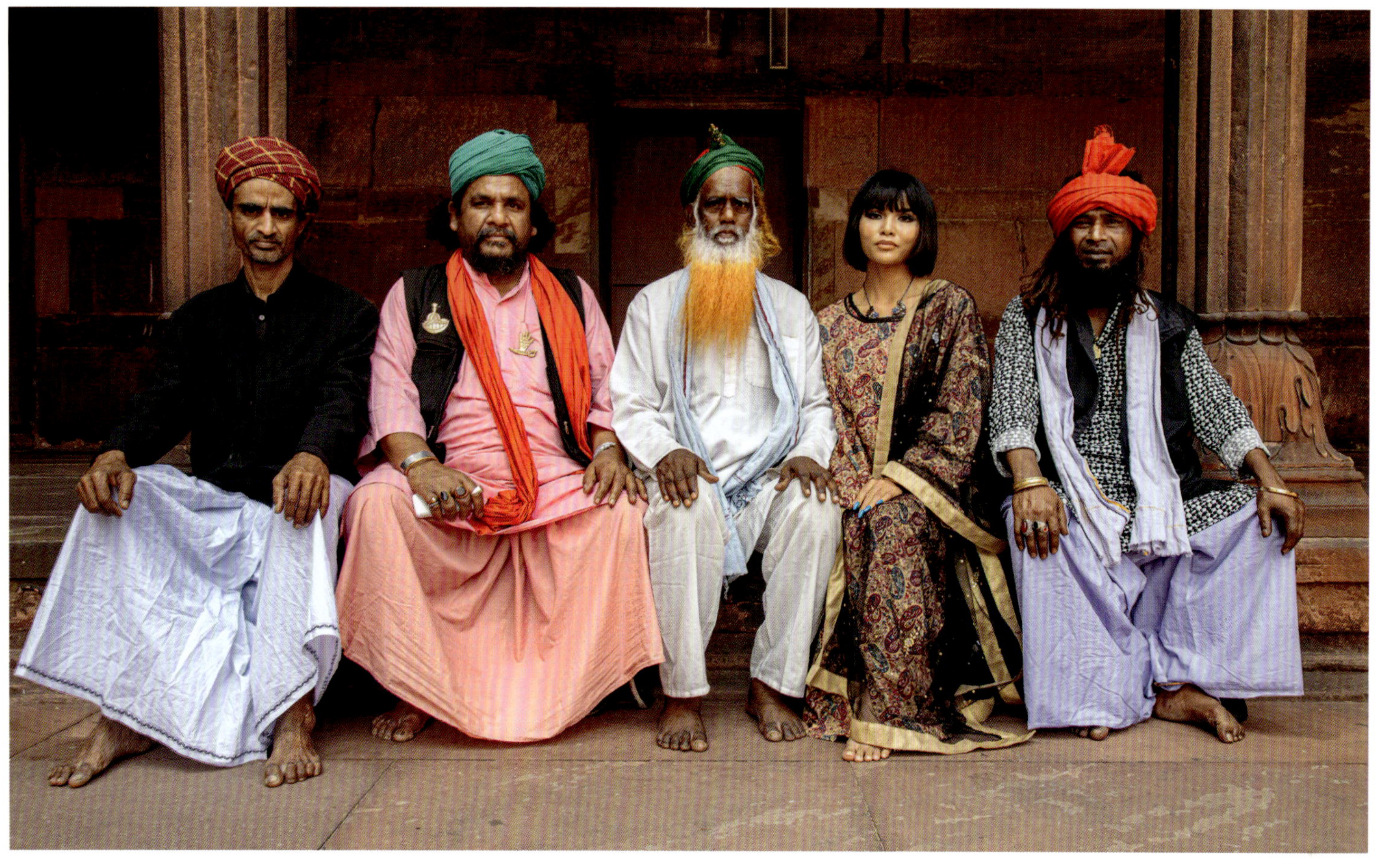

I am often asked by photographers, "How do you find your portrait subjects?" and "How do you approach a subject and ask them to pose for you?" More often than not, I walk up to a given subject and ask directly. Or, if language is an issue, I point to my camera and then to their face. But sometimes subjects approach me, or if I am working with a model, they approach the model and then ask if they can take a picture together.

Following a morning shoot at the Jama Masjid (the Red Mosque) in Old Delhi, India, my model and makeup artist, Nattakun Plaengdee, and I were approached by a group of men who were also visiting the mosque. One of the men asked if I would take a picture of him and his friends while seated "with the lovely and beautiful model." After getting Natt's consent, I did take several shots of the men but with the understanding that after shooting their group portrait with Natt, I would be afforded the opportunity to photograph individual portraits of each of the men. As evidenced by the portraits shown here, my request was granted.

◘ Nikon D850, NIKKOR 24–120mm lens, *f*/8 for 1/160 sec., ISO 200, Daylight/Sunny WB

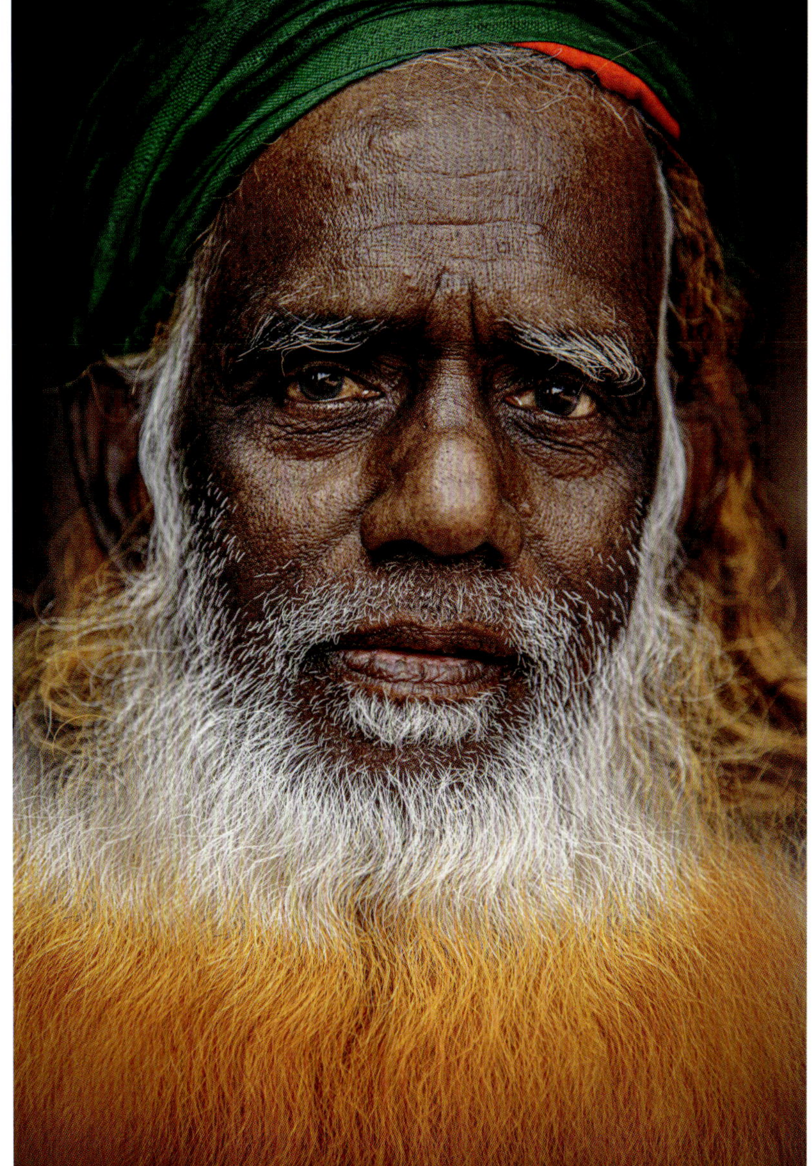

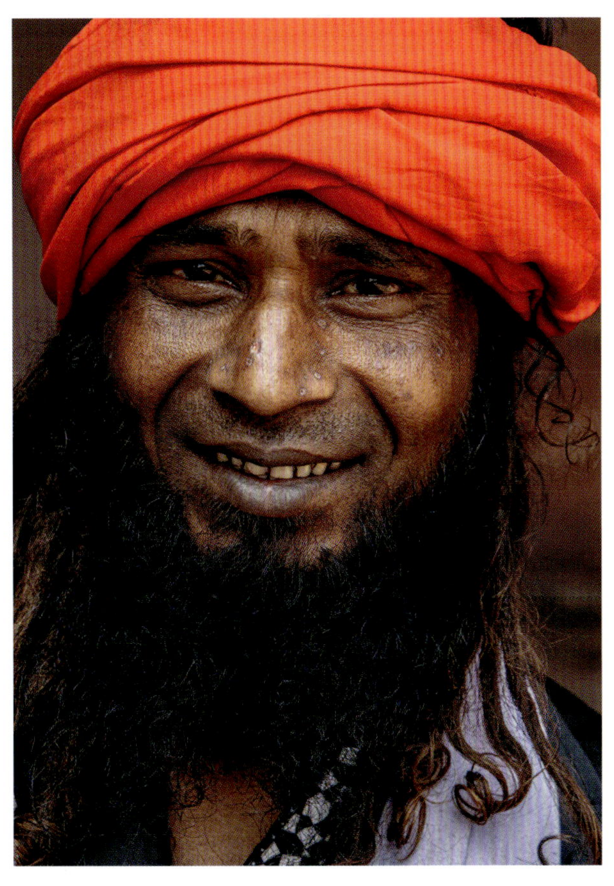

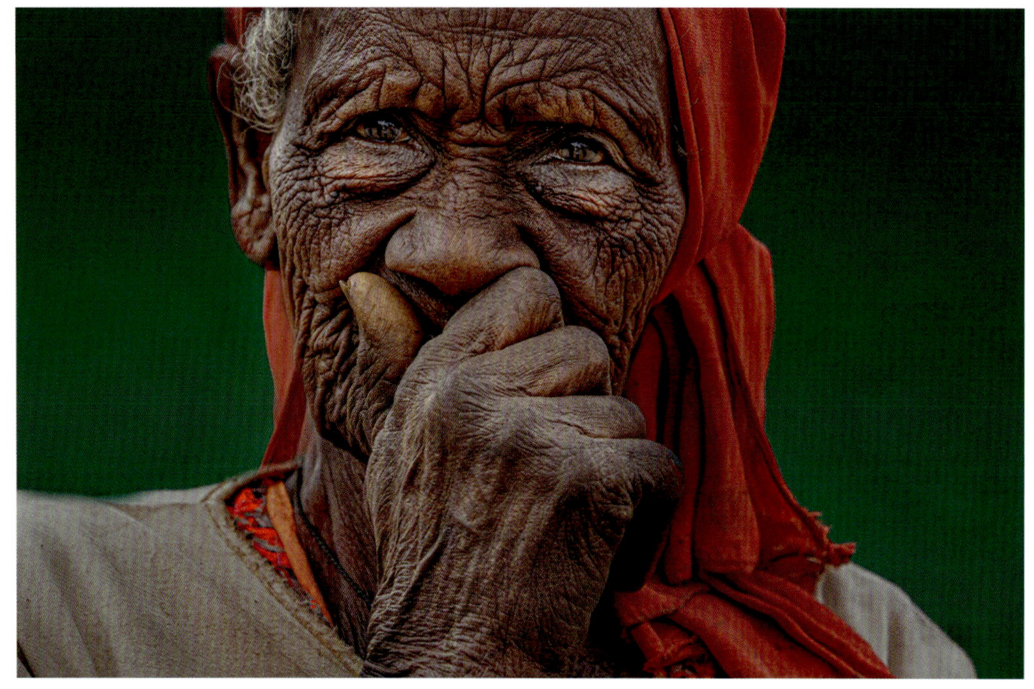

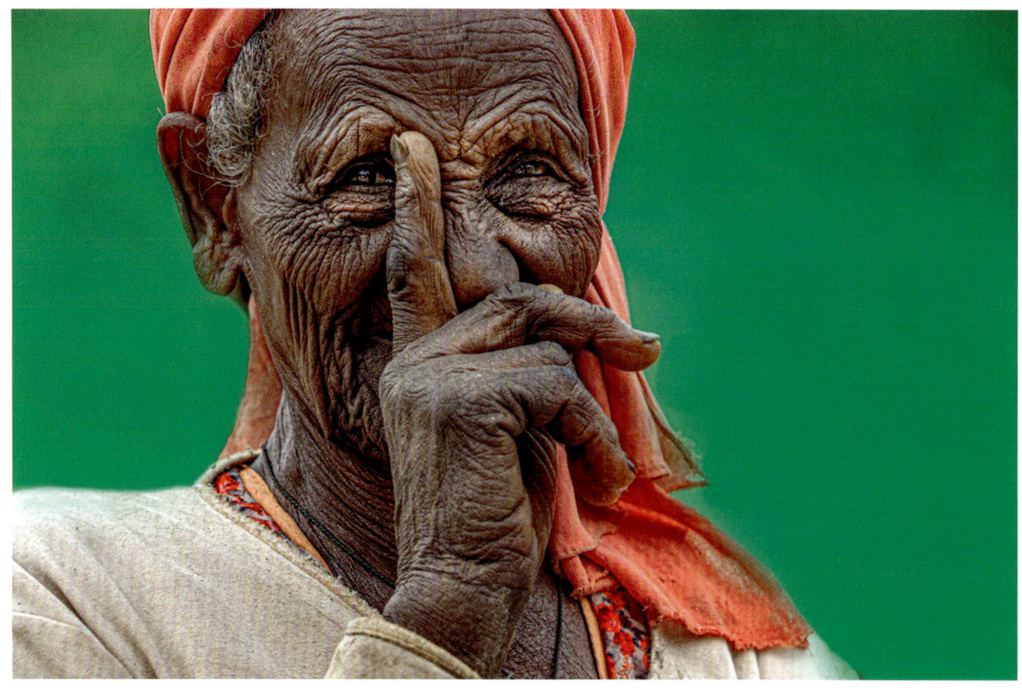

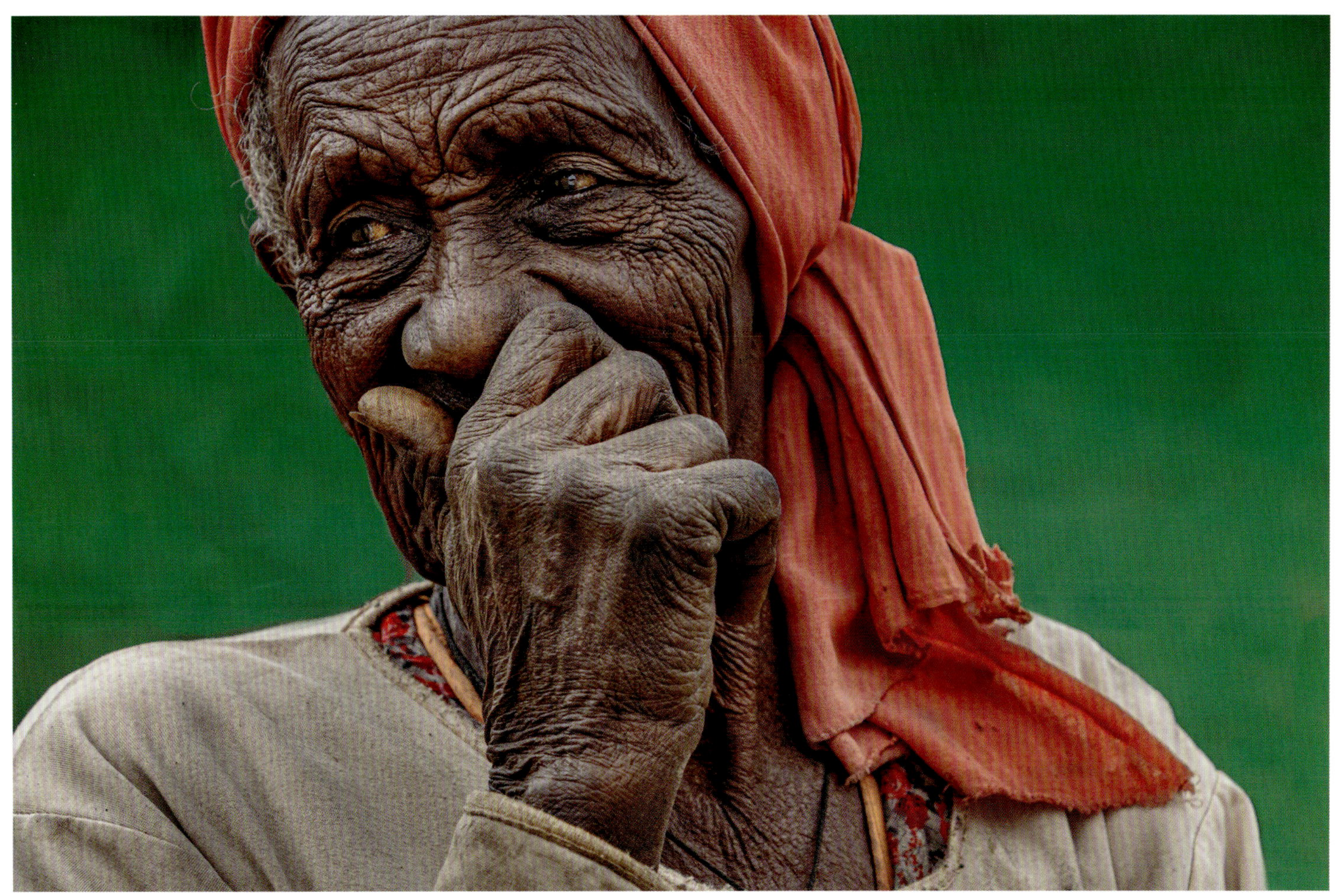

When I feel it is warranted, I do enjoy the challenge of photographing a person while simultaneously carrying on a conversation with them, as it often produces fleeting gestures that would be almost impossible to recreate in a more formal setting.

While shooting and conversing with this elderly woman in a small farming community just outside Addis Ababa, Ethiopia, I asked, "What one piece of advice would you offer anyone who wanted to live a full life?" I ask this of almost everyone I photograph, regardless of age, and her quick, emphatic reply left no doubt that she was committed to this one piece of advice, which resonated with me as well. With the aid of my interpreter, she said, "Whatever you do with your life, if it doesn't make you nervous, if it doesn't make you afraid or anxious, then it's *not* worth doing!"

For more than forty years, almost without fail, I have awakened each day to a nervous excitement, anxious to make new discoveries with my camera, often afraid that on this particular day my vision will fail me, I will miss the ultimate shot, or a desired subject will say an emphatic no to my request to photograph them or their pet. This anxiety fuels my passion, my vision, and my love of image-making. I am a self-employed miner on a constant search for the mother lode, and I still dream daily of one day finding it. It's my wish that all of you also leave your house feeling nervous, anxious, and afraid as you embark on your next photographic outing.

◘ Nikon D850, NIKKOR 24–120mm lens, *f*/8 for 1/320 sec., ISO 400, Daylight/Sunny WB

Although it happens rarely, I have had people, both young and old, approach me on streets around the world and simply ask if I would take their picture. And just to be clear, I am not referring to a couple on the beaches of Maui extending their arm, ready to hand over their iPhone so I can take their photo, but rather people who genuinely seem to feel that they could be just the subject I am looking for, as odd as that might sound. One such instance took place in Kibish, an incredibly small and remote village in Ethiopia near its southern border with Sudan. Every day a fierce gold trade begins in Kibish before dawn, the miners lining up outside a large corrugated structure, anxious to enter and sell yesterday's haul to the buyers, while the waiting buyers seem ever-anxious to learn if today will be the day when some lucky dreamer will enter their structure with something larger than the usual tiny flecks of gold that weigh no more than two-tenths of an ounce.

On this particular late afternoon, I had just finished photographing a group of young men playing pool, and as I walked out into the open courtyard I felt a soft but hurried tap-tap on my left shoulder. I was quick to turn around, thinking that perhaps I had left a piece of photo equipment behind in the pool room, only to see a young girl of fourteen from the nearby Surma tribe, her hair partially covered in a wreath of flowers, a not uncommon look created for foreigners with cameras—a photo opportunity offered in exchange for something of value.

"Photo!" she said. Several minutes later, I walked with her to a nearby hotel wall with fading red paint, knowing this would make for a clean background. With the help of my interpreter, I asked her to stand near the wall and give me some attitude—and attitude I got!

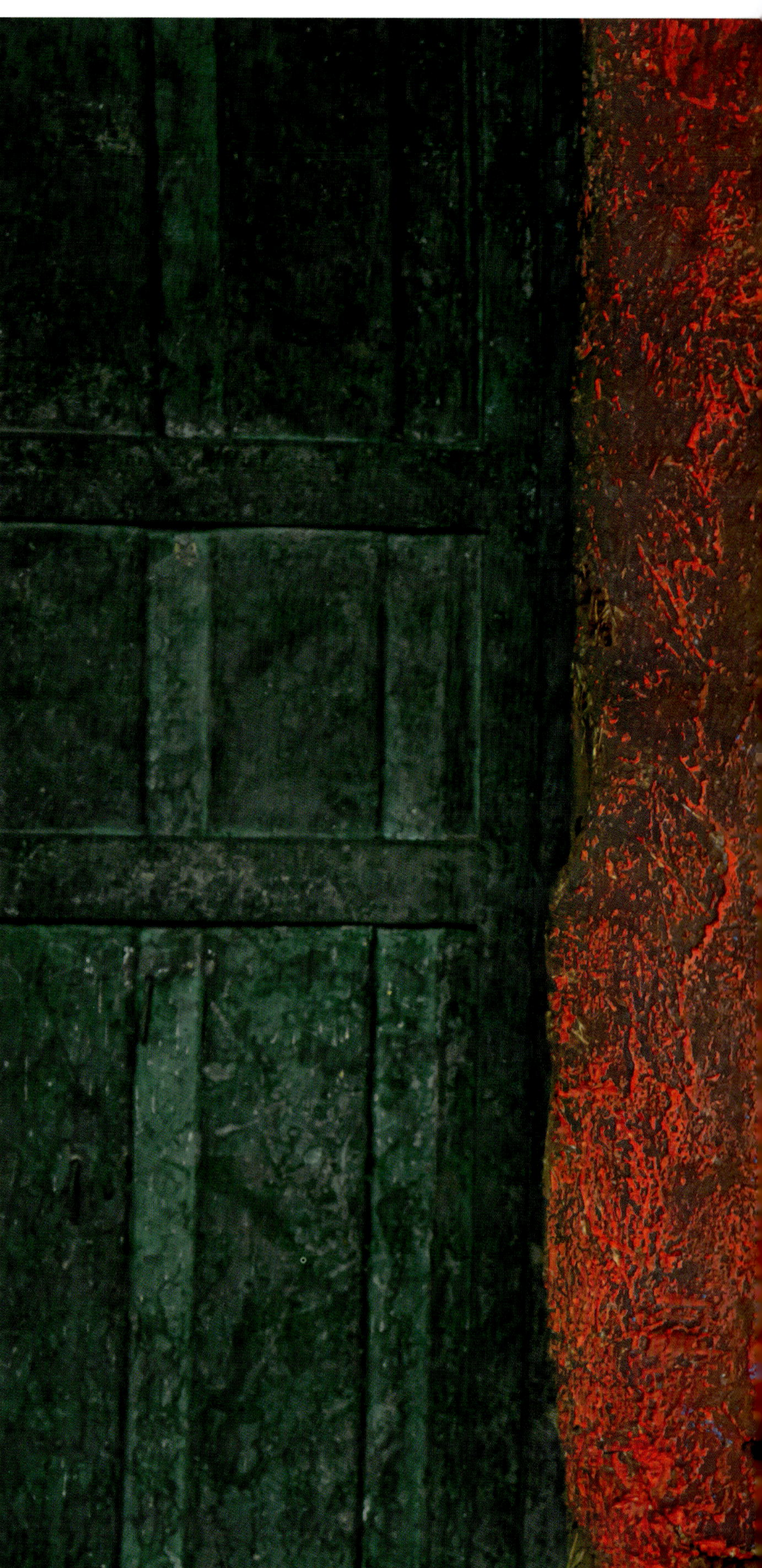

◘ Nikon D850, NIKKOR 24–120mm lens, *f*/8 for 1/200 sec., ISO 400, Daylight/Sunny WB

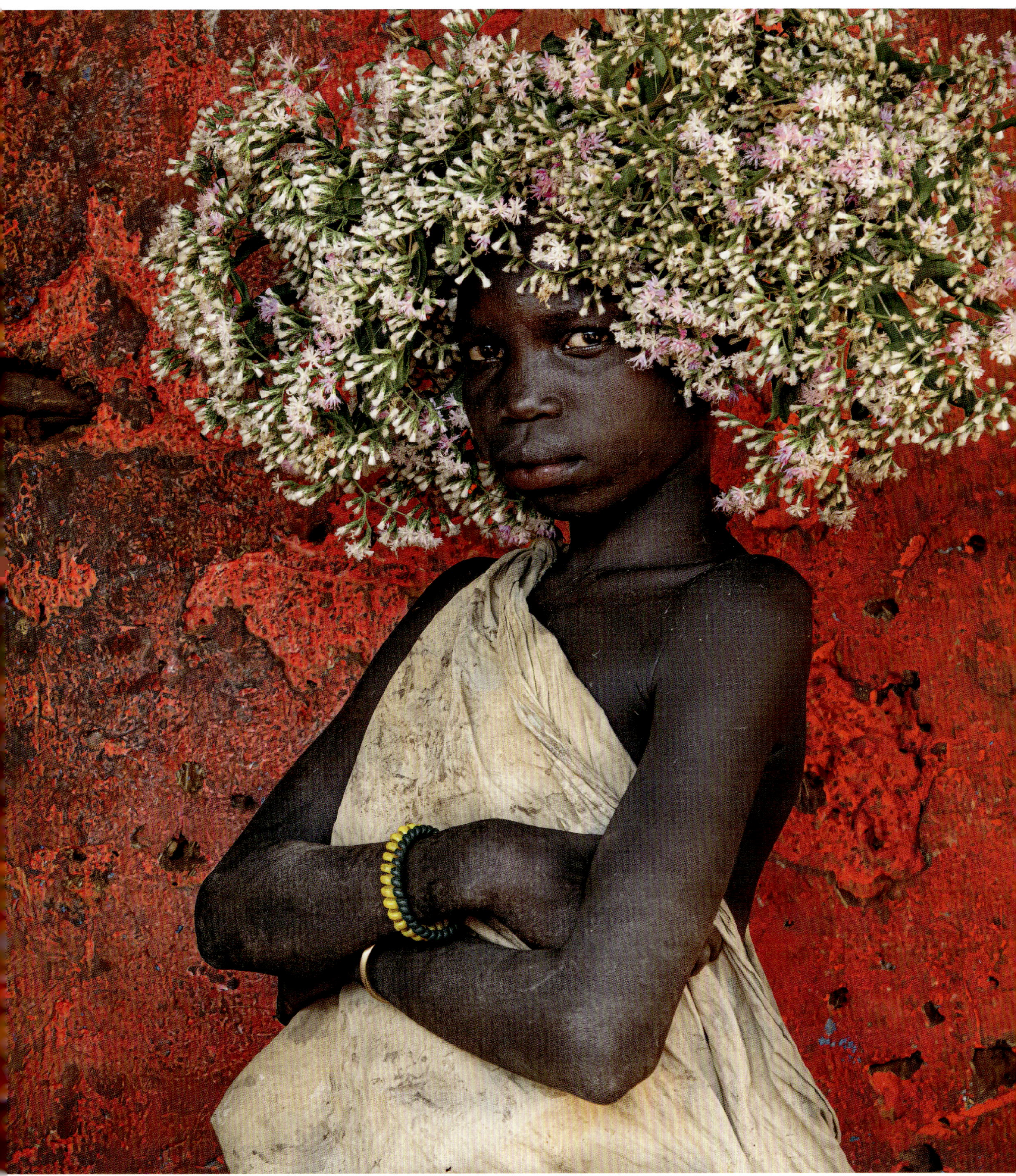

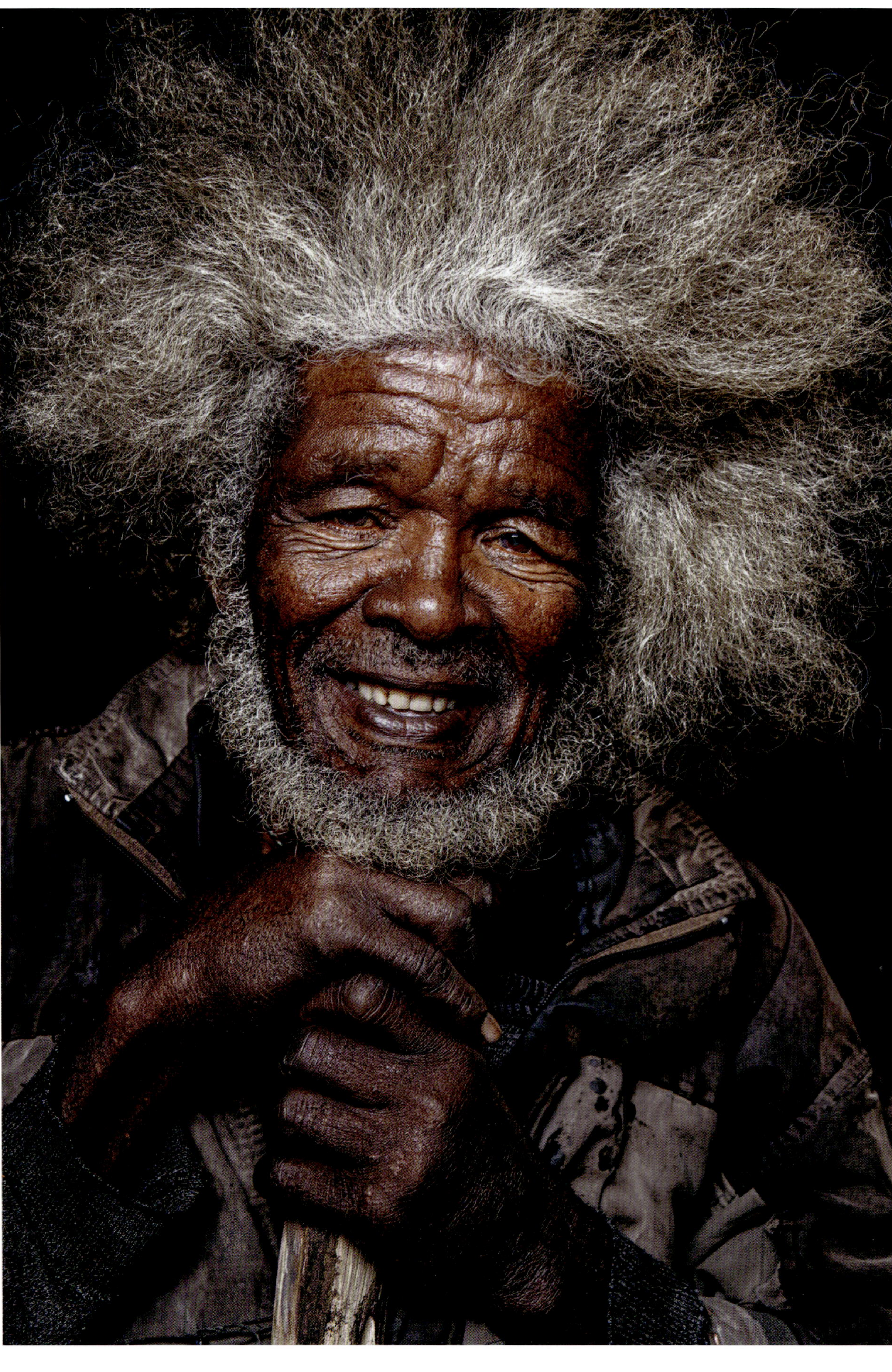

Several days after arriving in Addis Abba, Ethiopia, and after an eighteen-hour car ride, I arrived at Chebera-Churchura National Park, which was but a forty-five-minute walk from the Konta tribe. Once I had my tent set up, I walked to the Konta village, where I was lucky enough to meet the tribe's most famous man, a 107-year-old who just two weeks before had had his picture taken with the prime minister of Ethiopia. In his younger years, this man had served in the Italian army; then he worked as a tailor for forty-two years and a woodworker for the next twenty-two years. Since the age of eighty-four, he has been a farmer, living off the land. He has outlived four wives but "lives joyfully" with a number of his children, grandchildren, and great-grandchildren. It wasn't long until I asked the obvious: "What advice can you offer that just might allow others to experience a long life?"

Without hesitation, as if it were his daily mantra, he said, "Let go of envy. It is poison! A life without envy means better sleep. A life without envy means you can taste your food. A life without envy means you will live in the present. But most of all, a life without envy means you can accept love from others and give love just as freely. In other words, without envy, you will experience freedom of the mind, body, and spirit, and you can now enjoy life's daily wonders!"

I photographed him in an empty shed, a rare concrete structure that I used as a makeshift studio, covering the back wall with black cloth. His face was pointed toward the one rather high open window, the soft northern light illuminating his incredibly kind, young face that was unlined by any trace of envy.

◘ Nikon D850, NIKKOR 24–120mm lens, *f*/11 for 1/100 sec., ISO 400, Daylight/Sunny WB

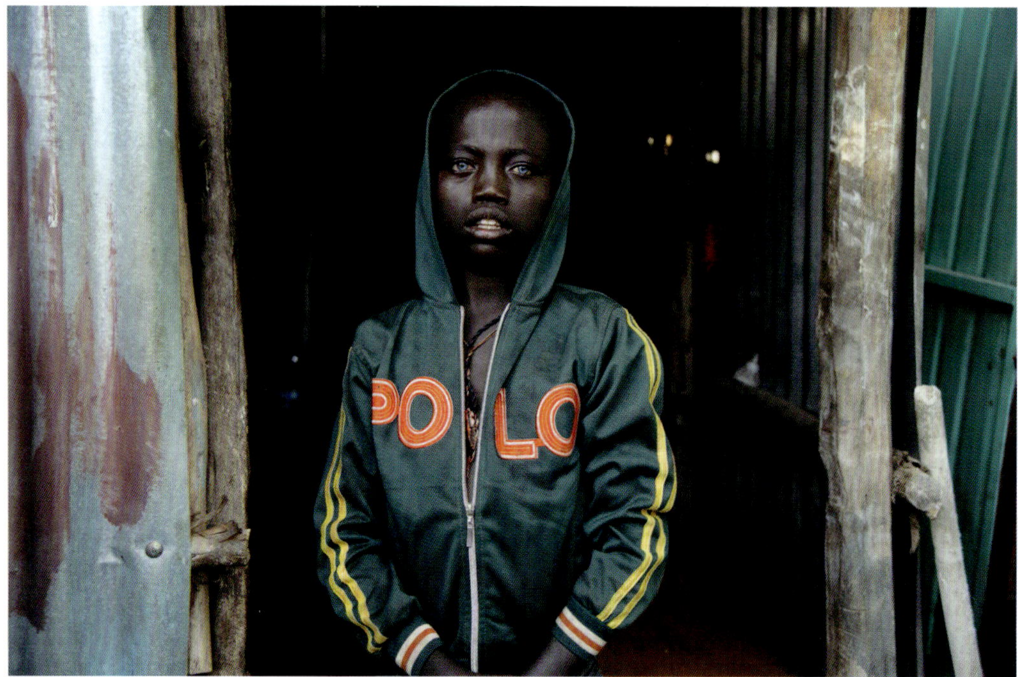

Abushe, a twelve-year-old who lives in Jinka, Ethiopia, has 20/20 vision but was born with a genetic mutation called Waardenburg syndrome, which can affect the pigmentation of hair, skin, and eyes; it occurs in an average of one in every forty thousand births. Abushe's father is dead and his mother works far from Jinka, and for many years he lived on the streets.

Over the past several years, Abushe and his vivid cyan eyes have been "discovered" by camera-toting tourists who find themselves in Jinka on their way to visit the Mursi tribe (known internationally for the "lip plate" ornaments worn by many Mursi women), as well as by several noted professionals, including Eric Lafforgue. One day, Abushe approached my students and me about a block from our hotel, on the main street that runs through the small town. Within minutes I found a storage shed under open shade and asked Abushe to pose in the narrow doorway, knowing that if I exposed for the natural light on his face, it would render the darker background interior of the shed as a black background.

When we said goodbye, we filled Abushe's pockets with birr notes (totaling about US$20), about a week's salary in local terms. I happened to see Abushe again the following year; he now is living with a relative in a nearby house and attending school, though as soon as each school week ends he is out on the streets of Jinka, ready to model all weekend long! I am confident he will realize many of the dreams he shared with us, including a desire to go to college and become a physician.

◘ **Nikon D850, NIKKOR 24–120mm lens, *f*/8 for 1/200 sec., ISO 400, Daylight/Sunny WB**

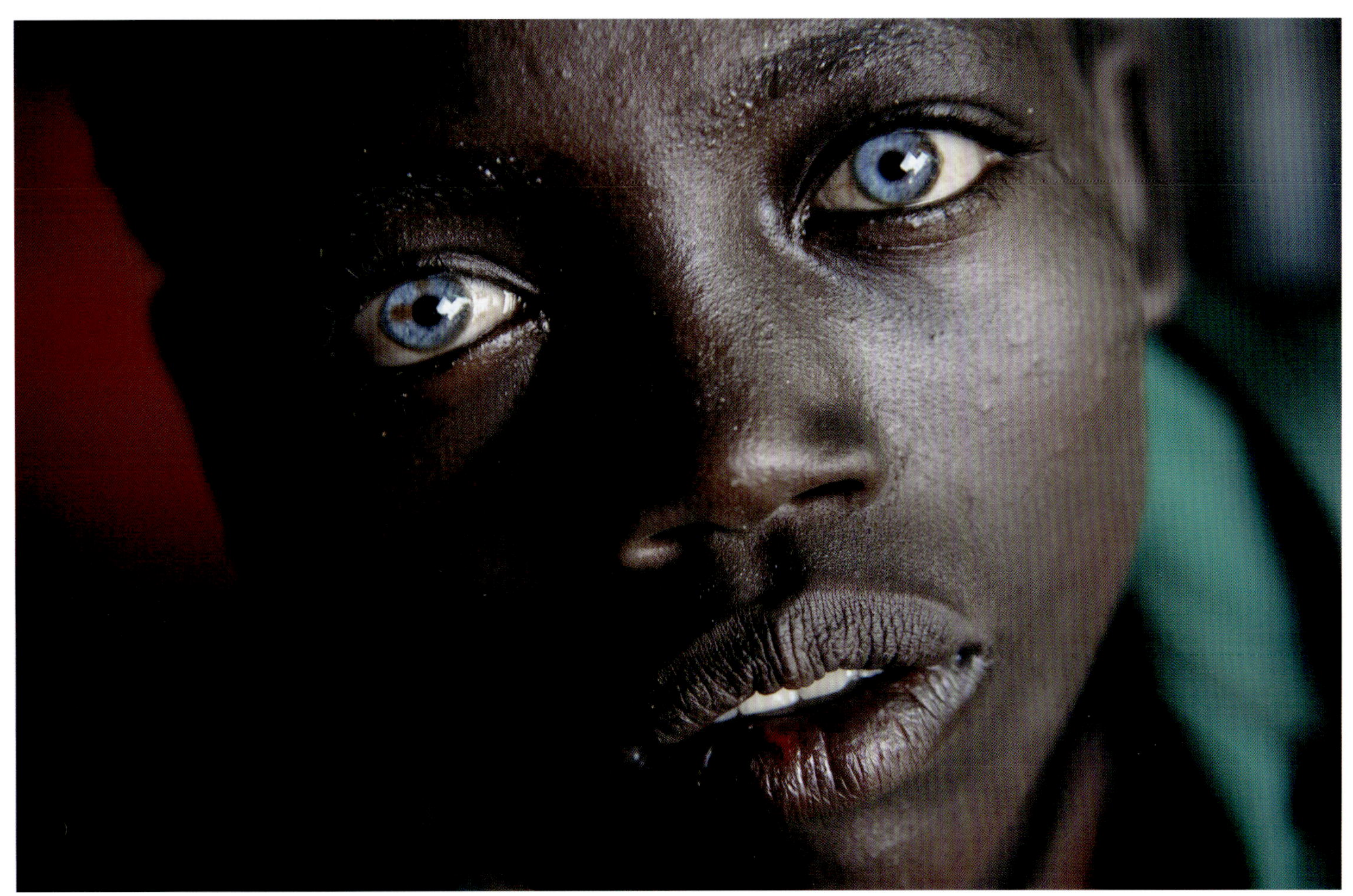

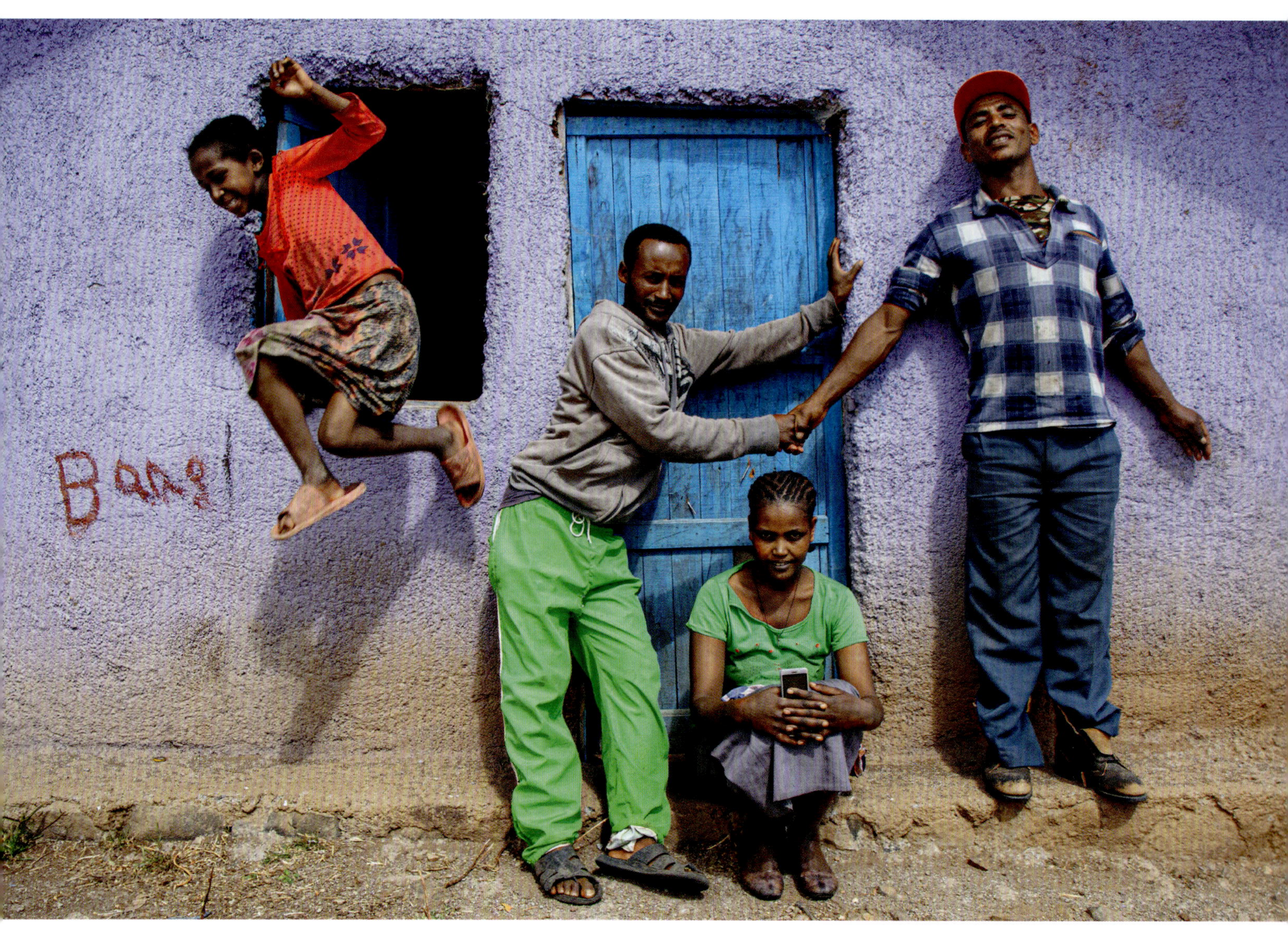

Several minutes prior to shooting this frame of a married couple and the husband's brother, the couple's daughter (the jumper) scrambled through the window into their lavender farmhouse to hide from my camera, fearful of seeing the ghost of herself. As I began shooting various compositions of her mom, dad, and uncle, she became so frightened of the sound of my camera's motor drive, convinced it could somehow still penetrate the wall to capture her ghost, that she bolted out the window, making this a far more interesting narrative! Yet she also expressed a nervous laugh, thus explaining the "smile." It felt to me that she was not that scared as much as she was simply shy. It was her mother who explained her behavior after I was done shooting that it was possibly attributable to her daughter's fear of having her soul "stolen" by the camera.

Fortunately, I had set my exposure for a "Who cares?" *f*/11 composition, with everything at the same focused distance and depth of field not an issue. This combined with my ISO of 320 to produce a shutter speed of 1/400 sec., fast enough to freeze the surprised young girl as she leaped out of the window.

◘ Nikon D500, NIKKOR 18–300mm lens, *f*/11 for 1/400 sec., ISO 320, Daylight/Sunny WB

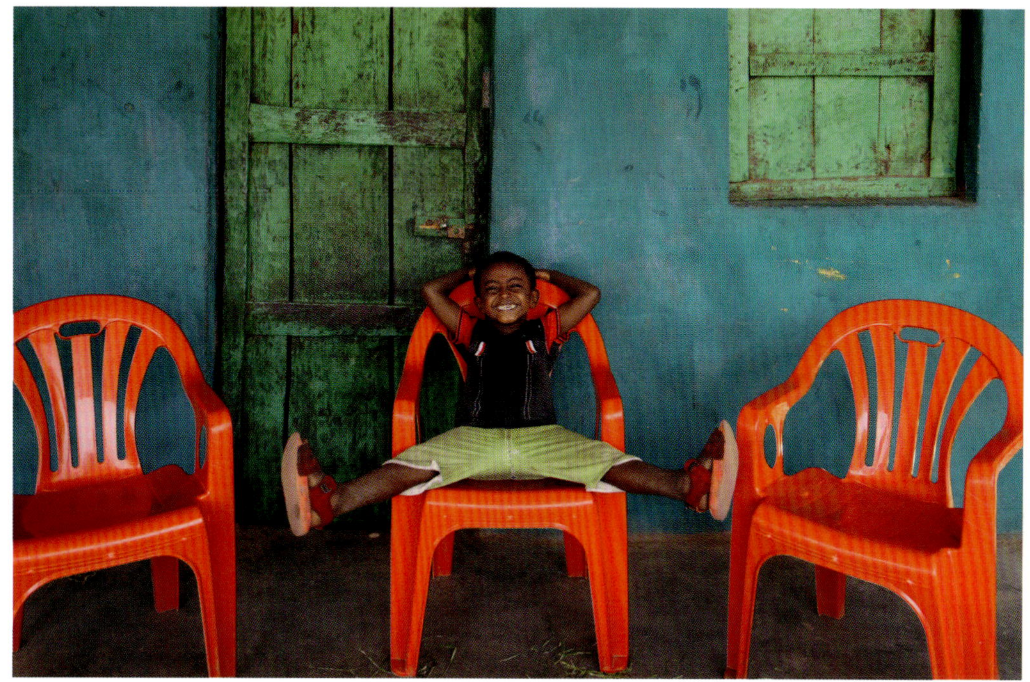

If not for the demands of hunger, I might never have known about Woito, Ethiopia, one of the smallest towns I have ever had the pleasure of visiting in all of Africa. This first visit to Woito was solely to stop and eat at the rest station, one frequented by truck drivers transporting fuel and cotton. Sometimes I saw these trucks lying on their sides along the northern route toward Konso, having failed to navigate the steep downhill turns.

My belly full of Ethiopia's most popular dish, injera, a crepe-like pancake that you fold to scoop up mashed red beans and hot chiles, I welcomed the short walk to the nearby town. It didn't take long for me to once again felt like the Pied Piper, a group of kids crowded at my sides and behind me, some curious, others recognizing the camera and clamoring to have their picture taken. It is normal for me to compensate many of my photographic subjects in my world travels, especially in the more impoverished areas. Compensation is sometimes money—20 to 50 cents, a dollar tops—but whenever possible, I prefer to give away pens, pencils, lollipops, even bars of soap—items that many people seem to prefer over 20 cents.

As I learned on that first trip to Woito and which was borne out in all of my successive trips (eleven and counting), the town always offers willing subjects. On this afternoon, something unexpected happened. Just after I had finished arranging three bright orange chairs outside a local coffeeshop for myself and two companions, a young boy ran over and jumped on one of the chairs. Mere seconds later, his mother, the owner of the coffee shop, grabbed him by the arm, pulled him off the chair, and scolded him as she sent him on his way—but not before I managed to grab my camera and capture this fleeting moment of a young boy's absolute delight in seeing three strangers from another world—just like my delight in seeing him! Several minutes later I shared the image with his mother to make certain she was okay with it, and in fact she was more than okay with it, as it brought a big smile to her face. About six weeks later, I returned to this same town and presented her with a print of the photo, which she proceeded to hang up in her café.

◘ Nikon D850, NIKKOR 24–120mm lens, *f*/8 for 1/320 sec., ISO 640, Daylight/Sunny WB

Sunrise was still ten minutes away, but there I was, in a dark, narrow back street several blocks from the Jama Masjid (Red Mosque) in Delhi, India, when I heard the faint sound of water streaming from a faucet into a kettle (or was it a teapot?). The sound was coming from behind colorful exterior walls and a large hanging tapestry. I also could hear groaning and a shuffling of feet—the sound of someone struggling to fit into a pair of shoes. Just seconds later, a head popped out from behind the tapestry, followed by a fully clothed yet disheveled elderly man who, understandably, looked very surprised to see a stranger standing just outside the entrance to his home. Within minutes we managed to speak just enough English (actually, mainly gestures) to convey my request to take his portrait, but just that initial fleeting portrait still resonated in my mind, of his head popping out of the busy tapestry like the cork of a champagne bottle. This was a classic composition that found me calling on the "Who cares?" aperture of *f*/8. In the low light, an ISO of 5000 was necessary to shoot at a fast enough hand-holdable shutter speed.

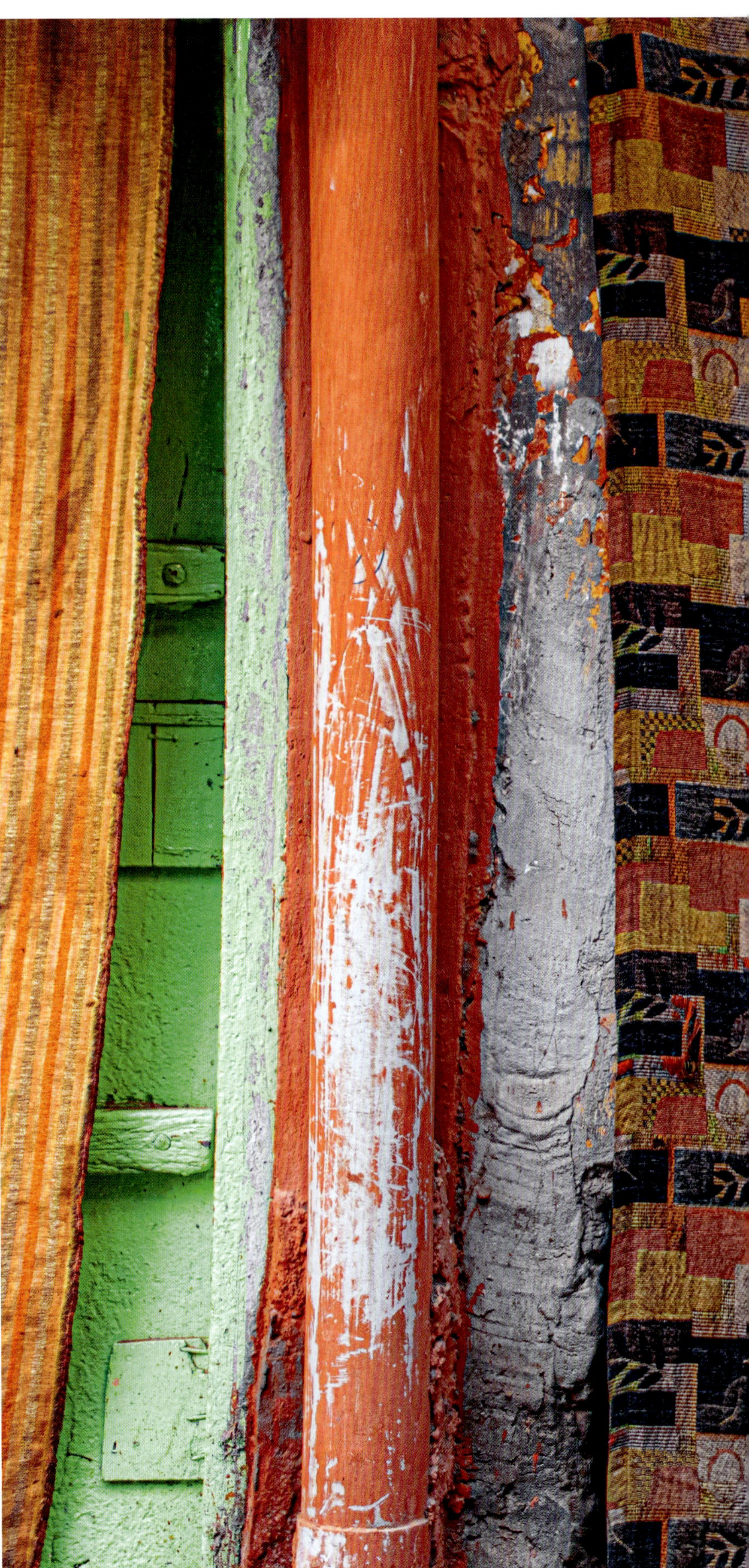

◘ Nikon D850, NIKKOR 24–120mm lens, *f*/8 for 1/100 sec., ISO 5000, Daylight/Sunny WB

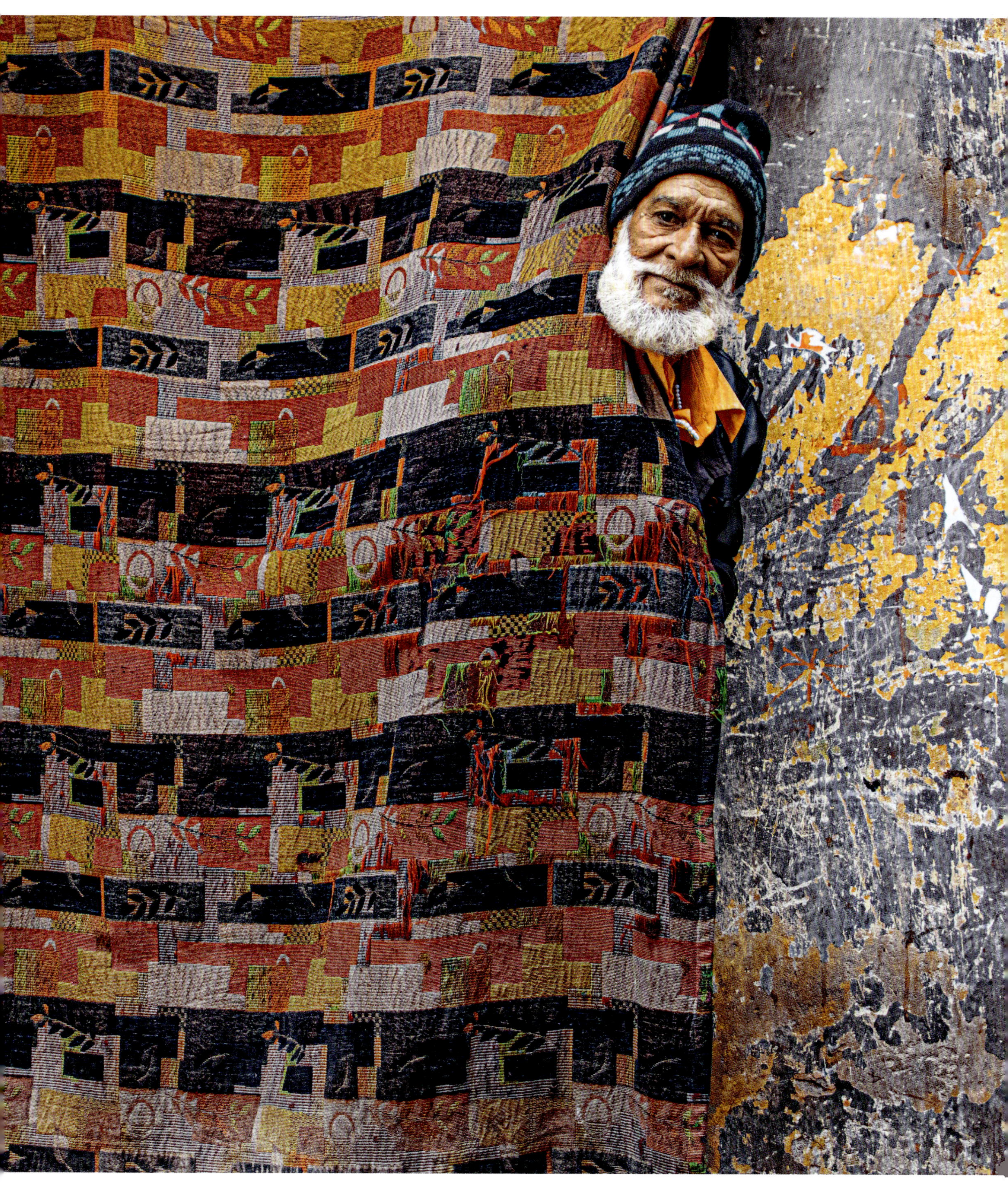

Candid

Unlike posed portraits, *candids* are usually pictures of people who were unaware that their picture was being taken, or—and this is where the debate gets really interesting—pictures in which the subjects *appear* to be unaware that their picture was being taken. In "true" candids, the subjects are not directed or told what expression to convey; they are just being themselves at that moment in time. At no time is the presence of the photographer actually felt.

Am I fan of shooting candids? It is *not* my favorite approach, but it is sometimes the only way I can get the shot, such as of a bicyclist I pan as he flies by me through Times Square, or a person or group of people engaged in an activity that I can't interrupt. More often than not, I am far more comfortable introducing myself and engaging with the subject, thus gaining their trust and usually giving me more time to get the hoped-for shot.

Recently I was discussing favorite images with a writer from India, and he was surprised to learn that one of my favorites was, in his words, "an image without color." I was quick to point out that technically this is an image of *all* colors, since white is the result of all color wavelengths reflecting off of a given subject.

It was a Sunday morning during the Epiphany celebration in Addis Ababa, Ethiopia. Thousands of worshipers were spread out on a soccer field with their backs to me, giving their undivided attention to the priests giving sermons, one at a time, on the distant stage. Within seconds, I felt a growing desperation to see one of the ladies turn around, preferably looking in my direction, which I knew would create an image of stark contrast. But as the minutes ticked by (about ten minutes, to be fair), all eyes remained focused on that distant stage. I could feel my desperation reaching that critical point of now or never, when I almost always choose *now*, and it was then that I shouted, "Excuse me!" I shouted this not once, not twice, but maybe five times before the woman you see here turned around for all of two seconds—and I couldn't have been more ready! After that ten-minute wait, which felt like a lifetime, it all came down to a mere 1/200 sec.!

Granted, I probably violated a number of taboos here, but I reasoned that most of the people at this Epiphany celebration were far more consumed by Epiphany than the crazy guy in the crowd, and my brief episode of shouting was forgotten two minutes later. I am not suggesting you run shouting down the aisle at the next Christmas invocation at the Vatican; I am a believer in respecting local customs and religious ceremonies and have since concluded that this was a mistake, but mistakes happen, and I am quite certain I won't make that one again.

When exposing for a frame-filling composition of white, overexpose your manual exposure by at least 1 stop (or, if in Aperture Priority mode, set your auto-exposure override to +1). All light meters think the world is neutral gray, so when your light meter is confronted with white, it suggests or sets an underexposure to record gray instead. Given that you don't *want* the white to look gray, you need to override your light meter by 1 full stop. While composing all that monochromatic color, look for contrast, such as the face turned toward me here. And don't forget to set your camera to CH shooting mode before firing away, since the glimpse is often fleeting.

◘ Nikon D500, NIKKOR 18–300mm lens at 300mm, *f*/16 for 1/200 sec., ISO 200, Daylight/Sunny WB

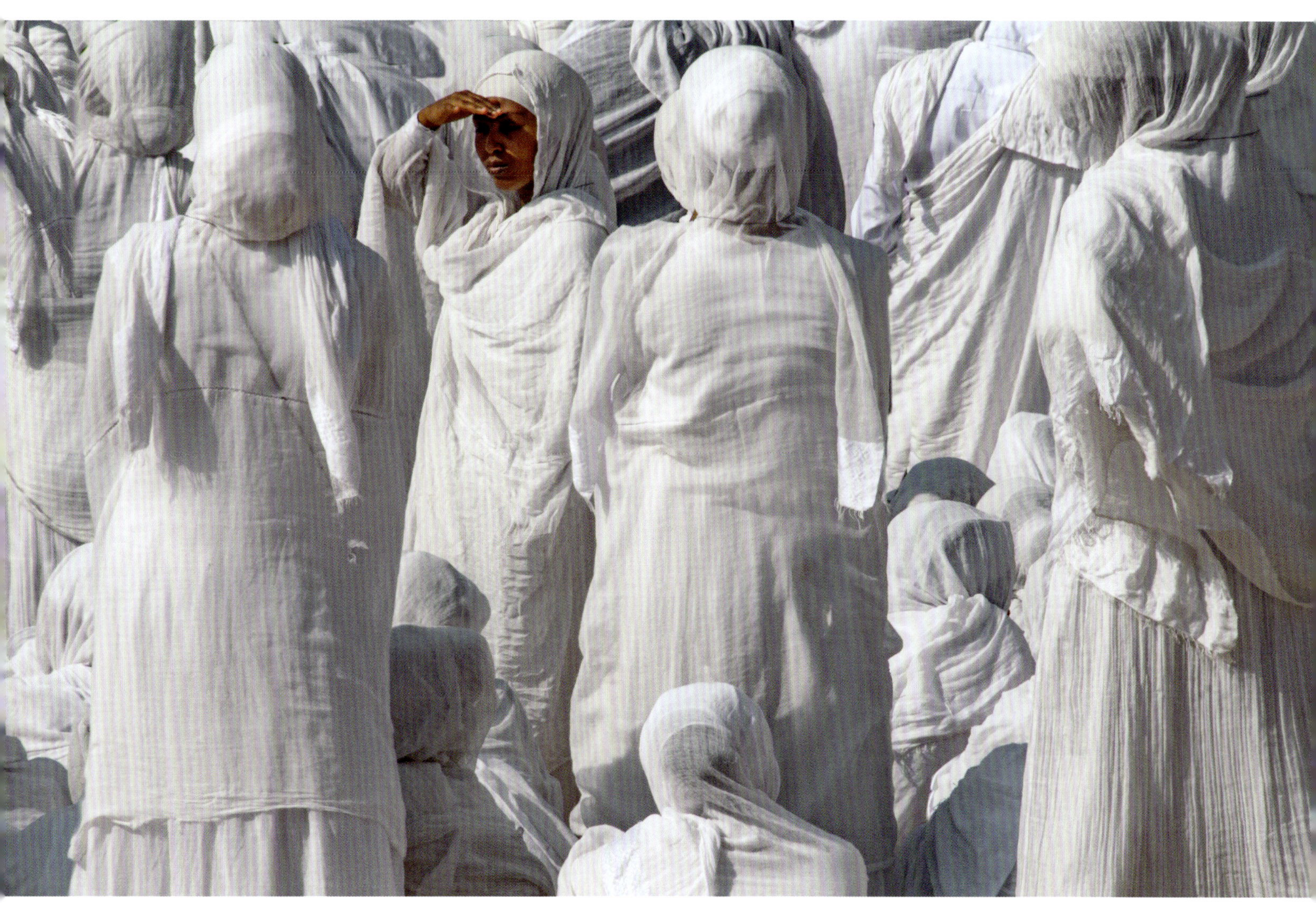

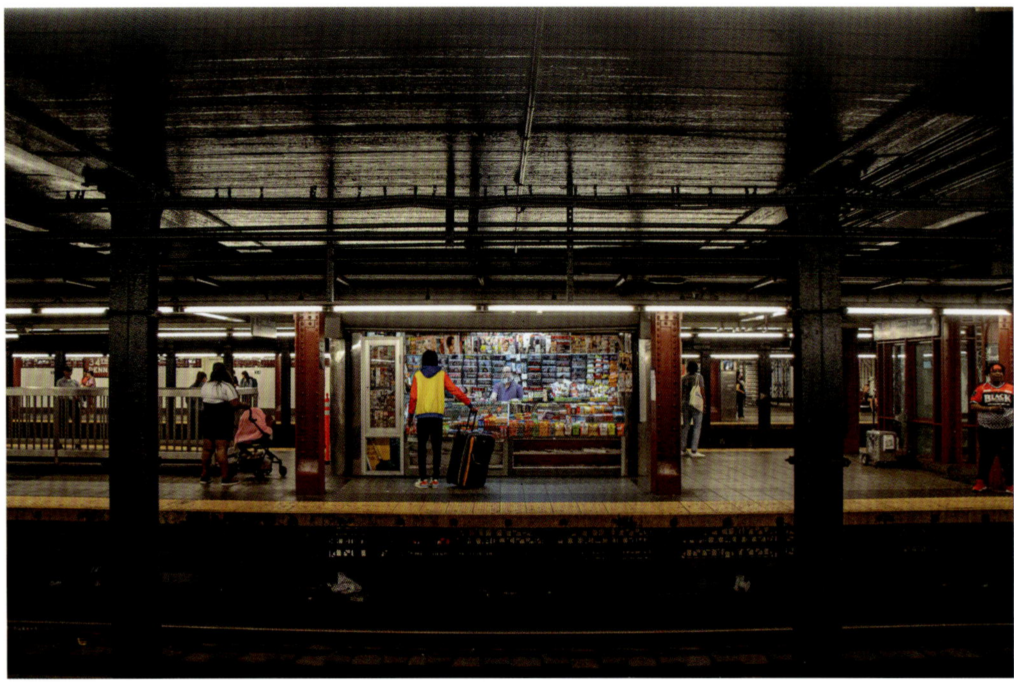

Exposing for White and Black

Your camera's built-in light meter is responsible for telling you how to set a correct exposure. It reads the light reflecting off any subject and indicates what a correct exposure will be, combining aperture, shutter speed, and ISO—at least, most of the time it does.

Your camera's light meter has been programmed to interpret *all* reflected light in the world as if it were *always* reflecting off of a neutral gray surface. That's right: it sees the world as colorless. It never sees those passionate reds, cheerful yellows, or stable blues, not to mention black or white.

Needless to say, we don't share the same vision as our camera's light meter; we live in a very colorful world. And the reflected light in our world is not a level playing field, because not all light is reflected equally. For example, the light reflected off of snow or a bride's white gown is, at a minimum, twice as bright as gray. But when your light meter is presented with a composition that is largely white, it does what it *only* knows how to do: turn all of that white into tones of gray. What the light meter is actually doing, without any intervention from you, is creating an image that is underexposed: dark white, if you will, or gray.

On the other end of the spectrum, the light reflected off of a black car or black dog is, at a minimum, twice as dark as gray. When your light meter is presented with a composition of largely black, it again does the only thing it knows how to do: turn all of that black into tones of gray. This time the light meter creates an image that is *over*exposed, making it "light black," or, yes, gray. The built-in light meters of all cameras today are based upon this simple law.

But here is where you come in! When shooting white subjects, be sure to *over*expose by at least 1 stop, allowing the shutter to stay open at least 1 stop longer (or setting the aperture 1 stop larger). When shooting black or very dark subjects, *under*expose by at least 1 stop, making the shutter speed 1 stop faster (or setting the aperture 1 stop smaller). That's right: although it sounds counterintuitive, you should overexpose when shooting white subjects to avoid underexposed gray, dark-white whites. And you should underexpose when shooting black or very dark subjects to avoid overexposed gray, light-black blacks.

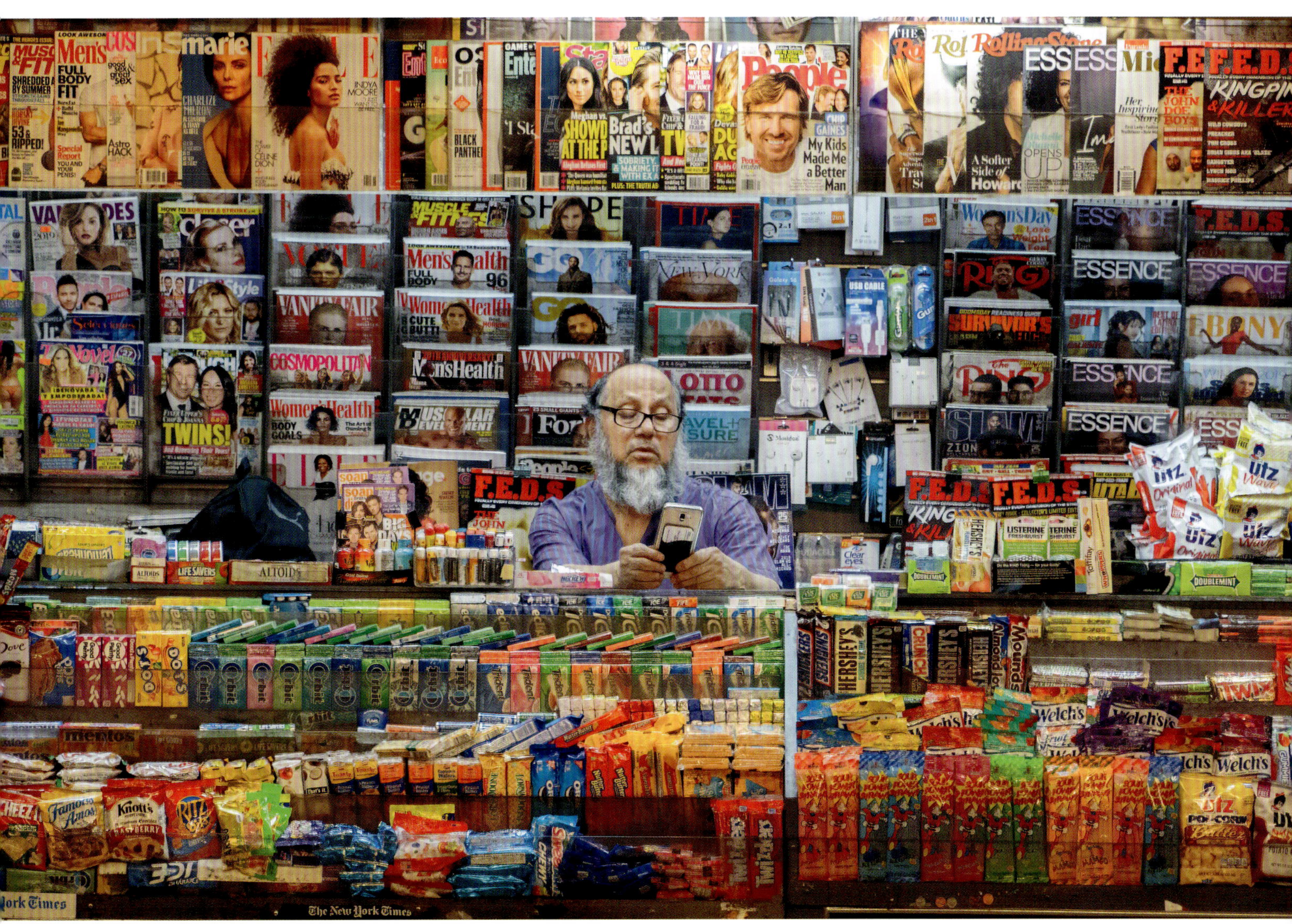

As I came up the stairway at the 34th Street subway station in Midtown Manhattan, my eyes were immediately captured by the newsstand directly across the tracks. What was instantly intriguing was the "wall of information," a testament to the information age, in which questions find answers and answers lead to more questions. And there amid that wall of information sat the magazine seller, who appears to be thinking, *Who needs magazines when all the news I need is right here on my phone?*

◘ **Nikon D500, NIKKOR 18–300 lens, *f*/11 for 1/125 sec., ISO 3200, Daylight/Sunny WB (shifted toward a Tungsten WB in post-processing)**

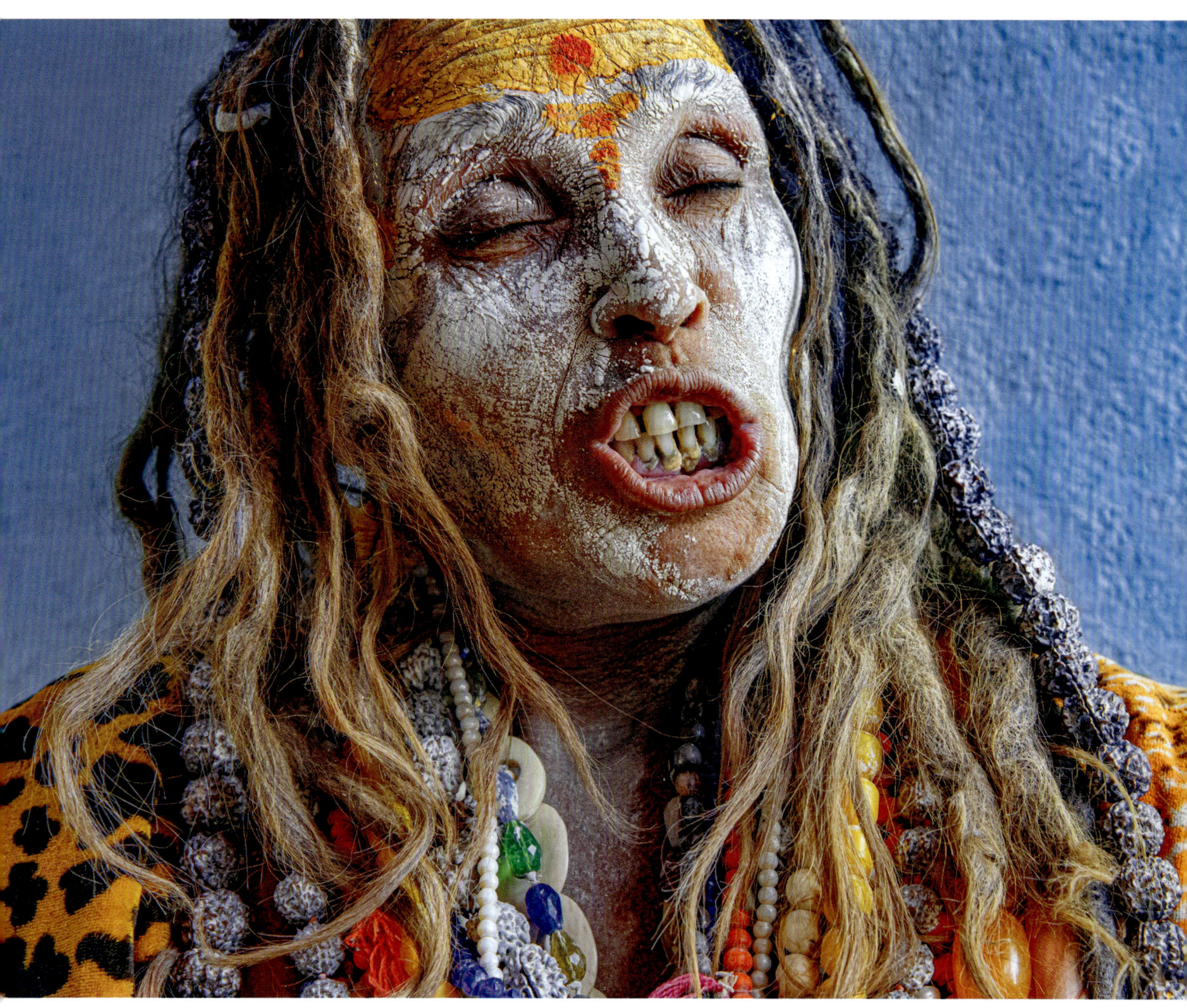

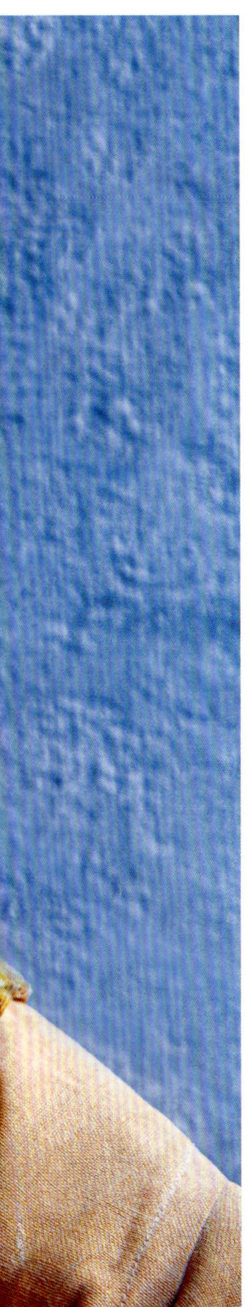

In Varanasi, India, a group of sadhus, or holy people, sat on carpets laid atop a small concrete terrace on the banks of the Ganges River. The thick smell of ganja hung in the air, and as I scanned the small group, all but one returned my smile. The one who did not, could not, as she seemed to have succumbed to a hypnotic trance, eyes closed, seemingly oblivious to my presence. She began to shake her shoulders, arms, and hands, and then moan, followed by "ish," more moans, more "ish," and so on. Her colorful jewelry, ashen face, and a smattering of yellow across her forehead created a picturesque composition against a quietly soothing wall of cyan blue. Wasting little time, I walked closer to her and zoomed in with my lens to fill the frame with her "ish." Since everything was at the same focused distance, it was a classic "Who cares?" exposure.

I sometimes struggle over the question of whether to photograph someone who is clearly not consciously present, and often I decide, *Nope! Not now, maybe later.* But in this case, there was another sadhu nearby playing a flute, and her trance seemed an understandable response to the music. About forty-five minutes later I returned to the same spot and, seeing that she was more present, I shared the result with her. She and her friends broke out into laughter, expressing pleasure at the photo.

◘ Nikon D850, NIKKOR 24–120mm lens, *f*/11 for 1/160 sec., ISO 400, Daylight/Sunny WB

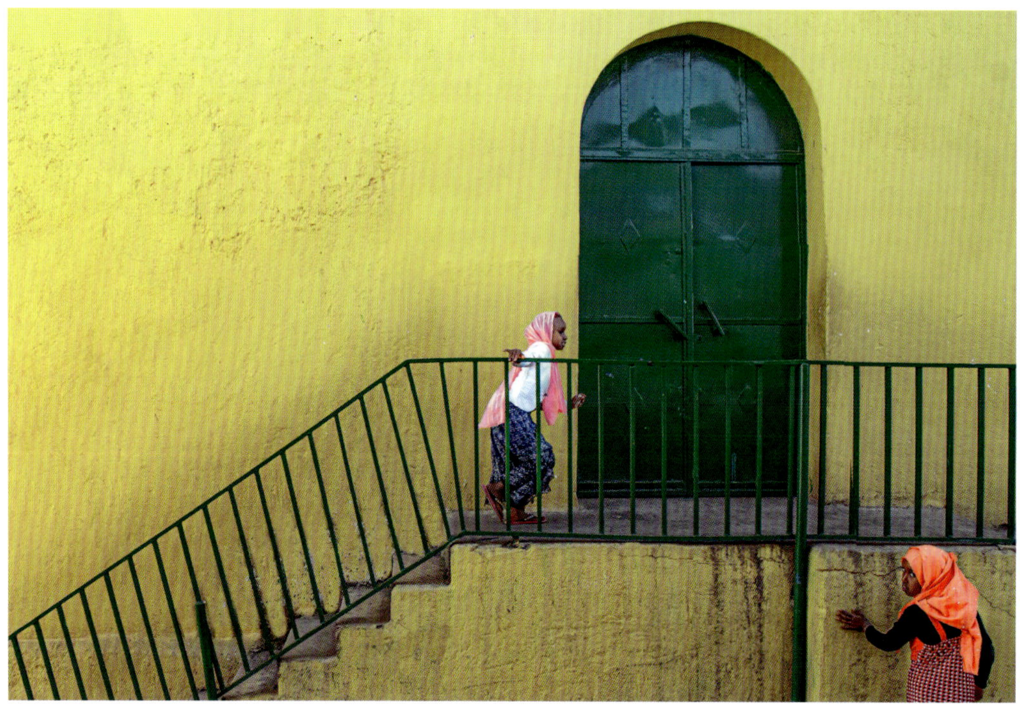

Years of shooting have left me absolutely convinced that any given day dedicated to simply being out and about with your camera will reward you with at least one unexpected and welcome image. Serendipitous moments are ours for the taking, and yet as elementary as it may sound, these moments of serendipity will always elude us if we are not in a position of anticipation, out on the streets with our camera at the ready instead of sitting at home watching another Netflix documentary.

On one Saturday in Harar, Ethiopia, I came upon this yellow school with a green entrance door. Knowing just how colorfully the women and young girls dress in Harar, I could only imagine the kind of photo possibilities that might enter or exit through that green door. But it being a Saturday, there was no school, and I had to fly back to Addis Ababa the next morning. Wait—what was that noise? Several young girls were coming down the narrow lane to my left. One of them stopped at the base of the yellow wall while the other ran up the steps. I begin firing as, without breaking stride, the girl in pink continued down the stairs to the right, and just like that, she was gone. It was only later when I was looking at the images in Camera Raw that I saw the other girl at the base of that yellow wall, and what a pleasant surprise that she was looking at me!

◘ **Nikon D850, NIKKOR 24–120mm lens, *f*/11 for 1/500 sec., ISO 400, Daylight/Sunny WB**

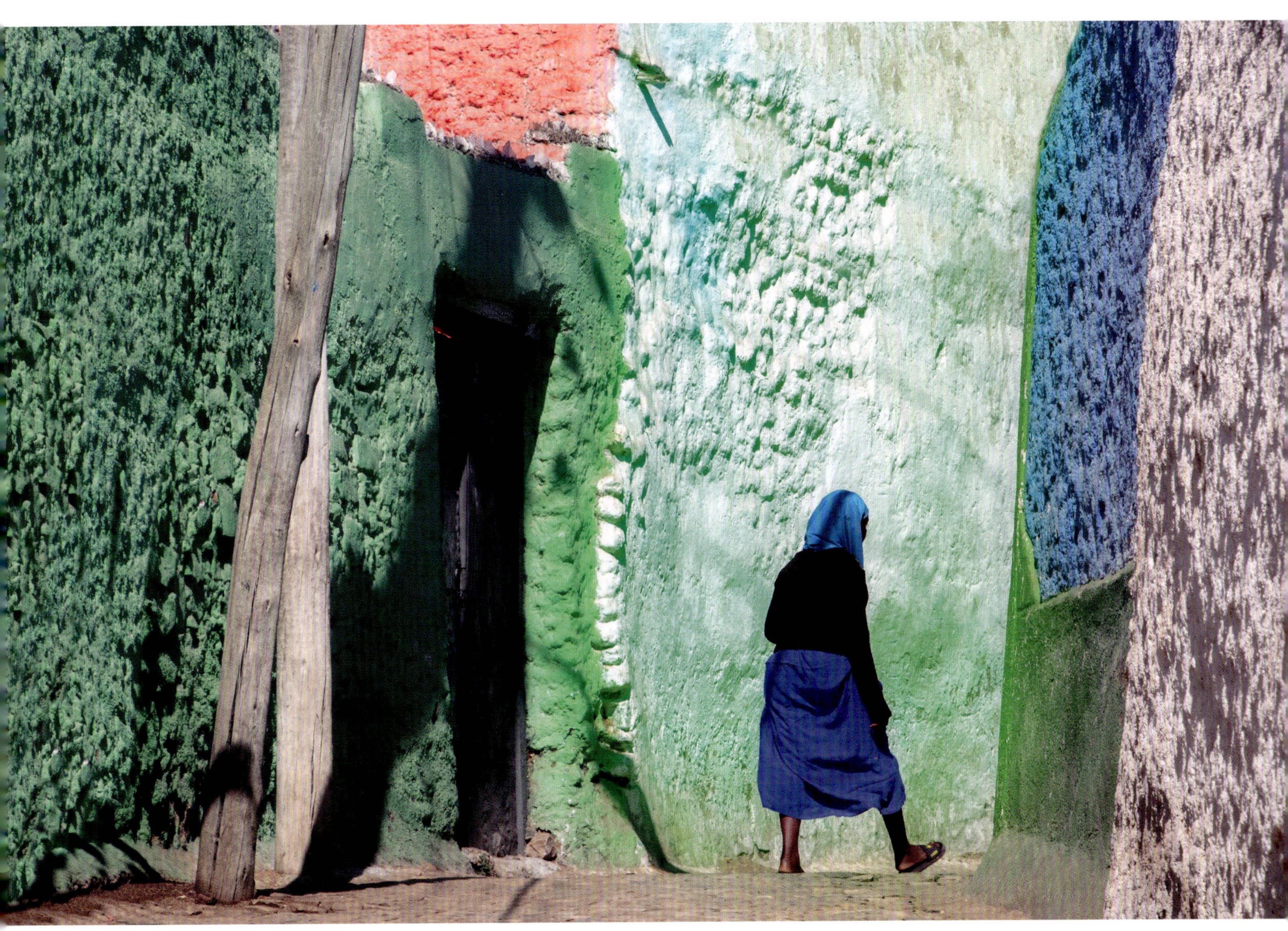

One afternoon in the incredibly colorful old city of Harar, Ethiopia, a small dog bolted out from behind a fifty-five-gallon drum. The dog was not coming at me but rather bolting after a cat, and as I turned around to witness the chase, I noticed this older woman, only three steps away from disappearing from view. I zoomed out to 300mm and, with my camera in Aperture Priority mode, quickly fired off several shots. Color, shape, texture: this is my kind of composition. Thank goodness for cats and dogs!

◘ Nikon D500, NIKKOR 18–300mm lens, *f*/11 for 1/250 sec., ISO 100, Daylight/Sunny WB

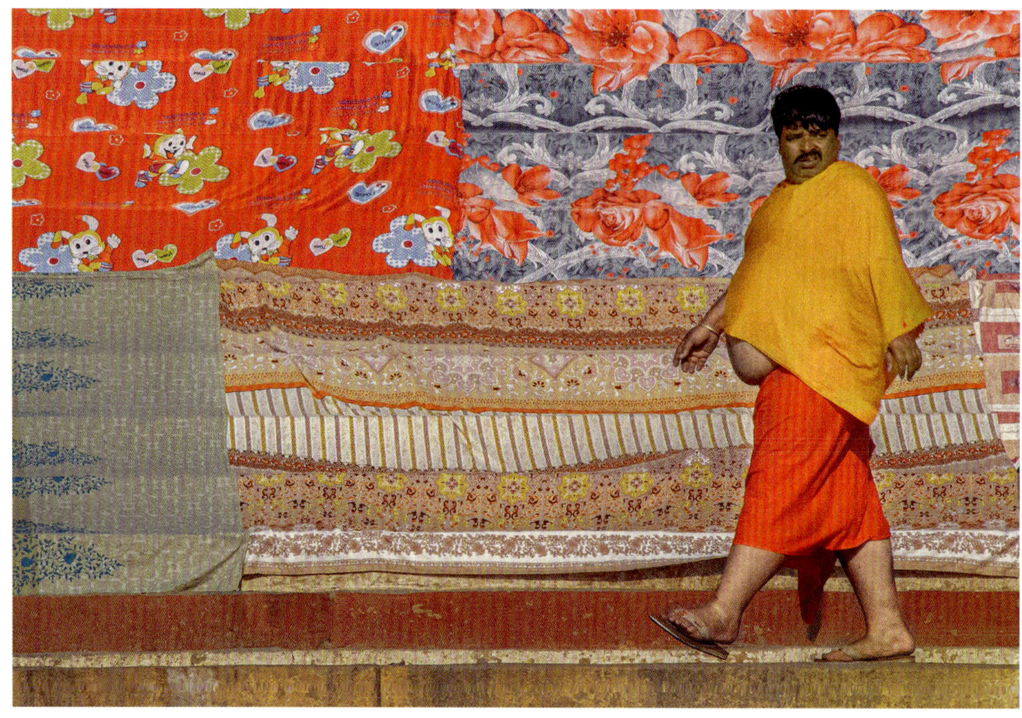

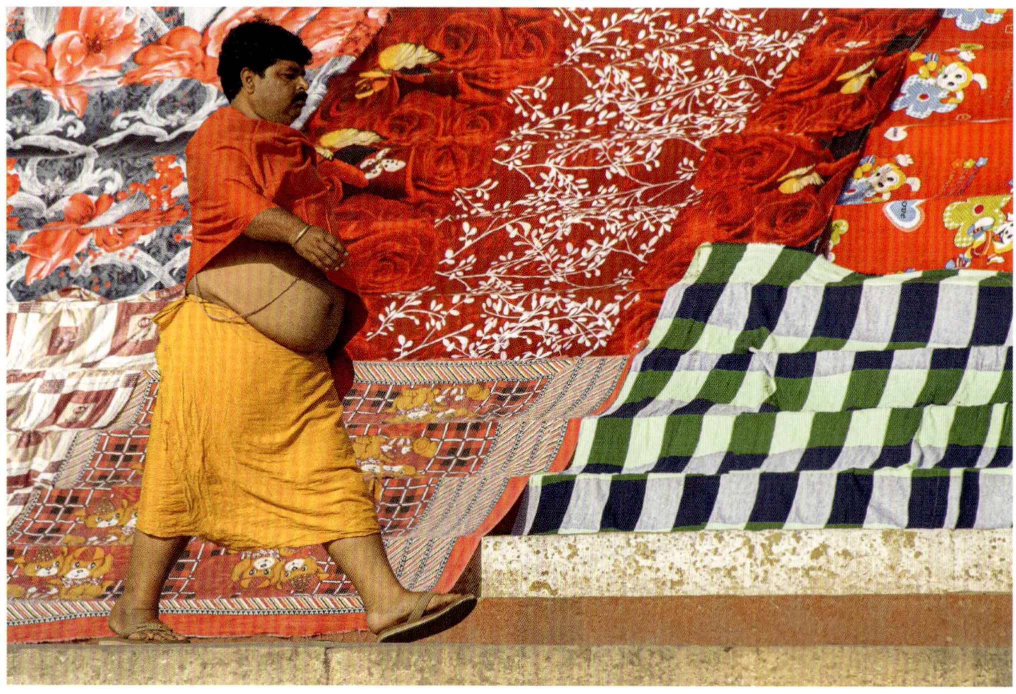

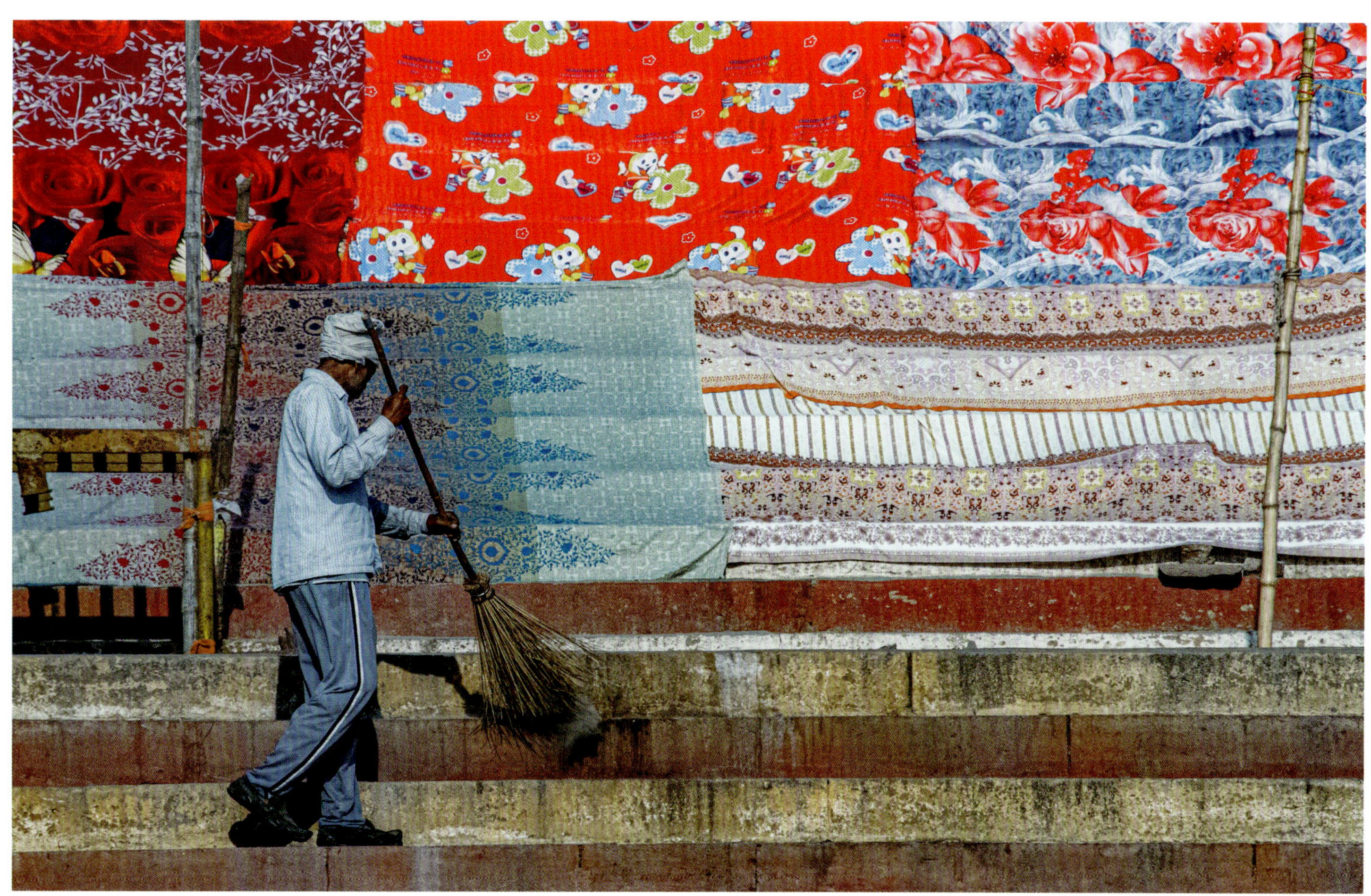

These are only a few of the many images I captured of the constant activity along the banks of the Ganges River in Varanasi, India, from my vantage point in a hired rowboat. At first glance it might appear you are looking at flags, but they are actually curtains, tablecloths, and sheets from the many nearby hotels draped out on the steps to dry in the hot sun after being washed in the river.

I have so many favorites, including one of an elderly man tasked with sweeping the few steps *not* draped with laundry, steps that make just one very long narrow path that parallels the river and allows locals to walk without trampling on the laundry. Although I was happy with this shot, a few seconds later (right about the time I was ready to tell my water taxi driver to row on), I spotted a man walking into the scene from my left, wearing a bright red shirt with a bright yellow skirt and then, seconds later, a man came in from my right dressed in just the opposite colors. Oh, how I wished they would have crossed paths at the same time within same frame, but that just wasn't to be. I looked at my watch and realized that I had already produced at least a half-dozen keepers, yet the sun had only been up for one hour, with most of the day still ahead. Lucky me!

◘ Nikon D500, NIKKOR 18–300mm lens, *f*/13 for 1/250 sec., ISO 200, Daylight/Sunny WB

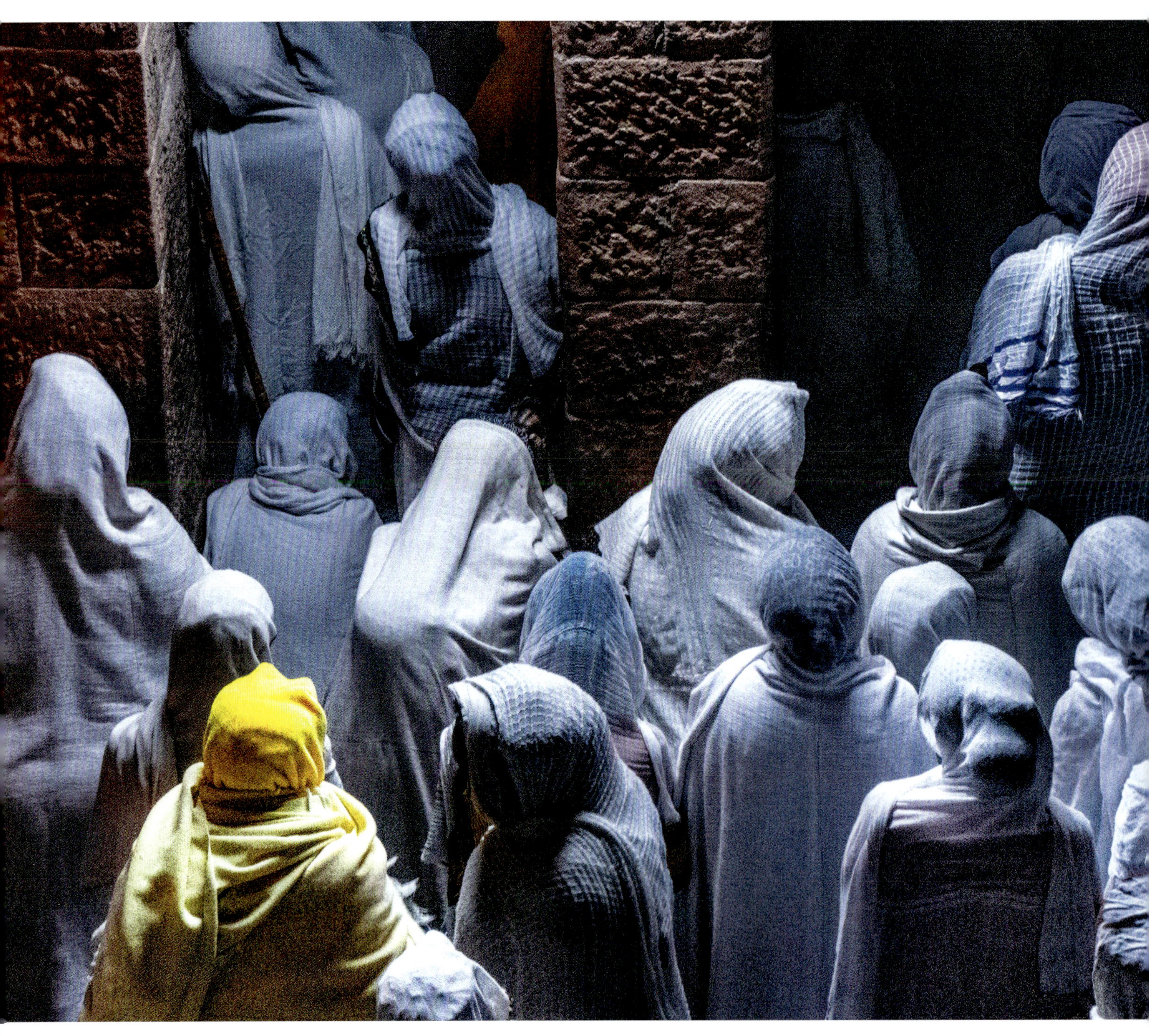

It was Sunday morning in Lalibela, Ethiopia, and my day had started with a 4 a.m. alarm. I arrived at one of the seven rock churches—literally carved out of the rocky terrain—as the morning church services began to unfold. I was able to perch on the surrounding rock ledge to one side of the church as women, clad in white and light blue, began to arrive. By now it was 5:15 a.m., still too early for natural light, and with only a few exterior lights surrounding this particular rock church, I was using an ISO of 6400. One by one the women arrived, then two by two, and soon the group began to swell in front of the women's entrance to the church. Suddenly the unplanned, unexpected moment: a lone woman appeared clad in yellow, breaking the calm of the white and light blue, much like the welcome contrast of a lone yellow sunflower against a clear blue sky. I sensed her impatience at finding the entrance to the interior of the church blocked. *She's going to exit left, out of the frame—no!* I thought. Quickly, I fired, and two seconds later, yep, she veered left and was gone.

◘ Nikon D500, NIKKOR 18–300mm lens, *f*/8 for 1/100 sec., ISO 6400, Daylight/Sunny WB

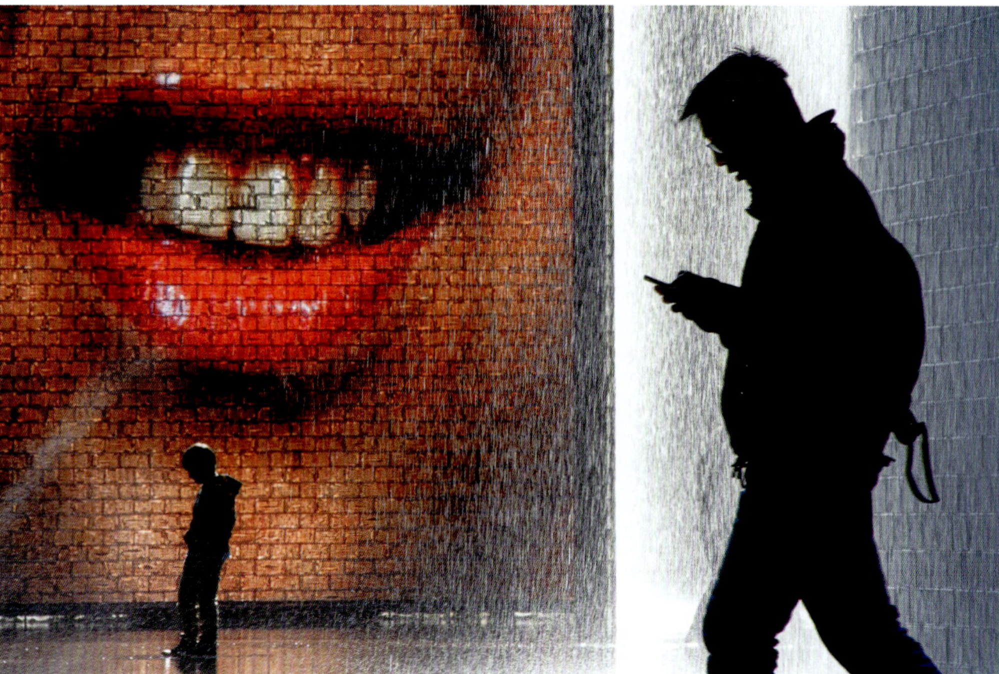

◘ **Nikon D500, NIKKOR 18–300mm lens, *f*/16 for 1/200 sec., ISO 640, Daylight/Sunny WB**

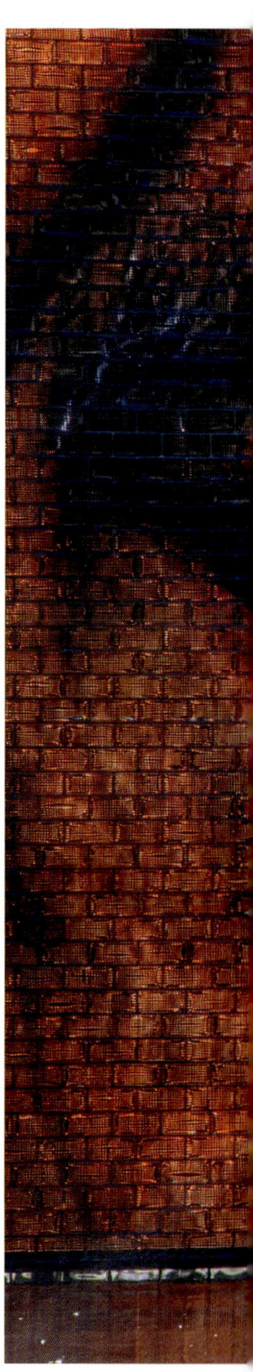

Although it was bitterly cold on this early spring day in Chicago, Crown Fountain was running at full strength, and there was no shortage of subjects. My students and I focused on creating splendid compositions of light and color, with silhouetted human forms adding personality to the overall scene. The combination of both backlight and front light is arguably the most killer exposure opportunity that one can come across. Here, the bright backlit sprays of water, the bright photographic image and the ice block stand in contrast to silhouetted figures walking in the foreground, creating strong graphic compositions.

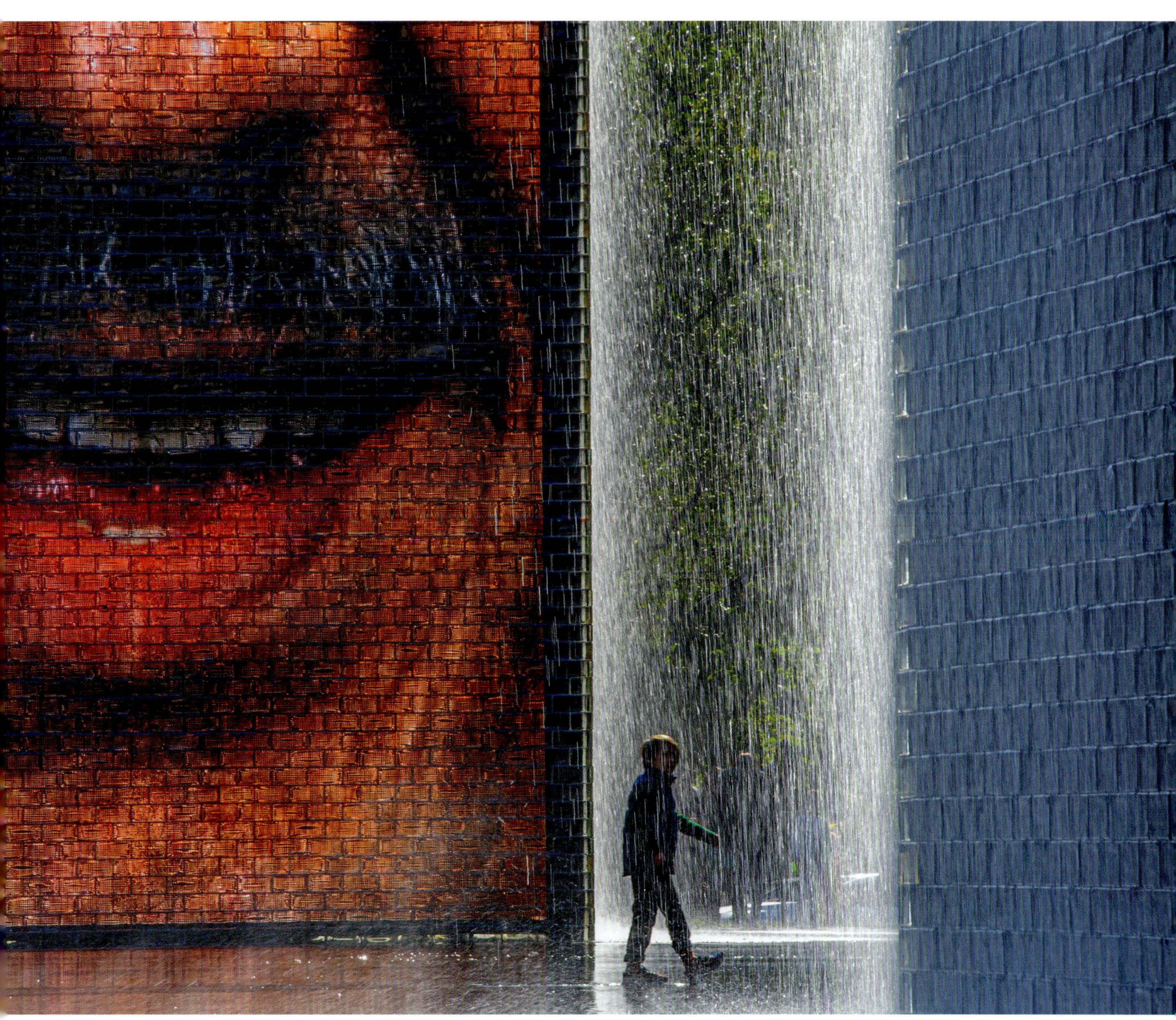

Nikon D500, NIKKOR 18–300mm lens, *f*/11 for 1/400 sec., ISO 640, Daylight/Sunny WB

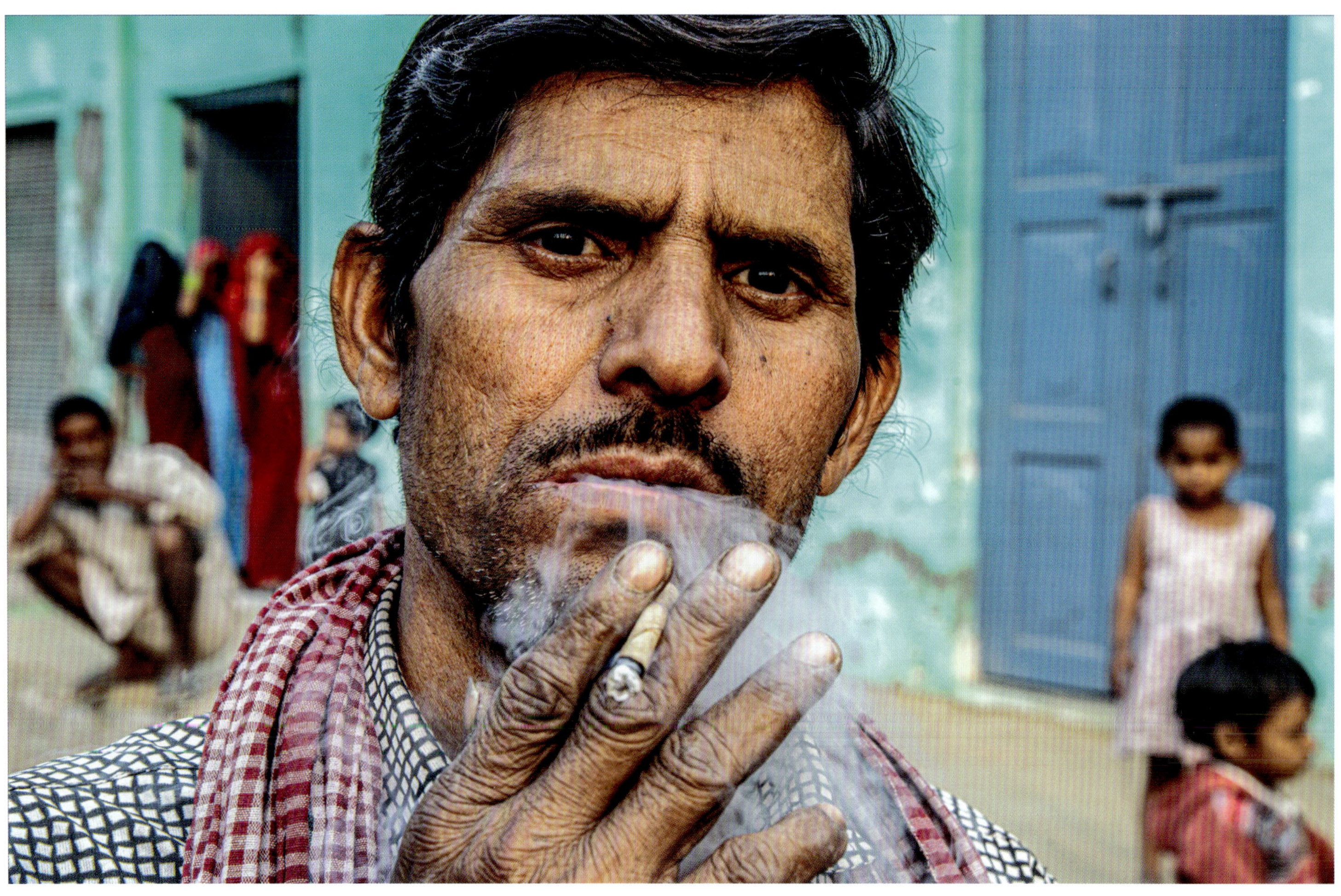

Although I do not normally walk up to total strangers and shove a camera in their face, I have done it on occasion, and this morning in a small, impoverished village outside of Agra, India, was one of those moments. Earlier I had been walking through the village and, as often happens, attracted the attention of several children, some of whom I photographed. It wasn't long before a very angry adult in the village took issue with my photographing the children. It was one of the few times when I honestly felt I might have to dodge left or right to avoid a closed fist, but for reasons that I cannot explain, I quickly raised my camera to my eye and started shooting this man, perhaps expecting that I could block the force of the anticipated punch with my camera—but the punch never came. I am sure he was just as surprised as I was when I started shooting, and instead of becoming even more agitated, he grabbed for the camera, not to take it from me but rather to see his picture. When I showed it to him, he began to laugh and was soon calling others over to look at his portrait.

The next thing I knew, he asked me to join him for a cup of tea, which I agreed to with the understanding that I would prefer to stay outside and drink it while sitting on some nearby steps. (I explained that it was too hot to be indoors, when in fact I was honestly a bit concerned about being cornered once inside the house.) I'm still not quite certain whether there was ever really a threat or whether it was simply a case of my imagination going into overdrive.

When in doubt about whether to photograph children in public parks or in city streets, either don't do it or find the parent and ask permission, with the promise of sending them a copy.

◘ Nikon D850, NIKKOR 24–120mm lens, *f*/5.6 for 1/1250 sec., ISO 400, Daylight/Sunny WB

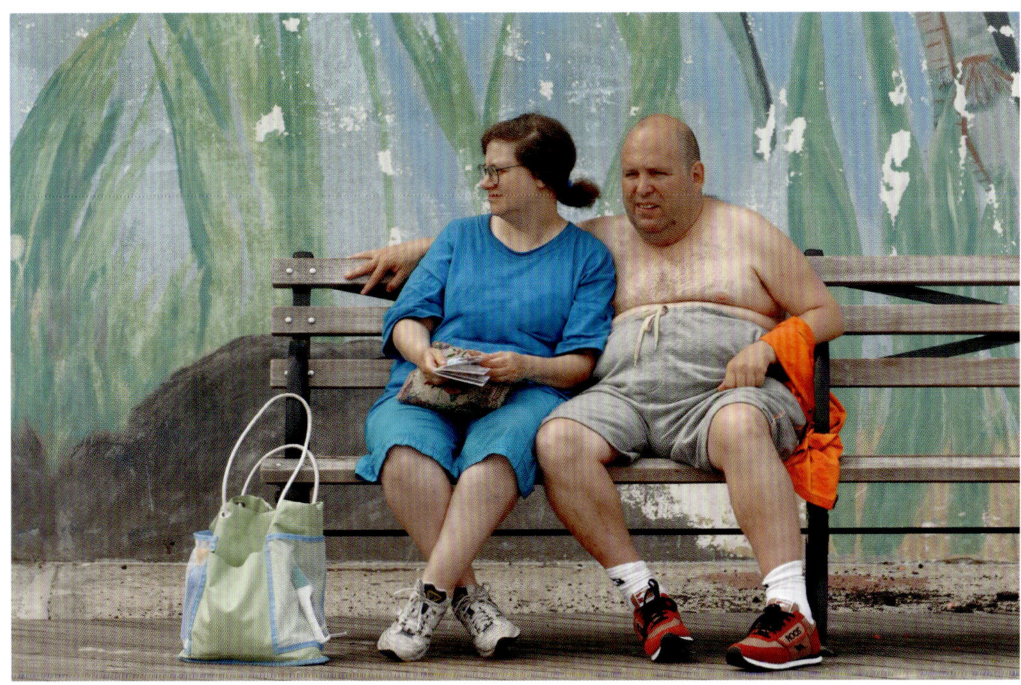

An effective photograph arouses our emotions, and in this case, I succumb rather quickly to the urge to smile, followed by a slight chuckle—not to make fun of but rather to enjoy this endearing couple, seemingly without a care in the world, seated on a bench in the shade on one of those dog-day August afternoons in New York's Coney Island. To love and be loved: it's why most of us are here.

◘ Nikon D810, NIKKOR 24–120mm lens, *f*/11 for 1/200 sec., ISO 320, Daylight/Sunny WB

There is something about this image, taken of a group of women celebrating something in Paris, that I have always found troubling—not the content, but the overall starkness of colors. I am a color guy, so it is surprising to admit that even I might be put off by "too much" color. Or was it simply a reminder of my life back in the late 1960s and early '70s, full of parties with ever-present fluorescent paints and black lights that I would rather forget? I showed the image to some friends, asking, "What single adjective best describes your reaction to this photo?" The responses ranged from "jarring" to "garish," "arresting," "astonishing," "tacky," and "snazzy."

Two years have since passed, and I have come to really like this image, perhaps partly because it is so divisive; one either loves its stark, garish, comic-book feel or hates it. Interestingly enough, this is about as "straight out of the camera" as an image could possibly be. I even avoided adding any use of Selective Color. Note that because this was taken a bit late in the afternoon, the exposure is a wee bit under Sunny 16.

◘ Nikon D500, NIKKOR 18–300mm lens at 28mm, *f*/16 for 1/160 sec., ISO 200, Daylight/Sunny WB

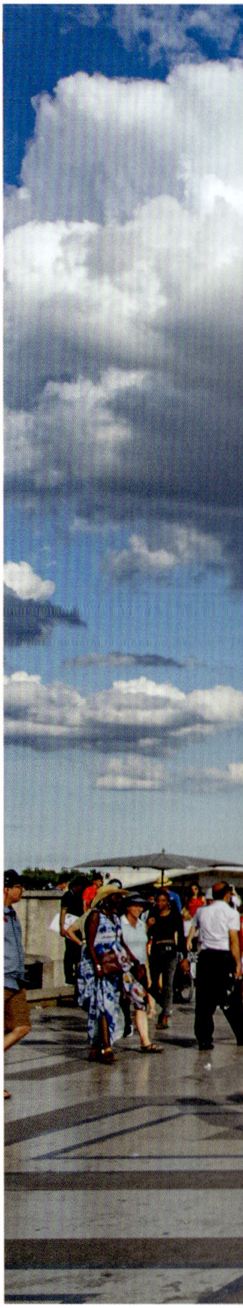

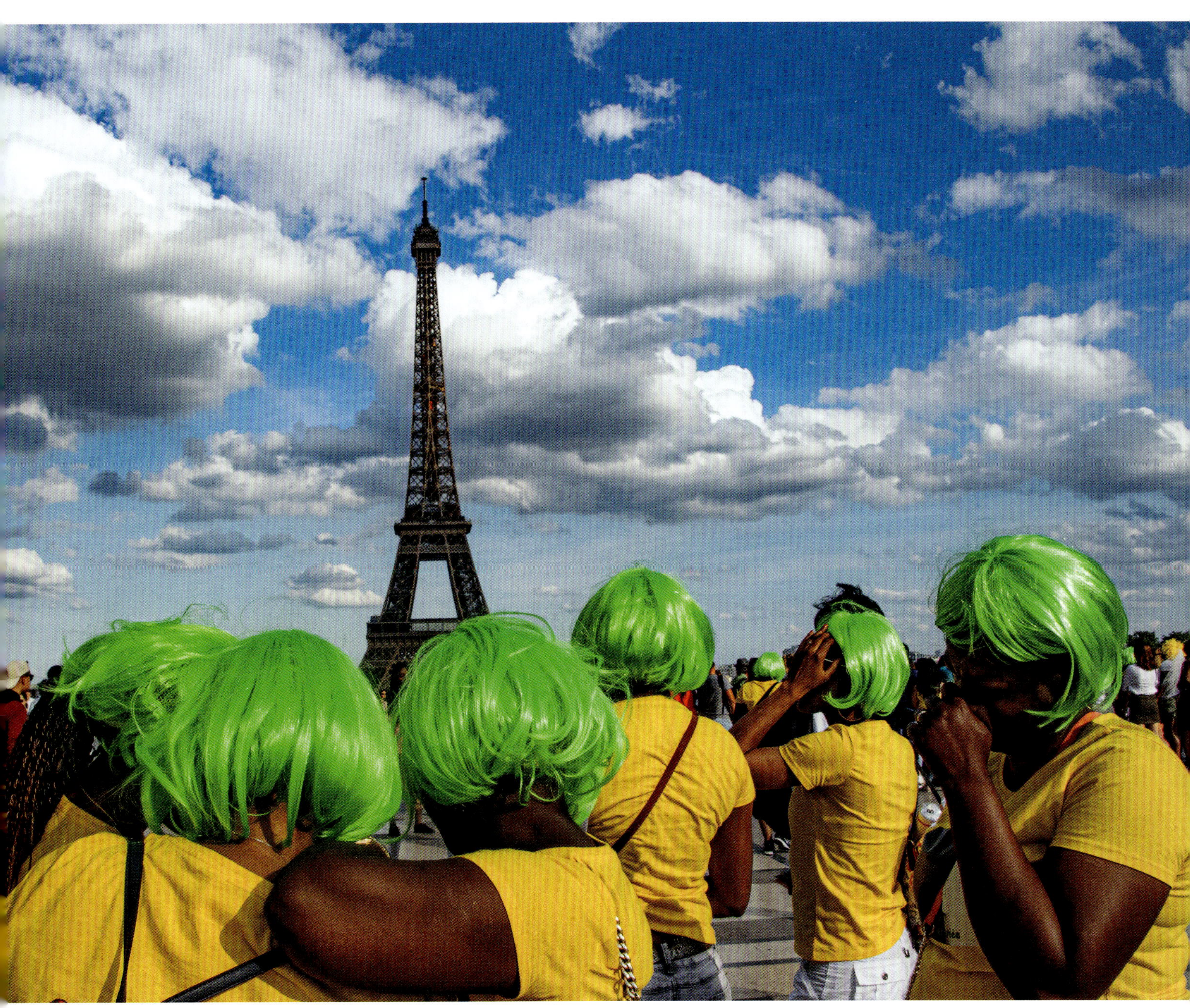

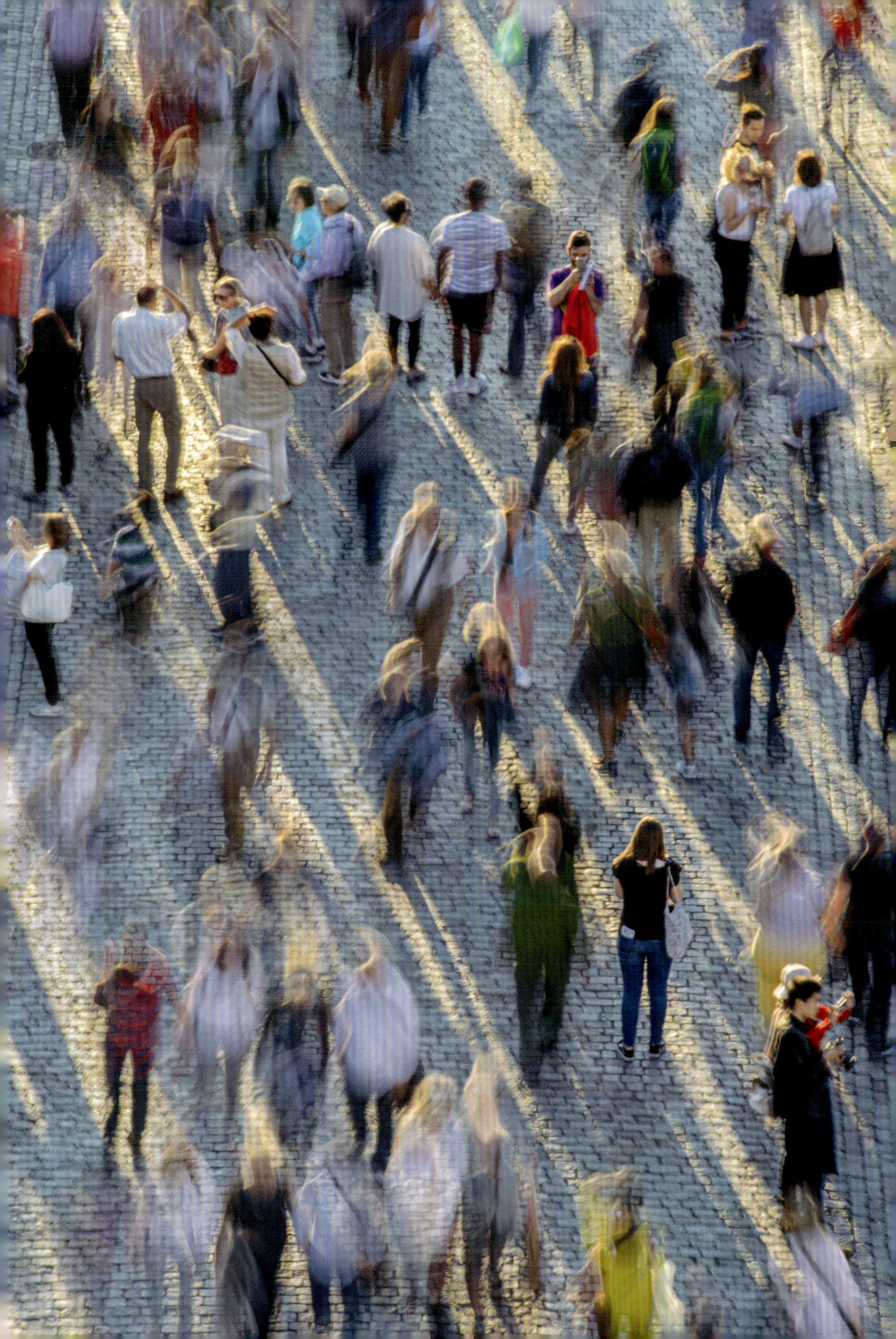

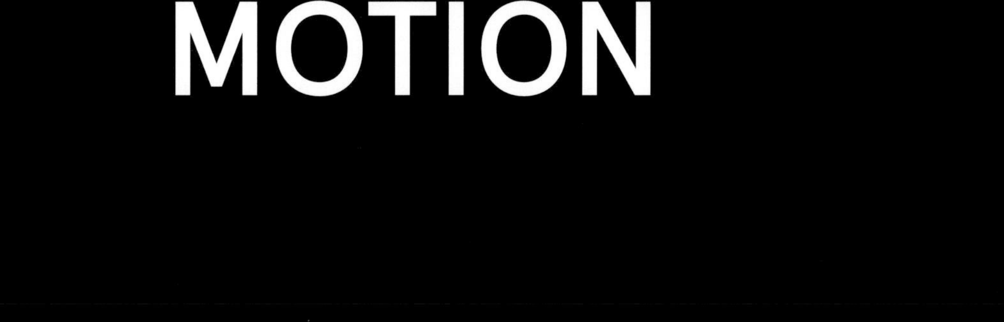
MOTION

Freezing Motion

Motion-filled opportunities are present all around us: on the streets, at the park, outside our office building, in the corner deli. No one's world is motionless. And it is in this very motion where photographic gold awaits to be mined.

There is perhaps nothing more satisfying than an image of action frozen in crisp, sharp detail, allowing us to scrutinize and analyze every nuance. At the risk of dating myself, it brings to mind good ole Sergeant Joe Friday on the television show *Dragnet*. ("*Dragnet*?" you ask. Google it!) Joe was famous for saying, "Just give me the facts." Any attempt to blur the truth with Sergeant Friday was quickly met with the facts. And there is certainly no blurring of the truth when freezing action-filled compositions.

There are many keys to freezing action shots. At the top of the list is using the right shutter speed. To freeze most outdoor action-filled shots—whether jumping, falling, leaping, stumbling, slipping, kicking, or sliding—a shutter speed of 1/500 sec. or 1/1000 sec. is best. Another key choice is your ISO, since the greater the ISO, the greater the likelihood that you'll be able to use both a small aperture and a fast shutter speed. Focusing needs to be fast, and the added depth of field created by an aperture of *f*/16 or *f*/22 may come in handy if you aren't spot-on with your focusing. Finally, the use of a motor drive (Continuous Shooting mode) is essential, as it's best to start shooting just prior to the anticipated peak of action and continue until just after, with the best image usually somewhere in the middle of the sequence of shots.

Understanding Shutter Speed

Choosing the right shutter speed to capture motion is, for many shooters, a hit-or-miss proposition, but it doesn't have to be if you ask yourself the following three questions: Do you want to freeze the action in crystal-clear sharpness? Do you want to convey a heightened sense of speed or urgency? Do you want to capture the ghostlike presence of people against an otherwise sharply focused scene?

Freezing the action of moving subjects is a relatively easy exposure; a shutter speed of 1/500 sec. or 1/1000 sec. will freeze most activities. Panning subjects is easily accomplished with shutter speeds between 1/60 sec. and 1/15 sec., depending on the speed of your subject. And if you want to record a blurred brushstroke of motion in contrast to a sharp subject, a shutter speed of 1/4 sec. will often do the trick.

No matter which shutter speed you use, don't forget to adjust your ISO for a well-balanced exposure. If you're freezing action with a fast shutter speed, your ISO will need to be high, perhaps 400. If you're panning, you'll want a lower ISO, around 100. And if you're using a very slow shutter speed to capture ghostlike figures, your ISO will need to be as low as possible, either 50 or L1.0 as is often indicated, perhaps even with the addition of a 3-stop ND filter.

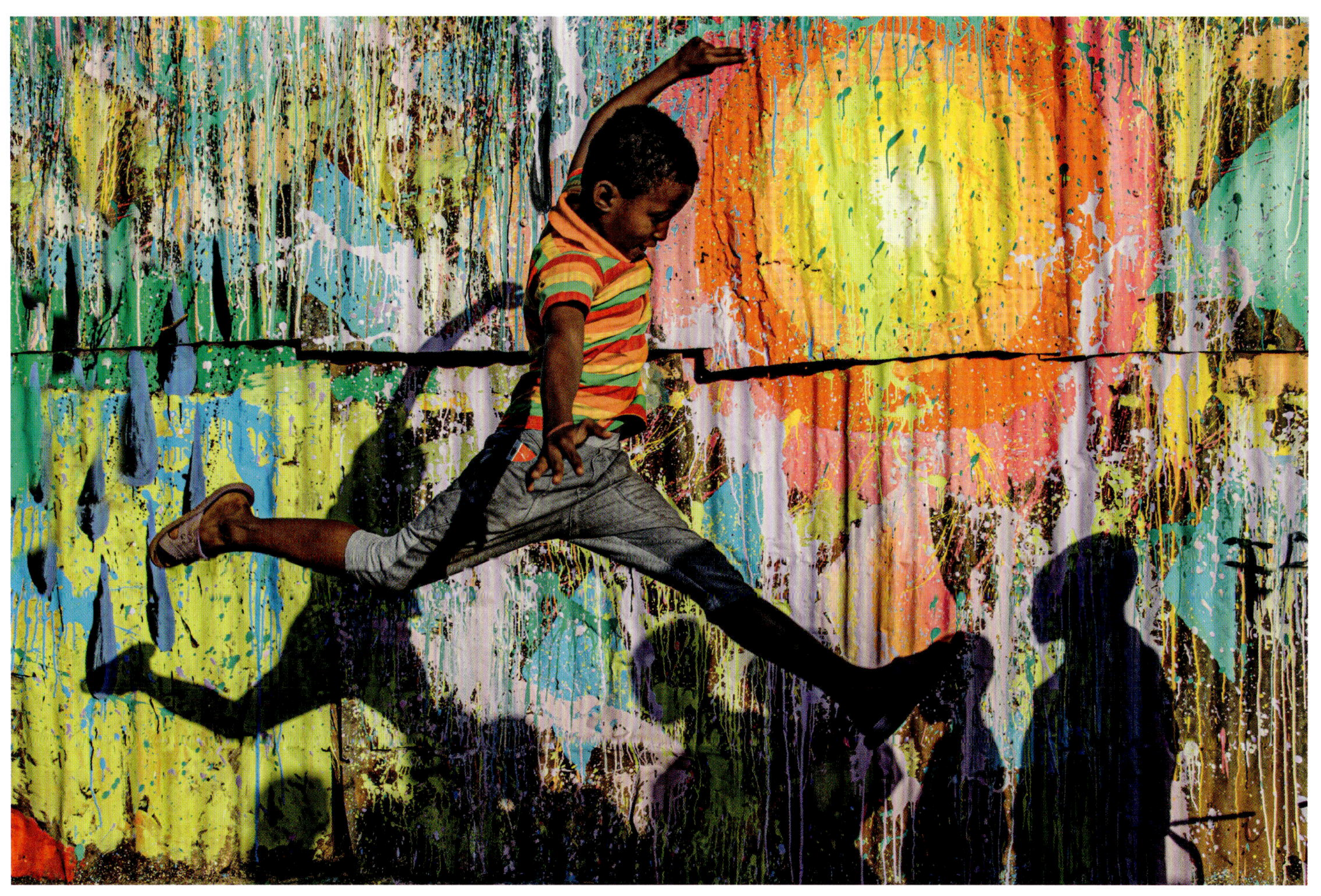

In Arba Minch, Ethiopia, a crowd of kids had gathered around me, their shouts of "Take my picture!" drowning out three nearby barking dogs. "Okay!" I replied, with equal excitement. I asked them to come in close behind me, so their shadows would run a bit up the colorful corrugated metal wall, and then for each of them to jump in front of the wall, one at a time. "Yes, perfect, like that," I said encouragingly. "Okay, one, two, three: *jump*!"

◘ Nikon D500, NIKKOR 18–300mm lens, *f*/11 for 1/1000 sec., ISO 640, Daylight/Sunny WB

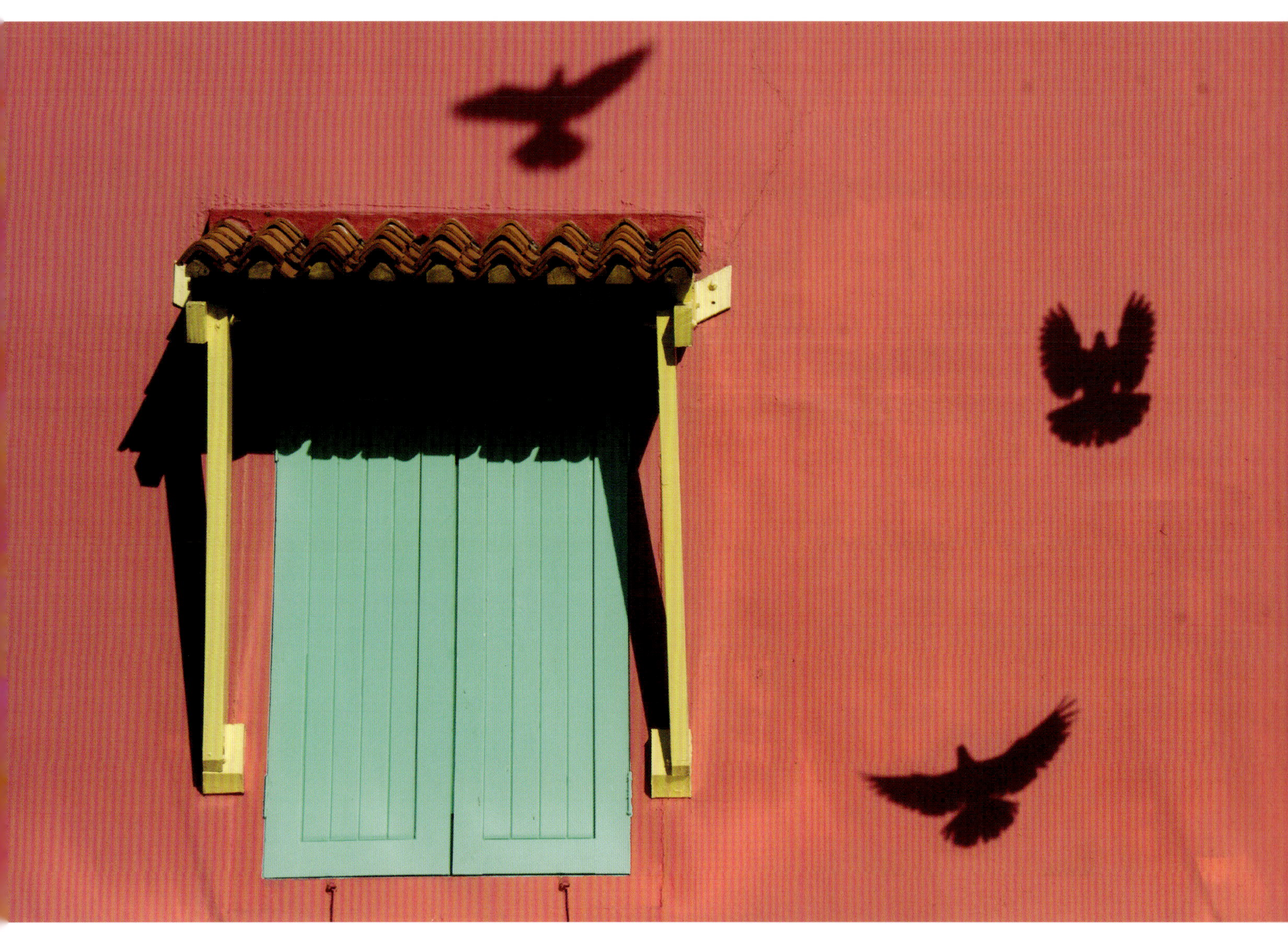

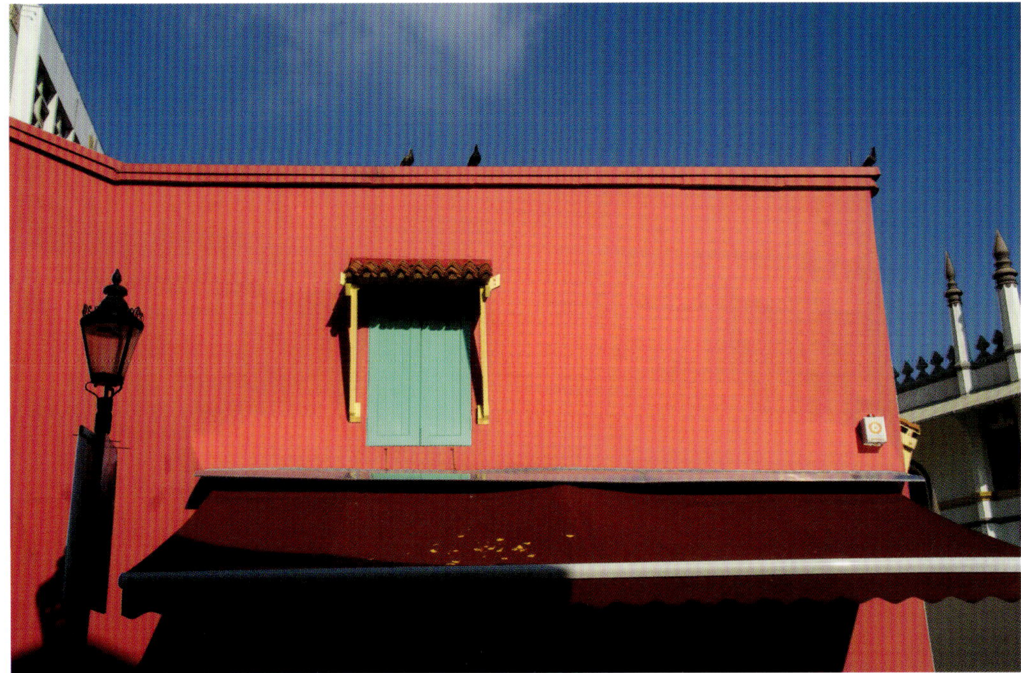

It was a lone pigeon's brief shadow racing up the side of this vivid magenta wall in Singapore that caught my attention. Along with another pigeon, it now sat perched atop the wall—and thus began the challenge! How could I get them (along with seven more pigeons perched on a nearby wire) to fly above that lone window and brightly painted wall, leaving only their shadows?

I took a quick walk to a nearby 7-Eleven and bought a bag of Doritos. Returning to the scene, I placed some Doritos atop the awning below the window (shown above). Within minutes, far more than nine pigeons appeared and descended on the awning. Every so often I waved my arms while quickly jumping, scaring the birds up past the wall, and then firing in CH mode. After more than eighty frames, I ended up with four that looked pretty cool, the one on the previous page being one of them.

◘ Nikon D500, NIKKOR 18–300mm lens at 135mm, *f*/11 for 1/800 sec., ISO 400, Daylight/Sunny WB

Blurring Motion

Motion is everywhere, yet many students miss it, which is why I tell all of them to try and imagine that they'd fallen asleep just *before* the wheel was invented, and then woken up today. Chances are good that they would be filled with fear and running for cover! Of course, we were all born into a whirl of nonstop motion and because of that, most of us have developed a blind eye to it, not to mention a deaf ear to all the noise it creates.

As for myself, I am motion obsessed. One of my favorite assignments that I teach in my online photography school (bpsop.com) is the process of creating compelling compositions with colorful "brushstrokes" created by motion-filled subjects. When you blur motion on the street, it can be even more believable: "Wow, that city bus is on the move!"

Many street photographers are reluctant to shoot blurred motion because, truth be told, firm camera supports are seldom there when you need them and the idea of lugging a tripod around is an even greater deterrent. All of this means that only a few of us are capturing these truly compelling compositions, but at the risk of turning a field that is currently not crowded at all into one that is, here is my very short list of recommended shutter speeds for turning everyday moving objects into brushstrokes: 1/15 sec., 1/8 sec., or 1/4 sec. There are exceptions to this list, of course; let your own experience determine whether you need to adjust these shutter speeds upward or downward. Enjoy!

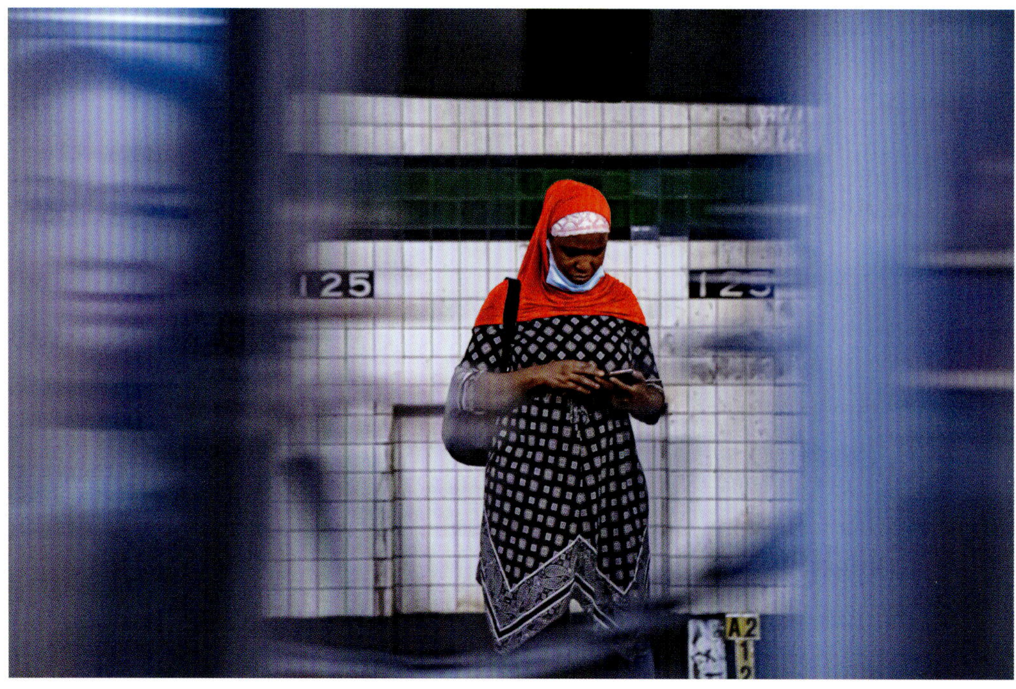

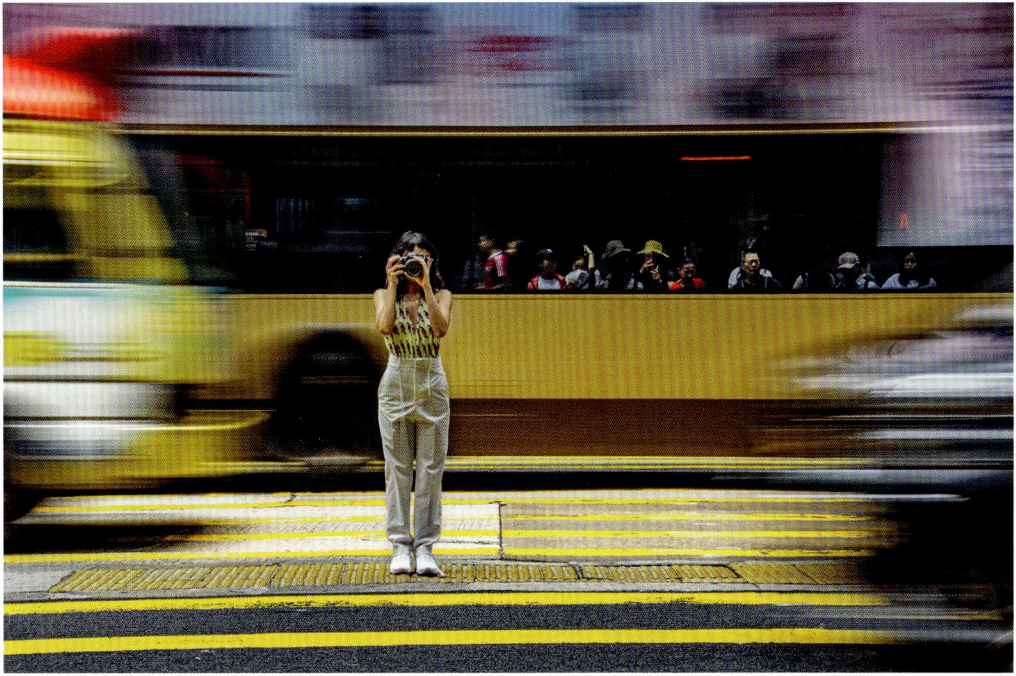

I am drawn to photographing chaos—a noted feature of most cities, whether large or small. Shutter speed plays a vital role in capturing scenes like this, as does serendipity. As much as I can control the motion effects of my photographic techniques, I have zero control over the size, color, volume, or mass of all that motion as well as its direction as it moves freely across my frame during these 1/2-sec. exposures. For this photo, the one thing I controlled was the lone model, whom I asked to pose and hold steady during the more than fifty 1/2-sec. exposures I shot over the course of fifteen minutes. How fortunate that in one of these exposures, a streaking bus passed through, against a backdrop of pedestrians awaiting the "safe to cross" signal. At first glance, the pedestrians appear to be passengers on board the bus, raising the question "How is that possible?" But now you know they are not on the bus, but waiting to cross the street. Further proof that despite all the planning and visual know-how, street photography is quite often reliant on serendipitous moments.

◘ Nikon D500, NIKKOR 18–300mm lens, *f*/22 for 1/2 sec. with a 4-stop ND filter, ISO 50, Daylight/Sunny WB

Contrast is often vital to a photograph's success; in many cases, it's the element that elevates one photograph over another. It can be contrast between tone or color, between sharp and dull textures, between light and shadow, or, as in this photo shot in a New York City subway station, between motion blur and crystal-clear sharpness. Here I got the added and completely unexpected bonus of an advertisement featuring a young woman on the passing subway car, adding another layer of contrast between the blurred woman and the in-focus woman—who also happens to be wearing red, which contrasts with the tiles behind in red's color complement, green.

◘ Nikon D500, NIKKOR 18–300mm lens on a tripod, *f*/14 for 1/15 sec., ISO 1600, Daylight/Sunny WB (fine-tuned in post-processing to eliminate a greenish cast caused by the artificial lighting)

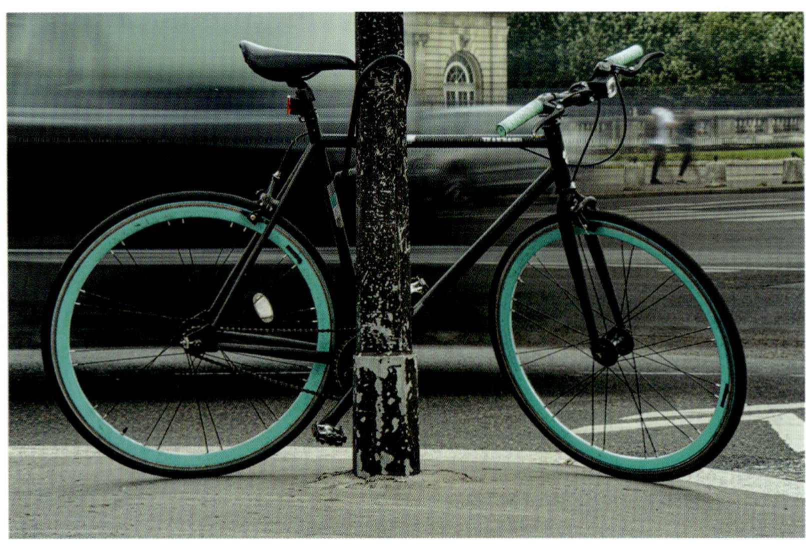

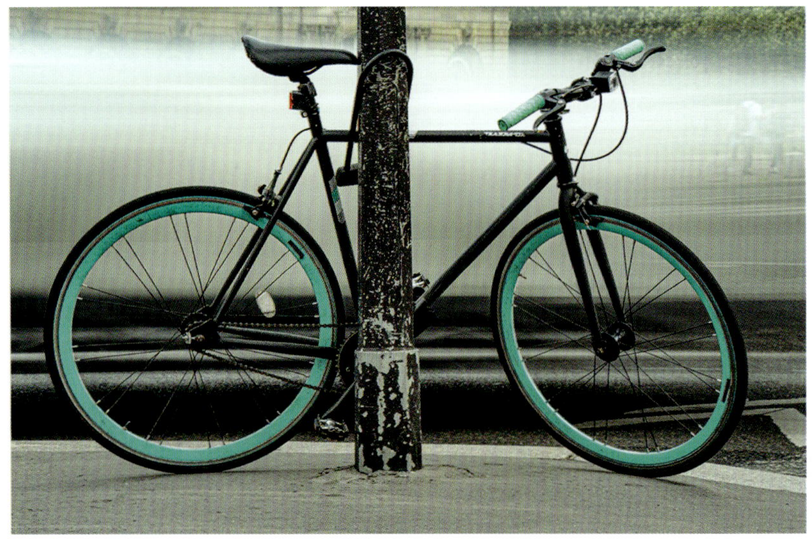

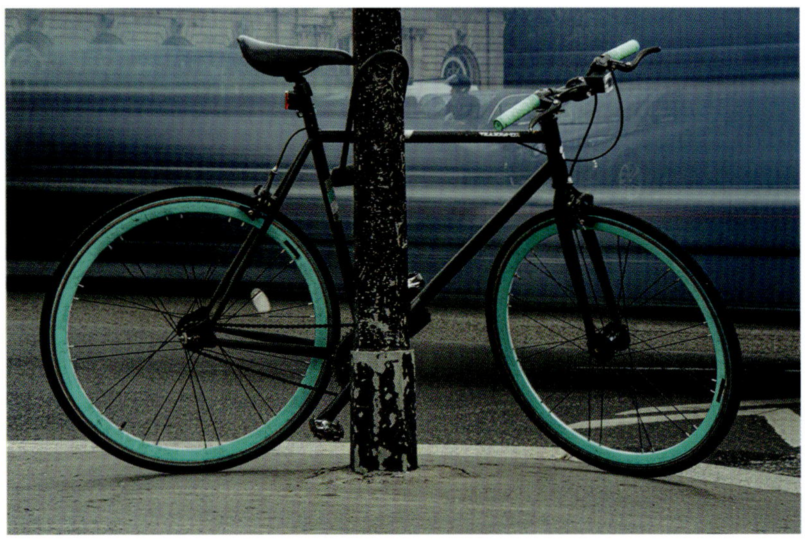

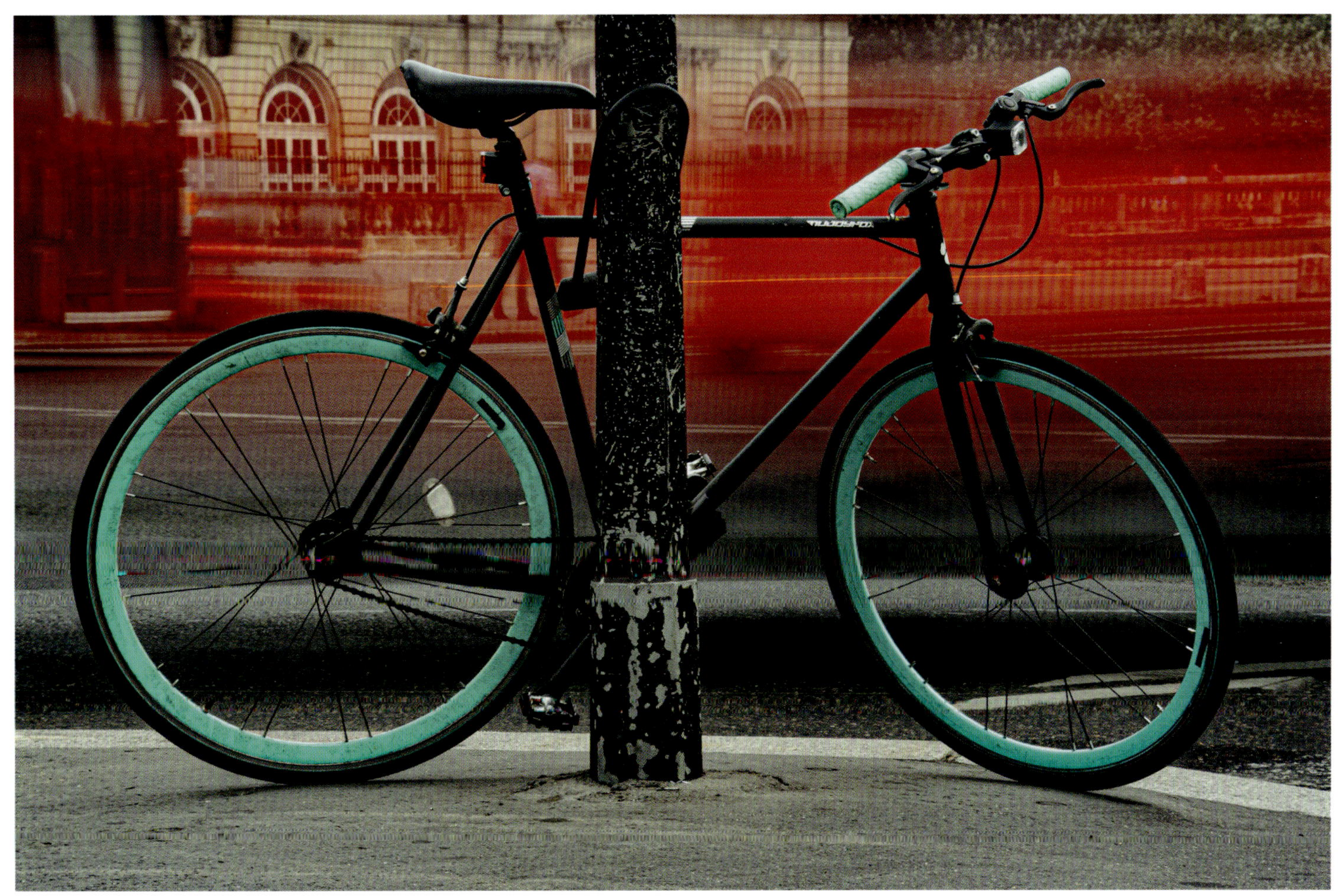

Would it surprise you to discover that this image of a turquoise bicycle is a thirty-minute exposure? Read on to discover how you, too, can make such long exposures.

I remain convinced that motion-filled images are "e-motion-ally" charged, as with this bike on a Paris street. I was immediately taken by the unexpectedly bright and colorful bike and was quick to frame it, crouching down on the sidewalk with my camera mounted on a tripod and waiting for the "whoosh" of a car behind it. But the wait was soon to challenge me. Photographic patience is not a strength of mine; many of my exposures are created in one second or less. That's been my approach for the last forty years: frame, shoot, move on, frame, shoot, move on. So why not shoot and move on in this case?

As you can see in three other exposures, the challenge wasn't just finding motion—there was plenty of that. But my standards are much higher than settling for black, white, or dark blue brushstrokes. I was holding out for a *red* car. Finally, at about the thirty-minute mark, there it was. Click! And just like that, I moved on with a huge smile on my face, thrilled with my "thirty-minute" exposure. As usual, it is always worth the wait when everything falls into place. True, most street photographers are equally familiar with those times when, despite the wait, everything does not come together, but when it does, it serves as the motivation to keep putting one foot in front of the other.

◘ Nikon D500, NIKKOR 18–300mm lens, *f*/16 for 1/4 sec., ISO 50, Daylight/Sunny WB

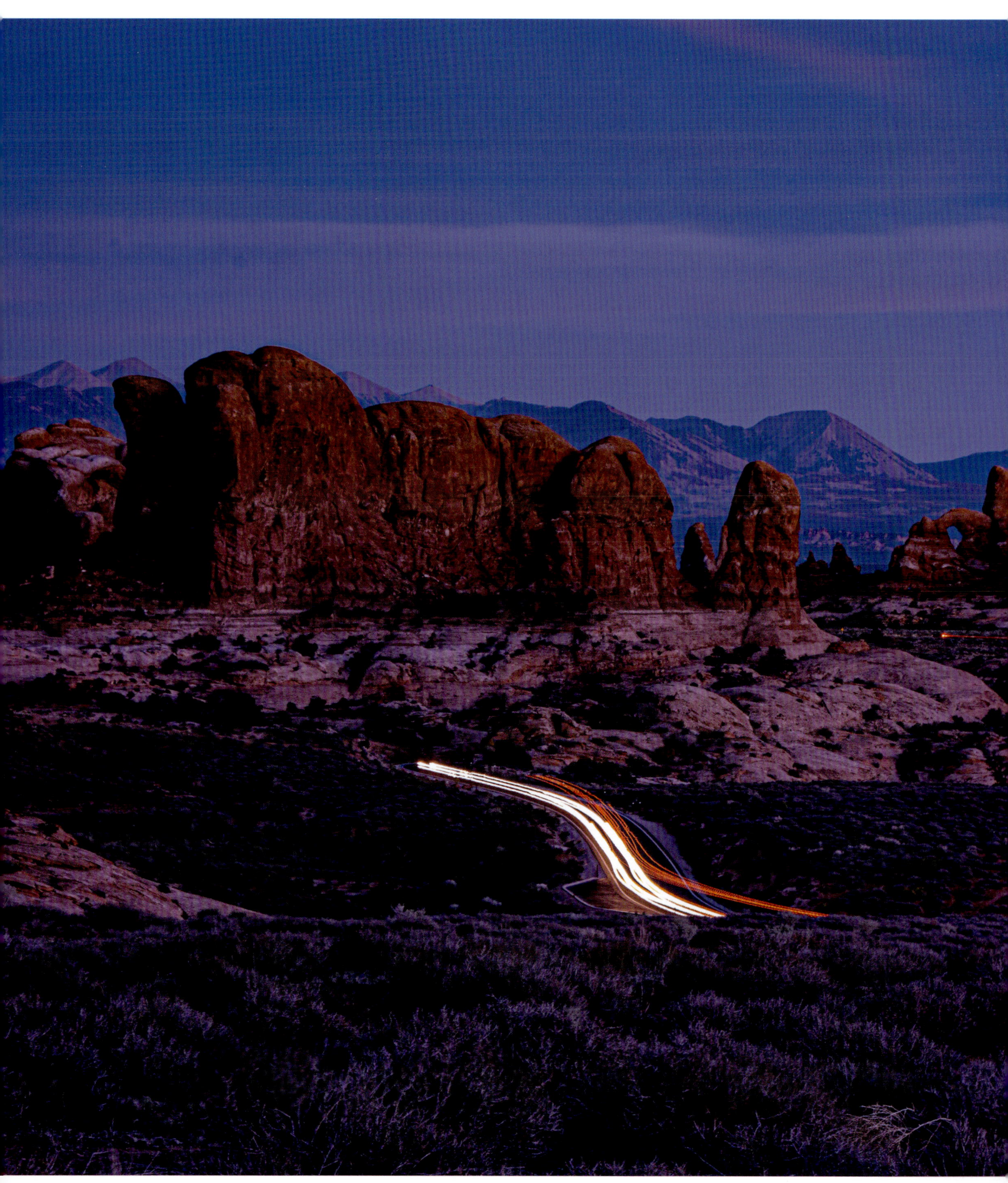

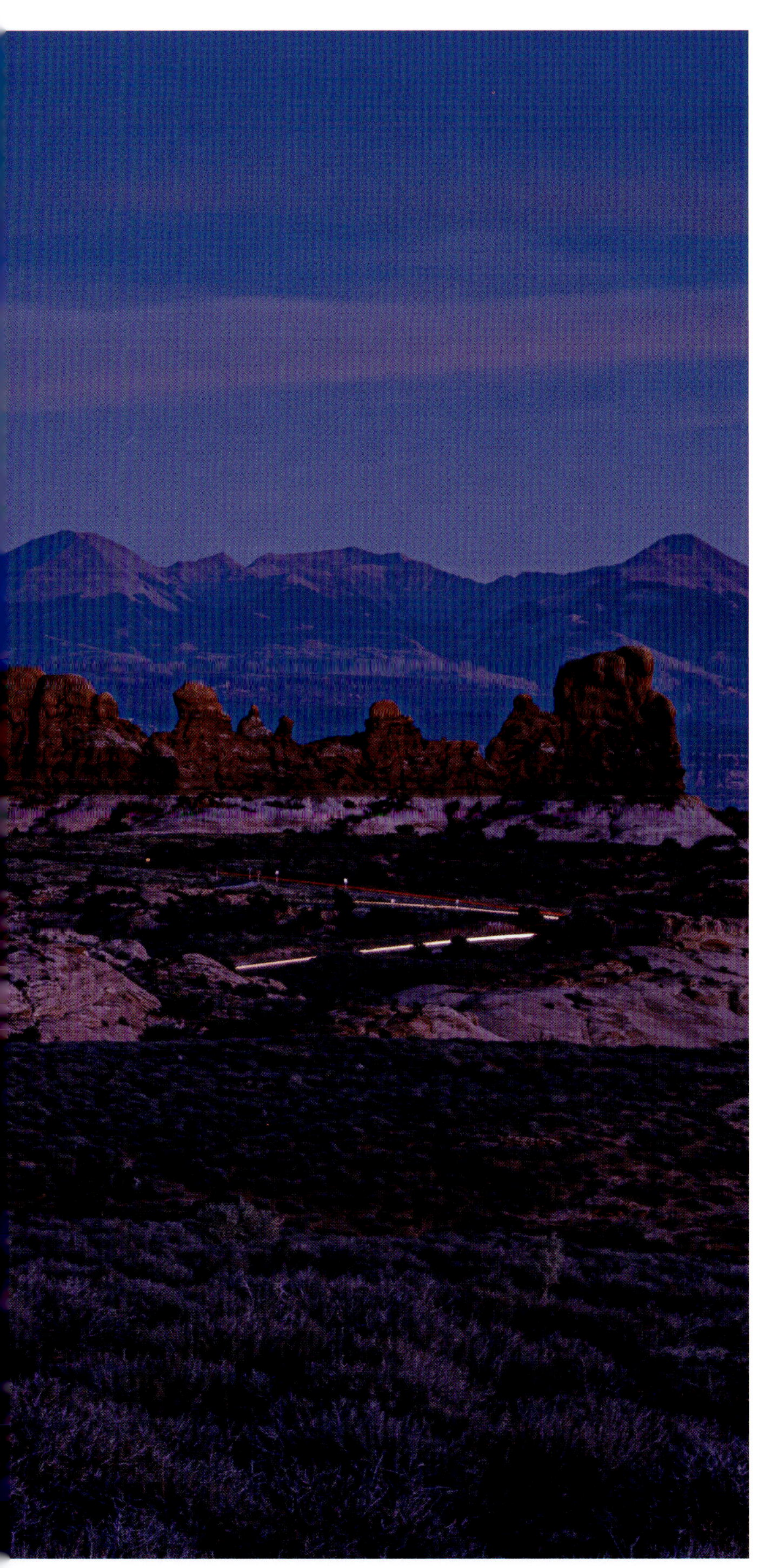

On this particular day, my students and I had just finished shooting the sunset to the west and planned to shoot the Milky Way later that evening. In the meantime, I suggested we take advantage of the very dramatic photograph opportunity to the east. "But there is nothing there to shoot but the mountains!" my students objected.

Since we had nothing else to shoot for at least an hour, I was quite firm in insisting that everyone set up their tripods and, using a moderate telephoto lens, compose the mountains to include a strip of highway. I suggested an 8-second exposure and the Custom Fluorescent WB setting (see page 68). You could hear the groans as they set up their tripods, but about fifteen minutes later, all you could hear was "That is so cool!"

One of the pitfalls of street photography is thinking that cities are the only places images can be found, when obviously this street is anything but. No matter how seduced you might be by a nature scene in front of you, don't forget your street smarts, especially when you have a street right in front of you!

◘ Nikon D500, NIKKOR 18–300mm lens, *f*/16 for 4 seconds, ISO 50, Fluorescent WB

Rain deters many photographers; some argue that the rain can ruin their gear. But that is a weak argument with today's DSLRs, most of which are darn near waterproof. Rain in the city means wet streets, and wet streets mean dramatic reflections—reason enough to grab your umbrella and venture out.

Of all of the cities where reflections can be found on the wet streets and sidewalks, two urban areas come immediately to mind: the Ginza District in Tokyo and Manhattan's Times Square. Some have suggested that Las Vegas, Nevada, is also great for reflections, but man, is it ever difficult to predict when rain will fall in Las Vegas. If you are headed to Vegas for some fun, check the weather, and *if* rain is forecast, take your camera for some unique reflection opportunities.

Several years ago, a hurricane warning for New York ended up bringing mostly remnants of the storm—heavy rain and wind. During a lull in the rain, I found myself out and about in Times Square, where I soon fixated on some vibrant colors reflected on the sidewalk from a neon sign. Shortly after composing the empty sidewalk ramp, I caught sight of two extremely colorfully clad women coming my way. I was ready, intent on using a moderately slow exposure to record some ghosted movement of their legs and possibly feet as they walked through my composition of color, texture, and motion.

◘ Nikon D810, NIKKOR 24–120mm lens, *f*/8 for 1/20 sec., ISO 400, Tungsten WB

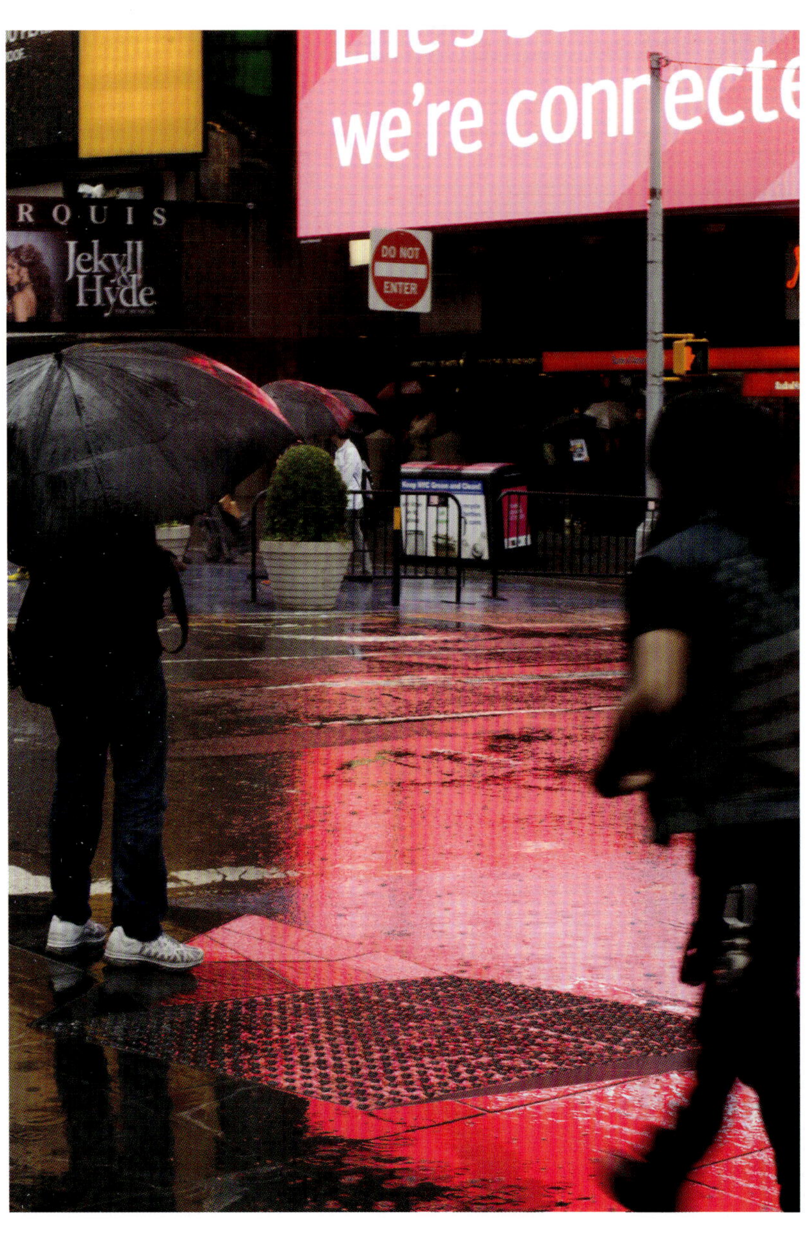

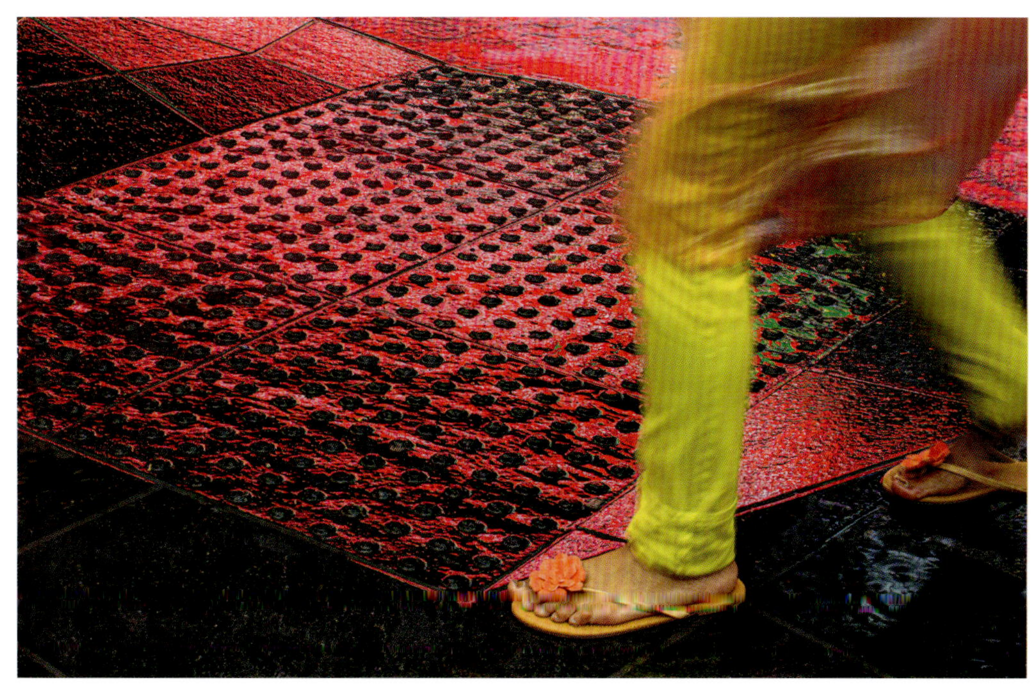

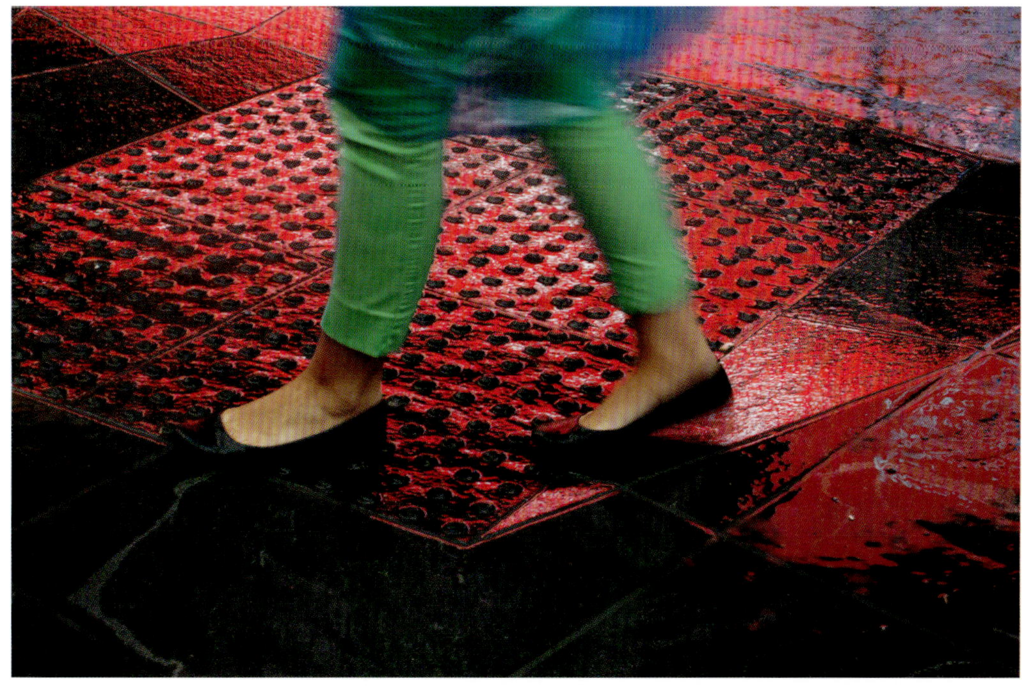

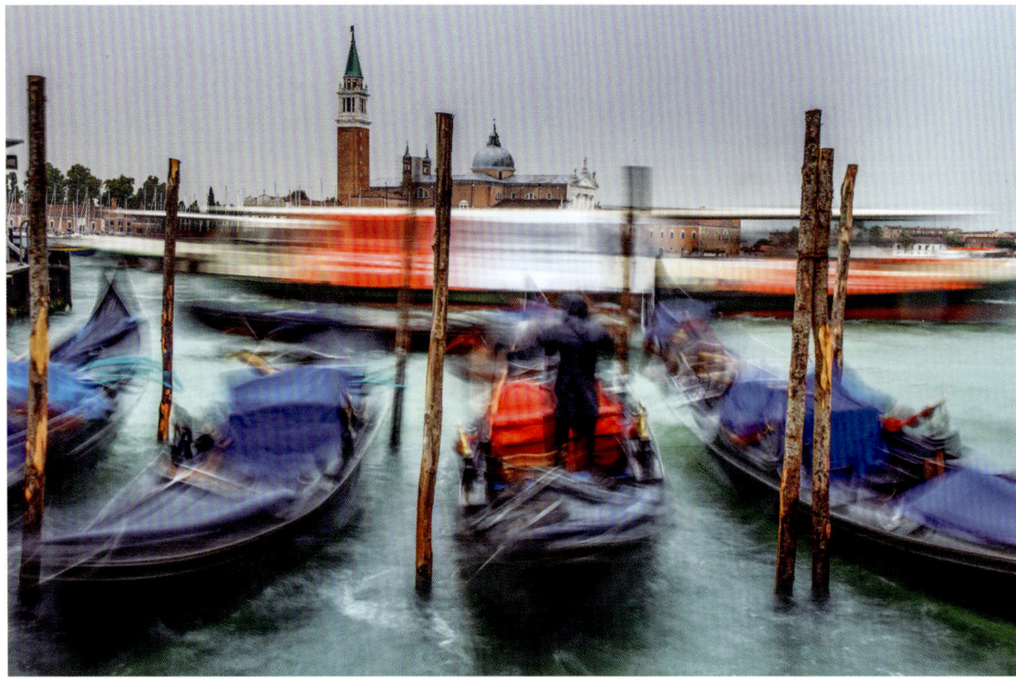

Rain, wind, rough seas, red boat traffic, and bouncing blue gondolas: a great opportunity for a motion-filled long exposure! On this morning in Venice, Italy, the harsh inclement weather found most of the photographers inside warm cafés, drinking cappuccino and waiting out the rain. I had this entire waterfront to myself. Let the wind blow and the rain continue to fall!

When it comes to attempting a long exposure to blur motion, remember this: the lowest ISO will always force the longest possible shutter speed in conjunction with the smallest aperture. But what do you do if even that does not result in a long enough shutter speed? Putting an ND filter on your lens will reduce the intensity of the light even further, just like a pair of sunglasses, making a longer exposure possible without overexposure. In this case, although the light was already reduced because it was a stormy day, a 3-stop ND filter reduced the light even further and enabled the 2-second exposure seen here.

◘ Nikon D810, NIKKOR 24–120mm lens at 31mm, *f*/16 for 2 seconds with a 3-stop ND filter, ISO 50, Daylight/Sunny WB

Several years ago, on a late afternoon in early September, I stood atop one of the lookout spires on the Charles Bridge in Prague and shot numerous exposures of the crowd crossing the bridge below. Setting my camera on a tripod, I combined a low ISO of 50 with a small aperture of *f*/22 and a 6-stop ND filter to allow slow shutter speeds of 1/2 sec. and 1 second. This kind of shooting is always unpredictable, since you can't control the stop-and-go movements of the crowd, leaving so much to chance—all the more reason to feel elated when you get one or two good shots. It was around the twenty-minute mark when I got the shot you see here.

◘ Nikon D500, NIKKOR 18–300mm lens, *f*/22 for 1/2 sec. with a 6-stop ND filter, ISO 50, Daylight/Sunny WB

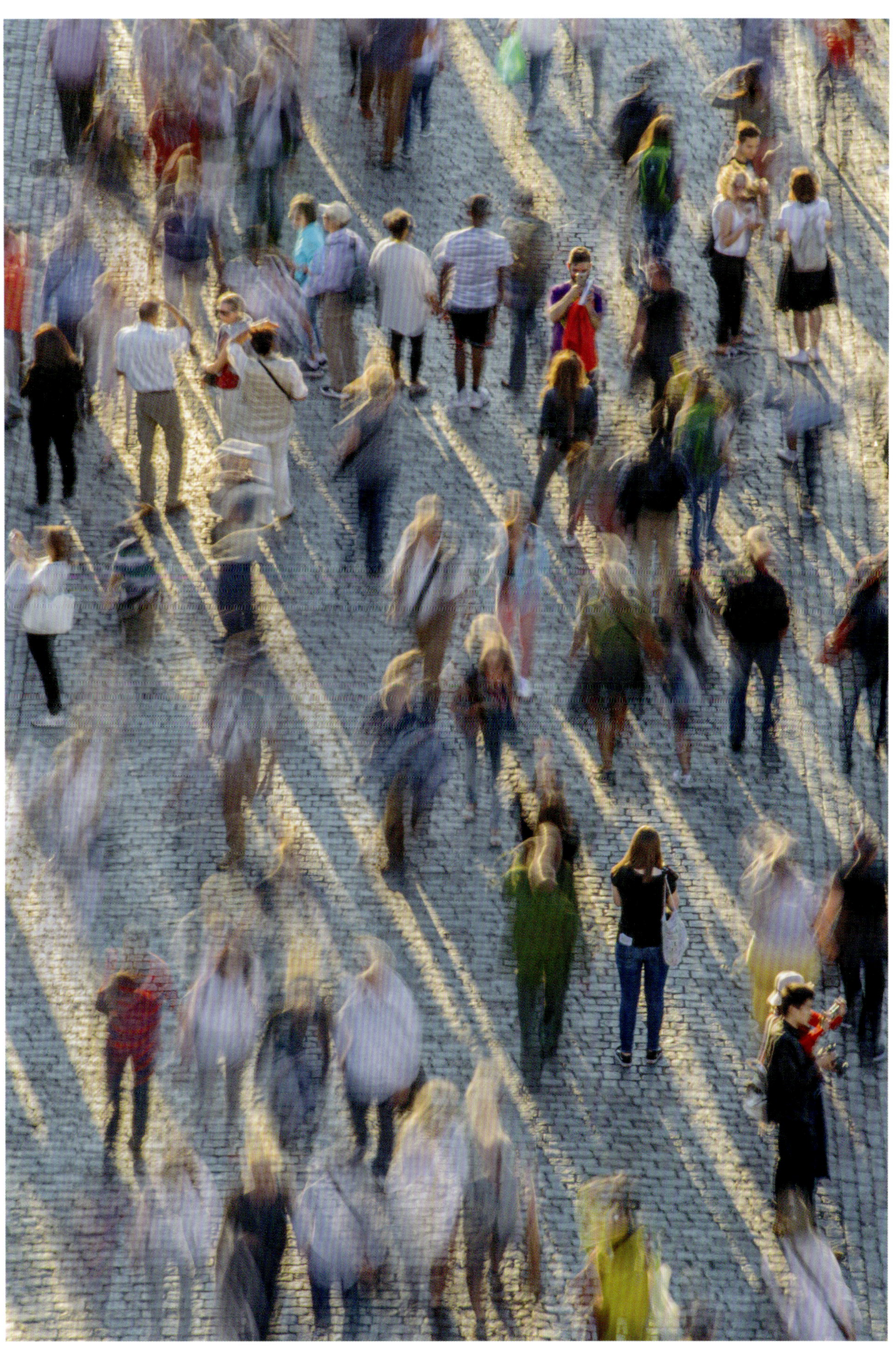

While in New York City's Times Square, I stood atop bright red stairs and watched the huge crowds. With my aperture stopped down all the way to *f*/32 and the addition of a 3-stop ND filter, I was able to get a correct exposure reading at a 1/2 sec. shutter speed with my ISOset to 50. As I pressed the shutter, I swiped from left to right while zooming the lens from a focal length of about 35mm to the longer focal length of 100mm. Swiping is nothing more than moving the camera up, down, left, right, or even in an S-shape movement *during* a slow exposure of 1/2 sec. or 1 second, with a twist. The result is this high-energy crowd shot. Are we having fun or what?

Swiping was perhaps first done as an artistic technique by nature photographers. The first swipe I saw was way back in 1987, a swipe of aspen trees in fall color. Today the technique is applied to just about anything, but for some reason it is seldom used by street photographers. Try it while shooting crowds on the streets or at outdoor sporting events such as college games, NFL games, or Major League Baseball games. It might be just the thing to wake up any number of otherwise ho-hum subjects that you would normally walk on past.

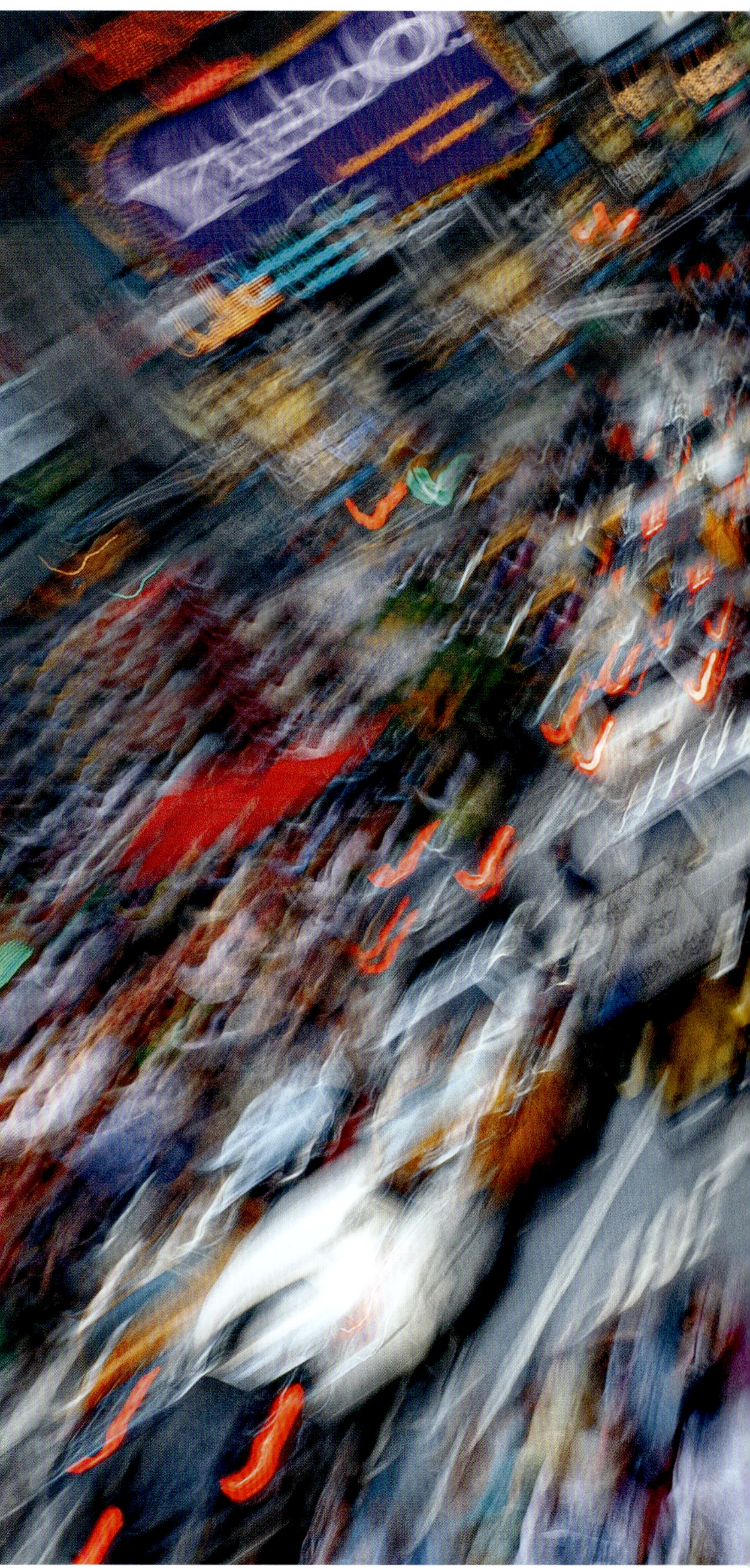

◘ Nikon D500, NIKKOR 18–300mm lens, *f*/32 for 1/2 sec. with 3-stop ND filter, ISO 50, Daylight/Sunny WB

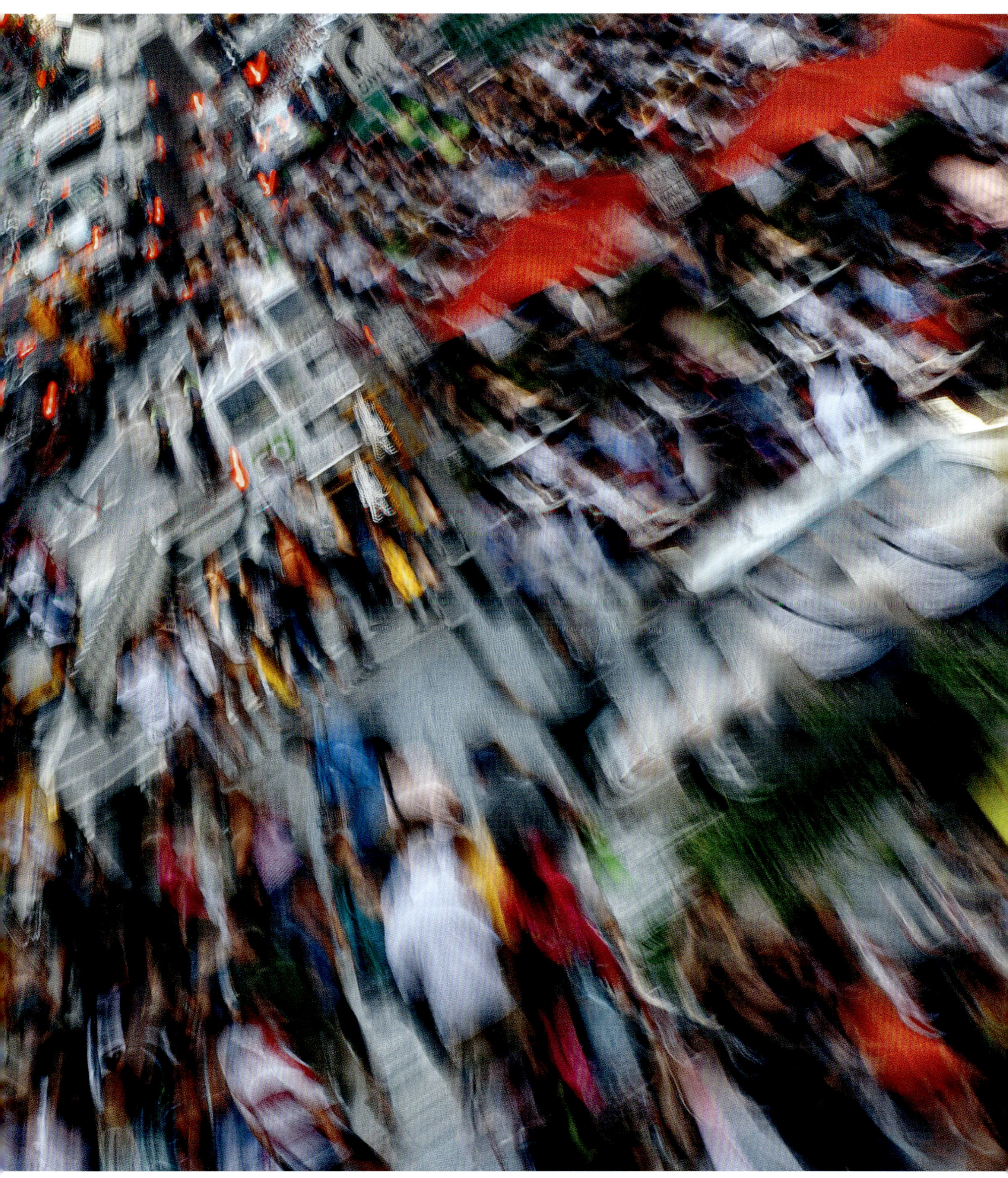

Panning

Panning is using a somewhat slow shutter speed while following the path of a moving subject with your camera and pressing the shutter release as the subject flies past. If you have tried your hand at panning, then not only do you understand the potentially deep level of frustration, but it's also entirely possible you have given up all hope of ever succeeding with it! I want to stress, however, that it's important to get back out there and fight on. Am I suggesting that panning is difficult? Absolutely! It is one of the most difficult creative shutter speed techniques. But I have witnessed many times the deep joy that comes when a student finally accomplishes what some might consider a monumental feat in the photographic world.

Here are the keys to panning:

1. Cradle the camera so the base sits flat in the palm of your hand. Use your other hand to hold the camera firmly from the side. If your lens has an image stabilization (IS) or vibration reduction (VR) switch, make sure it is in the "on" position, as this will help stabilize the camera.
2. Choose an area of moving subjects that can be framed against a busy background, such as a wall of graffiti or city storefronts. Do not attempt to pan against a solid-colored wall, since effective panning relies on contrast between the moving subject and the background.
3. As the subject enters the frame, move in the same left-to-right (or right-to-left) direction and *at the same speed* as the subject. If possible, always keep the moving subject in the first third of your frame.
4. Consider shooting a series of shots at 1/30 sec., 1/25 sec., 1/20 sec., and 1/15 sec. You will see a clear difference in overall sharpness of the moving subject as well as a difference in the streaked background.

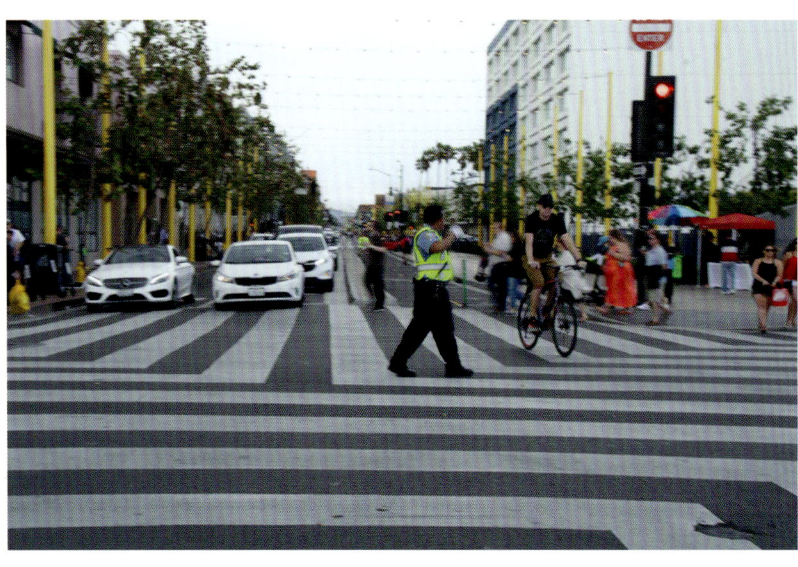

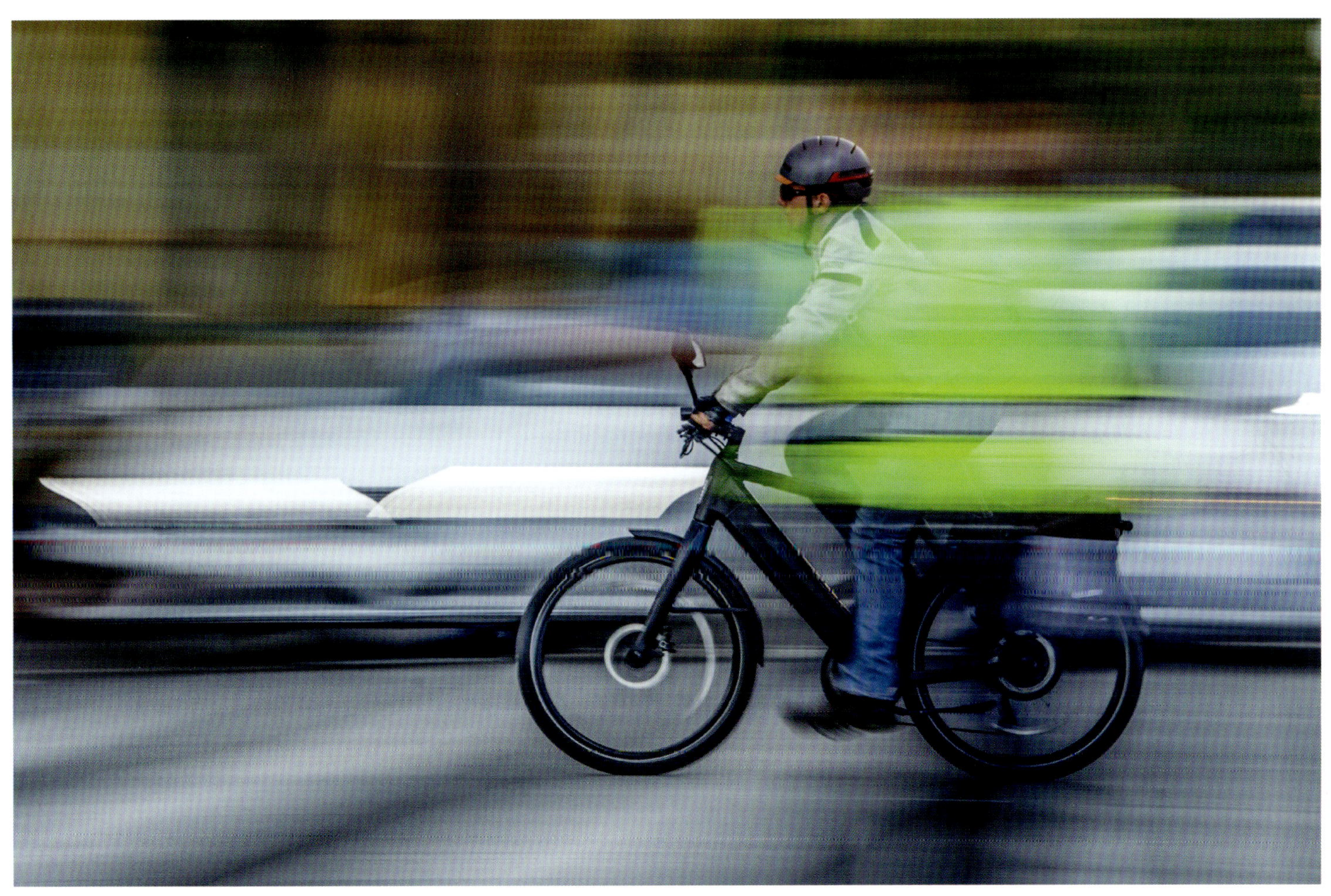

I was on the streets of Santa Monica, California, photographing skateboarders and bicyclists, my back to the entrance to the famous Santa Monica pier. Many people were out on this summer Sunday afternoon under high overcast skies. As I panned a passing bicyclist, moving my camera from right to left, I was absolutely *not* expecting that my moving camera would also record a police officer directing traffic in a greenish-yellow safety vest, creating a welcome whoosh of color that elevates the overall composition. (You can see the police officer I am talking about in the photo on the previous page.) The street continues to be my greatest photography teacher, offering up a plethora of unexpected lessons that I can put in my notebook and call upon later, wherever I am.

◘ Nikon D850, NIKKOR 24–120mm lens, *f*/22 for 1/15 sec., ISO 50, Daylight/Sunny WB

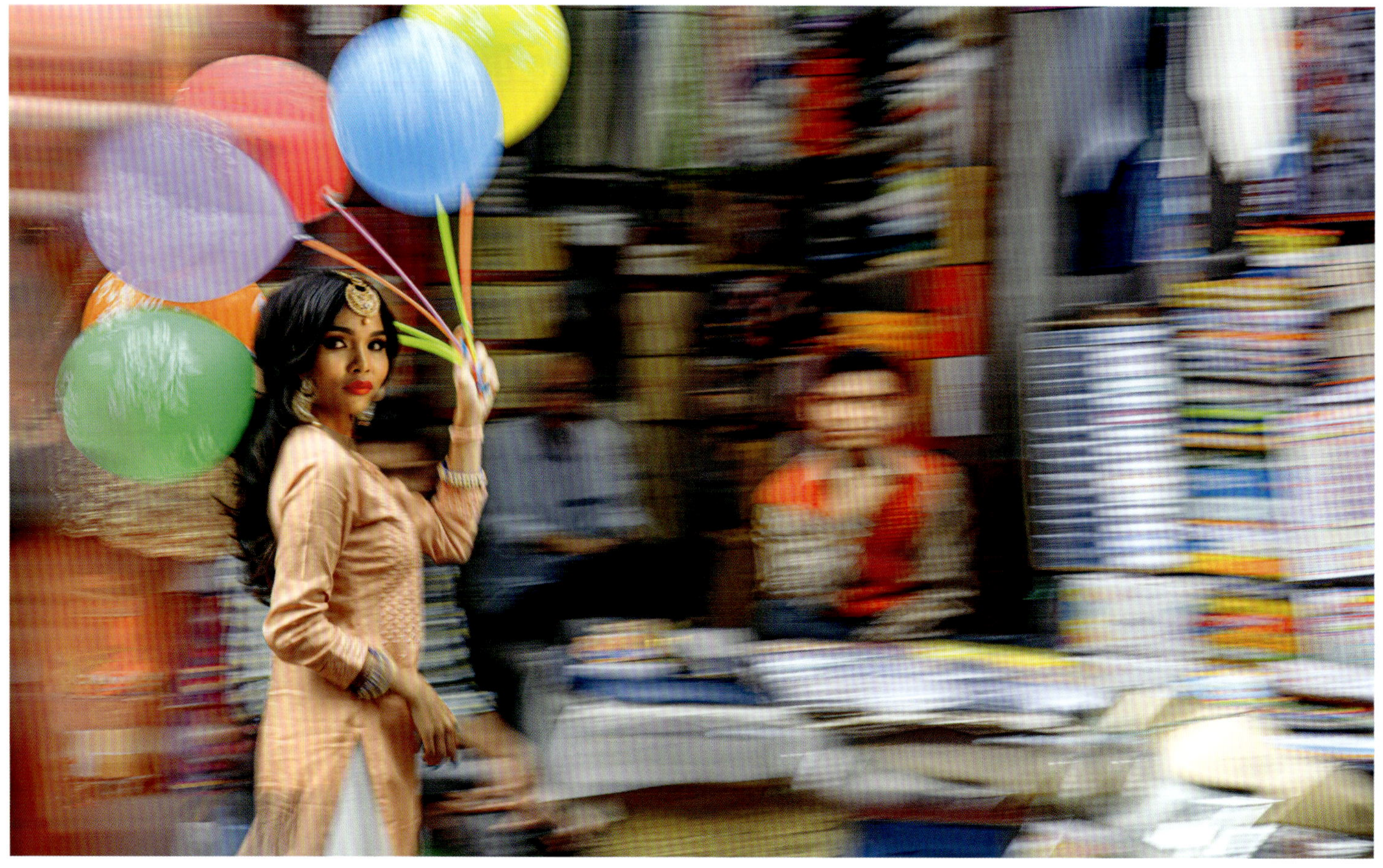

They say the secret to convincing everyone just how talented you are is to destroy each and every failed image, sharing only the really great ones. I don't know whether anyone actually destroys their failures, but I do believe that it is important to show only your best work. As an instructor, however, I find it useful to also share the failures when it serves a purpose.

Here, you can see the "winning" image of makeup artist and model Nattakun Plaengdee walking down the streets of Chandni Chowk, in Old Delhi, India. I've also included two images that fell short—and these are actually just two of the more than thirty images that failed for reasons of focus or exposure. Failures like these are especially common when shooting action and motion sequences. Even though this is a staged shoot, the nature of panning involves an incredibly high failure rate, which is why shouts of joy are often heard in my workshops when a student records a successful pan.

After purchasing a cluster of colorful balloons, I asked Natt to walk back and forth, passing in front of the many businesses while I panned her. I followed her with my camera, moving left to right (or right to left), all the while shooting in Aperture Priority at *f*/16, with an ISO of 50, which produced shutter speeds of 1/20 sec., 1/15 sec., and 1/25 sec. at various times. The photo above is the *only* one of more than thirty attempts that was perfectly executed; Natt's face is sharp, while everything else around her is a streaked blur, to a lesser or greater degree. As you may know, I am fond of saying "You keep shooting!" and this is certainly a very good example of why.

◘ Nikon D850, NIKKOR 24–120mm lens, *f*/16 for 1/20 sec., ISO 50, Daylight/Sunny WB

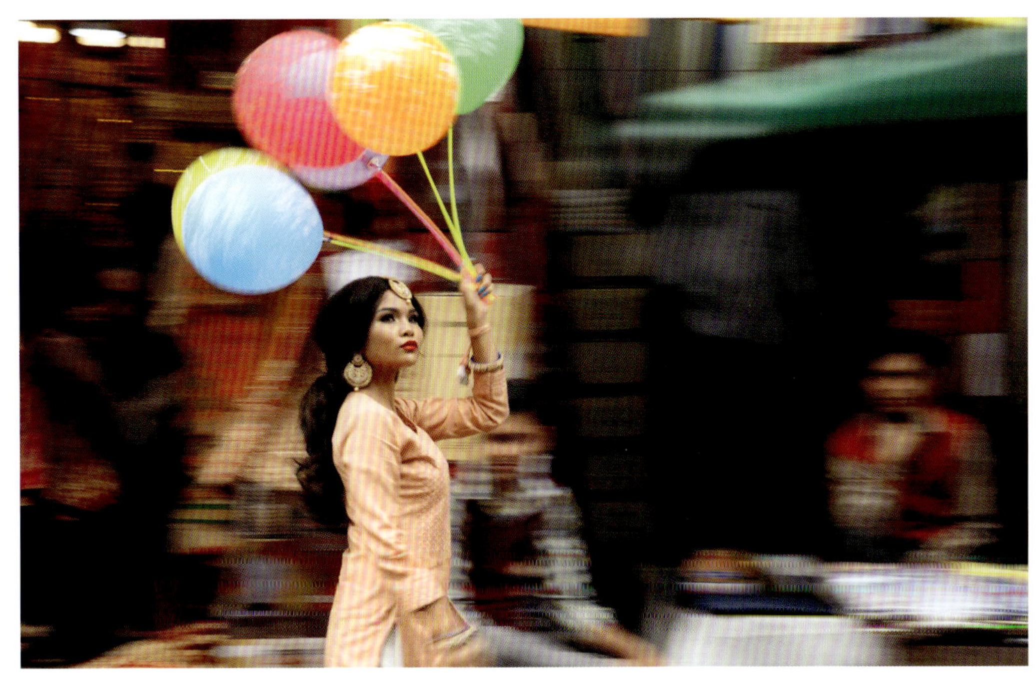

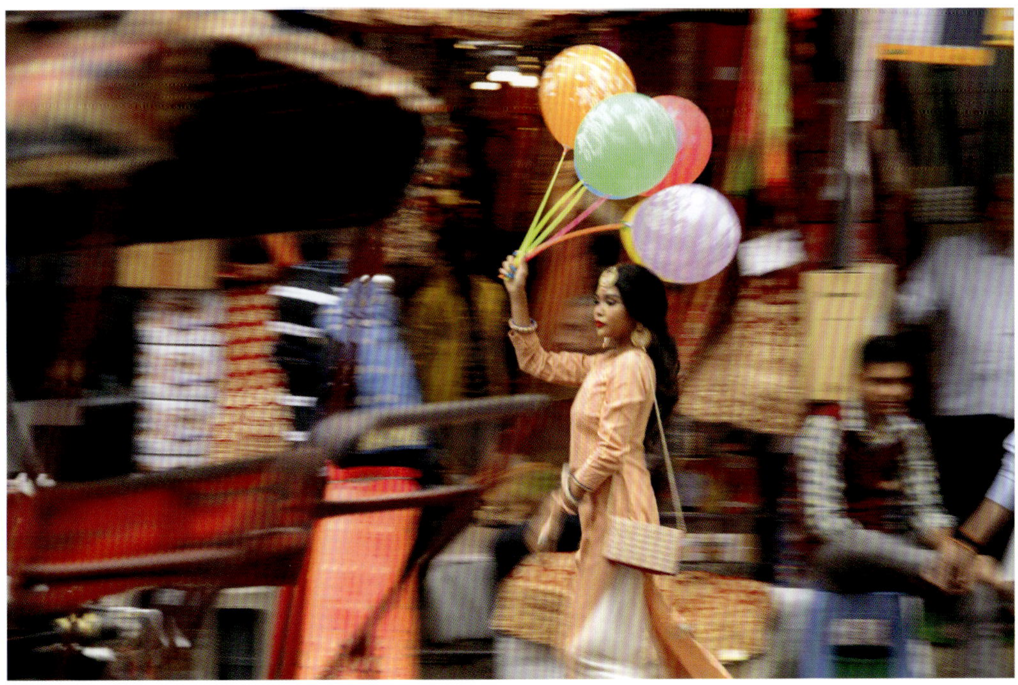

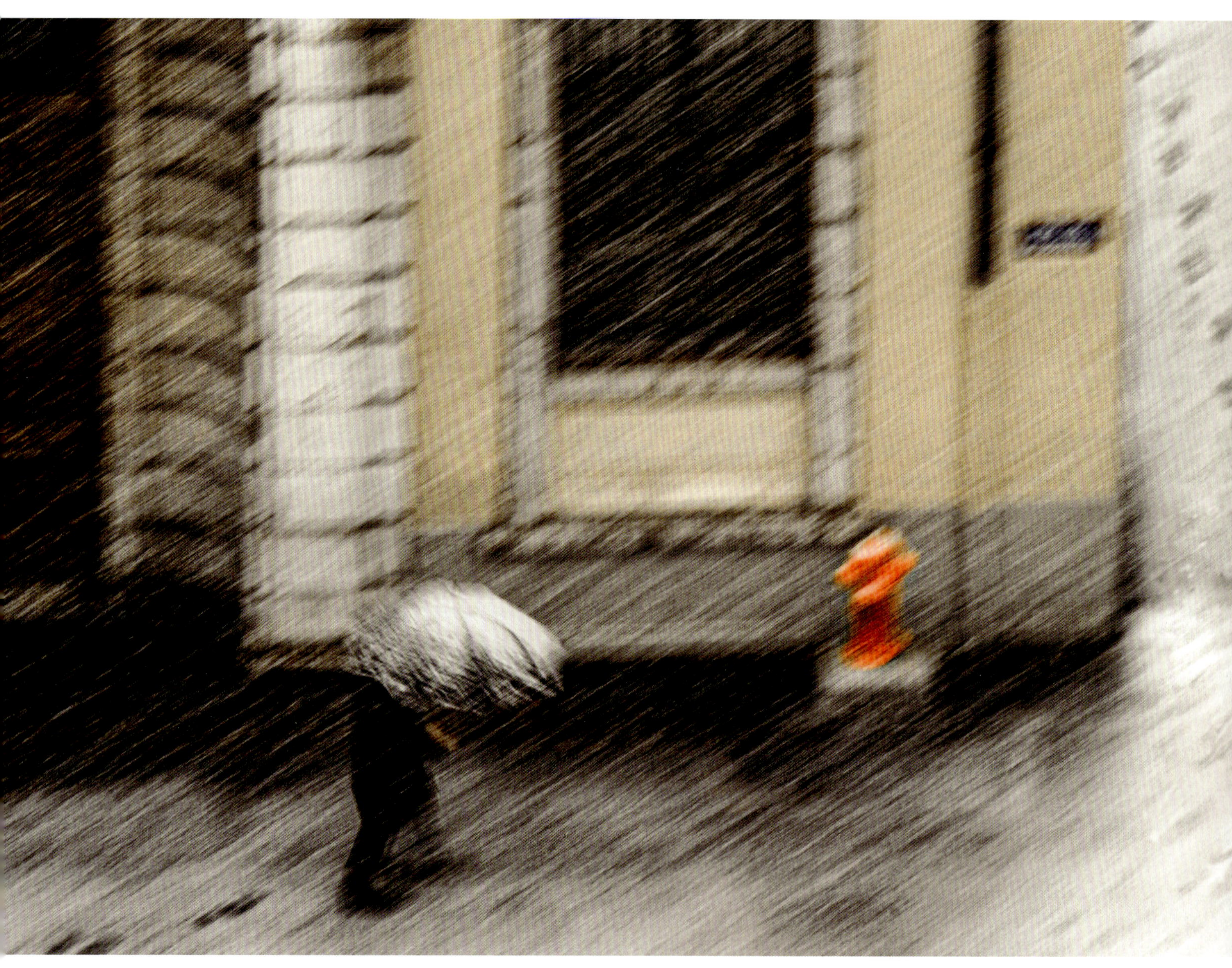

During one memorable trip to Lyon, France, we had a few days of extreme cold. How cold was it, you ask? It was so cold that the pickpockets were sticking their hands into strangers' pockets just to stay warm. It was so cold you could hear my 88-year-old neighbor's dentures chattering in the glass. It was so cold the politicians had their hands in their *own* pockets. But I digress!

I did find time to shoot the storm, even if I did so mostly from the deck of my hotel room, shooting for a few seconds, then dashing back inside to warm up, then going outside again. But cold or not, people were out on the streets, and one man with his trusty umbrella made it worth my venturing out. While shooting for 1/30 sec., I also panned the camera in the same direction he was walking, which happened to be the opposite of the driving snow, thus rendering even longer streaks of snow.

◘ Nikon D300S, NIKKOR 35–70mm lens, *f*/22 for 1/30 sec., ISO 200, Cloudy WB

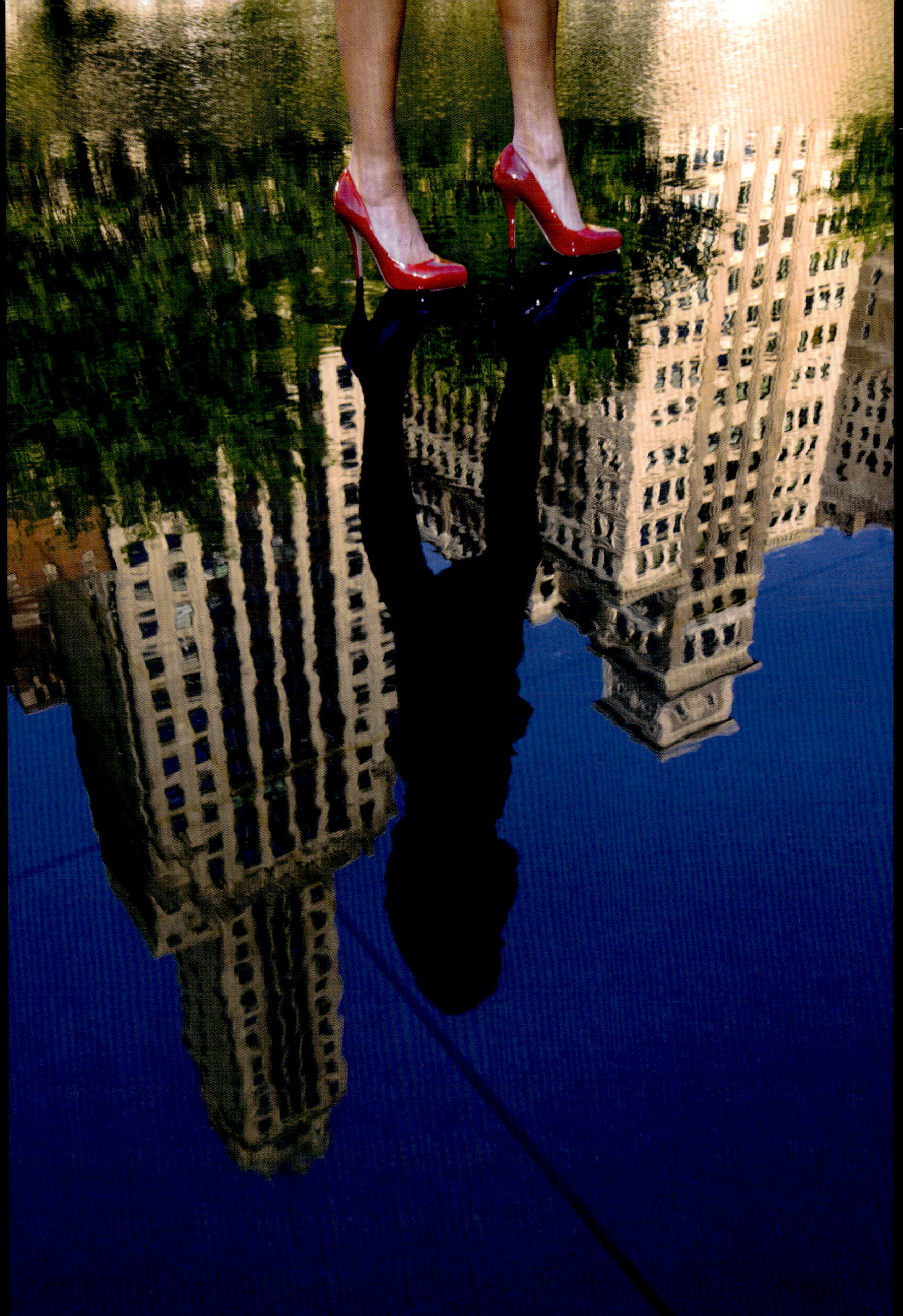

SEEKING THE ABSTRACT

Abstracts

Cities are filled with so much material that any street shooter with a love of abstracts, textures, and graffiti will have no reason to travel elsewhere other than falling victim to that old adage, "familiarity breeds contempt." Seriously, I have been known to spend an entire week in a single automotive junkyard, only reluctantly moving on to other matters that needed my attention.

Junkyards, found on many city streets, are a paradise of color and texture, line and shape. Graffiti provides colorful, often poignant opportunities to incorporate only a portion of the work, enabling the photographer to create their own art piece. There are abstract opportunities in high-rise buildings, reflections that are often a warped and distorted view of the actual surroundings. And of course, there is the glass itself, streaming or beaded with rain at bus stops and storefronts, as well as textured and wrinkled plastic. Textures provide abundant artistic material, and when used as background the abstract element of texture often contributes more to the success of an image than the identifiable subject does. Let's take an abstract journey and expand the possibilities of street photography.

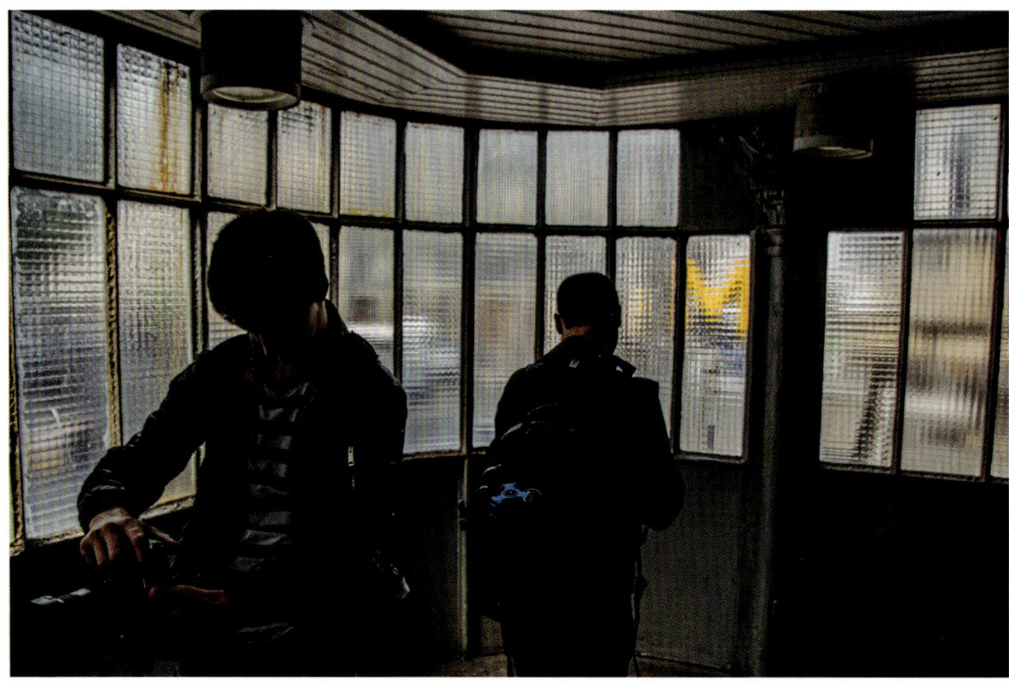

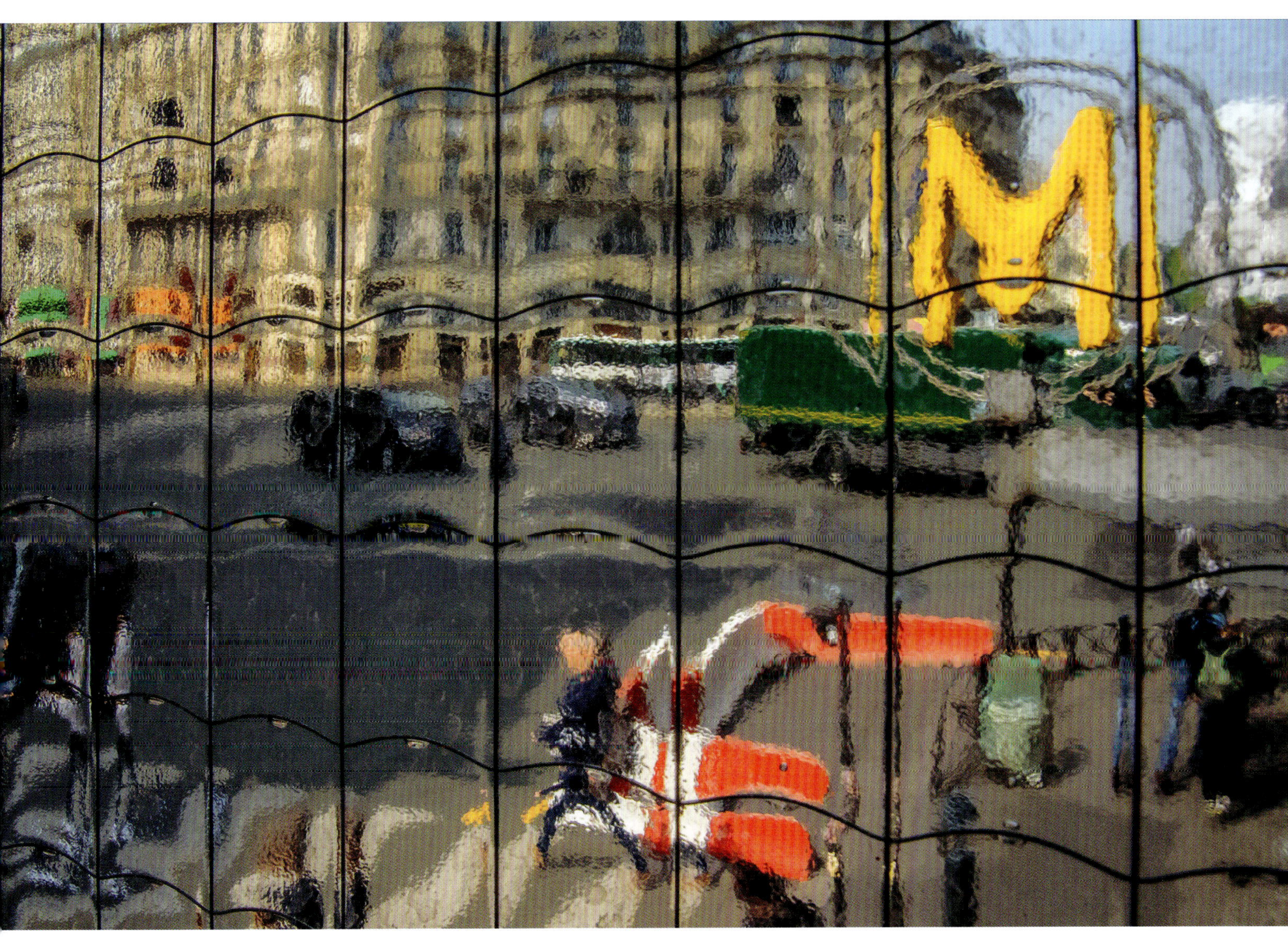

Two of my students and I had just come up the steps at a metro station in Paris when I caught sight of some really old-style windows made of glass and wire mesh (see previous page). It was surely an abstract opportunity, and our goal was to combine this textured foreground with the Parisian street in the background.

What was most critical for a shot like this was a massive depth of field to render any semblance of an interesting background in focus, so I set my aperture to *f*/22 on my 10–24mm lens, shooting at the focal length of 13mm and focusing on the foreground glass window. The resulting image revealed an abstracted view of the street beyond the textured window, just as I had hoped.

◘ Nikon D500, NIKKOR 10–24mm lens at 12mm on a tripod, *f*/22 for 1/100 sec., ISO 320, Daylight/Sunny WB

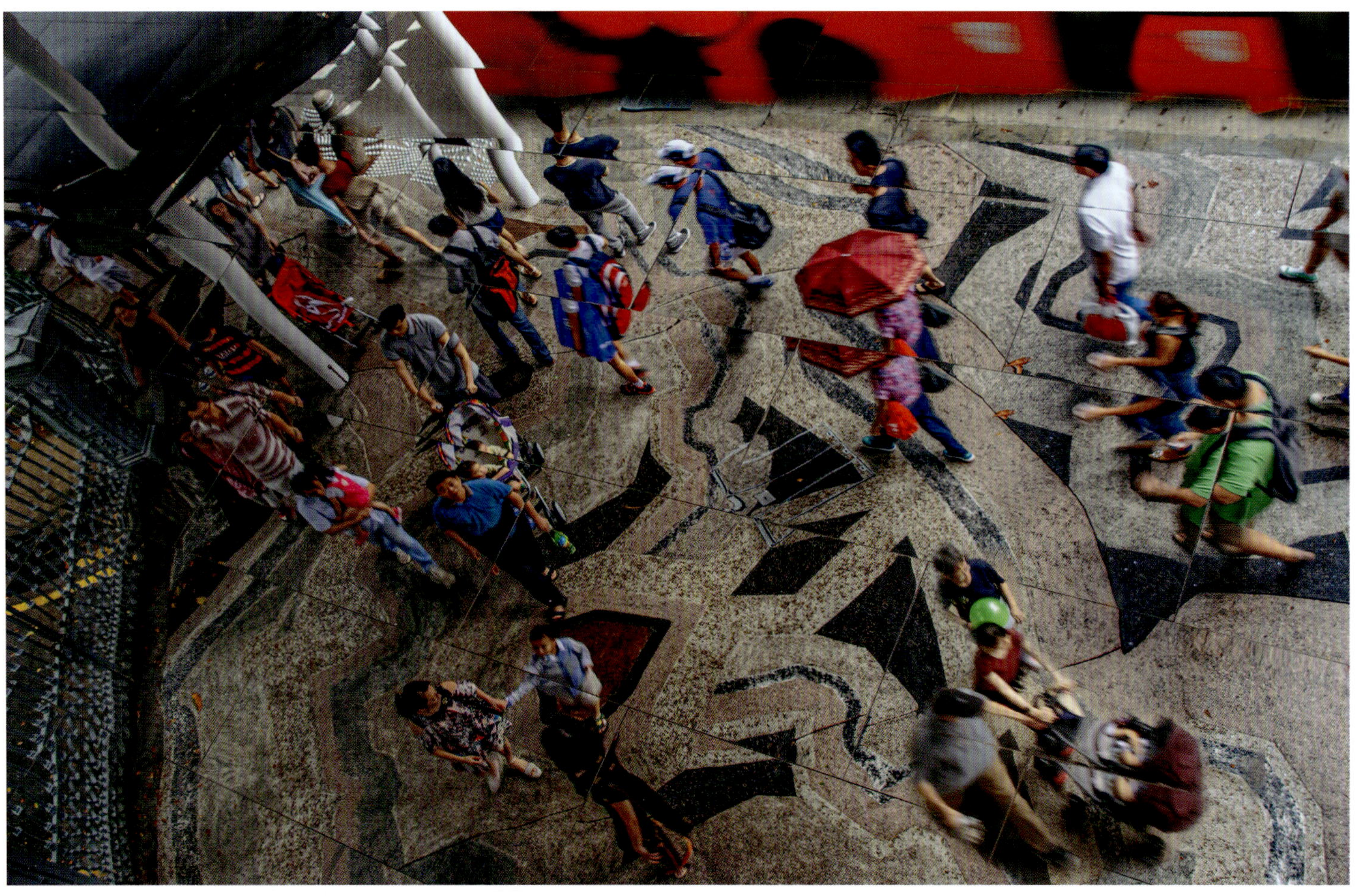

Expanding your vision has much to do with understanding and embracing the unique visions of the various lenses most photographers carry as we walk about the world we live in, hopeful of returning with spoils from the hunt. How well do you know your 16–35mm lens, your 24–70mm lens, and your 70–300mm lens? When we reformulate our conventional vision with the unique visions of our lenses, from super wide to super telephoto and super close-ups, compelling images really are plentiful. Combine this with a willingness to look at not only what's in front of you but also what is below and above you, and the world begins to really open up! Here is an example of simply looking up and discovering that a wonderful abstract was mine for the taking, thanks to a mirrored ceiling at a bus stop in Singapore.

◘ Nikon D850, NIKKOR 24–120mm lens, *f*/14 for 1/320 sec., ISO 640, Daylight/Sunny WB

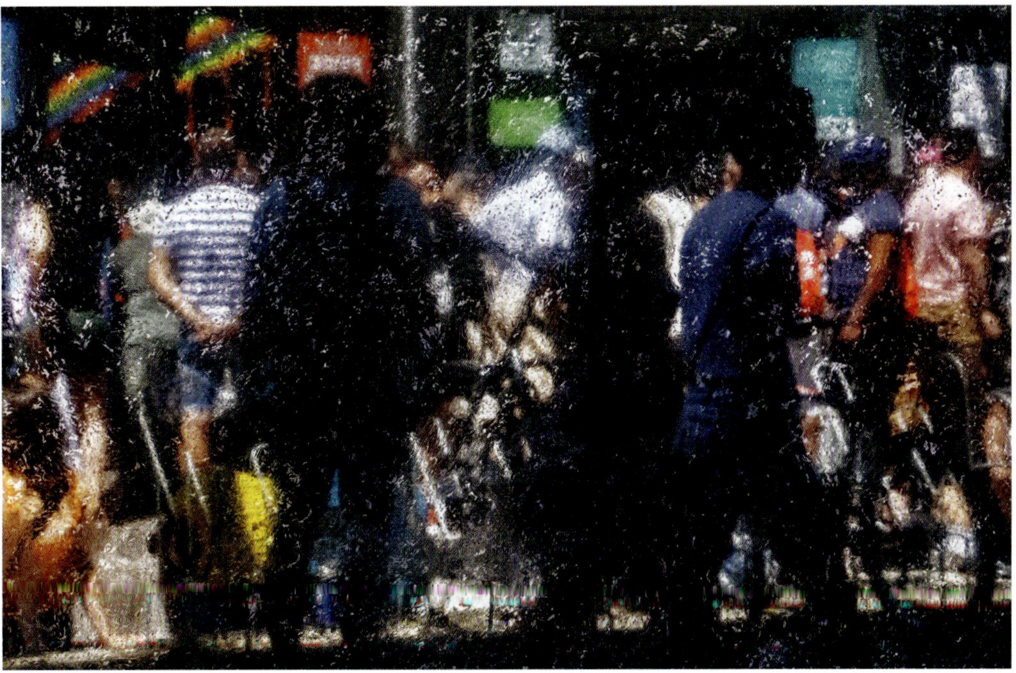

During one Turinto workshop, I shocked a couple of my students by calling attention to the shots they were both passing up. As I explained that the shot in question was right in front of them, the first student replied, "The only thing in front of us is a black granite wall."

"Yes," I said, "it is a black, shiny, *highly reflective* black granite wall. Look again. Do you see the reflections of the people on the street?"

"Not really," was the unified reply.

I showed them how to use the smallest aperture available on their lens and focus on the surface of the granite, setting their exposure to at least -1 to compensate for the meter's wish to overexpose all that black into gray. My students' initial reluctance was soon followed by exclamations of "Oh my God!" and "Oh wow, that's cool!"

A black, shiny granite building: who would have thought it held any photographic potential? It's safe to say that now two of my students do—and perhaps you do as well.

◘ Nikon D500, NIKKOR 18–300mm lens, *f*/36 for 1/40 sec., ISO 400, Daylight/Sunny WB

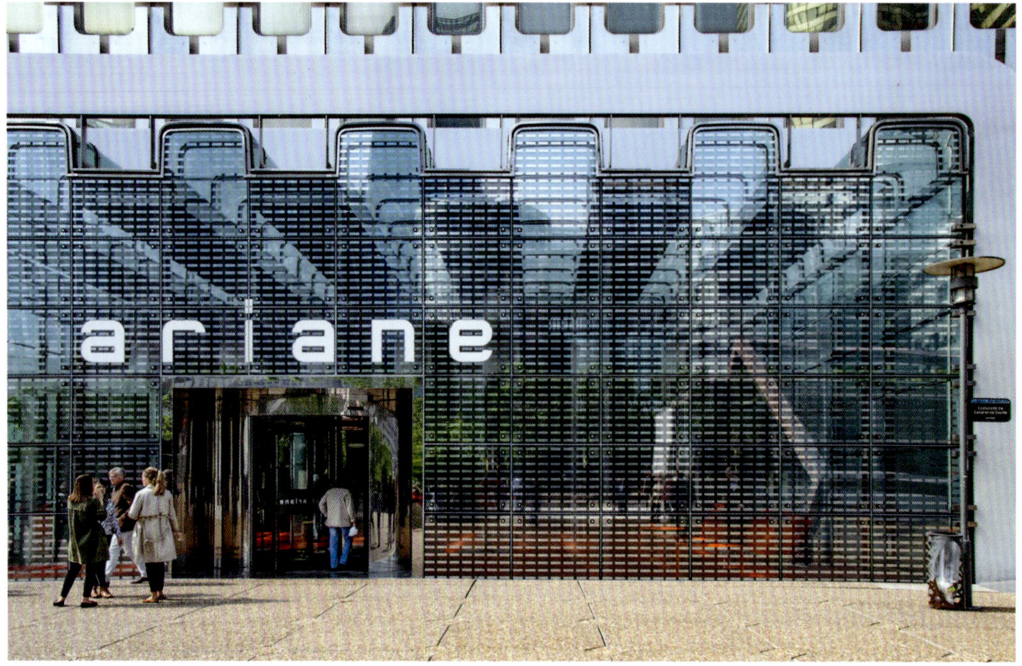

Even in the smallest towns and cities, reflections in the windows of ground-floor offices abound, even if only of the grocery store or gas station across the street.

I was looking for photographic opportunities in the La Défense area of Paris, an ultra-modern office park with a number of skyscrapers. One particular office building stood out; it was not all that tall, the exterior windows had a white checkerboard pattern, and thanks to a well-lit interior, I was able to see subjects inside at the same time as reflections in the glass of people passing by outside. It was a dream location with vast potential, but it was also a frustrating location, since on this day, over the course of more than two hours, not many people were inside or passing by outside. It was like *knowing* you were at the perfect fishing hole but, for whatever reason, the fish were simply not biting. I did eventually get one shot that I really liked, shown on the next page. It was lucky that the interior furnishings of the building were red, offering contrast to the lone woman dressed in black reflected in the window. Without these red furnishings, I do feel this image would have fallen flat.

◘ Nikon D500, NIKKOR 18–300mm lens, *f*/16 for 1/320 sec., ISO 400, Daylight/Sunny WB

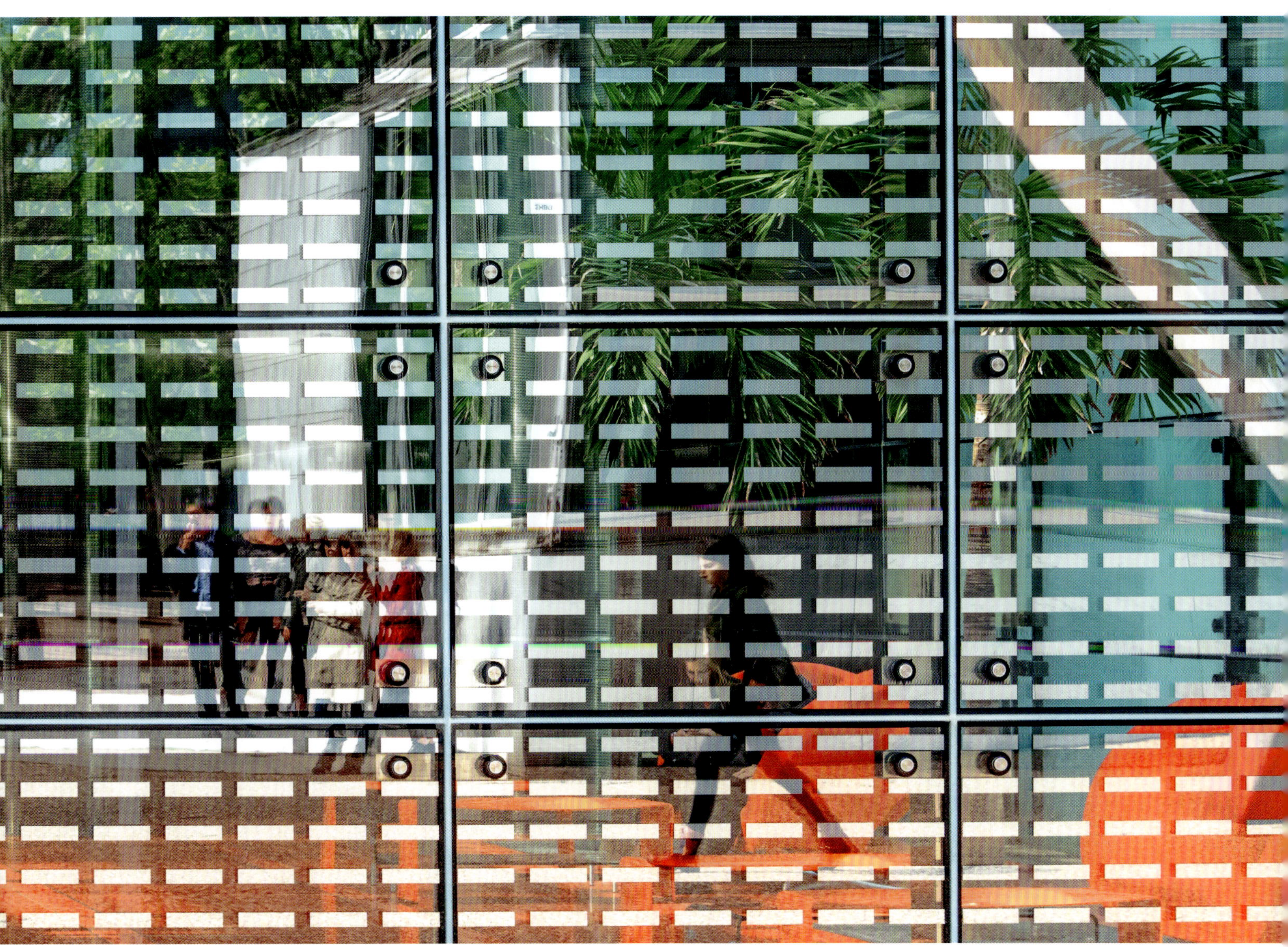

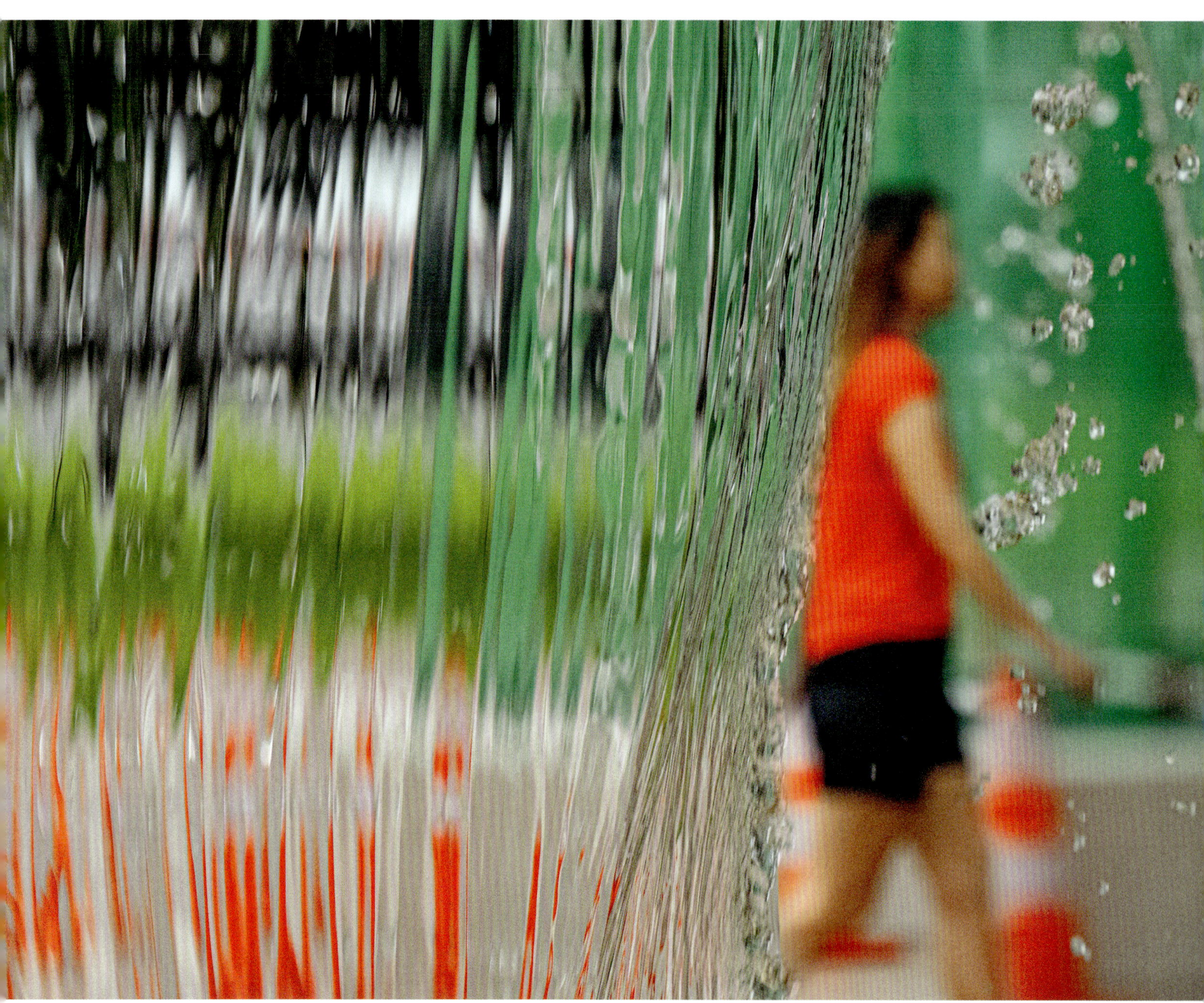

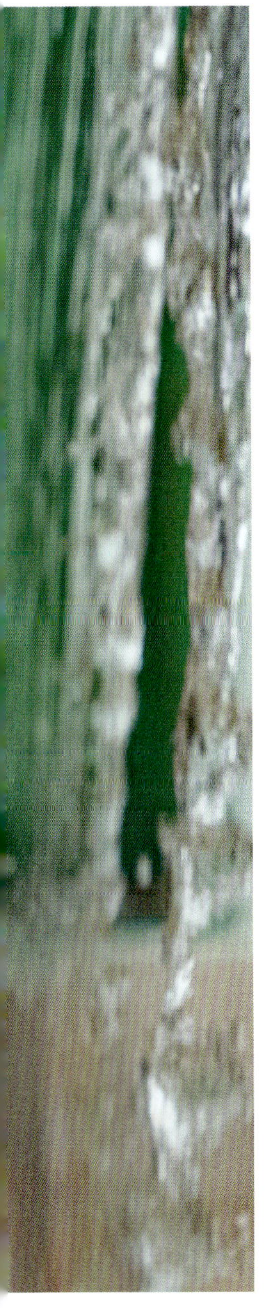

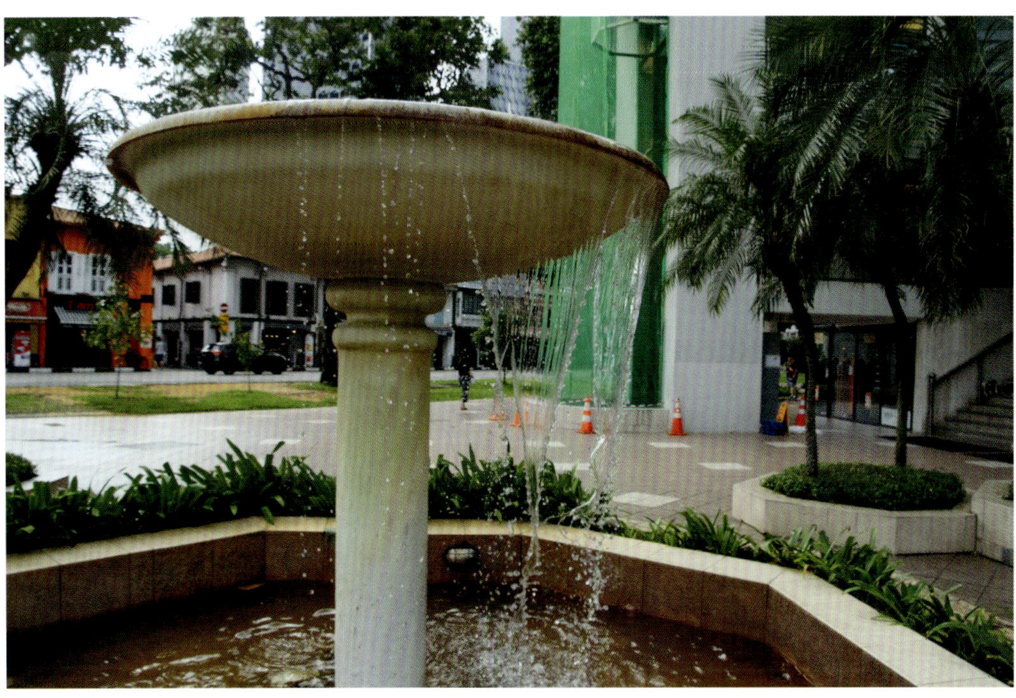

City fountains, particularly those with several overflow bowls, can be used to create a clear shower-curtain effect as the overflowing water cascades downward. If there is some degree of wind, an open "doorway" or two will often develop in that wall of water, as with this fountain I photographed near Arab Street in Singapore. My chosen composition was this open doorway, and it took a lot of patience to wait for a passerby to walk through it in the background.

Freezing action was more important than depth of field, so I first set my ISO to 400, then my shutter speed to 1/1000 sec., and adjusted my aperture until a correct exposure was indicated at *f*/10 on this moderately overcast day. The resulting image is a play of texture and colorful shapes in what may appear at first glance to be a kind of abstract reflection but in fact was a tightly controlled composition.

◘ Nikon D500, NIKKOR 18–300mm lens, *f*/10 for 1/1000 sec., ISO 400, Daylight/Sunny WB

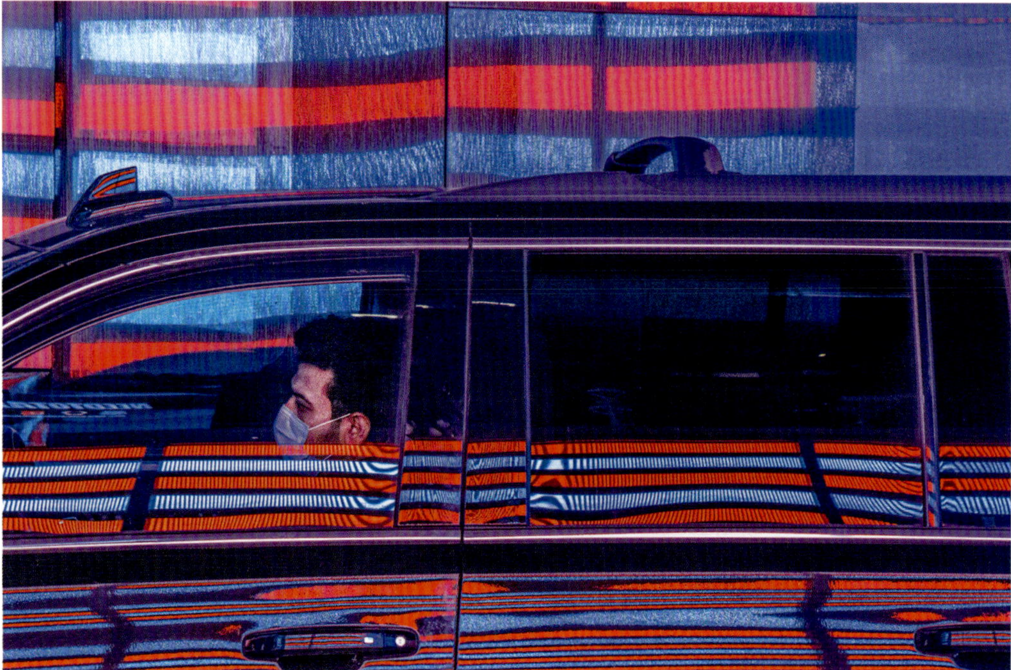

It was a Tuesday night in Manhattan, and I was outside of the Marine recruiting office in Midtown where a large illuminated American flag shines brightly onto the passing cars. When the nearby streetlight turns red, the moving cars come to a stop, unknowingly becoming patriotic flag-draped cars and trucks. Note the rare Auto WB setting, due to an overwhelming mix of light sources.

◘ Nikon D500, NIKKOR 18–300mm lens at 230mm, *f*/8 for 1/160 sec., ISO 1600, Auto WB

It is a given that Millennium Park and the adjoining Crown Fountain will be on every Chicago street photographer's shoot list, as both are magnetic locations offering a constant stream of photographic opportunities. On this day, one such opportunity was provided by an excited young woman visiting from the Czech Republic proudly posing for her boyfriend in her newly purchased red shoes. Unbeknownst to both, I was focusing solely on her red heels and her silhouette reflected in the water's shallow sheen, along with the reflections of several high-rise buildings on nearby Michigan Avenue.

Several minutes later, I introduced myself, and a conversation ensued, in which they shared their elation at discovering Nordstrom Rack (where she'd scored the red shoes), a feeling I am sure many others can appreciate. Of course, I sent the couple copies of the photos several days later; a few weeks afterward, the woman replied, saying that their time in Chicago had been a summer to remember.

◘ Nikon D810, NIKKOR 24–120mm lens, *f*/22 for 1/200 sec., ISO 400, Daylight/Sunny WB

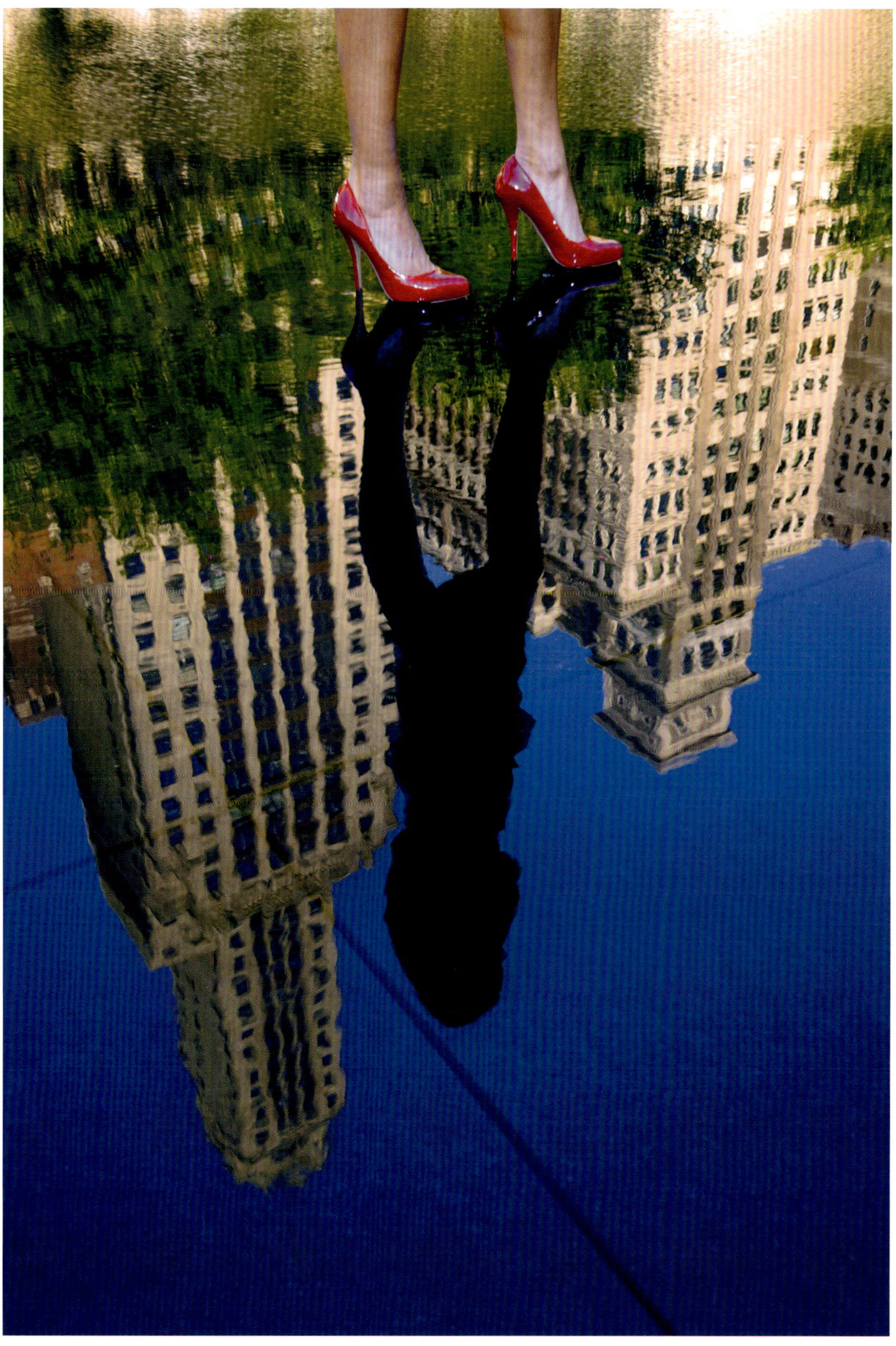

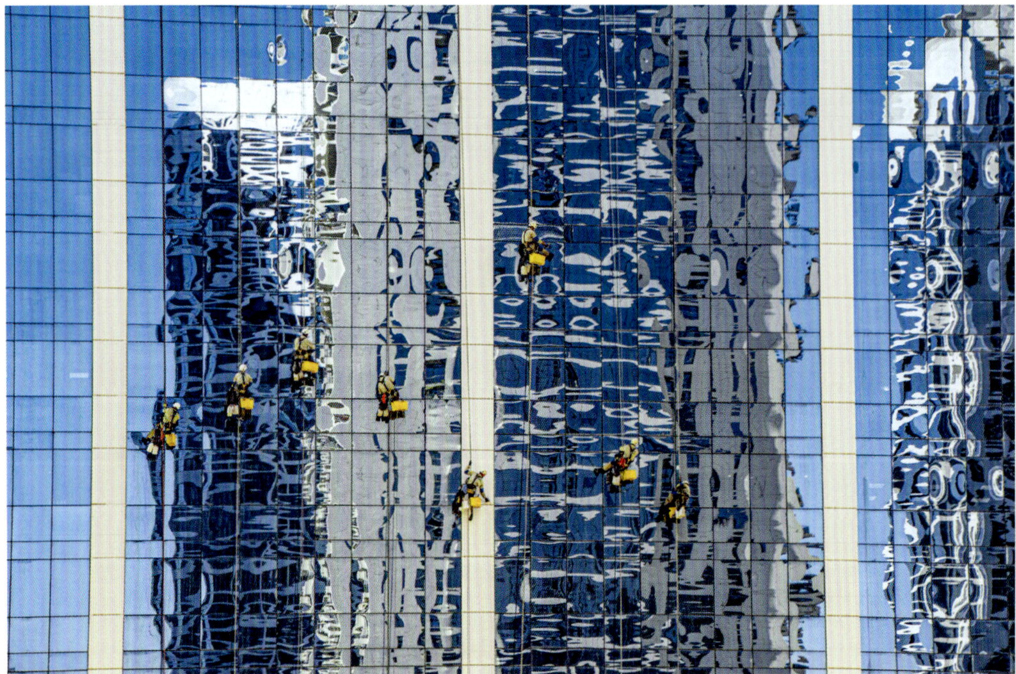

Photographic opportunity presents itself in any number of ways, not the least of which is by looking up—way up. Sometimes you get lucky and see the perfect cloud, or a murmuration of acrobatic starlings creating rolling black waves near sunset, or a tall building that showcases the reflections of neighboring buildings, rendering them as abstract textures. And then on this day: window washers!

This was a classic "Who cares?" aperture choice of *f*/11, shot in Aperture Priority. Shoot, shoot, shoot, shoot—don't stop until they stop. With each and every move, they present you with a unique and different composition. Another example of why "you keep shooting!"

◘ Nikon D500, NIKKOR 18–300mm lens, *f*/14 for between 1/250 sec. and 1/640 sec., ISO 640, Daylight/Sunny WB

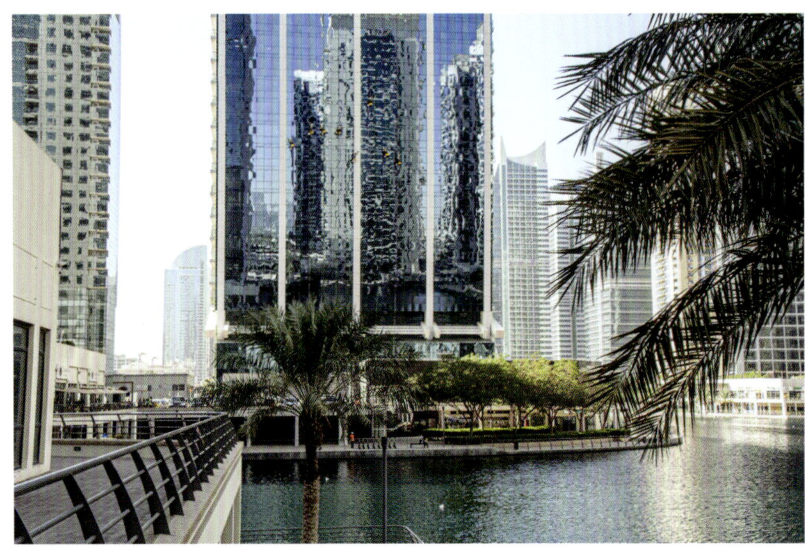

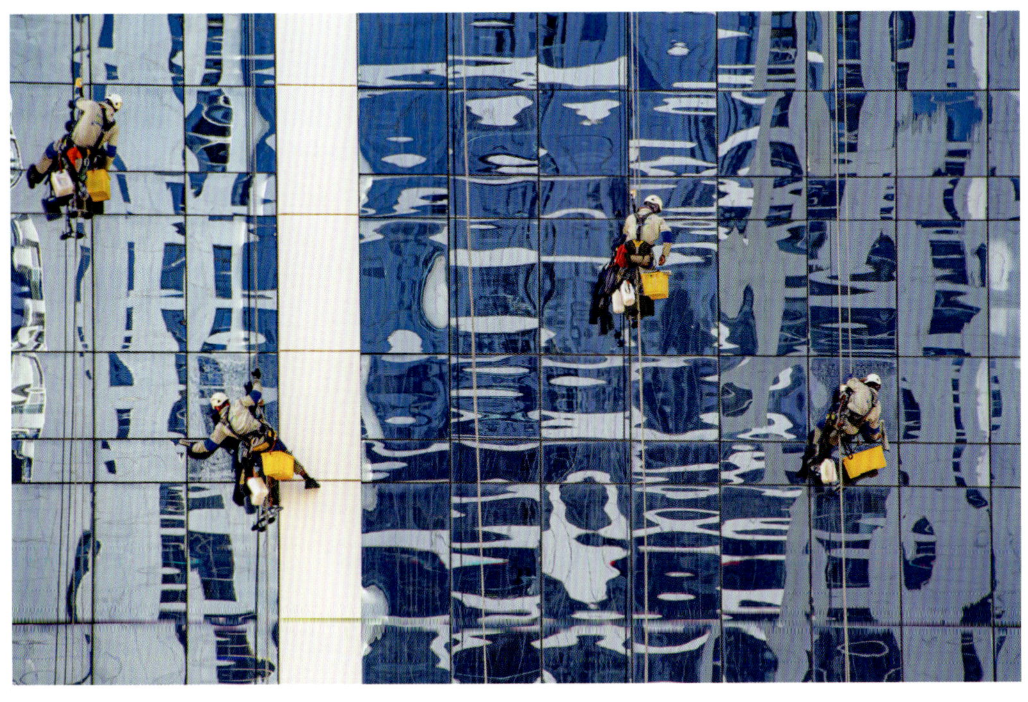

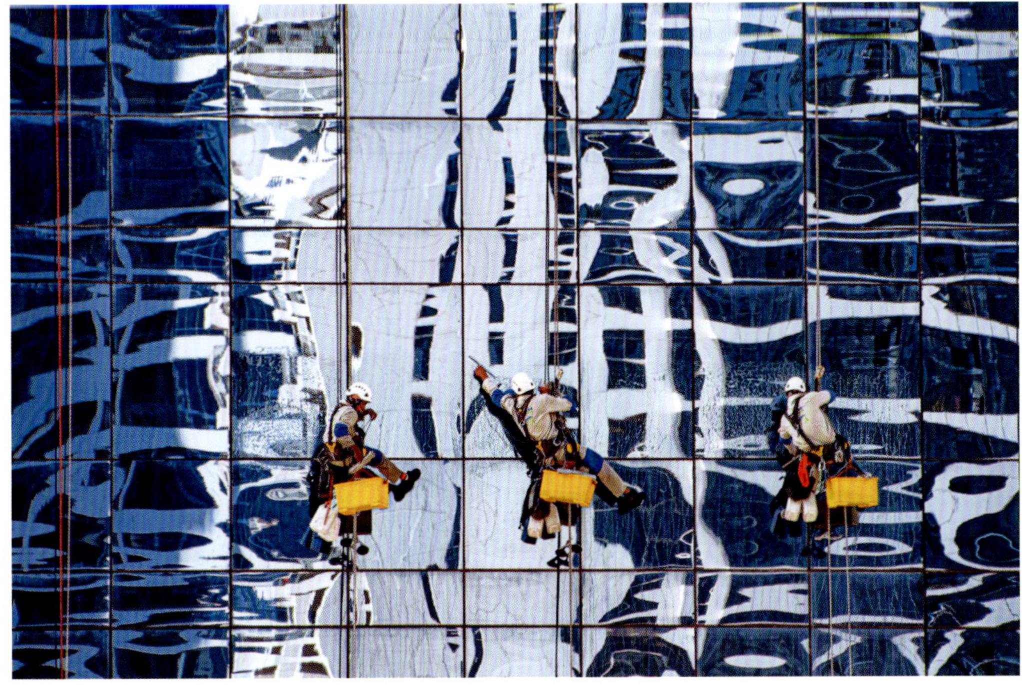

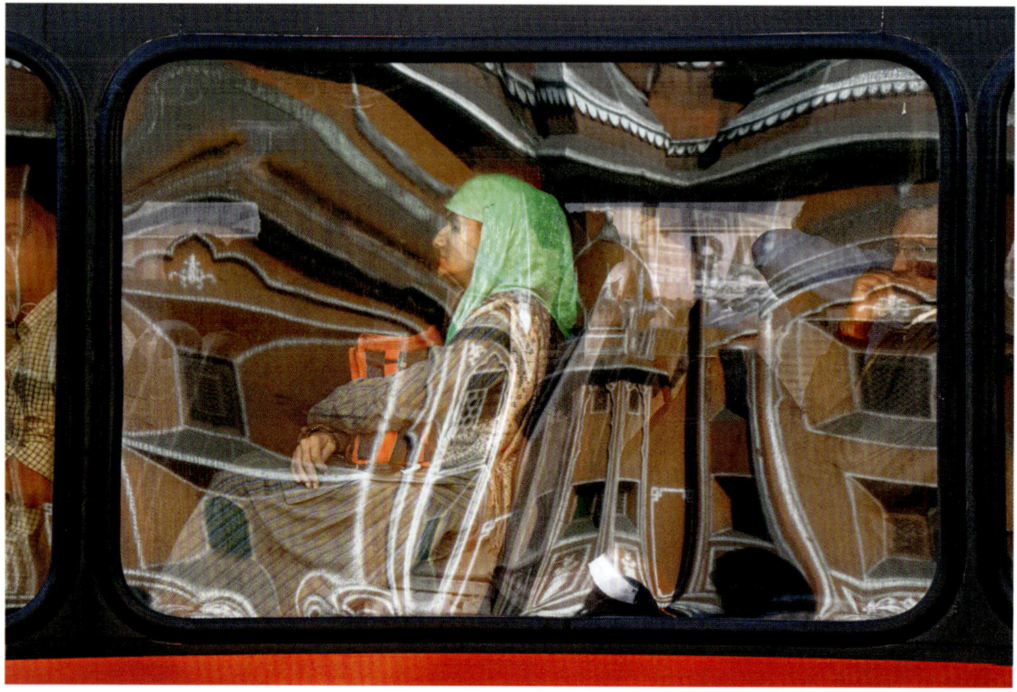

The famed Hawa Mahal palace in Jaipur, India, is a marvel of architecture and well worth visiting and photographing. But for the better part of one hour, I had my back to the palace, opting instead to shoot its reflection in the windows of buses at a bus stop across the street. When one bus was stopped due to traffic congestion, I was able to get a double exposure of sorts: an abstracted view of the palace with its pink and red sandstone, the lines of which were turned into a kind of patterned blanket, and sitting as still as can be amongst the chaos, a woman passenger on the bus, looking straight ahead and paying no mind to either the palace or me.

◘ Nikon D500, NIKKOR 18–300mm lens, *f*/16 for 1/100 sec., ISO 200, Daylight/Sunny WB

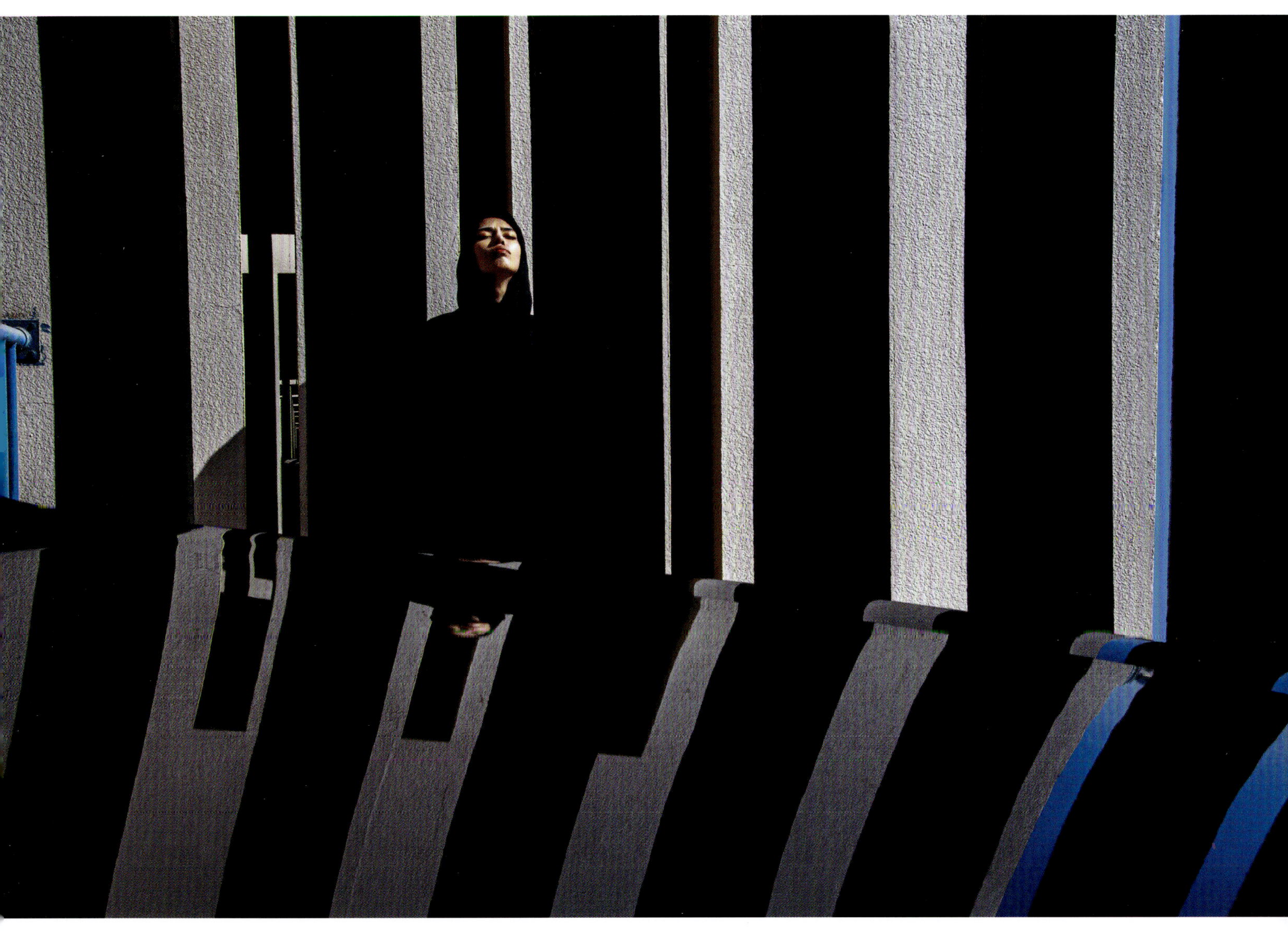

Our intention was simple: to ride the elevator to the highest floor of the parking garage and then make our way to the corner, where we hoped for an unobstructed view of the Dubai streets below. But as we stepped off the elevator, I was soon distracted by some wonderful reflections on one of the cars parked on the floor, reflections that called to mind a zebra's stripes. Soon I was taking advantage of this serendipitous opportunity, using the tried-and-true Sunny 16 exposure formula. (In post-processing, and after clicking on BASIC in Adobe Camera Raw, I intensified the contrast between light and dark by moving the black slider to the left, adding about 30.) In hindsight, I so wish that my model was wearing a red hooded sweatshirt.

◘ Nikon D850, NIKKOR 24–120mm lens at 24mm, *f*/16 for 1/100 sec., ISO 100, Daylight/Sunny WB

Texture and Macro

Whenever I speak about macro, or close-up, photography, almost without fail, everyone thinks I'm referring to nature subjects. Shooting macro on the streets has more to do with the abstract—the nicks, dings, scrapes, and dents found on cars and newspaper boxes, in parking garages, and on glass and weathered signs. When we turn our attention to the really small, forgotten details that truly are everywhere, the world of photographic subject matter quickly becomes a thousand times greater!

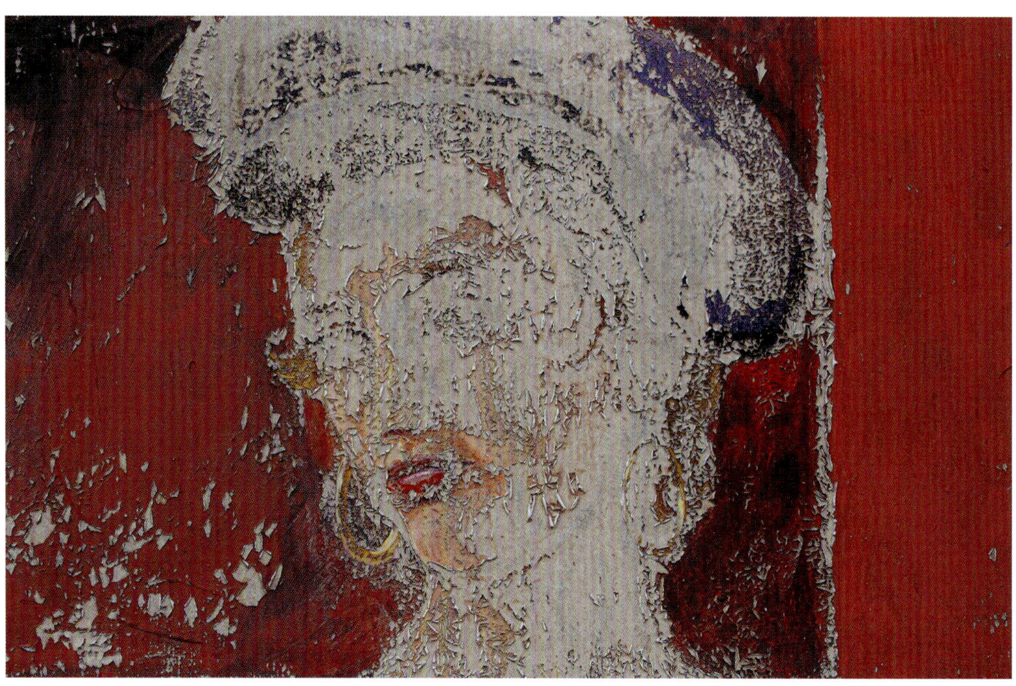

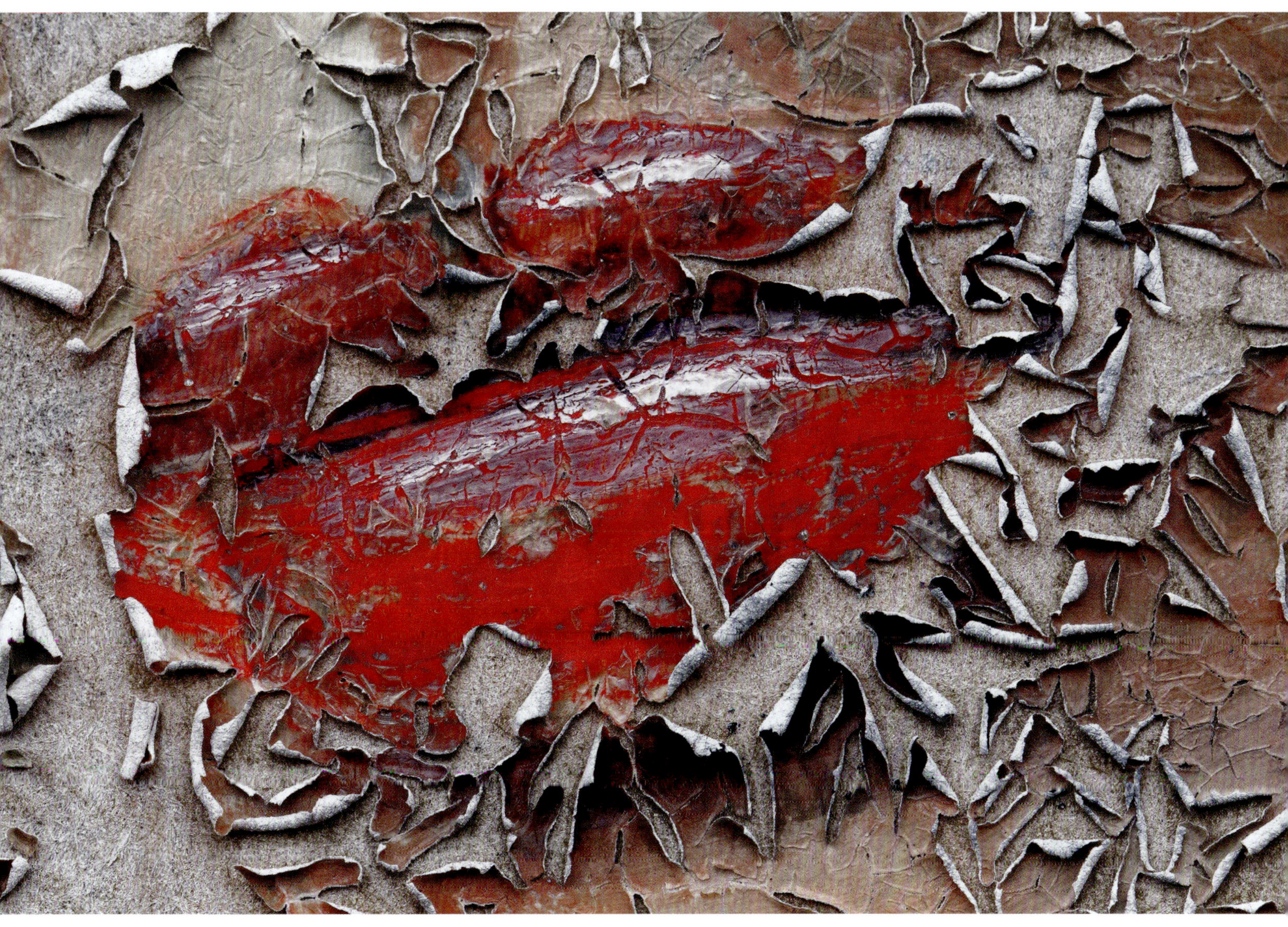

I was in Ashland, Wisconsin, when my eyes caught sight of this "chapped lips" image. Note, the photo above is an expanded view of a small detail in the photo on the previous page; so often photographers miss the macro shot, as they are too seduced by the bigger picture.

◘ **Nikon D500, Micro-NIKKOR 105mm lens, *f*/18 for 1/200 sec., ISO 400, Daylight/Sunny WB**

In my workshops around the world, one photographic subject that students continually walk past is the many reflections found on parked cars, especially dark blue or black cars. Even after I point out the reflections, students often ask, "Where? I still don't see them." But once they spot them, there is no turning back. Before you know it, they are seeing reflections in cars on every block!

One such car we came upon was in Philadelphia, and even I felt a kind of childlike enthusiasm, because this was one really colorful reflection—and you know that I love color. As with almost every abstract subject, make it a point to fill the frame with *just* the abstract, leaving no hint of the actual object the viewer might be looking at. Also, a reflection is deep, meaning that it is distant. It is *not* on the surface of the car. Therefore, you will want to use a smaller aperture for scenes like this, such as *f*/16, if not *f*/22, to grab enough front-to-back depth of field.

◘ Nikon D500, NIKKOR 18–300mm lens, *f*/22 for 1/200 sec., ISO 400, Daylight/Sunny WB

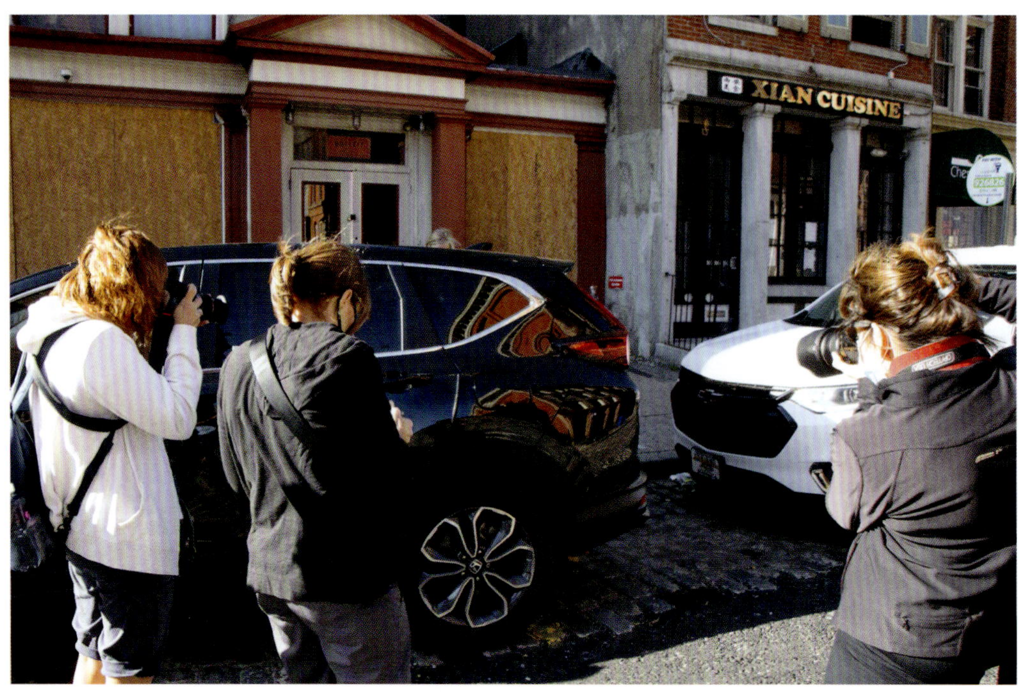

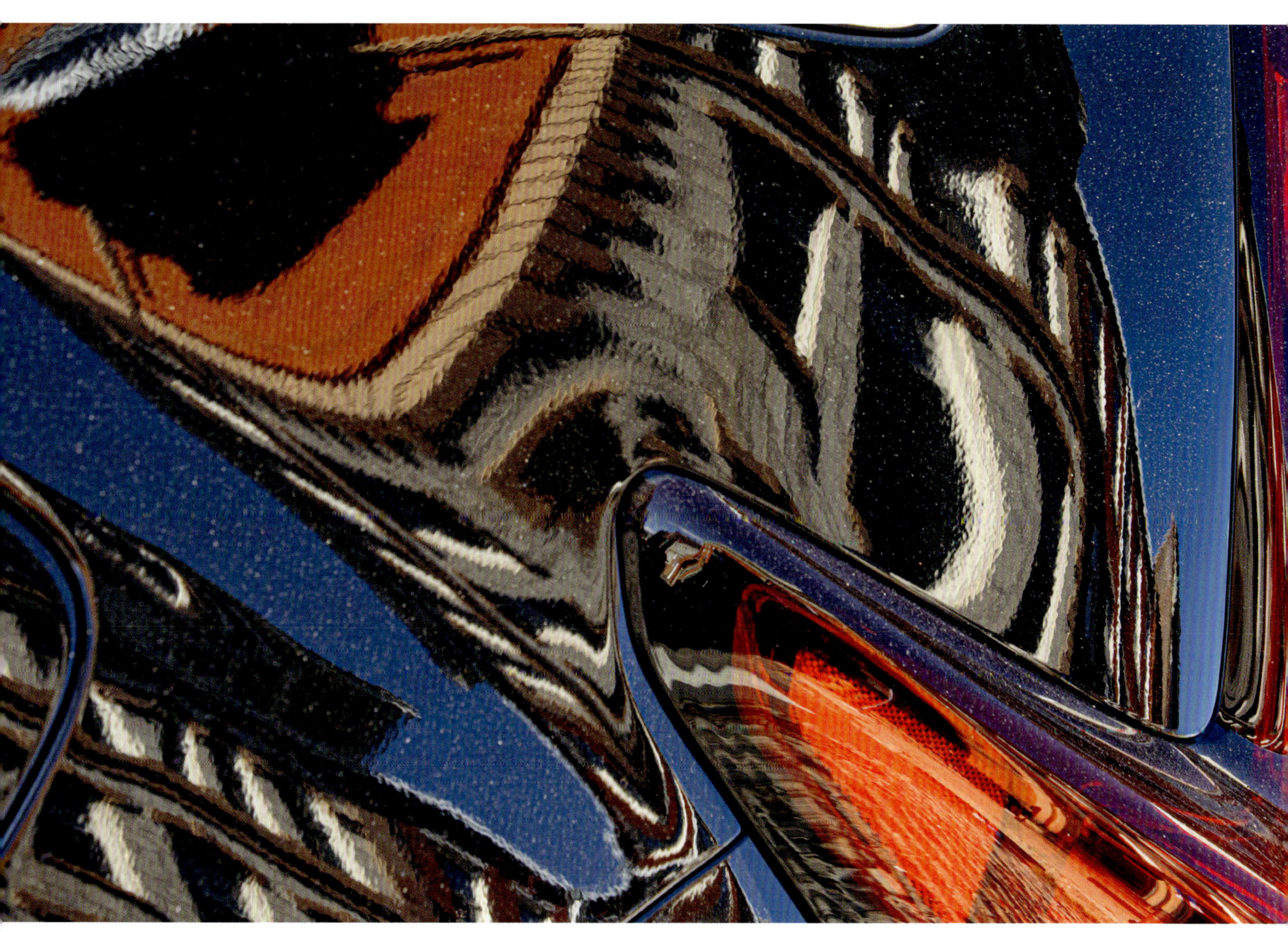

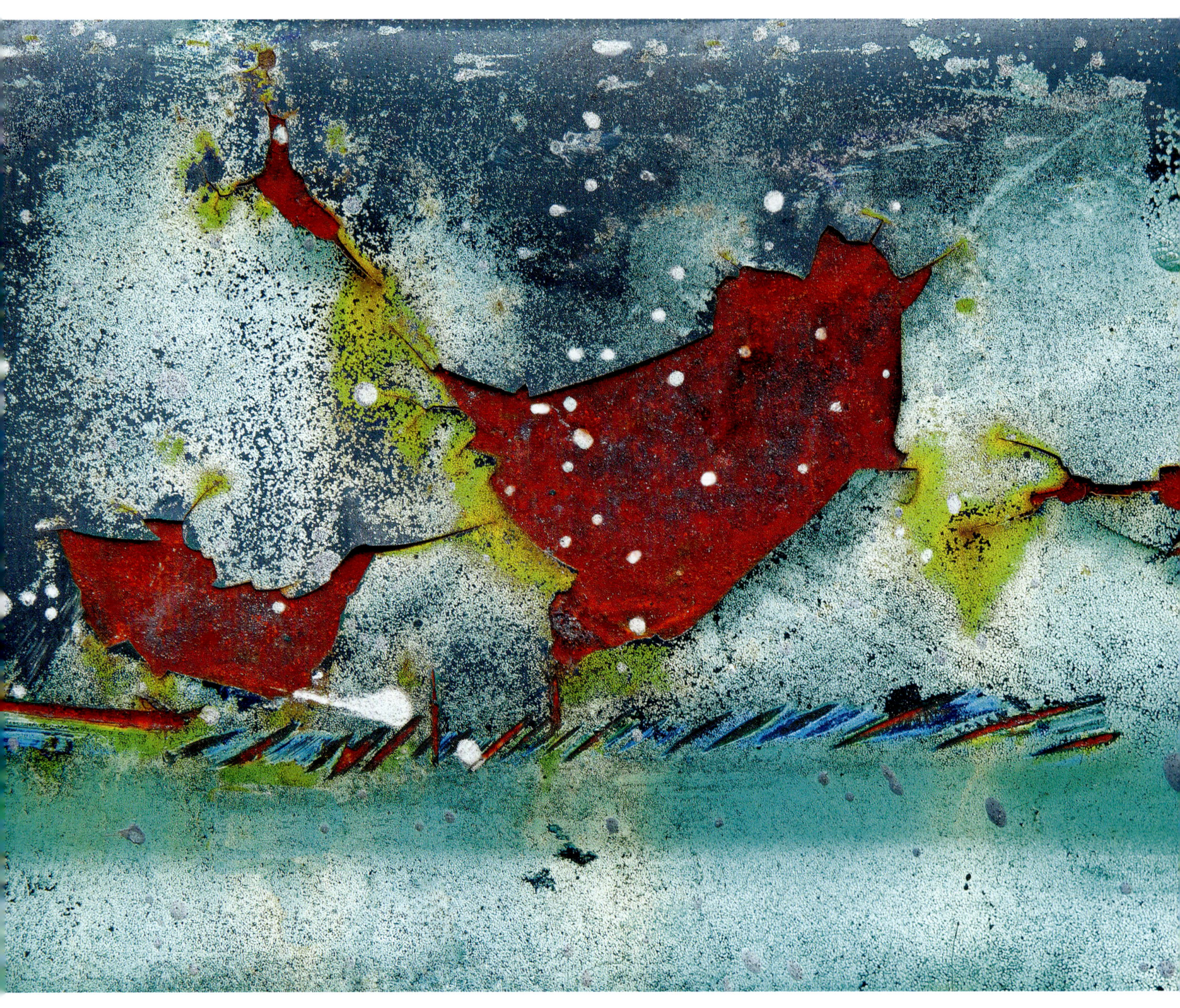

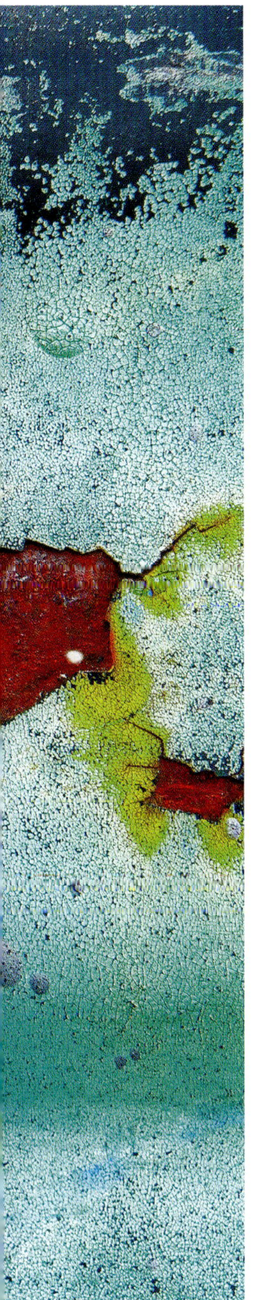

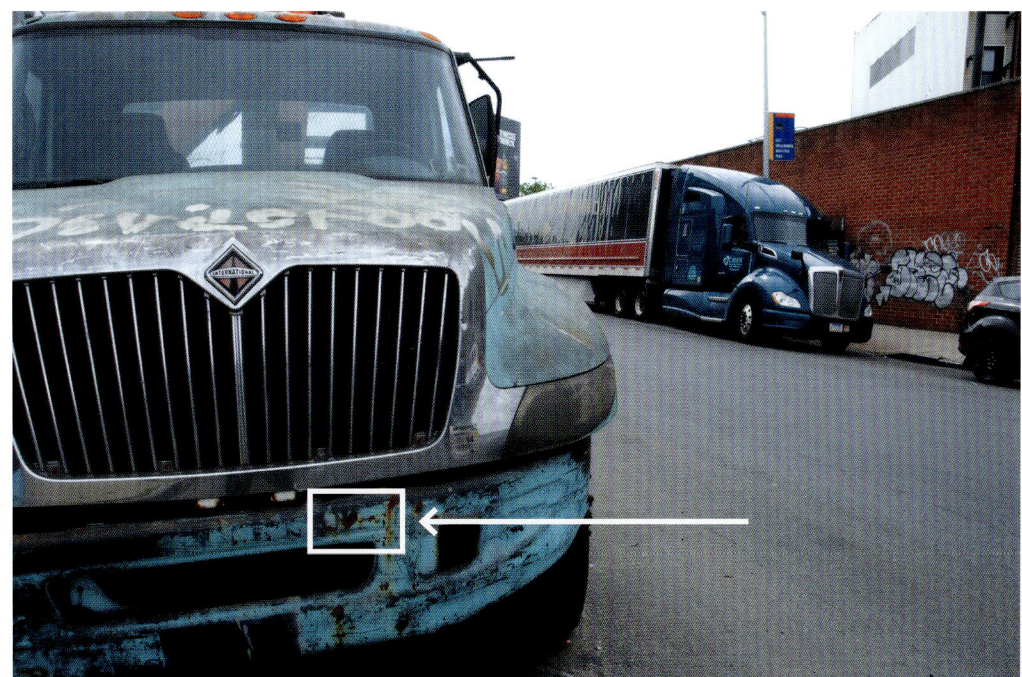

"Brutal ful" subjects are those that are often ignored or discarded in favor of more "beautiful" photographic opportunities, yet on closer inspection a certain beauty can be found in the visually discarded. As soon as my eyes caught sight of this front bumper of a really old, abandoned tow truck in Brooklyn's Flatbush neighborhood, I wondered how many altercations, collisions, bumps, and bruises it had taken for this beauty to be revealed. It is beautiful for sure, at least in my mind. And although I am hesitant to share what I see for fear of influencing you, in the middle of this composition, I do see a mama cat leaping in the air on a star-filled night.

Open your eyes to the battered and bruised, and don't be surprised if you discover a world with endless photographic potential.

◘ Nikon D500, Micro-NIKKOR 105mm lens on a tripod, *f*/13 for 1/30 sec., ISO 100, Daylight/Sunny WB

Graffiti

If I were to walk into any art gallery, photograph a painting, and then share it as "my" art, most of you would be quick to say, "That's not your art! That's a photograph you took of a Rembrandt/Matisse/Pollock/Dali/Picasso." I would of course agree, yet many photographers have no problem photographing the outdoor art created by graffiti artists around the world and claiming it as "their" art when in fact they did nothing more than take a photograph of it.

I have photographed a lot of graffiti over the years, but with an important criterion: to use the graffiti as *part* of my art. Meaning, make it into an out-of-focus yet vibrantly colorful background, combine it into a humorous composition, blend a portrait into it, consider it for a moving background to contrast with a moving foreground subject that you are panning, and so on. Graffiti is an often striking, stop-you-in-your-tracks kind of art, but don't just shoot it—add your mark to it, making it about *your* creative process whenever possible.

In Dublin, Ireland, I came upon an area of some truly fantastic wall art, including this vibrant and colorful mural that was in marked contrast to the five distinct silhouetted human-like shapes. With their arms raised, it seemed to suggest to me that I was amidst a joyful, party-like atmosphere, thus my immediate motivation to invite one of my students to "join the party"! I asked her to stand in front of the stark shapes with her head bent down, and on the count of one, two, three, "throw your head and hair straight up toward the sky." This sent her hair flying, and with my blazingly fast shutter speed, I had no trouble conveying the idea that she was very much rockin' out with the stark shapes in that mural.

Freezing action here was vital, so without any hesitation, I was quick to choose my shutter speed of a 1/1000 sec. and then adjust the aperture until a correct was indicated at *f*/10. When shooting the very quick action of a tossing head of hair, it is just as important to also set your camera to the highest frame rate, often referred to as the setting "Continuous High." In conjunction with that 1/1000 sec. shutter speed, your camera will be recording exposures of at least five frames per second.

◘ Nikon D500, NIKKOR 18-300mm, *f*/10 for 1/1000 sec., ISO 320, Daylight/Sunny WB

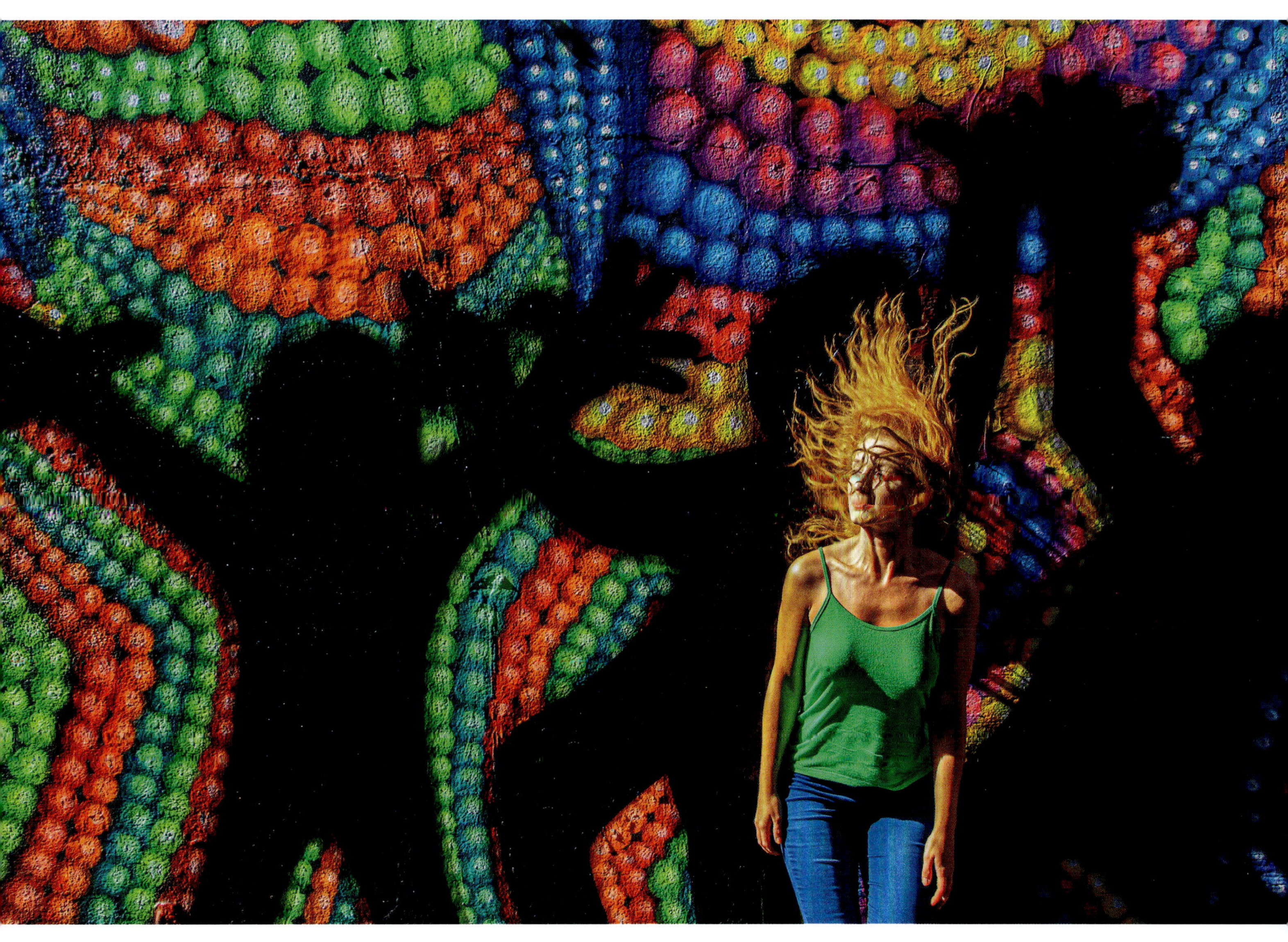

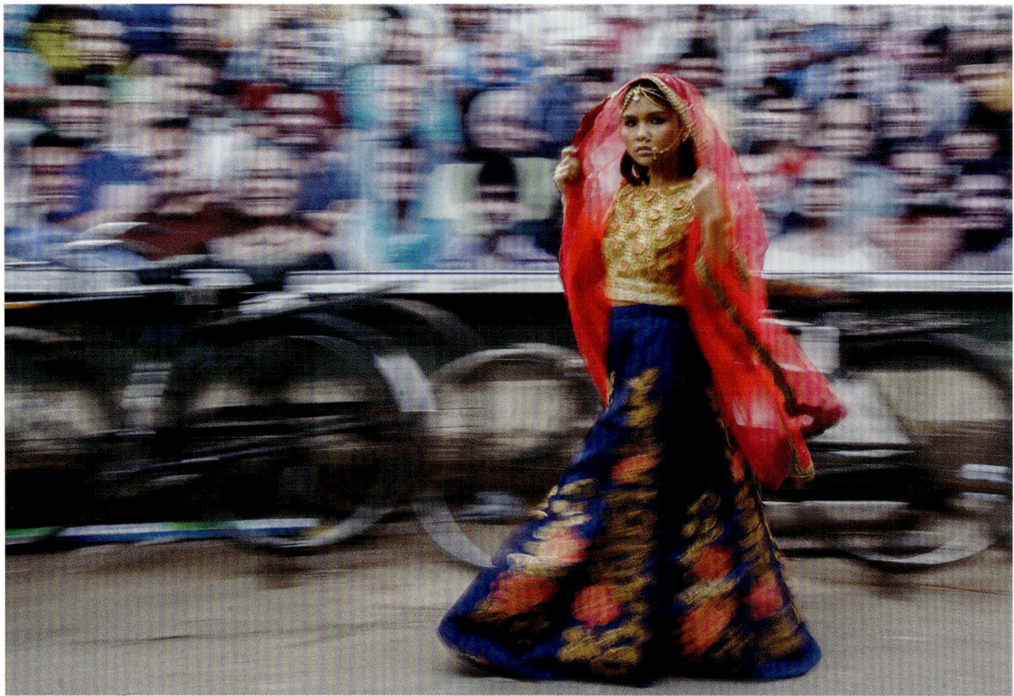

We had just finished an entire afternoon of shooting in Delhi and were on our way back to the hotel when my model, Nattakun Plaengdee, and I discovered several large pieces of graffiti near our hotel. One of the walls of art showed a crowd of people sitting in a grandstand, and although I could not understand the significance of what appeared to be a political statement, I did understand how this crowd could form an almost believable backdrop if they were blurred to look like a crowd watching a parade, with the focus on the subject in that parade. I decided that the following morning we would return to this location, a mere five-minute walk from our hotel. Return we did, with Natt as our "princess" for the parade, though we were short on marching bands, clowns, and elephants. With my exposure set to *f*/22 for 1/15 sec., I panned Natt as she walked down the narrow street. And as you can see, the crowd behind her was spellbound!

◘ Nikon D810, NIKKOR 24–120mm lens, *f*/22 for 1/15 sec., ISO 200, Daylight/Sunny WB

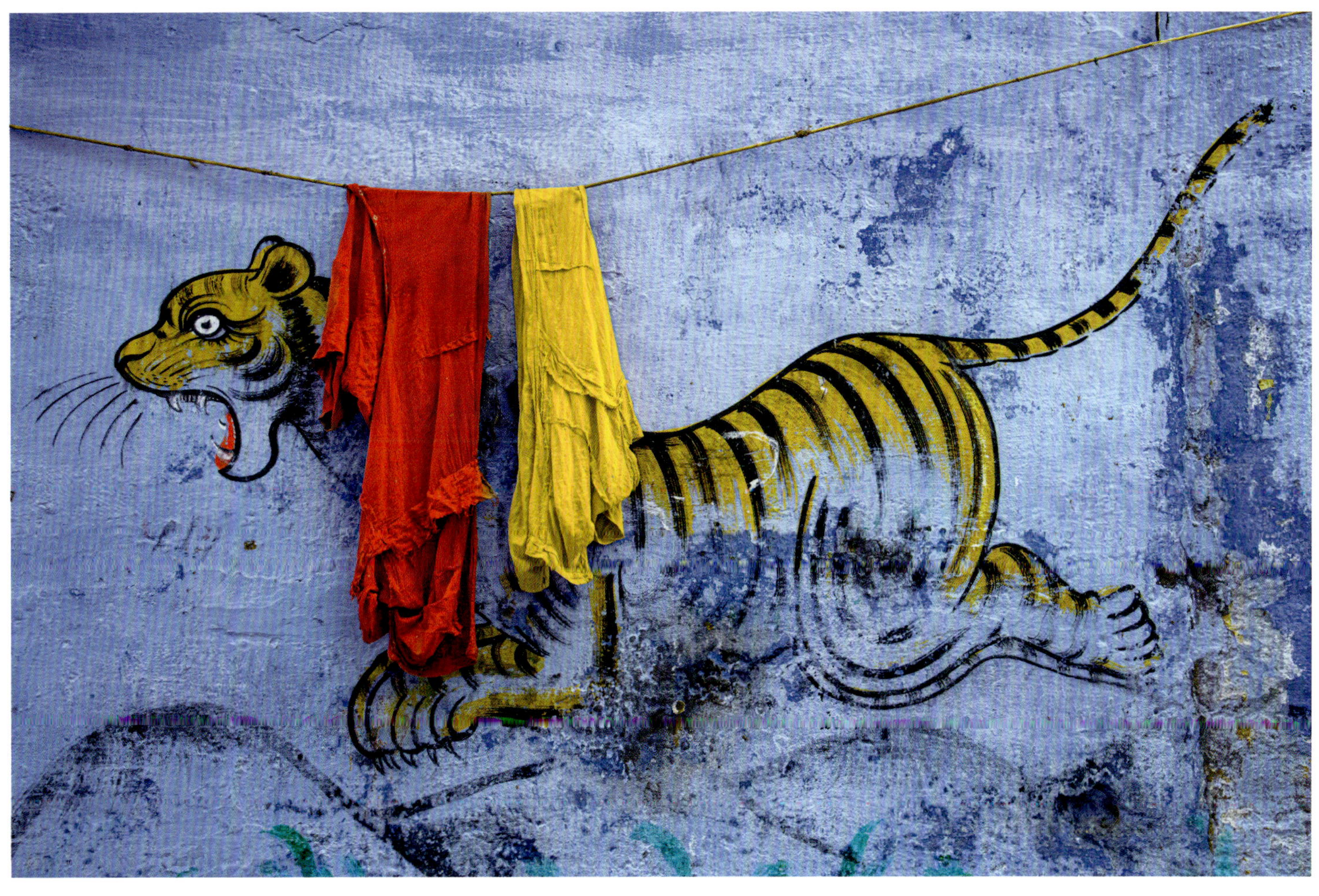

I turned toward the sound of children laughing,which drew me into a narrow lane in the back streets of Varanasi, India. Thirty feet farther, I spotted this colorful composition of red and yellow, times two, against the somewhat complementary cyan and blue wall. A shout-out to the artist who painted the tiger, another to the person who hung the laundry, and of course an extra shout-out to the children whose laughter brought me to this serendipitous and colorful encounter.

◘ Nikon D850, NIKKOR 24–120 lens at 58mm, *f*/11 for 1/200 sec., ISO 640, Daylight/Sunny WB

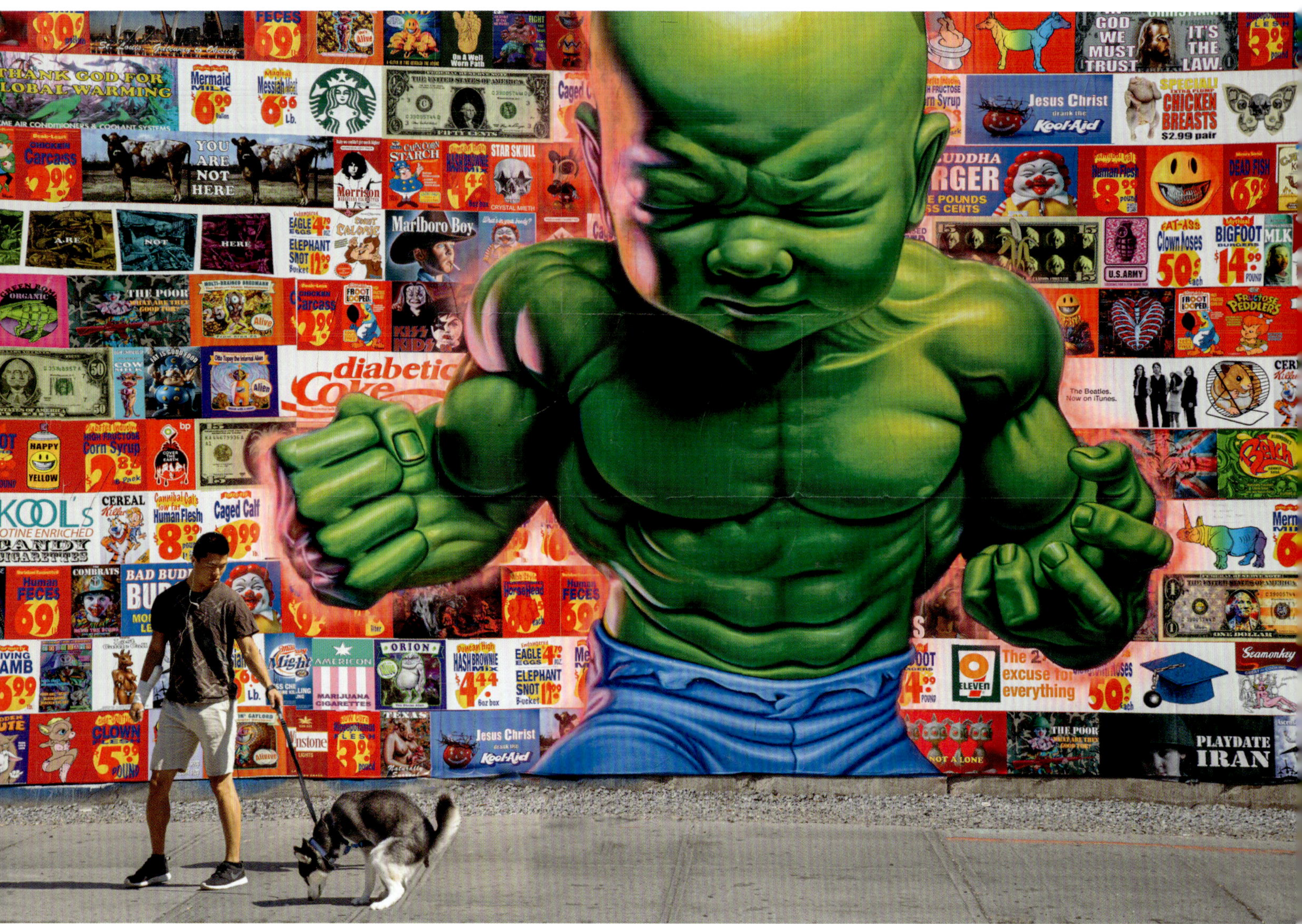

If patience is a virtue, then street photography is the place to become virtuous! In all my years of shooting, nothing else has come close to challenging my patience more than street photography. It's similar to shooting wildlife on the plains of Africa, where almost everything is up to chance. And just like staking out a known watering hole where wildlife gather, I chose to stake out this "watering hole," a large wall of graffiti art on the corner of the Bowery and Houston streets in New York City, and wait for . . . something. Two hours later, my patience was rewarded with a brief encounter that resulted in this humorous shot.

◘ **Nikon D500, NIKKOR 18–300mm lens at 105mm, *f*/11 for 1/500 sec., ISO 200, Daylight/Sunny WB**

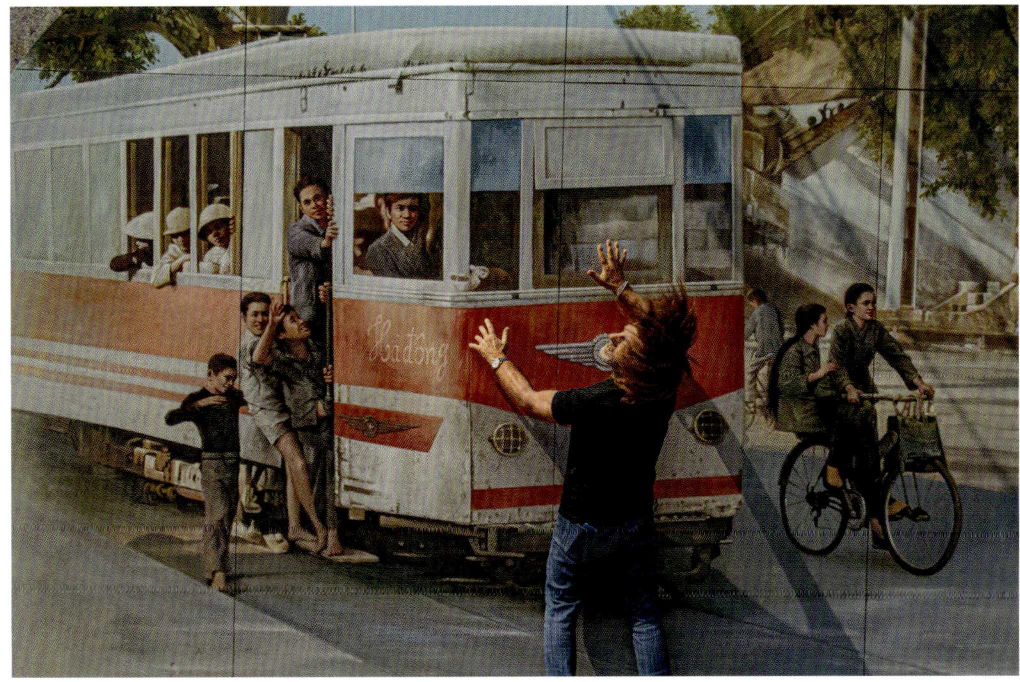

Within seconds of seeing this mural of an old-style electric bus in Hanoi, Vietnam, I knew I wanted to take a selfie that would capture the dangers of crossing the roads in Hanoi. (Granted, the real danger is not from old electric buses but from the more than eight million motorcycles—but as one who continues to choose life, I opted for comedic danger over real danger.)

With my camera on a tripod and my self-timer preset to take nine consecutive exposures, each at *f*/11 for 1/500 sec., I repeatedly snapped my head back. After the first nine attempts, I still wasn't quite satisfied, so I shot another series of nine, and it was then that I got two usable shots, including this one. This time I chose to freeze the action of the subject (yours truly), freezing my head and hair in such a way as to suggest that I have just been hit head-on by the bus.

◘ Nikon D850, NIKKOR 24–120mm lens, *f*/11 for 1/500 sec., ISO 400, Daylight/Sunny WB

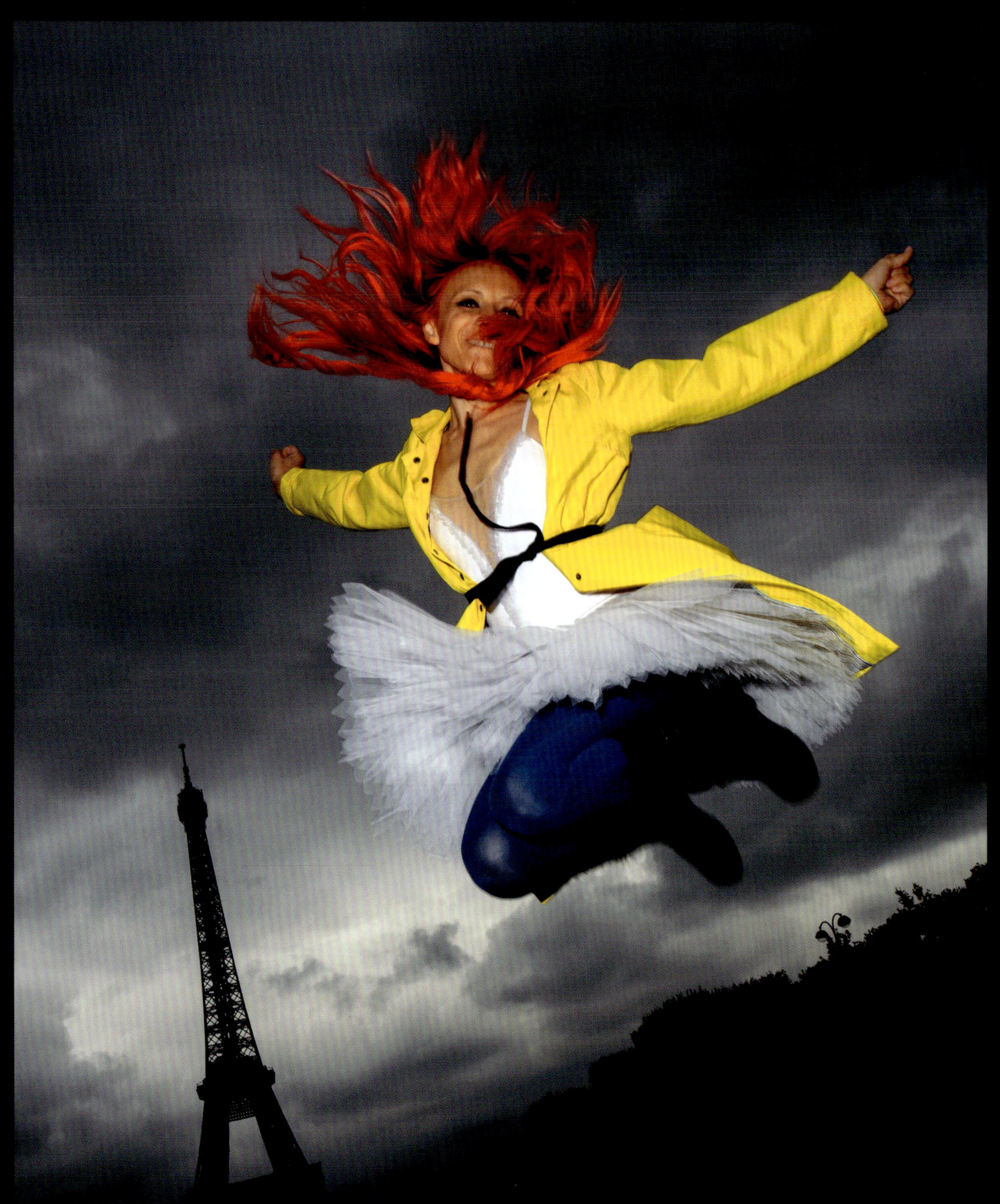

USING FLASH

Flashes of Inspiration

Flash is a necessary and immensely creative tool that will increase your creative opportunities one hundred-fold! Once you fully understand portable flash and how it works, you will have a tool in your hands that changes how you approach and photograph your street photography subjects. No more walking away from situations where the light is too contrasty, too dark, or too weak and flat. You can use a portable flash to reduce contrasty sunlight and even simulate sunlight when the sun isn't out. It can be used to freeze a moving subject and prevent blurring, to recreate the style of a traditional studio portrait, and to create light in ways limited only by your imagination. When you combine what you already know about available light with what you are about to learn about artificial light, you will be unstoppable!

What I am about to tell you regarding the use of portable flash may come as a shock, but it is true. There are only *two* kinds of photographic opportunities in which using your flash makes sense, and there is but one *absolute* setting for the camera and one *absolute* setting for the flash; yet combined, these options can unleash an endless stream of compelling images.

The two photographic opportunities in which using your flash makes sense are (1) when you want to "kill" the ambient light completely, rendering a composition whose sole light source is the flash, and (2) when you want to combine the light of the flash with the natural light that is also present.

As far as the one *absolute* setting for the camera, you will be consistently successful each and every time when your camera is in the Manual mode. For the one *absolute* setting for the flash, always shoot in TTL (through the lens) mode.

And that's it. So how and when do we put these two simple principles to work on the street? Let's find out!

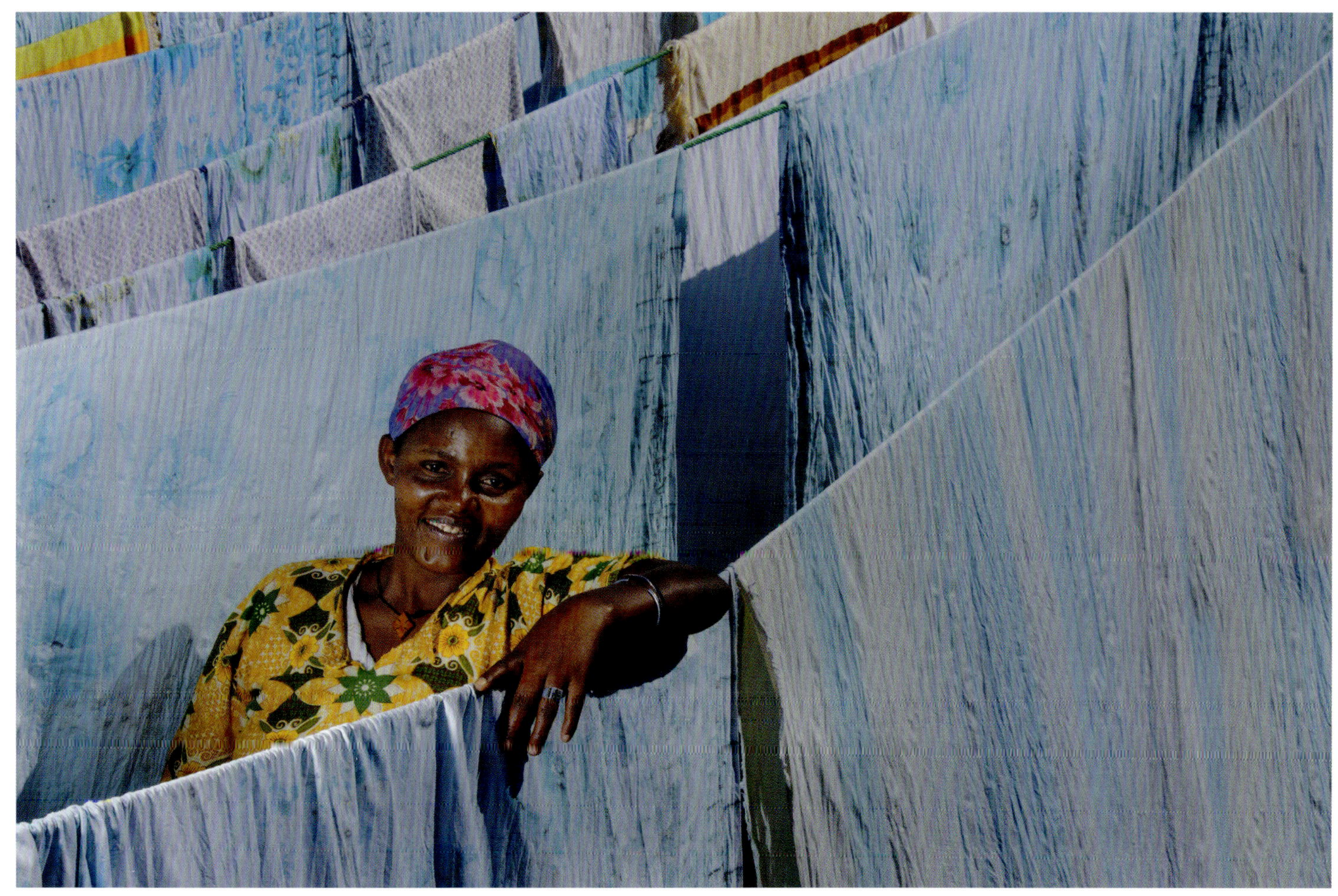

When shooting a portrait in midday sun, a flash can provide welcome fill light to reduce the contrast of the harsh overhead light, which can cast dark circles under your subject's eyes ("racoon eyes"), hiding much of their detail and color. Such was my dilemma when I spotted this young hotel employee in Jimm, Ethiopia, doing the laundry. Her infectious smile caught my attention, snapping me out of a lethargic mood. And her deep yellow blouse and the red in her bandana were a fabulous contrast in the expanse of blue. I told her I liked to make pictures and she gave me permission to take hers. But it was 1 p.m., with the sun directly overhead, so I explained that I would need a few minutes to set up. I set a flash onto my portable light stand, placing it to her right (my left) and attaching a light amber gel. I returned to the elevated deck and asked her to strike a confident pose, suggesting she lean on the laundry line as if to say that she was in charge of this "office space."

With my Velo remote TTL transmitter mounted to my camera's hot shoe and the other Velo TTL trigger mounted under my flash on the light stand, I set my exposure for the ambient light of the sky, since that was the same light that was on the woman's face, and reduced the power of my flash to 1/4, which proved just enough fill to eliminate those raccoon-eye shadows, while still recording a correct exposure of the ambient light.

◘ Nikon D810, NIKKOR 24–120mm lens, *f*/22 for 1/125 sec., ISO 200, Daylight/Sunny WB, Nikon SB-900 flash at 1/4 power

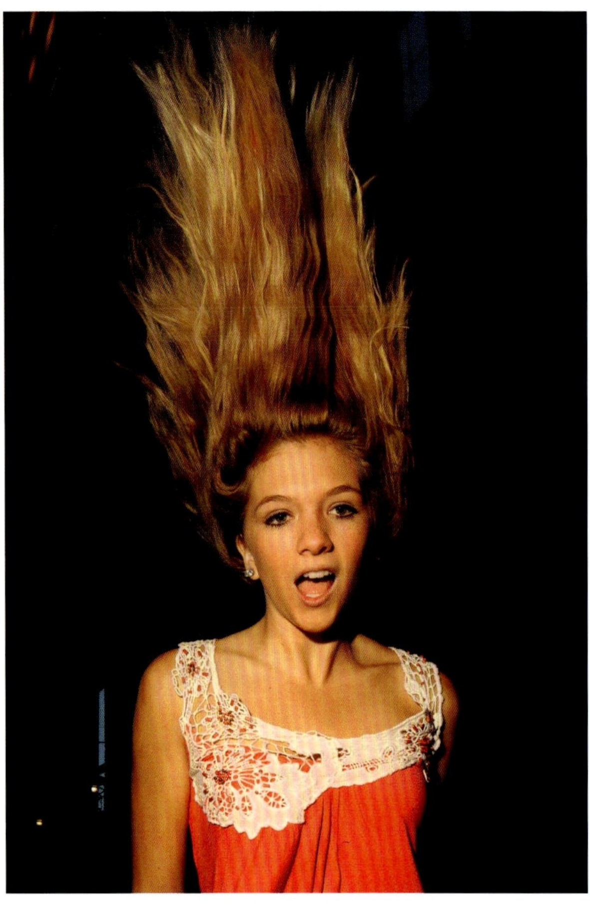

On the streets of Brooklyn, a large warehouse in open shade was the perfect backdrop to offer up some welcome contrast as I photographed model Emily Carlson with my camera and a Nikon SB-900 flash. Before taking Emily's photograph, I set my camera to Manual mode and chose an aperture of *f*/11, since depth of field was not going to be any concern, then adjusted my shutter speed until 1/15 sec. indicated a correct exposure for the building behind Emily. I knew that if I adjusted the shutter speed to 1/250 sec., I would record a *severe* underexposure of the building, which I confirmed by taking a test shot. At *f*/11 for 1/250 sec., the building was all but black, other than a few windows reflecting a bit of distant light from the morning sky. I then asked Emily to walk toward me with the flash on a light stand to my left. On the count of three, I fired the flash with a remote trigger as she bent her head over and then quickly snapped it back, stopping to look right toward me. My hope was to record a composition of her "lit" with vertical flying hair, and it's fair to say I got the shot. I should also note that the flash had a small diffuser over it to soften the light as well as a warming gel, accounting for the overall warmth of the flash output seen in the tones of Emily's skin and hair.

◘ Nikon D850, NIKKOR 24–120mm lens, *f*/11 for 1/250 sec., ISO 200, Daylight/Sunny WB, Nikon SB-900 flash

Understanding Flash Photography

There are three factors that go into creating a dynamic flash exposure: (1) choosing the right aperture, (2) making certain your subject is at the right flash-to-subject distance, and (3) using a shutter speed to either include ambient light present in the scene, deliberately underexpose it, or kill it entirely.

1. As with any image, start by selecting the right aperture, whether for a storytelling composition (*f*/16 or *f*/22), a composition with a very limited focus (*f*/4 or *f*/5.6), or a "Who cares?" composition (*f*/8 or *f*/11).
2. Once you have determined which aperture makes the most sense, and with the flash in TTL mode, you will see a *flash range* indicated on the back of your flash. The wider the aperture, the longer the reach of the flash range (for example, three to eighteen feet at *f*/11, versus six to thirty-nine feet at *f*/5.6). This range is telling you that at *f*/11 if your subject is within three to eighteen feet from your flash, you'll get a "perfect" flash exposure. Your flash range will also be influenced by the ISO, but as a general rule, most flash exposures can be achieved with an ISO of 100 or 200. If your subject is closer than three feet or much farther away than eighteen feet, the flash exposure will be either overexposed or underexposed.
3. Finally, determine whether you want to include the ambient light *or* cancel all the ambient light, then set the shutter speed accordingly. In other words, either choose the correct shutter speed for the ambient light or set a shutter speed that severely underexposes the ambient light, resulting in a flash exposure surrounded by all black.

Overcast days provide opportunities for one of the easiest flash exposures you will ever make, and one that often results in a dramatic exposure. First, set your camera in Manual mode. With your aperture set to *f*/22 and your ISO to 100, point your camera at the cloudy sky and adjust your shutter speed until a 2-stop underexposure is indicated. Usually this will result in a shutter speed between 1/30 sec. and 1/200 sec., depending on the time of day, with a greater chance of obtaining the "dark sky" effect in the early morning or late afternoon. Take a test shot of this natural light; your sky should appear darker than normal. Now, attach your flash to the camera's hot shot or tether it to the hot shoe via a TTL flash cord and set it to the TTL mode. Once you're set up, lie low to the ground and ask your subject to jump in the air as if in great excitement. While looking up with your wide-angle lens, fire away. Voilà! A beautifully lit subject against the backdrop of a severely underexposed sky. If you have a cloudy weekend in the forecast, you have just discovered a reason to celebrate! Thanks to one of my students, Olga Zemetra, for this joint collaboration in Paris a few years ago.

◘ Nikon D800, NIKKOR 24–85mm lens, *f*/11 for 1/160 sec., ISO 100, Daylight/Sunny WB, Nikon SB-900 flash

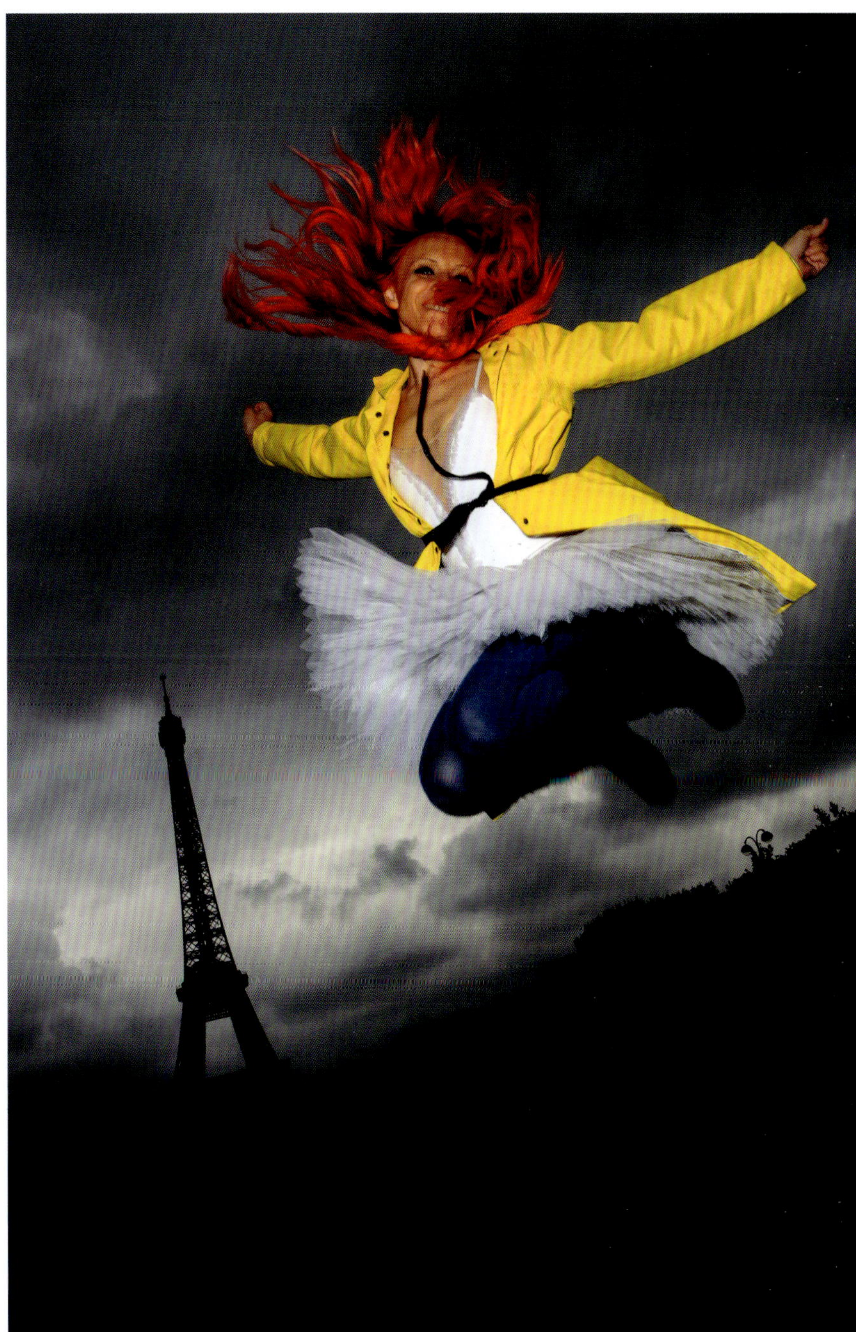

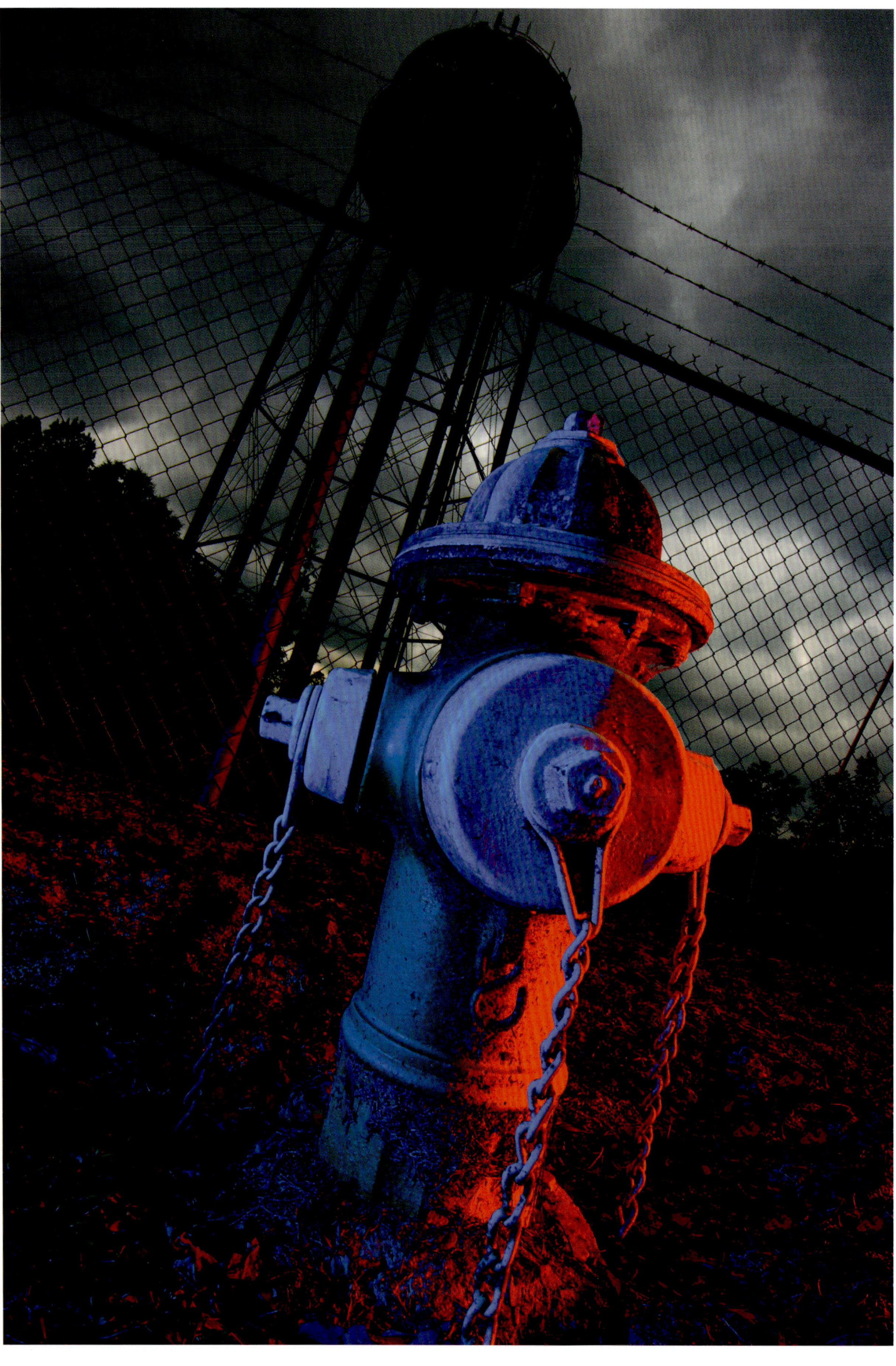

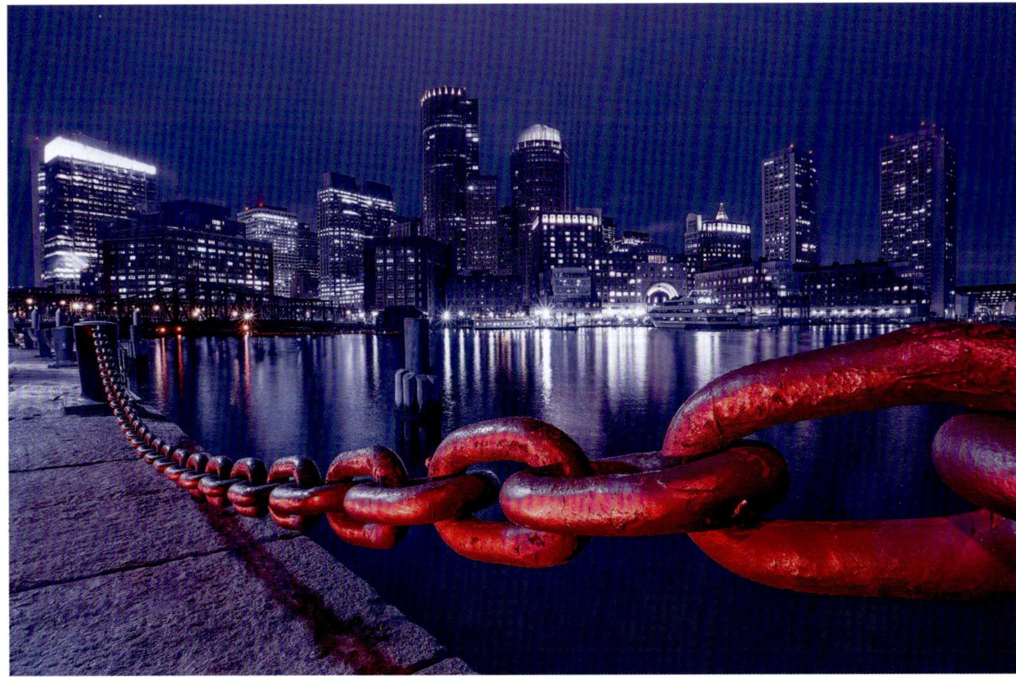

The desire to do something different, to create an image that is not expected, that surprises—that desire never goes away. To be sure, not all of my attempts to create something fresh succeed, but with each failed attempt I get one step closer to one that does. I am driven to succeed, in part, by my peers. There is so much incredible photographic talent in this world, and each time I venture onto the internet, I know that I will see incredible work that I wish were mine, always inspiring me to try new things and up my game.

The last time I was in Boston, I was shooting a section of the skyline near the courthouse, where there is a long expanse of a chain safety barrier at the water's edge. As the blue hour arrived, the "what ifs" kicked in: *What if I shoot the same composition that has been done many times before, using a wide-angle lens and framing the chain in the foreground as a leading line, but this time use a flash with a red gel, and light up the entire chain?* I set a 15-second ambient exposure and manually fired the flash by pressing the test button every four feet as I walked down the length of the chain, with the flash raised high enough so it would not be visible. In this way, I was able to throw a seamless series of red lights onto the chain from beginning to end, and it worked beautifully!

◘ Nikon D850, NIKKOR 14–24mm lens, *f*/22 for 15 seconds, ISO 200, Daylight/Sunny WB, Nikon SB-900 flash

Think of the flash as a portable sun that you can call upon anytime you want, creating sunlight where none existed or adding more to a given area. And if one flash can do all that, can you imagine what *two* flashes can do?

On a long, overcast weekend with lots of time to think, ponder, analyze, and entertain the many "what ifs" born out of boredom, I thought, *What if I pretend to be a graffiti artist and start tagging stuff in the neighborhood with colorful "sprays" of blue and red light?* So out the door I went with my camera, flashes, and blue and red gels.

Shooting with flash on an overcast day is a simple procedure. Set your camera to Manual mode, choose an aperture of *f*/22 and a low ISO of 100, and then, pointing your camera at the sky, adjust your shutter speed so your meter reading is 2 stops underexposed. Set your flashes in TTL mode and to fire remotely. For the image on the previous page, I also attached a colored gel to each flash. I placed one flash on either side of the fire hydrant, about two feet away, and fired away. The result is a patriotic fire hydrant (doing my part to make America's fire hydrants great again) against the backdrop of a foreboding urban scene, made even more dramatic with the 2-stop underexposure for the ambient light.

◘ Nikon D810, NIKKOR 24–85mm lens, *f*/22 for 1/160 sec., ISO 100, Daylight/Sunny WB, two Nikon SB-900 flashes with Rogue gels

About the Author

Bryan Peterson is a professional photographer, internationally known instructor, and founder of the Bryan Peterson School of Photography. He is also the bestselling author of *Understanding Exposure*, *Learning to See Creatively*, *Understanding Portrait Photography*, *Understanding Color in Photography*, and his most recent book, *Bryan Peterson Photography School*. His trademark use of color and strong, graphic composition have garnered him many photographic awards, including the New York Art Director Club's Gold Award and honors from *Communication Arts Photography Annual* and *Print* magazine.

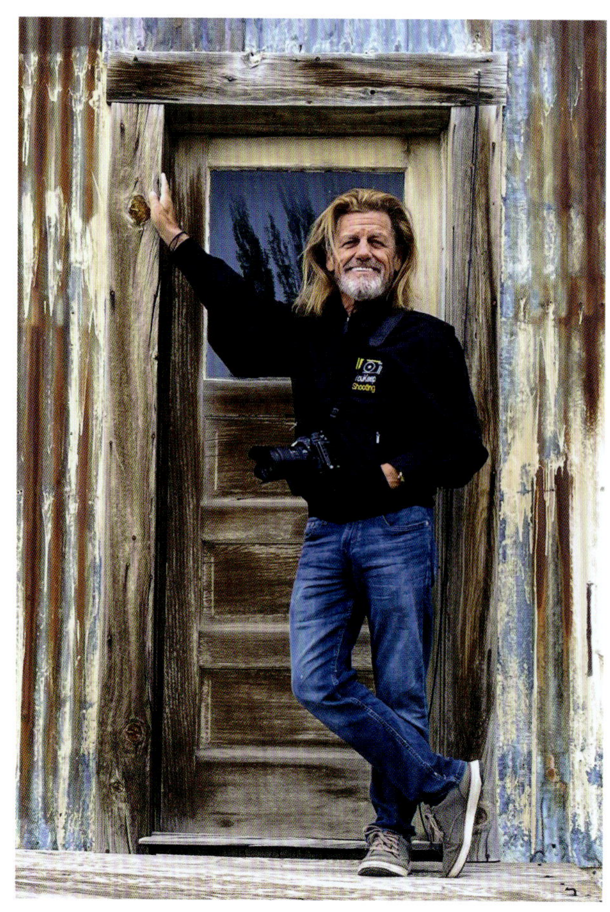

Index

A
abstracts, 150–54, 157–58, 160, 162–63
anxiety, role of, 95
apertures
  choosing, 44
  definition of, 8
  depth of field and, 44
  f-stops, 8
  singular-theme, 44
  storytelling, 26, 44
  "Who cares?," 11, 31, 44, 87, 102, 104, 111, 160, 180

B
backlight, 22–23, 25, 27, 69, 118
black, exposing for, 108, 153
blurred motion, 130–31, 133, 135–36, 138, 140

C
camera, seeing like a, 6, 8
candids, 106, 109, 111–13, 115, 117–18, 120–22
children, photographing, 120
color
  composition and, 78, 80–82, 84–85, 87, 117
  connections and, 46, 47, 49–51
  "too much," 122
  transparent, 22, 25, 27
composition
  color and, 78, 80–82, 84–85, 87, 117
  connections, 46–47, 49–51, 53
  framing with a frame, 54–58, 60
  mergers, 38–39, 41–42, 44–45
  pattern and, 78–80
  point of view, 62, 64, 67, 69, 71
  Rule of Thirds, 33
  scale, 72–74, 76
  storytelling, 26, 44
connections, 46–47, 49–51, 53

D
dappled light, 28–31
depth of field, 26, 44

F
flash, 178–81, 183
framing with a frame, 54–58, 60
f-stops, 8

G
Golden Section, 33
graffiti, 150, 170, 172–74, 183

I
ISO, 8

L
light
  back, 22–23, 25, 27, 69, 118
  dappled, 28–31
  meters, 34, 108
  and shadow, 32–34
  See also flash

M
macro photography, 164–66, 169
mergers, 38–39, 41–42, 44–45
motion
  blurring, 130–31, 133, 135–36, 138, 140
  diagonal lines and, 64
  freezing, 126–27, 129, 170, 175
  panning, 142–44, 147
  shutter speed and, 126

P
panning, 142–44, 147
pattern, 78–80
photographic triangle, 8
point of view, 62, 64, 67, 69, 71
posed portraits, 90–92, 95–96, 99–100, 102–4, 179

R
rain, 136, 138
red, 16
reflections, 18, 136, 150, 153, 154, 158, 160, 162, 163, 166
Rule of Thirds, 33

S
scale, 72–74, 76
shadow
  light and, 32–34
  pockets, 6–9, 13
shutter speeds
  definition of, 8
  motion and, 126
  range of, 8
silhouettes, 6, 11, 13, 15, 16, 20, 22, 23, 25, 27, 51, 74, 118
starburst effect, 22, 25, 27
storytelling apertures, 26, 44
street photography
  characteristics of, 1
  definition of, 1
  finding subject matter for, 15
  photographic gold and, 1–2
  popularity of, 1
subject matter, finding, 15
Sunny 16 rule, 11–13, 16, 18, 20, 41
swiping, 140

T
texture, 164–65

W
white, exposing for, 106, 108
white balance (WB), 68, 69
"Who cares?" aperture, 11, 31, 44, 87, 102, 104, 111, 160, 180

Z
zoom lenses, 26

Many thanks to the best editor ever, Julie Mazur Tribe, and to Emma Rudolph, Isabelle Gioffredi, Jane Chinn, and the gang at Ten Speed Press.

Published in the United States by Watson-Guptill Publications, an imprint of Random House, a division of Penguin Random House LLC, New York.
www.watsonguptill.com

Library of Congress Cataloging-in-Publication Data
Names: Peterson, Bryan, 1952-author.
Title: Understanding street photography : an introduction to shooting compelling images on the street / Bryan Peterson.
Description: First edition. | New York : Watson-Guptill Publications, an imprint of Random House, a division of Penguin Random House LLC, [2022] | Includes index.
Identifiers: LCCN 2021053704 (print) | LCCN 2021053705 (ebook) | ISBN 9781984860583 (trade paperback) | ISBN 9781984860590 (ebook)
Subjects: LCSH: Street photography.
Classification: LCC TR659.8 .P483 2022 (print) | LCC TR659.8 (ebook) | DDC 778.9/4—dc23/eng/20211220
LC record available at https://lccn.loc.gov/2021053704
LC ebook record available at https://lccn.loc.gov/2021053705

Trade Paperback ISBN: 978-1-9848-6058-3
eBook ISBN: 978-1-9848-6059-0

Printed in China

Acquiring editor: Emma Rudolph
Designer: Isabelle Gioffredi
Typefaces: Colophon Foundry's Apercu Pro by The Entente, Phil's Fonts' Freight Pro by Joshua Darden, Grilli Type's GT Alpina by Reto Moser
Production designers: Mari Gill and Faith Hague
Production manager and prepress color manager: Jane Chinn
Copyeditors: Julie Mazur Tribe and Kristi Hein | Proofreader: Karen Levy | Indexer: Ken DellaPenta
Publicist: Feliz Cruz | Marketer: Windy Dorresteyn